Early Christianity

D1280892

254

Early Christianity

ORIGINS AND EVOLUTION TO AD 600

In Honour of W H C Frend

Edited by

IAN HAZLETT

ABINGDON PRESS
NASHVILLE

PALM BEACH ATLANTIC UNIVERSITY
WARREN LIBRARY
900 SOUTH OLIVE AVENUE
WEST PALM BEACH, FL 33401

EARLY CHRISTIANITY:
Origins and Evolution to AD 600

Copyright © 1991 by Ian Hazlett

First published in Great Britain 1991 by SPCK,
Holy Trinity Church, Marylebone Rd., London NW1 4DU.

Published in the U.S.A. 1991 by Abingdon Press

All rights reserved.
No part of this work may be reproduced or transmitted in any form or by
any means, electronic or mechanical, including photocopying and
recording, or by any information storage or retrieval system, except as may
be expressly permitted by the 1976 Copyright Act or in writing from the
publisher. Requests for permission should be addressed in writing to
Abingdon Press, 201 Eighth Avenue South, Nashville, TN 37202.

This book is printed on acid-free paper.

Library of Congress Cataloging-in-Publication Data

Early Christianity: origins and evolution to AD 600: in honour of W.H.C.
Frend/edited by Ian Hazlett.
    p. cm.
Includes bibliographical references and indexes.
ISBN 0-687-11444-6 (alk. paper)
    1. Church history—Primitive and early church, ca. 30-600.
I. Frend, W. H. C. II. Hazlett, Ian. 1944 .
BR162.2.E37 1991
270. 1—dc20   91-12730

Typeset by Rowland Phototypesetting Ltd.,
Bury St. Edmunds, Suffolk.

MANUFACTURED IN THE UNITED STATES OF AMERICA

Contents

Contents

Contents

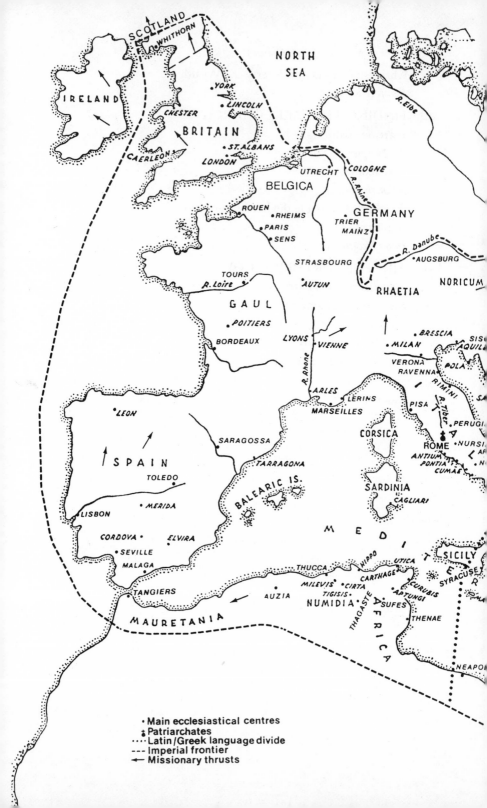

SCOTLAND

IRELAND

WHITHORN

YORK

LINCOLN

CHESTER

BRITAIN

ST. ALBANS

CAERLEON

LONDON

NORTH
SEA

R. Elbe

UTRECHT

COLOGNE

BELGICA

GERMANY

ROUEN

RHEIMS

PARIS

TRIER

SENS

MAINZ

R. Rhine

STRASBOURG

R. Danube

AUGSBURG

TOURS

R. Loire

AUTUN

RHAETIA

NORICUM

GAUL

POITIERS

BORDEAUX

LYONS

VIENNE

R. Rhône

BRESCIA

MILAN

VERONA

RAVENNA

SISI

AQUIL

POLA

ARLES

LERINS

MARSEILLES

PISA

RIMINI

R. Tiber

PERUGI

LEON

CORSICA

ROME

NURSI

SARAGOSSA

SPAIN

TARRAGONA

ANTIUM

PONTIA

CUMAE

AF

TOLEDO

BALEARIC IS.

SARDINIA

LISBON

MERIDA

CAGLIARI

M E D I

CORDOVA

ELVIRA

SEVILLE

MALAGA

THUCCA

HIPPO

UTICA

SICILY

TANGIERS

AUZIA

MILEVIS

CIRTA

CARTHAGE

CURUBIS

SYRACUSE

TIGISIS

APTUNGI

SUFES

R

MAURETANIA

NUMIDIA

THAGASTE

THENAE

A
F
R
I
C
A

T
E

NEAPO

• Main ecclesiastical centres

⚑ Patriarchates

⋯ Latin/Greek language divide

--- Imperial frontier

← Missionary thrusts

THE ROMAN EMPIRE
AND THE CHURCH
in the fourth century A.D.

IN GENERAL, MODERN RATHER THAN ANCIENT NAMES ARE USED

SARMATIA

DI

MURSA

BELGRADE

SIRMIUM

DACIA

R. Danube

MOESIA

NAISSUS

SARDICA

CRIMEA

SEBASTOPOL

BLACK SEA

TITYUS

BOSPHORUS

MTZKETHA

TBILISI

GEORGIA

VALARSHAPAT

ARTASHAT

MACEDONIA

PHILIPPI THRACE

THESSALONICA

EDESSA

GREECE

ATHENS

CORINTH

PATMOS

LACEDAEMON

CRETE

ADRIANOPLE

CONSTANTINOPLE

CHALCEDON

NICOMEDIA

LAMPSACUS

NICAEA

ASIA

SMYRNA

EPHESUS

TRALLES

SARDIS

COLOSSAE

ARYCANDA

SINOPE

PAPHLAGONIA

BITHYNIA

GANGRA

ANCYRA

GALATIA

PHRYGIA

HIEROPOLIS

PHILOMELIUM

ANTIOCH

ICONIUM

CILICIA

TRAPEZUS

PONTUS

SATALA

NEOCAESAREA

SEBASTE

NYSSA

CAPPADOCIA

NAZIANZUS

CAESAREA

SAMOSATA

ANAZARBUS

TARSUS

CYRRHUS

CNOSSUS

ANTIOCH

LAODICEA

ARMENIA

ASHTISHAT

MOKH

EDESSA

OSRHOENE

NISIBIS

MESOPOTAMIA

R. Tigris

ARBEIA

PERSIA

SALAMIS

TRIPOLI

CYPRUS

SYRIA

BERYTUS

LEBANON

TYRE

DAMASCUS

R. Euphrates

DURA

PALMYRA

SELEUCIA-CTESIPHON

NEAN

SEA

OLEMAIS

CYRENE

CYRENAICA

LIBYA

MARMARICA

ALEXANDRIA

SCETIS

MEMPHIS

EGYPT

THMUIS

PHAENO

AILA

PALESTINE

SAMARIA

BOSTRA

CAESAREA

LYDDA

JERUSALEM

GAZA

ARABIA

PERAT

GULF

R. Nile

LYCOPOLIS

TABENNISI

The Contributors

[Select publications listed]

Rev. Dr James S Alexander. Lecturer in Ecclesiastical History, St Mary's College, University of St Andrews, Scotland. Contributions to the *Theologische Realenzyklopädie* and *Augustinus-Lexikon*.

Doz. Dr Irena D Backus. Maître d'enseignement et de recherche, Institut d'histoire de la Réformation, Université de Genève, Switzerland. *The Reformed Roots of the English New Testament: the influence of Theodore Beza on the English New Testament* and *Logique et théologie au XVIe siècle: aux sources de Martin Bucer*.

Mrs Diana Barclay. Part-time Tutor in Ecclesiastical History, University of Glasgow, Scotland.

Prof. Timothy D Barnes. Professor of Classics, University of Toronto, Canada. *Early Christianity and the Roman Empire* and *Constantine and Eusebius*.

Mr Gerald Bonner. Emeritus Reader in Theology, University of Durham, England. *God's Decree and Man's Destiny: studies on the thought of Augustine of Hippo* and *St Augustine of Hippo: life and controversies*.

Dr Sebastian P Brock. University Lecturer in Aramaic and Syriac, Oriental Institute, Oxford, England. *Syriac Perspectives on Late Antiquity* and *Holy Women of the Syrian Orient*.

Rev. Prof. Stuart G Hall. Formerly Professor of Ecclesiastical History, King's College, University of London, England. Rector of Pittenweem and Elie, Scotland. Co-editor of the *Theologische Realenzyklopädie*; editor of *Saint Melito of Sardis: On Pascha, and fragments*.

Dr Jill Harries. Lecturer in Ancient History, St Salvator's College, University of St Andrews, Scotland. *Religious Conflict in fourth-century Rome: a documentary study*.

Rev. Dr William Horbury. University Lecturer in Divinity, Fellow of Corpus Christi College, Cambridge, England. Co-editor of *Suffering and Martyrdom in the New Testament*.

Prof. Joseph F T Kelly. Director and Professor of Inter Religious Studies, John Carroll University, University Heights, Ohio, USA. *Why is there a New Testament?*

Prof. Noel Q King. Professor of History and Comparative Religion, Merrill College, University of California, Santa Cruz, USA. *The Emperor Theodosius and the Establishment of Christianity* and *African Cosmology: an introduction to religion in Africa.*

Mr Andrew Louth. Reader in Religious Studies, Goldsmiths' College, University of London, England. *The Origins of the Christian Mystical Tradition* and *Denys the Areopagite.*

Prof. Luther H Martin. Professor of Religion, University of Vermont, Burlington, USA. *Hellenistic Religions: an introduction* and *Technologies of the self: a seminar with Michel Foucault.*

Dr Jane E Merdinger. Visiting Assistant Professor, Department of History, University of California at San Diego, USA.

Mr Kenneth S Painter. Formerly Deputy Keeper, Department of Greek and Roman Antiquities, British Museum, London, England. *The Water Newton Early Christian Silver.*

Boniface Ramsey OP. Adjunct Professor, School of Theology, Seton Hall University, South Orange NJ, USA. *Beginning to Read the Church Fathers* and *The Sermons of St Maximus of Turin* (editor).

Rev. John Riches. Senior Lecturer in New Testament, University of Glasgow, Scotland. *Jesus and the Transformation of Judaism* and *The World of Jesus: first century Judaism in crisis.*

Prof. Dr Adolf M Ritter. Professor of Church History, University of Heidelberg, Germany. *Charisma im Verständnis des Johannes Chrysostomus und seiner Zeit* and *Das Konzil von Konstantinopel und sein Symbol.*

Dr Philip Rousseau. Associate Professor of History, University of Auckland, New Zealand. *Pachomius: the making of a community in fourth-century Egypt* and *Ascetics, Authority, and the Church in the Age of Jerome and Cassian.*

Prof. Dr Kurt Rudolph. Professor of the History of Religion, Philipp's University of Marburg, Germany. *Gnosis: the nature and history of ancient religion* and *Theogonie, Kosmogonie, und Anthropogonie in den mandäischen Schriften.*

Prof. Dr Knut Schäferdiek. Professor of Church History, University of Bonn, Germany. Editor of *Missiongeschichte als Kirchengeschichte,* vol. 2/1; co-editor of *Theologische Realenzyklopädie.*

Rev. Prof. G Christopher Stead. Formerly Professor of Divinity, University of Cambridge, England. *Substance and Illusion in the Christian Fathers* and *Divine Substance.*

Rev. Prof. Maurice F Wiles. Regius Professor of Divinity, University of Oxford, England. *The Making of Christian Doctrine* and *The Remaking of Christian Doctrine.*

Rev. Prof. Rowan Williams. Lady Margaret Professor of Divinity, University of Oxford, England. *The Wound of Knowledge: Christian Spirituality from the New Testament to St John of the Cross* and *Arius: heresy and tradition.*

Mr David F Wright. Senior Lecturer in Ecclesiastical History, New College, University of Edinburgh, Scotland. Editor of *Common Places of Martin Bucer,* co-editor of *The New Dictionary of Theology.*

Rev. Prof. Frances M Young. Professor of Theology, University of Birmingham, England. *From Nicaea to Chalcedon: a guide to the literature and its background* and *The Use of Sacrificial Ideas in Greek Christian Writers from the New Testament to John Chrysostom.*

Editor: Dr W Ian P Hazlett. Lecturer in Ecclesiastical History, University of Glasgow, Scotland. Contributor on Early Christianity in the *Encyclopaedia of World Faiths;* and Reformation Studies.

ABBREVIATIONS

NE J. Stevenson, ed., *A New Eusebius. Documents illustrating the history of the Church to* AD *337.* Revised with additional documents by W H C Frend. London, SPCK 1987.

CCC J. Stevenson, ed., *Creeds, Councils and Controversies. Documents illustrating the history of the Church* AD *337–461.* Revised with additional documents by W H C Frend. London, SPCK, 1989.

PG *Patrologia Graeca.* Ed. J-P Migne. Paris, 1841ff. (Original Greek sources).

PL *Patrologia Latina* Ed. J-P Migne. Paris, 1841ff. (Original Latin sources).

Preface

William Frend occupies a special place among historians of the ancient Church, in particular by his professional interest in archaeological finds and also by his sympathetic concern for those who dissented from the *Ecclesia Catholica* – Donatists, Monophysites, and others. The panorama he has unfolded in his big work of synthesis, *The Rise of Christianity*, has its detailed focus in a large number of particular studies. That these studies have provoked discussion and disagreement is a testimony to their importance. Only scholars with very significant things to say are paid the high compliment of sustained and courteous argument to defend a contrary or at least an alternative view. The flow of younger students wishing to be guided by him in their research has been constant. His books and the point of view which is there represented will long remain a marker.

No writer on early Christian history has been more aware of the wider social dimension of the Christian mission, so that the dynamic ideas and beliefs may at times appear secondary to the social structures which they reflect and justify. Hence the paradox that a historian with much admiration for cohesion and order has presented a case for finding the roots of these virtues in a Catholic reaction against tightly knit dissenting groups. The groups were cohesive, but wholly lacking in universality. We are left with a rare paradox that universality is singularly difficult to reconcile with coherence and order.

In this volume of essays colleagues and friends of Professor Frend have joined to salute a scholar whose productivity has been continuous and even now in his seniority shows no sign of abating. *Ad multos annos!*

Henry Chadwick
Peterhouse
Cambridge

xiii

Introduction

While William Frend's activity as a prolific scholar is widely acknowledged and appreciated, his primary function was that of a teacher. During the height of his career in this respect he worked at the University of Glasgow, in the dual framework of Trinity College and the Faculty of Divinity. It was within this context that his impact and influence were most immediate and unmistakable. His erudite, humane, humorous, and gently ironic approach to ecclesiastical history was valued by a whole generation of students who were largely aspiring ministers of the Church. His relatively unconventional approach to the subject provided a definite palliative for the pains of those struggling with the perceived inconstant abstractions of biblical criticism and dogmatics. Like all good historians, William Frend had the gift of presenting persons and issues as they often in reality were – untidy, flawed, fallible, inconsistent, and sometimes farcical. The fact that as a lay rather than an ordained ecclesiastic he had no particular theological or ecclesiological axe to grind helps to account for his liberal and earthy approach to church history, as well as to explain his appeal to theology students. His ability to discuss matters of the past as 'real-life' problems of the then Church and Society earned him the reputation of being 'the best professor of practical theology in Scotland'.

William Frend's avowed concern with attracting students to the study of church history and disseminating knowledge of it more widely has been one of the main considerations determining the nature of this book, offered to him on the occasion of his seventy-fifth birthday. It was decided not to follow the style of the traditional *Festschrift* with its usual conglomeration of specialized and sometimes arcane studies appealing only to the few. Instead, a new concept and a new genre was groped for. This was to provide a book authored by a variety of specialists which would have an appeal to a clientele other than other specialists, scholars, and advanced students (though if it appealed to these as well, so much the better).

And while the needs of divinity students approaching the subject have been obviously in mind, so also have those of curious inquirers who are located at related or quite different positions in the educational spectrum.

The aim then has been to devise an alternative means of informed access to the history of Christianity during its first six hundred years or so, at a time when serious religious, biblical and historical knowledge is being relegated rapidly to the general educational and cultural basement. And so the keynote is introductory but not elementary; for while basic descriptive information is offered, the incorporation of some of the fruits of current critical research, negative or positive, has also been envisaged. Further, a coordinated topical, that is a thematic approach rather than the traditional continuous narrative-form has been adopted. It is believed that this 'pegs' format may enable readers inexperienced in the field to come to terms swiftly with its scope and complexity by establishing points of orientation as well as tools of interpretation. Therefore within such a multi-authored book there is inevitably a wide variety of styles, presuppositions, methods and interests. This however also reflects the modern reality that there is no one standard way of doing the subject, as is the case in any discipline. There is no reason why outsiders or newcomers to the subject should be shielded from such diversity. This approach is of course light years away from the normative one bequeathed to Christianity by the patriarch of Church History, Eusebius of Caesarea, even if the study of the period still very much stands on his shoulders.

On one or two features of the contents a word of explanation is necessary. The topics within the Church and Society section are of course only select and exemplary, for there are a host of other topics which one could have included there. Also, the last article, on 'The Early Church in the Renaissance and the Reformation' has been included for two reasons. Firstly, modern studies of the early Church and 'patristics' originate not, as some vainly imagine, in the nineteenth, but in the fifteenth and sixteenth centuries. Secondly, one of William Frend's secondary teaching areas has been the Reformation, and in a sense he resembles many of the adogmatic Christian Humanists of that era who propagated the notion of recourse to the authentic original sources and remains of early Christianity.

As editor of this book I would like to thank the contributors for

their uncomplaining cooperation within the uncomfortable restraints of a sort of designer book; I owe special thanks to Rowan
Williams who stepped in at a late stage to take over the task allotted
to the brave late Richard Hanson; also to Kurt Rudolph for taking
over from Elaine Pagels who was incapacitated by a series of family
tragedies; to Philip Law, my editor at SPCK who helped to generate
the concept behind this book; to Leslie Milton MA BD, research
student at Glasgow, who compiled the Chronology and Conspectus;
and to the Rev. Valerie Watson MA BD STM, Minister of Kelvinside/
Hillhead Parish Church, Glasgow, who gladly undertook the task
of furnishing the indexes.

Ian Hazlett
Glasgow 1990

PART ONE

---

*Why Study Early
Church History?*

1

Why Study Early Church History?

JOSEPH KELLY

In writing an essay about 'Why Study Early Church History?' in a book dedicated to William Frend, one has mixed feelings. Surely such a topic is appropriate; but, on the other hand, surely such a topic is irrelevant. Does anyone reading a book such as this need to be told that the study of early church history is important? Phrases such as 'carrying coals to Newcastle' and 'selling iceboxes to Eskimos' come instantly to mind. What I should like to do, then, is not to justify such study to those of us engaged in it but rather to suggest how such study can be justified to those outside, to our students and colleagues in other disciplines.

Perhaps the word 'student' needs qualification here. To be sure, there are some students who plan to make a career of teaching and doing research into early church history; they are a delight to have in class and one of the rewards of the discipline. I am, unfortunately, not referring to them. Rather I refer to the vast majority of students who have no inclination to the field: graduate students who need to take a course in church history and for whom the patristics course is offered at a convenient time, seminarians who want to meet the needs of today's Church but who must endure learning about the great -isms of the first few centuries, and, finally, the overwhelming numbers of college and university students who have little or no interest in courses in religion – or in religion itself for that matter – and for whom the college's early church historian is just one more quaint person who could not make a success in the more 'relevant' disciplines such as economics or computer science.

There are clearly serious dangers facing the study of early church history. The teaching of ancient languages has largely disappeared from the pre-college curriculum, so that prospective students, who may or may not know the requisite modern languages, find quite daunting the prospect of having to learn at least Greek and Latin, if not something even more arcane. The many new disciplines, such as communications and the business disciplines (what a colleague of mine calls 'the servile arts') compete strongly with the traditional ones for students and for *Lebensraum* (literally, 'living space') in the general or core curriculum. But surely the most important threat is the unhistorical attitude not only among the young but also among many supposedly educated people. The old British tradition of waiting until fifty years after the event to consider it worthy of historical study would evoke wonder and ridicule today. For an astonishing number of Americans, studying the Kennedy administration passes for history; the ancient Greeks, Romans, Jews, and Christians have become characters in gigantic movie spectacles. Indeed, every year professors who teach about the ancient world exchange idiocies which appear on examinations: Punches Pilot, the biblical profits, the Quest of the Hysterical Jesus, Oedipus was a patient of Freud, and, my own favourite, the suit of Dionysius (pronounce it!).

The foregoing was not meant to depress, but rather to awaken us to the need to convey to others the importance of what we do. If we simply presume the obvious importance of our discipline and are indifferent to what our colleagues and students think of it, we may find ourselves going the way of other disciplines – reduced budgets, smaller staffs, decreasing influence. We do not want to fulfil the second-century pagan critic Celsus' caricature of the Christians as frogs sitting about a pond, croaking to one another.[1] We must convince not only ourselves but also others as to why one should study early church history.

Let us begin with our attitude toward the discipline. Do we really think it worth studying, or do we simply consider this a personal idiosyncrasy, fortunately shared by enough people so that we can get teaching positions? Have we resigned ourselves to a decreasing influence and fewer students? Do we truly consider what we do irrelevant to the modern world? We must ask these questions because the future of our discipline depends upon them.

Why did we take up the study of early church history? Because we found it fascinating. But if we did, why should we take a defensive attitude and presume that others will not? On the contrary, we should take the view that this can interest others as much as it interested us in our student days and still interests us today. Instructors who approach a topic apologetically will never convince anyone of the topic's value. To be sure, few of our students will ever become patristic scholars, but we should not have that as a goal. This is a specialized field and, like all such fields, the province of only a few. But if we believe the study of early church history to be important, we must want to convince others that even a passing acquaintance with it is worthwhile. Indeed, if we carry out our task properly, we will find students who took the initial course wanting to take a second or even a third course. I have had such experiences myself, and I know other patristic scholars with similar experiences.

What, then, did we find so fascinating? Clearly, that will depend on the individual, but some common factors will emerge. For example, early church history tells a story with some romance and adventure. To be sure, a patristics scholar reading an article about the manuscripts behind a critical edition of some obscure Syriac Father may have some difficulty finding the romance and adventure, but we must prescind from the particulars so essential to our work to the larger picture. The story of the Church begins at Pentecost with a frightened group of disciples wondering what will happen to them; it progresses through an almost frenetic attempt to win over the outside world before the Second Coming; it focuses on an epic struggle with the most powerful empire of the ancient world; it reaches its high point with the conversion of that empire to the new faith; it closes with the gradual decline of a great civilization and the emergence of a new world. It has a large canvas and broad brush strokes. While we must pay meticulous attention to the particulars, we must never forget the general, for that is probably what attracted us. Indeed, anyone who has read William Frend's *The Rise of Christianity* will understand what I mean.

Within this larger picture are many smaller ones which can also be fascinating. Although this may surprise some, my students have always enjoyed learning about the establishment of the New Testament canon. For most of their lives, they have heard passages from the New Testament, and most have heard expositions of New Testament passages, but when I ask them how the Church determined which books belong to the New Testament, they do not know and they rather enjoy finding out. Marcion and Montanus particularly intrigue them, the former by the audacity of his personal canon and the latter by his sad attempt to revive prophecy.

As a corollary to this, when I teach about the canon of the New Testament, I also teach about its text. When they learn that we do not have the originals (autographs) of any New Testament book, they quite naturally ask how anyone knows what the books said. I have prepared a sort of beginner's guide to textual criticism, and the class and I basically establish a text. We do all this in the context of the growth of authority in the early Church so that they can see the relation between the canon and text of the New Testament and the rise of the episcopal office, the *regula fidei* (the rule of faith, often a creed), and the first synods.

In addition to considering what first attracted us to the discipline, we should also think about the relevance of our discipline as a means of attracting students.

Most historians recoil at the word 'relevant' and often with good reason. An astonishing assortment of fools and frauds has performed an equally astonishing assortment of foolish and fraudulent things under that guise. Often historians think relevance means the here and now, and thus the false or at least strained relating of some past event to a current problem. Surely no one wants to see articles like 'The Fathers and the Depletion of the Ozone Layer'.

Yet the word need not always have a pejorative meaning. Indeed, if we think about what we are doing, we are always concerned to be relevant. We speak of history, not of antiquarianism. Antiquarianism is the study of the past for its own sake, and surely most historians are personally antiquarians – we would rather read a book about the fourth century than about the twentieth. On the other hand, history has always had contemporary implications. These run the gamut from the Roman ideal of history as training in citizenship through the Augustinian idea of history[2] as a record of divine activity in the created world to modern warnings about the price of neglecting history; the contemporary implications may differ, but they are there. We consider someone ignorant of history to be boorish and ill-informed, to be lacking in any sense of where he or she is in time, to be unaware of what forces from the past are driving people today. While we should forcefully reject the nonsense associated with 'relevance', we should simultaneously recognize that we study and teach history because we think it relevant in the very best sense of the term, that is, that it enables us better to understand the contemporary world.

Such a recognition aids us in our endeavour. For example, we study the history of the Church. This means that we must have an ecclesiology, but it should also mean that the historian of the Church be cognizant of contemporary ecclesiology. We must never forget that our students hear the word 'Church' in many contexts, not just in our class, and frequently our approach says little about the Church as they understand it. In the old days, that is before ecumenism, a simpler situation obtained. Roman Catholics knew that the Church consisted of those in communion with the Bishop of Rome; Protestants knew that the Church consisted of God's elect. Thus one could do church history in a simple albeit appalling way. Today we see the Church as the whole people of God, saints and sinners, lowly and significant, educated and illiterate, within and without the institutional confines.

Our church history must acknowledge this and work with it. Historians who still see the discipline as the Church–State conflict or the analysis of the great -isms of antiquity are speaking from and to a different generation. Clearly one must never overlook topics like these, but they must be seen in a broader, more comprehensive, context. No matter how fascinating we might find the conflict between Ambrose and Theodosius,[3] we must still acknowledge that tens of millions of early Christians lived their lives with little or no interest in the Church–State problematic, and they, too, were members of the Church. History which focuses on Ambrose and Theodosius but which excludes these others is simply not good history.

Ecumenism, that is, an interest in all members of early Christianity, represents the broadest base, but other important contemporary topics claim the historian's attention. Women, long relegated to decorating altars or forming 'ladies' auxiliaries' to men's Christian groups, now claim their right to full participation in the Church. No church historian can ignore this. Intellectual honesty and the rights of the students demand that this topic find a place in every church history course. To be sure, a patriarchal Church in a patriarchal world denied women a great role, and many historians fear that some scholars, attempting to wear the feminist mantle, will construct in the classroom a church which never actually existed. One must concede these points, but, on the other hand, one must also recognize that the limited role of women in early church history is a product not just of ancient churchmen but also of modern church historians who had little or no interest in finding women's roles in the past.

It is too easy just to say that the Church limited women's role and therefore there is nothing to study. Recall what happened when this

7

kind of thing was done before. For generations, confessional historians portrayed the Gnostics as heretics whom Irenaeus and other orthodox writers put in their place, that is, outside Cyprian's ark of the Church. Today we recognize Gnosticism as a powerful spiritual as well as intellectual movement in the second century and later, and, although we can still smile at some of the Gnostic fantasies, we take Gnosticism very seriously as an authentic if aberrant Christian movement.

The same applies to other Fathers and 'heretics'. Today we recognize that Jerome had serious personal problems with delusions of grandeur and fear of persecution, and now his virulent attacks on Pelagius, Jovinian, et al. seem less like defences of orthodoxy than the ravings of a frightened man. And where do we stand today on the 'heresies' taught by Jovinian and Pelagius? Does any modern Christian truly consider marriage a secondary state for those poor ravenous lechers who cannot embrace perpetual virginity? And do we really believe that God will whisk all but a select few off to eternal damnation as Augustine claimed in denouncing Pelagian enormities?

Confessional concerns have routinely got in the way of history. The English Roman Catholic writer Philip Hughes seriously claimed that the participants in the early ecumenical councils considered them ecumenical because the popes accepted them as such, as if the eastern bishops felt they needed the approval of an Italian bishop who could not even read the conciliar proceedings in their original language![4]

To return now to the role of women in early Christianity, let us realize that the historiography which coloured our views in the past does so still. Early church history will continue to revolve around the great men like Origen and Augustine, but if it is to relate to a contemporary Church, it must also consider early Christian women. It is not a man's Church today, and it never was, theologically or historically. We must dig a little deeper, use different methods, and, where necessary, adopt a different attitude.

Another relevant topic which the early church historian might consider is the plight of the very many people not only of the Third World but also of the United States and the European Economic Community who live in destitution and filth and with little or no prospect of a better life. Here is an area with abundant evidence from early Christianity, starting with Our Lord who repeatedly expressed

8

his concern for the poor, and with Saint Paul who worked on the collection to help the poor of Jerusalem. At the end of the second century, Dionysius, bishop of Corinth, praised the Roman community for its good works. Gregory Thaumaturgus made the ransoming of barbarian captives a Christian duty. Basil the Great expressed concern about eremitic monasticism because the hermit denied the basic Christian sense of community. Perhaps the best testimony comes from Christianity's imperial critic, Julian the Apostate, who complained to his fellow-pagans that 'the impious Galileans [his contemptuous name for Christians] support not only their own poor but ours as well . . .'.[5] Indeed, this is a fruitful area not only for the teaching of early Church history but also for research as well.

At this point, the church historian may well say that all this is just fine, but there is still the problem of getting students into the classroom in the first place. After all, why should they take classes in early church history when they can take classes in more modern fields such as contemporary theology, ethics, or comparative religions? My answer is that students consider more than just the particular subject; they also consider the particular instructor. Every campus has instructors who can offer courses in just about anything at any time of day and still bring in the students. Who among us does not have fond memories of teachers whose subject matter did not interest us particularly, at least not before we took the class? And what did we respond to? Effective teaching.

Some traits transcend the discipline. Students always appreciate teachers who are learned, who come to class prepared, who have a sense of balance and a sense of humour, and who care for students. But if even these virtues do not suffice, there are still technical steps which the church historian can take, and I know just the person who can guide us in this area.

William Frend was a visiting professor at our university in the fall semester of 1981. He taught a graduate class in North African church history, and also an undergraduate introduction to early Christianity, a class opened not only to students concentrating in religious studies but to any students who wished to fulfil their requirement in religious studies with this class. Both classes were successful, not just because of William Frend's ebullient personality and vast learning, but also because of his approach to the students. The modern student, for better or worse (usually worse), is brought

9

up on television. University professors and other professional educators might join in a chorus of woes, but lamentations teach precious few students. When William Frend came to us, he brought with him hundreds of slides of various early Christian sites, including, of course, many he had seen and even excavated himself, especially in North Africa. These both delighted and intrigued the students, and the slides enabled him to make the class material more immediate to them. Let me explain.

As just noted, the students of today are very visually oriented. In so many of their classes, they see slides, videotapes, documentary films, or laboratory demonstrations. To ask them to sit for a semester while the great visiting scholar besieges them with a plethora of names and dates is to deter them from any interest in church history. The professorial lecture is still the heart of any college course, but the effective instructor supplements that wherever possible. Furthermore, the slides also have a strong scholarly content; for example, classes on early Christian prayer can use slides of the *orantes* (those praying) from the catacombs to demonstrate that the first Christians prayed from a position of strength and emphasized the communal nature of prayer. Representations of the cross but not of the crucifixion demonstrate the character of early Christian Christ piety, while representations of Christ in the imperial purple demonstrate the close relation of Church and State. Furthermore, I argued earlier that we must pay attention to all in the Church, not just the great figures such as the Fathers. It is easy to pay attention to Origen or Augustine who left behind so many writings, but how does one get in contact with those who did not write? I suggest that the art, which reflected the concerns of so many people, does that; for example, the simple drawings on the gravestones in the catacombs which serve as memorials for otherwise unknown Christians link us in an effective, almost tangible, way with our forebears. Finally, we must also recall that much early Christian art is just that, and a student can respond to the artistic as well as the historical or iconographic[6] content.

Let me add to all this an advantage which scholars on the eastern side of the Atlantic have over those of us on the western side. They can arrange field trips for the students to a local site, if there is one, to let students see the *realia* (the physical remains) of the early Church and to give them some sense of Christianity's impact on their own history. Clearly our Italian colleagues can do this almost with a vengeance, especially in Rome, but there are sites in the British Isles which would admirably fit the bill.

It is surely worth mentioning that the instructor can also make use of early Christian music, albeit to a far lesser extent than the visual arts.

I must mention that when William Frend showed these slides, he also repeatedly enthralled the students with personal stories of how he worked at particular sites and some of the difficulties encountered. The effect was almost magical as the students were able to share his sense of discovery. They learned not only what happened in early Christianity but also how modern scholars have learned about it. Indeed, they even got a glimpse into how the occasional professorial idiosyncrasy affects a discipline!

William Frend has always stressed the importance of interdisciplinary work. This, too, has a positive effect upon students. When they have decided to concentrate on a particular field, they do not object to its narrowness, but in other fields they appreciate a broader approach. There was precious little which students interested in chemistry or French literature could find in his class, but when he discussed the historical, geographical, economic, and social factors behind the rise of Christianity, many students recognized a kindred spirit. Other scholars can profit from this approach.

Another of his pedagogical virtues is his sense of humour. Church historians naturally take their discipline very seriously – What scholar does not? – but it never hurts to recall that those outside find some of this material humorous, if not actually ludicrous. The picture of the learned and saintly patriarchs of Constantinople, Antioch, and especially Alexandria engaging in intrigue, intimidation, and bribery at the Council of Ephesus always amuses students. They also enjoy episodes from the *Sayings of the Desert Fathers*, especially those intended to weed out pride in the young monks. 'On a journey a monk met some nuns, and when he saw them, he turned aside off the road. The abbess said to him, "If you had been a perfect monk, you would not have looked so closely as to see we were women." '[7]

On one occasion, William Frend told a class that an Arian bishop was acting so dreadfully that 'the emperor should have had him sacked and sent down'; I still smile at the image of a patristic patriarch being treated like a truculent undergraduate.

On a 1981 visit to an American Catholic university, he told the assembled faculty and students, who theologically would have been Chalcedonians,[8] that the Christian faith taught us that Christ had two natures before the incarnation and one after it. He then kept on speaking, waiting for his audience to recognize the implications of his words. Naturally it took some time for them to realize he had preached monophysitism to them, and even then, bearing in mind their distinguished guest's reputation, they were not ready to contradict him too quickly!

I mentioned earlier that it sometimes helps to tell students how modern scholars arrive at their conclusions; it also helps to show the human side of modern scholars. For example, in the spring semester of 1979, the late R P C Hanson told a class at our university how H M Gwatkin, the great historian of doctrine, had told his students that he had gone to Egypt looking for beetles but instead found Mrs Gwatkin!

The foregoing has attempted to justify academically the study of early church history and to suggest pedagogical methods which may aid us in interesting non-specialists in our discipline. Let me close by suggesting a theological or at least a Christian reason for the study. Christianity is an historical religion. It is Christian belief, based on the Old Testament, that God acts in human history. From the opening verses of Genesis to the closing verses of the Apocalypse, the Bible affirms the created world as a theatre of divine activity. This theme played a major role in early Christian thought, most prominently in the works of Augustine but in other Christian writers as well.

Linked to this is the notion of the communion of saints, that is, that there is an organic link between the Christians of different generations. When Irenaeus attacked the Gnostics, he claimed support not from a succession of episcopal office-holders but from a living link of which he was a part (John to Polycarp to Irenaeus). The desert monks confidently put sayings in the mouths of the famous *abbas* (Fathers), so strong was their identification with the heroes of the past. Fourth- and fifth-century bishops of Rome claimed that not they but the apostle Peter himself spoke in their writings.

Many theologians, from radical to conservative, speak of the unity of the human race and of the Christian oneness with all peoples of the world. This claim should not be limited just to our contemporaries. The southern transept window of the cathedral of Chartres shows the four evangelists seated on the shoulders of the four great

12

prophets (Isaiah, Jeremiah, Ezekiel, and Daniel) to represent the living relationship of the Old and New Testaments. I suggest we borrow that image to visualize how we relate to those Christians who have gone before us. The least we owe them is some knowledge about them and their world.

NOTES

1 Celsus, *On the True Doctrine: A Discourse against the Christians*, tr. R J Hoffman (Oxford and New York, Oxford University Press, 1987), p. 79.
2 Saint Augustine's idea of history is found in his *The City of God*, available in many translations.
3 Ambrose was bishop of Milan in the late fourth century, and Theodosius was the Roman emperor; they collided several times over the relation of the Church to the State.
4 *The Church in Crisis*. London, Burns & Oates, 1961.
5 Cited in CCC, p. 57.
6 Iconography means literally 'writing in images', and when scholars try to recreate Christian life via art, this is called iconography.
7 *The Sayings of the Fathers*, IV. 62, ed. Owen Chadwick in *Western Asceticism*, Library of Christian Classics, vol. 12 (Philadelphia, Westminster, London, SCM, 1958), p. 58.
8 That is, adherents of the Council of Chalcedon (AD 451) which taught that Christ was one person with two natures, human and divine, in opposition to the Monophysites who taught that he had only one nature.

PART TWO

Context and Origins

2

The World of the Roman Empire

JANE MERDINGER

In 31 BC, the Roman Empire was born. Off the north-west coast of Greece, Octavian, great-nephew of Julius Caesar, decisively defeated his arch-rivals, Mark Antony and Cleopatra. Upon their flight to Egypt and subsequent suicide, Octavian became, at a mere thirty-two years of age, master of the Roman world. The realm that he inherited was an exhausted one, torn and bleeding from years of intermittent civil war. Rome's march to greatness in the preceding two centuries had been impressive, but the problems inherent in expansionism had caused the republic to totter. It was Octavian's lot to pick up the pieces and forge a new system of government.

In fact, he proved more than equal to the task. With remarkable political acumen, Octavian assumed control over the army, the senate, and the treasury – the major sources of power in the commonwealth. The price of peace was high – the demise of the republic – but from its ashes he created an empire that would endure five hundred years. In grateful acknowledgement of his services, the Senate voted him the title of Augustus, an appellation both exalted and semi-religious in tone, designed to underscore his supreme status in the Roman world.

What was this Empire like, that Augustus had fought so long and so hard to gain it? It is difficult for us in the twentieth century to comprehend the sheer magnitude of its embrace. From the rain-soaked coasts of Brittany to the glistening beaches of Greece, from the white-hot sands of Morocco to the steely peaks of the Alps, the Empire was vast. Under Augustus' successors, it reached even further. Britain came under its sway, Mesopotamia and eastern Europe too. The monuments of its glory are still with us, mute testimony to its enduring greatness. Hadrian's Wall, to this day, stands guard in northern England, moss-covered now, a once-mighty bulwark against the ferocious Picts. In a quiet corner of

17

France, under azure skies and bright sunshine, the Pont du Gard still rears up proudly, a marvel of Roman engineering. Sixty million people lived within the Empire, perhaps even seventy million: Celts, Berbers, Italians, Greeks, Syrians, Egyptians, Arabians, Thracians, and more. Numerous customs, languages, and traditions peppered the countryside, for the Empire ever remained an amalgamation of the various peoples whom it had conquered. Local deities were worshipped, age-old gods and goddesses who brought their devotees comfort and relief alongside newer Roman deities.

For all its diversity, however, the Empire boasted important marks of unity. Latin was the official language in the western part of the Empire, Greek in the east. Knowledge of those two tongues alone could carry a person all the way from Britain to Mesopotamia, a remarkable fact when one considers the map of Europe today. All government business and legal matters were conducted in Latin or Greek; the army, needing a single common language, insisted solely on Latin throughout its ranks. Many educated Romans were bilingual, though in the latter days of the Empire, as troubles began to gnaw at its foundations, fewer people could afford the luxury of learning a second language.

The legal system also contributed to uniformity throughout the Empire. Though not as gifted in philosophy or the arts as the ancient Greeks, the Romans displayed a real genius for jurisprudence. As early as 450 BC they had begun codifying the basic principles by which their society would operate. Originally associated with religious practices, Roman law gradually became a science of its own. Contact with the many peoples conquered by the republic forced Roman lawmakers to formulate broad conceptions of the rights and duties of humankind, giving birth to the precepts of natural law.

No essay on the Roman Empire would be complete without reference to the marvellous network of roads, bridges, tunnels, and aqueducts that crisscrossed its vast face. In feats of engineering, the Romans knew no rivals in the ancient world. Of primary importance were the roads. From early on, the Romans reckoned that military success would ensue only if soldiers could march quickly and efficiently to enemy territory. Dirt roads simply would not suffice; even in the best of weather, movement on them was slow, only about twelve miles per day. In foul weather, they could easily become impassable, clogged with puddles and mire. As early as the third century BC Roman engineers started to produce paved roads, undergirded by foundations four feet deep and capped with cobblestones or smooth flagstones. On such surfaces, rain or shine, soldiers could march thirty miles a day. Because speed was of the essence, Roman roads ran very straight, especially in open countryside. With an impressive 250,000 miles of Roman roads spanning the Empire, even citizens in the remotest of outposts heard, on occasion, the tramp of the legions' feet, the clatter of supply wagons, the braying of pack mules.

ROMAN SOCIETY

Society in the ancient world was primarily agricultural; in the Empire, over ninety per cent of the inhabitants lived in the country-side. Values were deeply conservative and highly patriarchal in tone. No emphasis was placed on progress; on the contrary, innovation and change were regarded with suspicion. What the Romans esteemed most of all was ancestral custom and tradition. Best to emulate the past, not to break with it. Had not courage, hard work, and loyalty conquered the world and placed it at the Romans' feet? The most brilliant poet of Augustus' day, Vergil, celebrated these virtues in Aeneas, mythical founder of the Roman nation. Aeneas was always, for Vergil, *pius* Aeneas; he always maintained a profound sense of duty and devotion toward the gods, his homeland, and his family.

In fact, the centrepiece of Roman society was the family. In this most fundamental of settings, children learned first-hand to worship their ancestors and honour their parents. Death masks of deceased relatives hung inside the home, watchful keepers of the *genius*, the guiding spirit of the household. Nearby, on the road leading into town or in the local cemetery, the family tomb stood proudly, site of annual solemn feats in memory of the departed. Presiding over the household was the father of the family, the *paterfamilias*. As the guardian and trustee of the family name and fortune, he possessed absolute power over all of his dependants: wife, children, and slaves. So important was his status in Roman culture that his grown children continued to be subject to his authority, even his married daughters, unless he specifically made provision otherwise. His wife was con-sidered to be the keeper of the hearth and the home; though less restricted in her comings and goings than other women in ancient societies, from a modern point of view her life was circumscribed by her husband and her culture. Until late in the Empire, every woman had to be under the control of a guardian, unless she earned a special exemption.

In many ways a woman's existence was much more precarious than a man's. Discrimination started early; infanticide was acceptable in Roman society, and more female babies were allowed to perish than male ones. A daughter, after all, would require a dowry in order to be married, an expensive proposition for most fathers. What is more, the free bread distributed to the masses in Rome – the grain dole – was given exclusively to males. As far as the government was concerned, women could not vote, so currying their favour with free handouts was a moot point anyway, and they were not likely to foment rebellion.

As for education, girls lost out to boys by a wide margin. In the ancient world, only middle-class and well-to-do parents could afford to educate their children, but whereas boys were encouraged to continue in school throughout their teens, girls were expected to cease their studies at the age of twelve and marry by the following year. Until age twelve, youngsters were taught the basic skills of reading, writing, and arithmetic. Boys then went on to learn grammar and literature and a smattering of geometry, astronomy, and music. Advanced education commenced in one's sixteenth year and focused almost exclusively on the study of rhetoric, although some philosophy might be taught as well. In a society that prized public speaking and verbal pyrotechnics, rhetoric was considered the crown jewel of one's education. The Mediterranean world lived in the out-of-doors, in the forum and in the marketplace, and great were the rewards for those who learned to captivate their audience with polished prose.

Middle-class and wealthy women, on the other hand, could not look forward to a career in the public eye; it was their lot in life to marry young and bear children. This was the expected, honourable, and virtually only option open to them. Marriage at such an early age, however, exacted its toll; from inscriptions on tombstones, it is clear that many young girls died in childbirth, their bodies unable yet to bear the pain of labour. But even older women died in childbirth, too; the Roman world was simply not equipped with the life-saving devices so familiar in modern, developed countries.

Lower-class women and female slaves did not lead the sheltered existence that their more prosperous counterparts did. They had to get out and work to earn their keep. Nonetheless, occupations open to them were limited, compared with opportunities available to men. Many of the jobs available to slave women were domestic in nature: nurse, maid, wetnurse, spinner, weaver, clothesmaker, hairdresser, and the like. Lower-class women were able to branch out a bit further; they became local shopkeepers, fishmongers, and butchers.

For most people in the Empire, male or female, life was not easy. Historians estimate that two per cent were wealthy; a mere eight per cent were middle-class; and the remaining ninety per cent lived virtually a hand-to-mouth existence. These are sobering statistics. Perhaps hardest for us to fathom is the tremendous gulf that existed between rich and poor. In the Roman Empire, the wealthy were stupendously wealthy. Some estates spanned thousands of acres, with several thousand slaves tilling the soil. One ranch alone in south-eastern Italy boasted 250,000 sheep, an impressive operation by any estimate. Augustus himself *owned* all of Egypt, not to mention other vast estates and plantations dotted all over the Empire. The poor, on the other hand, either crowded into the cities that hugged the Mediterranean shoreline or sought employment as tenant farmers on the estates of the rich. These *coloni*, as tenant farmers were called, worked the land and paid their rent with a percentage of their harvest or with their labour. Rent was not the only thing that they owed, however. There were taxes to be paid as well, which constituted an additional burden.

Nonetheless, with talent, ambition, and a bit of luck, a man could go far in Augustus' time. The two best routes for success were the civil service and the military, the backbone of the Empire. Civil service jobs mushroomed overnight when Augustus became emperor, and the city of Rome alone developed a huge appetite for such employees. People were needed to supervise the grain dole, the fire department, the police department, the water supply, street-cleaning, the upkeep of public buildings, the construction and repair of roads and sewers, etc. Add to that all of the work that had to be done out in the provinces: someone had to collect taxes, oversee supplies for the army, manage the emperor's private estates, supervise the imperial postal system, and inspect roads and bridges. The list is almost mindboggling. Nonetheless, this is where an enterprising individual could make his mark; we hear of numbers of freedmen who started out in menial jobs only to work themselves up into positions of great importance. A good head for figures, a sharp mind, a gift for flattery – any combination of these could propel a man from obscurity to prominence, if he was determined enough.

Life in the military promised, perhaps, less spectacular rewards, but a man could carve out a fine career for himself in it nevertheless. Legionaries were recruited from the older, more civilized provinces and served for twenty years. Hard fighting in Germany and the Balkans during the early days of the Empire took its toll, but thereafter peace reigned in most parts of the Mediterranean for almost two centuries. As a result, many a soldier assigned to the frontier found himself spending the bulk of his time not in combat but in building roads or barracks. Legionaries were forbidden to marry, since they might be transferred at a moment's notice, but most soldiers took up with a local woman near their camp and had children with her. Upon retirement, they collected a handsome bonus and often remained in the area with their family. The situation proved to be a satisfactory one all round: the government could count on her veterans in times of crisis to help ward off enemy attack; frontier towns gradually became more romanized through their presence; and the veterans themselves lived quite well off their discharge stipend.

Whatever a person's career choice, chances were good that sooner or later the ambitious individual would spend some time living at Rome. In a sense, all roads did lead there. Capital of the Empire, nerve-centre of the government, home to the gods, it was truly the most important place to be in the ancient world. For the first-time visitor, it must also have been the most thrilling spot to be, or the most nerve-wracking, depending on one's point of view. Rome was huge. At least 500,000 people lived there, perhaps even a million; no one knows for sure. What is clear is that by the second century AD, its population had far outstripped most of the other major cities of the Empire, only Alexandria being comparable. The noise was incessant. Chickens squawking, babies crying, merchants hawking their wares – every day was pandemonium, and night-time brought little relief. Merely walking from one spot to another could be an adventure in itself. Streets were narrow and twisted; pickpockets abounded; litters of the rich and famous easily knocked down the absent-minded. Juvenal, the famous satirist from the second century AD has painted an indelible portrait of the trials and tribulations awaiting the hapless resident of Rome. Nothing escaped his venom, or his eye. Sycophants, foreigners, diviners, social climbers parade through his satires like characters at a carnival, littering the landscape with their insouciance and their greed.

The wealthy, of course, lived much better than the poor at Rome. Apart from housing and civil status – being 'free' (a 'citizen') or 'unfree' (a 'slave') – the ultimate gauge of social class must have been food. The rich dined sumptuously. No extravagance was spared: no bird was too exotic to eat, no spice too distant to find, no pastry too delicate to concoct. Tables at dinner parties fairly groaned with silver platters, as course after course made its grand entrance. Fanciful decor was paramount: thrushes topped with a tasty sauce, cleverly ensconced in handmade nests; roasted peacock, its gorgeous plumage arrayed in a fan-like display; dormice rolled in honey and sprinkled with sunny poppyseeds. In vain did Augustus and his successors fulminate against lavishness by passing sumptuary legislation. No one paid any attention. The poor, on the other hand, ate very simply. Bread, fruit, and vegetables were their mainstay; meat they had infrequently, because of its expense. Everyone drank wine, with water to dilute it to taste. The aristocrats could choose fine wines imported from the Rhineland or southern Gaul, while the masses had to make do with cheap, local varieties. Virtually no one drank beer or milk; those were the beverages of the barbarians.

Rich or poor, everyone could take the advantage of the amusements and amenities which Rome proffered after hours. (Twentieth-century readers may be surprised to learn that the working day in ancient Rome ended shortly after one p.m., though it should be remembered that work commenced early in the morning.) Many made a bee-line to the baths, where they could relax in steam rooms, enjoy a massage, swim in hot or cold pools, and exercise in the gymnasium. Some of the larger baths were truly palatial. The baths of Diocletian, built in the third century AD, accommodated three thousand people and included a library, lecture halls, bars, restaurants, lovely gardens, and even an art museum. Admission was cheap, so even the poorest could partake. Actual upkeep of the baths was staggeringly expensive, but Augustus and subsequent emperors gladly shouldered the cost. They knew how important it was to keep the people content.

Romans loved spectacles, and the government spared no expense to provide them with this type of amusement as well. Wild beast hunts, gladiator fights, circus races, comedy and tragedy, mock sea battles – nothing was too extravagant or too dangerous to present to

23

the masses at Rome. The tastes of the people were not refined. Gladiatorial combats and wild beast hunts could be shockingly grisly; it was not uncommon for an unarmed combatant, tied to a stake, to be torn apart by a ferocious leopard, or for a gladiator armed to the hilt to cut down a defenceless opponent in cold blood. Oftentimes, an orchestra played throughout the fighting, and after the dead bodies were hauled away, attendants would sprinkle saffron on the sand to mask the stench of death in the amphitheatre. We do know that the more sadistic events were usually scheduled for the morning, when most people would be at work. Nonetheless, there was still plenty of gore at the afternoon games, and most Romans simply accepted such scenarios as a matter of course.

Far less gruesome but equally intoxicating for the masses were the chariot races, conducted at the Circus Maximus. Seven laps around the elliptical course won the prize, and competition was intense. Four-horse teams typically were the featured attraction, but other combinations thundered around the track as well. Betting was heavy, as fans shouted for their favourite colours to take the lead. So crowded were the viewing stands that the imperial government took the unprecedented step of tripling the seating capacity to 160,000.

Finally, the theatre offered its own special blandishments to the public. Both tragedies and comedies were staged, but the latter with their quick wit and ribald repartee easily attracted much larger audiences. For most Romans, tragedies were simply too austere and moralistic to be entertaining. Over time, comedies began to pander more and more to the crude streak in the masses and degenerated, for the most part, into music-hall shows, studded with tasteless lyrics and vulgar gestures.

THE LATER ROMAN EMPIRE

For two hundred years, the Mediterranean world basked in the glow of peace and prosperity. Augustus had done his job well; Rome seemed indomitable. The gods smiled daily on her: *Fortune favours the brave*. Toward the end of the second century, however, cracks began to appear in the facade. The emperor Marcus Aurelius spent most of his reign on campaign, waging savage battles against swarms of barbarians on the eastern front. He was successful, but the victories were hard-won, an ominous harbinger of times to come. In the third century AD, the Empire suffered a series of stunning disasters. Crippling inflation, devastating plague, famine, brutal wars with the Goths and the Persians all took their toll. People lost faith in the government; emperors came and went, as troops stationed in different parts of the Empire took matters into their own hands and raised their own generals to the purple. In the space of seventy years, twenty-seven different men were officially proclaimed emperor; this figure does not even begin to reflect the numbers of usurpers who vied for the throne as well. Of the twenty-seven, most were killed by their own troops, two committed suicide, and only four died a natural death. The nadir of Rome's fortunes occurred in AD 260, when the emperor himself was defeated in battle by the Persians and led away in chains as a prisoner, never to be heard from again. In the depths of such humiliation, the Empire was fighting for its very life.

Excellent generals, tough discipline, and hard fighting brought Rome back from the brink in the late third century. In AD 284, Diocletian ascended the throne, a rough Illyrian general who had worked his way up through the ranks. A born disciplinarian with a genius for administration, Diocletian reorganized the imperial government and the army. Reasoning that the Empire was simply too big to be governed effectively by one man, he decided to split it into two parts; he would govern the eastern half and his colleague, Maximian, would rule the west. Each would remain in his own territory, closely monitoring problems which cropped up there and devising appropriate solutions. No more military revolts in remote provinces – now an emperor would be within striking distance of any seditious activity. Furthermore, Diocletian reorganized all of the provinces in the Empire, cutting them up into much smaller units so that they could be more efficiently governed.

The other pressing need in the late third century was for a bigger, more flexible army to preserve the Empire from attack. More than ever before, barbarians were massing along the Rhine and the Danube, threatening to burst into the Empire at any moment. With his long years of military service, Diocletian was just the man to know what to do. He decreased the number of troops in each legion and then placed the new legions more evenly along the borders. In addition to these permanent garrisons, he created a new flexible attack force, cavalry squadrons that were primed to move rapidly to any trouble spot.

Such vast changes in administration and defence necessarily affected other areas of Roman society. Having halved the Empire, Diocletian succeeded in doubling its bureaucracy – and bureaucracies are very expensive to maintain. His reorganization of the army, together with the recruitment of new troops, placed an added strain on the economy. Someone had to pay for all of these programmes, and Diocletian found himself imposing harsh new taxes throughout the Empire as a result. Depending on the quality of the soil and the number of people living there, every farm was now assessed a set amount of wheat, olives, or grapes that it had to produce each year and hand over to the government. Unfortunately, what looked good on paper failed dismally in practice. In real life, people fall ill, floods occur, the sun fails to shine, crops die. Add to that the effect of erosion, soil depletion, and the absence of crop rotation – things that the ancient world never understood – and it is easy to see why Diocletian's scheme ultimately proved unworkable. When *coloni* could not pay their taxes and fell deeply into debt, many of them abandoned their lands and either indentured themselves to an affluent landlord or simply ran away. In a drastic move, Diocletian ordered local town councillors to shoulder the burden themselves; they now personally had to pay out of their own pocket any taxes defaulted on by neighbouring farmers. Such local magistrates were already feeling hard pressed. Despite war, famine, or plague, they had continued to be responsible for the upkeep of their town: the water supply, the baths, temples, the forum, roads for passing soldiers, the public postal system. What had once been a coveted honour had become an odious burden; men now tried desperately to avoid public office, for it spelt almost certain financial ruin.

In the early fourth century AD, Diocletian's successor, Constantine, capped the whole process by declaring certain jobs to be hereditary. Harsh times demand harsh measures; Constantine needed guarantees. The Empire had to be defended; grain had to be shipped from Africa to Rome; bread had to be baked for the masses. All jobs connected with shipping, baking, farming, and the military became hereditary, and stiff penalties were exacted from those who shunned their destiny.

Perhaps most insidious of all in the later Roman Empire was the tendency to allow barbarians to settle within the Empire's boundaries and to join the army. In such wise, the enemy without gradually became the enemy within. Since the second century BC, German tribes had clustered on the banks of the Rhine and the Danube, gazing across the waters at the magnificent civilization that lay on the other side. Three hundred years later, they began crossing over in earnest, pushed forward by the Huns from Central Asia and by their own desires. Battles ensued; when the Romans won, they thrust the barbarians back and breathed a little easier for a time. Often, however, the barbarians triumphed and in their hour of victory wrested steep concessions from the Empire: a huge indemnity of gold to be paid them each year, or land inside the Empire for them to settle on. With the Empire's population declining, it was only a matter of time before these early Germans settlers began signing on with the Roman army. A gradual barbarization of the ranks set in. By Constantine's era, even the officer corps was beginning to count barbarians amongst its members. How trustworthy all of these men were remained open for debate. In the fifth century, when new tribes came hurtling into the Empire looking for plunder and land, the more settled barbarians could have put up a better fight against them.

In the end, the western part of the Empire simply could not sustain itself against the onslaught. Military defences were stretched to the breaking point; city life collapsed; the sturdy Roman farmer disappeared, crushed by taxes, misery, and despair. In AD 476 a Goth, Odoacer, bloodlessly deposed the emperor, a mere slip of a boy. Henceforth, barbarian kings would rule Rome; the Empire of Augustus, Diocletian, and Constantine had fallen. But not quite all was lost. As civilized life gradually ebbed away, one vital force continued to pulse throughout the Mediterranean – Christianity.

BIBLIOGRAPHY

Balson, J P V D, *Rome: The Story of an Empire*. New York, McGraw Hill, 1970.

Brown, Peter, *The World of Late Antiquity from Marcus Aurelius to Mohammed*. London, Thames and Hudson, 1971.

Jones, A H M, *The Later Roman Empire*. 3 vols., Oxford University Press 1964.

Lewis, Naphtali, and Meyer, Reinhold, eds., *Roman Civilization, Sourcebook II: The Empire*. New York, Harper & Row, 1951; Harper Torchbook, 1966.

MacMullen, Ramsay, *Enemies of the Roman Order: Treason, Unrest and Alienation in the Empire*. Cambridge, Mass., Harvard University Press 1967.

3

The Birth of Christianity

JOHN RICHES

Appropriate metaphors for the origins and development of Christianity are not easy to come by. If we say that Christianity begins life as the offspring of a mother, already a number of powerful suggestions are being made which may mould our subsequent understanding of its history. At the very least we assume an identifiable mother and an identifiable child. We may be encouraged to see both mother and child as having each a single continuous history. We shall be disposed to cast our story of Christianity's development in terms of 'its' interaction with surrounding cultures and, depending on our views of human development, we shall see these external factors as contributing more or less to its formation. We may, moreover, be prompted to ask further questions: Was Christianity the only child born to this mother: was it not, in Alan Segal's powerful metaphor,[1] one of twins, like those born to Rebecca who already in the womb were struggling against each other and who came into the world, the one clutching the other's heel?

Such a metaphor, that is to say, is both fruitful and seductive. It enables us to discern patterns and connections in the seemingly random data of history; but at the same time it may blind us to other ways of reading the material. Above all, if we employ this particular metaphor then we must be on our guard against the too easy assumption that we are dealing with readily identifiable entities. There is a singularity about the phrase, the birth of Christianity, which may blind us to the sheer diversity of belief, practice and community, all of which might with good reason be identified as in some sense Christian, in the first century. We must not, that is, allow such a metaphor to divert us from the crucial question: What is it that gives unity to such diversity?

Let us take up Alan Segal's suggestion that Christianity is to be seen as one of twins born to the Judaism of the Second Temple period, the other being Rabbinic Judaism which emerged in the Academy at Jamnia after AD 70. One might develop this idea as follows: the Judaism of the Second Temple period, which runs from the return from exile in Persia in the late sixth century BC and the re-establishment of a Jewish state to the destruction of the Temple in AD 70, was in serious decline in the first century AD. Rome had established control over the Mediterranean, bringing Palestine under its control in the 60s BC. For the Jews this represented one further incursion by foreign powers and raised questions about their ability to maintain an independent Jewish state run in accordance with Jewish laws. Such questions were vital ones, for the Judaism of the Second Temple period was a thoroughly national religion. This conflict between Jewish ideals of a national, independent Temple–state and the desires of powerful neighbours to control the Middle East were tragically resolved at the end of the First Jewish Revolt (AD 66–70) by the destruction of the Temple, the central institution of that state. Without it, it simply could not function. What emerged from the ashes was, on the one hand, a communal form of piety, located in the home and the local community and focused on communal and private prayer, the reading and interpretation of the Scriptures; on the other a dynamic missionary movement which would sweep through the cities of the Mediterranean and within fewer than three hundred years be adopted as the official religion of the Empire.

The origins of these antagonistic twins pre-date the fall of Jerusalem. Christianity emerges from the preaching of a Galilean millenarian prophet and his followers, of whom the most prominent had not known him: Paul's entry into Christianity is occasioned by a vision or call-experience which leads him to abandon his 'persecution' of Christianity and to join the ranks of its wandering preachers. The Judaism of the Jamnia period has its precursors in the sages and the Pharisees of the Second Temple whose origins go back at least as far as the Maccabean revolt of the second century BC. More specifically, however, Jamnia has its roots in the later developments in the Pharisaic movement, as, in Jacob Neusner's phrase, it makes the transition 'from politics to piety', relocating the centre of the cult in the home and the local assembly by transferring some of the priestly rituals of the Temple to meals and prayers in the home.

Obviously such an account is schematic in the extreme. But before attempting to fill in some of the gaps, it is worth considering the strengths and weaknesses of such a general hypothesis. Its strengths are considerable. It relates the origins of Christianity and Rabbinic Judaism to the history both of Second Temple Judaism and of the wider Mediterranean world. It draws attention to the competitive nature of early Christianity and of Jamnian Judaism as they each seek to reshape Jewish traditions and create a new community after the destruction of Jerusalem. It connects developments in first-century Judaism prior to the fall of Jerusalem with those after it. But it also has its weaknesses. Attention to the wider political history of the time may divert from the inner religious dynamic, the sense of the 'holy' and its peculiar representation, which occurs within particular communities. Concentration on the competitive relations between early Christianity and Jamnia may lead the historian to overlook other complex cultural forces which both groups had to deal with. Tracing the origins of these two communities back to Jewish groups in the earlier part of the first century may simplify what was a more complex pre-history, fed by different sources and groups, including those from outside Judaism. Above all such a story may tempt us to see continuity and indeed unity where the connections are in fact more accidental. With such provisos, let me attempt to flesh out a little more such a picture of the birth of Christianity.

Judaism in the first century, the 'mother' of Christianity, was itself a very diverse phenomenon. This diversity, however, springs from a common stock. On the one hand, it can be traced to a set of common beliefs in Jewish election, the making of a 'covenant' between God and his people and the giving to them of the land. The Law[2] spelt out the terms of this relationship between God and his people and regulated their relations with each other. The priests administered the Law and the worship of the Temple which too was prescribed and regulated by the Law. In broad terms all groups might be said to have subscribed to such beliefs and indeed to the practices which they entailed. But of course the detailed working out of such beliefs can permit a great deal of variation and this occurs all the more readily where existing community structures and practices are under threat. Such diversity can however be held together in other ways than by shared beliefs. A shared history, a shared attachment to a particular territory, common descent and a common experience of the numinous in popular festivals and in the worship of the Temple: all these can weld a community together and hold them, even when their understanding of shared beliefs diverges quite sharply.

There were, that is to say, strong communal bonds holding the Jews of the first century together. But there were also strong forces undermining those bonds. Theirs was a national religion with a religious constitution which was being impugned, variously, by Roman rule, whether direct or indirect. Very crudely, we can say that there were four broad types of responses possible to such a situation. One was to look for a military solution, and this was pursued at various times by Jews, culminating in the First Jewish Revolt. Secondly, the Sadducees[3] sought to maintain at least a semblance of the Temple state by striking a compromise with the occupying powers. This meant accepting that the High Priests were appointed and dismissed at will by the Roman governor; and accepting the presence of a Roman occupying force in Jerusalem. But at least it ensured, so long as there was peace, the continuance of the Temple worship. Thirdly, a different way was taken by groups like the Essenes at Qumran and the Pharisees. They, in their various ways, withdrew, or began to withdraw, from the national political sphere. The differences between the two groups are of course considerable. The Essenes withdrew physically from Jewish communal life and set up an alternative community with its own rituals and worship, which they saw as a substitute for the atoning rites of the Temple, until such time as the Romans were defeated and they took control of the Temple themselves. The Pharisees gradually abandoned their hopes of influencing the life of the nation from the court or the 'Sanhedrin' and began to establish their own communities centred on Torah with again their own rituals, such as hand-washing before meals, taken over from the priestly rituals of the Temple. Here a very different experience of the numinous is being set at the centre of communal life, and it is this which will be intensively cultivated in the period after the destruction of Jerusalem.

There remains a fourth way, that of the millenarian prophets. Such figures, like John the Baptist, Jesus and a number of others of whom we read in Josephus and Acts,[4] looked to some divine act of intervention to restore Israel's fortunes and usher in a new age. And in announcing the onset of a new age, they also depicted in imagery, in ethical teaching and in story something of the quality, the theological and ethical assumptions on which the new age would be based. In one sense such figures are unpolitical, not concerned with the exercise of power, with courses of action which could effect the change which they so vividly announce. In another way their preaching may be of considerable political consequence in so far as it focuses a people's discontent, their sense of loss of identity and value, and fosters new hopes for national renewal.

Such figures are possessed by a particular sense of the numinous. They feel themselves called to proclaim their message regardless of the personal consequences. John the Baptist, Jesus, the Samaritan prophet recorded in Josephus, Theudas (Acts 5.36), all met violent deaths as martyrs for their cause. But while they are all possessed by their divine call, the message which they proclaim and their manner of life is by no means identical. Rudolf Otto, whose classic work *The Idea of the Holy*[5] attempted to define the sense of the numinous which in various forms lies at the heart of the religious experience of different communities, also in a less well-known work attempted to distinguish John the Baptist and Jesus as different religious types: John the ascetic prophet announcing the coming wrath and judgement of God; Jesus the charismatic figure possessed with a sense of present fulfilment and with a vision of the qualities which would spring from such a new life in God.

It is interesting to compare the way in which John and Jesus convey their vision of what is to come. John conjures up terrifying images of the 'stronger one' with his winnowing fork, of the axe laid to the root of the tree, ready to rise and fall, of the coming baptism of fire and spirit (Matt. 3.11f.). Jesus, by contrast, anticipates a coming messianic banquet in his meals with tax-collectors and sinners, and, in his stories of everyday life, teases people into a new understanding of the ways of God with his people. In his ethical teaching, not least in his command to love one's enemies (Matt. 5.43 ff.), he begins to work out what the way will be for those who follow a God who is merciful to all, who 'sends his rain upon the just and the unjust'. And this vision of the new world is linked with a call to people to follow him in a way that is costly and demanding. Such figures, because they are possessed by a God-given vision of a new age, can loosen the ties of their followers with the old age. In this sense they are deeply subversive. Secondly, because they are able to break with the old, they can sit lightly to old community loyalties and self-definitions, John can dismiss descent from Abraham (Matt. 3.9f.), not because he despises what God has done in the past but because of his overpowering sense of what God is about to do in the immediate future. Jesus shares meals with tax-collectors and sinners, an act which is clearly shocking to his contemporaries, indicating, as it does, that such people may enter the Kingdom of heaven before those who are still attempting to hold on to the new age.

In all this Jesus appears as a powerful charismatic prophet calling people to awake to the new dawn. He calls a group of people around himself, invests some of them with special authority (twelve to sit on the twelve thrones of Israel in the new Kingdom) and sets off to Jerusalem where he meets his death at the hands of the authorities, Jewish and Roman in some combination which it is hard to reconstruct. What, the perennial question runs, is the relation between Jesus and the Christian communities which sprang up around the Mediterranean world in the aftermath of his death? 'Jesus', as Loisy said, 'preached the Kingdom. What came was the Church.' In what sense can it claim to be his legitimate heir?

The question, though perennial, has not attracted undue attention in recent years, though in this respect William Frend is, as in so much, a refreshing exception to the rule. Answers to it must start, not with the attempt to prove the legitimacy of the Church's 'kerygma' from an examination of its historical origins in Jesus' teaching, but by considering the various ways in which the early Christian communities appropriated traditions about Jesus, forged religious symbols for themselves from his teaching and the stories and beliefs about his life and death, and institutionalized a specific sense of the numinous centred on him.

Such questions present themselves in the most problematic form with regard to Paul's relationship to Jesus. Paul, though by no means ignorant of Jesus' sayings, makes very little use of them, even when it comes to matters of ethics. He is not interested in knowing Christ according to the flesh (2 Cor. 5.16), but rather in experiencing and proclaiming the new life in Christ. Nevertheless there are significant links between Paul and Jesus, even if these are by no means straightforward.

Like Jesus, Paul expected that the existing order would shortly come to an end, but unlike Jesus he rarely made use of the term 'Kingdom of God' to express this expectation. Instead he talked about Jesus' death and resurrection: Jesus' own resurrection being the firstfruits and the guarantee of the general resurrection which Paul expected within the lifetime of his contemporaries. Thus for Paul an essential first stage in the turning of the ages had occurred through Jesus' death and resurrection, and so Paul clearly saw himself as being in a different situation from Jesus during his

33

lifetime. Thus he explains his own situation, not in terms of Jesus' preaching of the Kingdom, but of his own experience of liberation through the death and resurrection of Jesus Christ.

The two ages are now defined in terms of the old age originating in Adam, of bondage to sin, and the new age, brought about through Christ's death and resurrection, of liberty and righteousness (Rom. 5.12–21). Paul's hope that he will share in the benefits of this new age is grounded in what has been achieved in Christ. It is not just that Christ's death and resurrection is the necessary first step towards the resurrection of all; cross and resurrection already shape the existence of those who live in anticipation of the final fulfilment. Their present existence, that is to say, is 'christoform': it is conformed to Christ's own experience of bondage and liberation which is his by virtue of entering into the human condition, of his dying and rising again. For him to enter this world is to take upon himself the form of a slave (Phil. 2.6ff., probably quoting from an early Christian hymn); it is, in a striking phrase of Paul's own, for the one who knew no sin to be made sin (2 Cor. 5.21). In this way he shares men and women's enslavement to 'beggarly spirits' (Gal. 4.3). Christ's death is then the gateway to a new, risen life of glory and liberation from bondage. Those who believe share in that life by virtue of their baptism into Christ's death. Like him they then 'die to sin', 'walk in newness of life' and live in the hope of sharing in his resurrection (Rom. 6.1–11). Thus Christ, in Ernst Käsemann's phrase, 'bears our fate'[6] in a dual sense: that he enters the human condition and assumes its form; and that by his death and resurrection he transforms it and brings new life to those who are conformed to him.

This conformity with Christ embraces not only fundamental aspects of Christian initiation and hope: being buried with him, dying to sin, looking forward to rising with him; it also extends to the particular existence which Paul 'enjoys' as an apostle. He is commissioned by Christ as an apostle to the Gentiles, called to be an ambassador of Christ, to share in his work (2 Cor. 5.20). In this he specifically sees himself as sharing in the same call experience (even though the circumstances are significantly different) as the other witnesses of the resurrection (1 Cor. 15.1–8). He becomes a 'collaborator' (2 Cor. 6.1). Just as Christ's suffering brings comfort and salvation to Paul, so Paul's suffering brings comfort to the Corinthians. In this Paul experiences in his own life the nature of God, his mercies and comfort (2 Cor. 1.3–7).

In all this, Paul shares something of the same vision of God's justice and mercy as Jesus. The difference is that for Paul the vision of God is linked to a call to participate in the mission of the Church to the Gentiles, whereas for Jesus that vision is linked to a call to proclaim the good news of the Kingdom to the poor and the sinners in Israel. Significantly their vision of God is in each case linked to a prophetic experience of call, of being possessed and overpowered by the holy, as one receives a particular message and task. And in a remarkable way though the tasks to which they are called vary substantially, they are both related to a central perception of a God who is radically open to his enemies, to that which is opposed to him. That vision underlies Jesus' statement that he had not come to call righteous but sinners, his meals with tax-collectors and sinners, his command to people to love their enemies, and his rejection of purity laws; and equally it informs Paul's preaching of a God who justifies the ungodly, his preaching of reconciliation to the Gentiles, and his rejection of the requirement of circumcision and adherence to Levitical dietary laws. One might say that what connects Paul with Jesus most intimately is an essentially prophetic experience of God which fills him with a sense of the mercies of God, of his turning towards his enemies, to the ungodly. What distinguishes them is that Paul's vision is now mediated through his knowledge, in the Spirit, of Christ.

But we need to remind ourselves of the dangers of being so concerned with tracing the continuity between Jesus and Paul that we overlook the other forces which contributed to the development of Christianity.

Before his conversion, Paul was a Pharisee, engaged in transposing a religion based on the worship of the Temple into one centred on Torah and located in the local community. This leads to a strange dialectic in Paul: on the one hand he distances himself sharply from any attempt to centre Christianity on the detailed interpretation of Torah. 'The letter kills, the spirit makes alive' (2 Cor. 3.6). On the other, he wants to justify the new community which he is painfully bringing into existence in terms of the 'Scriptures'. His letters are peppered with scriptural allusions, using techniques he had learnt in his days as a Pharisee, and in the very chapter where he appears to dismiss Scripture so comprehensively, he goes on to argue on scriptural grounds of some considerable dubiety that the Jews when they interpret Scripture still have a veil over their hearts (2 Cor.

35

3.15). At the same time he invokes the authority of Scripture for his own preaching of the Lord, who is the Spirit (as opposed to the letter) and the source of liberty (2 Cor. 3.17).

Paul's communities, whatever the later Church may have become and however much he may have on occasion rued it, were communities where the prophetic voice had precedence over the written words of Torah, and in this respect as in much else they were conceived by contrast with the emerging communities of first-century Judaism. That contrast had to be maintained in sharp conflict with those 'Judaizers' who wished the Christian communities to mirror developments in the synagogue.

Again when Paul came to regulating the life of the community, he made strikingly few references to Jesus' ethical teaching, even where, as for example on the question of the believers' relation to the state, there were sayings of Jesus to which he might have appealed. Instead he appealed quite widely and indeed sometimes bizarrely (1 Cor. 11.14) to arguments from the popular ethical philosophies of his day. There is much, though by no means all, in his teaching which has its source outside the Jewish tradition, and the tendency to draw on Hellenistic[7] sources for ethical guidance will grow in the churches rather than not diminish.

In the end, trying to understand Paul's achievement in terms of sources, of contributions from one culture or community or figure, or another, can all too easily lead us to overlook his own contribution. Paul describes himself as an apostle and as free and links this with having seen the Lord (1 Cor. 9.1). Thus on his own account at least there is something at the centre of his religious experience which is deeply his own.

Yet the problem with such deeply personal experiences is that they cannot easily be demonstrated or replicated. They may, it is true, encourage sympathetic experiences in others who come directly into contact with the prophetic figure, but they are not of themselves able to provide the stuff from which long-lived religious communities can be made. Perhaps Paul's greatest achievement is to have forged the images of the cross and resurrection into powerful symbols which could mediate to his community that sense of the numinous which for him was so closely tied to his own call.

Such forging of symbols is ultimately a mysterious process. Certainly there are no prescriptions for it. Naturally the story of Jesus' cross and resurrection will have been told to Paul; it is not his own invention. There is evidence for it as forming part of the community's basic creed in 1 Cor. 15.3ff. It was celebrated in the Church's own Eucharist (1 Cor. 11.26). What Paul does is to allow those ideas to shape and inform his own experience of suffering and rejection by his former community and of conflict within his own churches. At the same time this linking of his own experience of suffering to the Christian beliefs about the cross and resurrection is itself an important part of giving further definition and meaning to those beliefs themselves. In this way the symbols of cross and resurrection come to stand for a rich and creative view of the world which will enable the community to grow and develop. Paul's letters are a remarkable witness to this process. As Paul reflects on his life in the light of the cross and resurrection, so those images are themselves fused together and enriched and become an enormously powerful and creative religious symbol, mediating the holy both to Paul and to his community, and giving shape and direction to the varied associations which the Church would spawn in the course of history. It was here, not in the old cultic symbols of Temple and sacrifice, nor in the newly emerging scribal communities based on the study and practice of the Law that the new community would discover and worship God.

There is of course much more to tell. The words and deeds of Jesus were also preserved by the early communities and eventually written down by the evangelists in a form which gives full weight to the passion and resurrection. Here there is a complex process whereby the communal memory of Jesus is being reworked in the light of the bewildering events of Jesus' last days and the subsequent trials and suffering of the earliest Christians. How far Paul's influence may be traced in all this is hard to say. Perhaps it was inevitable that in coming to terms with their own experience of rootlessness and persecution the community should give Jesus' death and resurrection a positive significance greater even than that accorded to his teaching and healing. Either way we can see the same process of symbol-making at work in the Gospels as in Paul. The community's sense of alienation, indeed of victimization, is overcome as they find it reflected and taken up into the story of Christ's own sufferings and strange triumph.

And, as in Paul, we can see in the Gospels a similar process of measuring oneself against developments in Judaism. This is particularly clear in Matthew where Jesus is presented both as the fulfiller of

37

the Law and also as the one who has freedom to transcend it. But it is there too in Mark in the controversy stories where Jesus' conflict with the scribes and Pharisees is regularly emphasized, whether this be Mark's contribution or that of his inherited tradition.

This same debate with the Synagogue is also clearly reflected in much of the Fourth Gospel, often in very shrill tones (chapter 8!). But beyond that, the Fourth Gospel is involved in the process of reflecting on the meaning of Jesus' life and death in terms which have at least as much resonance in the wider Hellenistic world as in that of Palestinian Judaism. The universal imagery of water, wine, bread, shepherd is deployed in a series of remarkable meditations which present Jesus as the heavenly figure come down to bring life and salvation, freedom from bondage and death. Little of his express teaching remains; the experience of liberation and fulness of life is projected back onto the person of Jesus; beliefs in some imminent disaster or crisis are now internalized to refer to the crisis in the individual's life as he or she comes into contact with the words and spirit of Christ.

What such further reflections, if drawn out, would suggest is something of the great diversity and fruitfulness of the symbols of death and resurrection as they help to shape and determine the life and thought of the emerging Christian community. They are, as Meeks has suggested,[8] metaphors which can form and give sense to the otherwise troubled and devalued existence of Christians. In so doing they also have the power to generate a great diversity of new self-understandings and communities. Above all they are able to give sense and direction to those who part company with the existing order, who break their ties with existing patterns of community and yet in their isolation find new hopes and new values for a new age. Here if anywhere lies the central force of emerging Christianity, which gives it both its extraordinary fecundity and a certain, if always elusive, unity.

NOTES

1 *Rebecca's Children: Judaism and Christianity in the Roman World.* Cambridge, Mass. Harvard University Press, 1986.

2 The Law, or Torah, was as it were the terms of the agreement or covenant between God and Israel. It was to be found in written form in the first five books of the Bible, the Pentateuch. Some Jews, notably the

Pharisees and their successors, the Rabbis, also held that there was an oral version which was contained in their oral traditions.

3 The Jewish priestly aristocracy who largely controlled the Temple.

4 *Antiquities*, 18.85–7; 20.97–8; 169–72; cf. *Jewish War* 2.261–3, and Acts 5.36; 21.38.

5 Oxford University Press 1923. His less well-known work was entitled *The Kingdom of God and the Son of Man: a study in the history of religion.* London, Lutterworth, 1938.

6 *Commentary on Romans* (London, SCM, 1980), p. 146.

7 A convenient term for the very diverse culture which pervaded the Mediterranean world and which was made possible by the spread of Greek as a lingua franca from the fourth century BC.

8 W Meeks, 'Social Functions of Apocalyptic Language', in D Hellholm, ed. *Apocalypticism in the Mediterranean and the Near East* (Tübingen, Mohr, 1983), pp. 687–705.

BIBLIOGRAPHY

Meeks, W, *The First Urban Christians: The Social World of the Apostle Paul.* New Haven and London, Yale University Press, *c.* 1983.

Riches, J K, *The World of Jesus: First Century Judaism in Crisis.* New York, Cambridge University Press, 1990.

Rowland, C, *Christian Origins.* London, SPCK, 1985.

Sanders, E P, *Jesus and Judaism.* London, SCM, 1985.

Segal, A, *Rebecca's Children.* Cambridge, Mass., Harvard University Press, 1986.

Theissen, G, *The Shadow of the Galilean.* London, SCM, 1987.

4

The Jewish Dimension

WILLIAM HORBURY

The Jews were an ancient and famous nation when Christ was born, and the Christians long continued to seem, by contrast, recent and obscure. For a correspondingly long time it would have sounded paradoxical to talk of a 'Jewish dimension' of Christian history. The boot was on the other foot, for pagans knew that Jews had a history, however it was to be interpreted, and that Christianity had modern Jewish origins. The Jewish population, also, was unmistakeably vast. To speak only of the Roman Empire, the Jews formed a very large minority, perhaps eight or nine per cent, a bigger proportion of the total population than was attained by the Jews in pre-1939 Europe. Their strength appeared in a formidable series of revolts;[1] until the fourth century Jews probably outnumbered Christians, and certainly exceeded them in standing and influence.

Externally, therefore, Christian life always had a Jewish dimension, which was also highly significant internally. The Jewish Scriptures were central in Christian life and thought, the founder of Christianity was Jewish, and Christianity could not be explained without reference to the Jews, who themselves disowned it. All these points emerge in the second-century defences of Christianity, culminating in Tertullian's *Apology*.[2] More generally, these and other Christian writings, including texts usually classified as Gnostic, show to what extent the Christians, despite their special tenets, formed a kind of sub-culture of the Jewish community. Thus at the end of the third century the first church historian, Eusebius, readily appeals to Jewish authority to establish the biblical canon, but also seeks to minimize Jewish political importance by stressing the disastrous failure of the three revolts.

This Jewish dimension, then, as perceived by early Christian writers, embraced both the external political importance of the Jews and their internal significance for Christian life and thought. These aspects are considered in turn below. Some account of the Jewish community and Jewish–Gentile relations in the times of the early Christians is followed by discussion of Judaism in the Roman Empire, Jewish–Christian links and Jewish–Christian controversy.

THE JEWISH COMMUNITY

The biblical view of Jewish exile as a punishment to be ended by a glorious return[3] was modified by Jews in the Graeco-Roman world. They also interpreted their dispersion[4] as a world-wide Jewish colonization, comparable with the colonial expansions of Greece and Rome. Hebrew words for 'captivity' were already rendered in the Septuagint by Greek *apoikia*, (colony), as at Jer. 29.1, 4, and Philo drew out the implications with near-imperial Jewish pride, for instance in his *Legation to Gaius*, 281–2.

This interpretation attests a sense of universality and unity as strong as that manifested by the Greeks. The Diaspora spanned the eastern frontier of the Roman empire. Its twin biblical foci of Assyria (Mesopotamia and Babylonia) and Egypt[5] were still of first importance. From the third century AD onwards Babylonia, beyond the Roman frontier, was the great home of Rabbinic study. It was rivalled in this respect by the mother-country, especially Galilee, the main centre of Jewish population in Palestine after 135. 'The Holy One, blessed be he, knows that Israel cannot bear the harsh oppression of Edom [Rome], and therefore he has exiled them to Babylonia'; yet 'the air of the land of Israel makes one wise'.[6]

The Rabbinic movement in these two regions moulded all subsequent Jewish history, for it originated the Hebrew and Aramaic writings which took shape in the fifth century as the *Jerusalem* (Palestinian) *Talmud*, and in the sixth as the *Babylonian Talmud*. Formally, both works are concentrated on the legal pronouncements and discussions of the early rabbis as presented in the *Mishnah*, compiled in Galilee about AD 200. Rabbinic exegesis and homily up to the fifth century is also and especially represented in compilations of *Midrash*, organized with reference to biblical books or the lessons read on sabbaths and festivals, and deriving their material mainly from Palestine. In these regions the figure of the rabbi and his teaching and preaching became important in Jewish life, now in connection with a highly developed form of the legal tradition handed down together with the Hebrew Bible, but in continuity with the teachers – especially those of the Pharisaic school – heard in the synagogues in earlier times.

Galilee was also the seat of the Jewish 'patriarch' (Hebrew *nāsî*', 'prince'), whose office gained recognition among Jews under Roman rule in the second century AD, and had come to an end by the year 429. His state was kingly enough to fit the biblical prophecies of Jewish rule, as appears from both Rabbinic and patristic sources. The *Mishnah* was completed under the aegis of the patriarch Judah I. The patriarch could in practice exercise the death-penalty; he represented the interests of the Jews under Roman rule to the government; and he collected moneys and controlled appointments in the communities through emissaries called apostles, armed with encyclical letters. The degree of resemblance between patriarchal government and apostolate in the New Testament did not escape contemporary Christian observers, for instance Jerome in his commentary on Gal. 1.1. With regard to the Jewish community it is more important that the Roman Diaspora again united in acknowledgement of exalted Jewish authority in the land of Israel, as in the old days of Jewish kings and High Priests.

The Empire included notable Jewish populations in Rome, Italy and Sicily, in Greece and the islands, and above all in the eastern provinces: Egypt and Cyrenaica, Syria and Arabia, Cilicia and Asia Minor. Further west, the importance of the Jews in North Africa emerges from Tertullian and Augustine, and among the earlier documents of Spanish Christianity are the canons of Elvira (about AD 306), forbidding Christians to eat or intermarry with Jews, or to have crops blessed by them.

In Graeco-Roman environments, 'the Diaspora of the Greeks',[7] the communities were organized along the lines of Graeco-Roman corporations, each forming a kind of city within the city; and many inscriptions commemorating their male and female office-holders in the classical manner survive. Their internal focus was the synagogue, for the public reading and exposition of the Law, prayers and communal meals (a pattern to which Christian worship was indebted), and for the settlement of disputes.

Synagogue buildings in the Diaspora could accommodate a hospice and a library. A Syrian inscription of the end of the fourth century shows that the synagogue, or part of it, could be called *naos*, 'temple'. Rabbinic claims for the destroyed basilica–synagogue of

Alexandria – 'He who has never seen the double colonnade of Alexandria has never seen the glory of Israel in his life'[8] – sound less excessive since the excavation of Diaspora synagogues at a number of sites. The remains at Sardis (over ninety metres long) stand out for size, those at Ostia for elegance, and those at Dura Europos on the Euphrates for magnificent murals. Despite the destruction of Herod's Temple, Judaism in the Roman Empire never lost the appeal of a 'holy and beautiful house'.

Vectigalis libertas, ('their liberty of worship is paid for by tribute'), was Tertullian's envious epigram on Roman protection of Jewish communal life. Government favour was of course not wholly unvarying. The poll tax to which Tertullian pointedly alluded was a punishment for the Jewish revolt of 66–70, and after the revolt of 132-5 Jews were excluded from Aelia Capitolina, the colony then founded on the site of Jerusalem by Hadrian. These adverse measures were far outweighed, however, by consistent acknowledgement of the Jews' way of life as legitimate. Tertullian could state without argument that, by contrast with Christianity, the Jewish religion was 'certainly lawful'.[9] Civil disabilities were imposed in the fifth and sixth centuries, and the building of new synagogues was prohibited, but the protection of existing synagogues was repeatedly confirmed by emperors and kings. This toleration contrasts with the contemporary repression of Christian heresies, and probably reflects not only respect for established law, but also the political importance of the Jewish communities.

Jews followed a wide range of occupations in town and country. In Egypt, for example, papyri from the second century AD and later mention Jewish field hands, tenant farmers, shipowners, a banker, and a woman of property named Tryphaena. In 404 Synesius of Cyrene sailed home from Alexandria in a ship with a Jewish captain and six Jewish sailors out of a crew of twelve. Jewish epitaphs from Rome commemorate Alexander the butcher or sausage seller (*bubularius*, indicating beef) and Eudoxius the representational painter (Greek *zōgraphos*). Jewish slaves are attested, notably in the aftermath of the revolts, but there was also considerable Jewish wealth. An early third-century enactment allowed Jews to become city councillors and magistrates, that is, to shoulder widely-avoided public financial burdens.

Both ends of the Jewish social spectrum are mirrored in Christian imaginative writing. The early third-century apocryphal Acts of

Thomas present the apostle as an enslaved Jewish carpenter and builder, who encounters a Jewish flute-girl; while the hero of the early seventh-century *Teaching of Jacob the Newly Baptized* is a Jewish merchant who in the past has taken both sides in the warring circus factions of the Blues and the Greens at Antioch.

JEWISH-GENTILE RELATIONS

Jews shared largely in the Graeco-Roman way of life, as their occupations suggest, and at least sometimes intermarried with Gentiles. Jewish customs were adopted in various degrees by people of mixed descent like Timothy,[10] or by non-Jews. The latter sometimes became proselytes, but more often, probably, had a looser attachment as 'godfearers', perhaps exemplified also in Acts, for instance by Justus.[11] At Aphrodisias in Caria a probably third-century list names three proselytes and fifty-four godfearers.

Culturally, the Greek language was a bond of union between Jews and Gentiles, as it was among the Jews of the Roman Empire themselves. Spoken Hebrew survived in the Holy Land, but needed encouragement in the face of Aramaic. Rabbi Judah the Patriarch is said to have recommended either Hebrew or Greek for use in the land of Israel.[12] Elsewhere in the Roman Empire Hebrew was probably not much used by Jews until the fifth century and later. Greek is the language of three-quarters of the many Jewish inscriptions of Rome (mainly third–fourth centuries), Latin that of nearly all the rest. The slow Christian acceptance of Latin in Rome and North Africa perhaps reflects a largely Greek linguistic background not unlike that of the Jews. In Galilee, Syria, and Mesopotamia Aramaic was common, once again, to Jews and Gentiles, and the dialect of Edessa, now known as Syriac, became an important language of Christian literature.

Good relations between Jews and non-Jews were none the less precarious. At Alexandria, it has been suggested, the Jews' linguistic assimilation misleadingly masked their real distinctiveness, and hence exacerbated anti-Jewish feeling. This suggestion could obviously apply more widely. The complex phenomenon of Jewish–Gentile friction was at any rate associated by contemporaries with the distinctive Jewish customs. This point was made particularly sore by the Gentile Judaizing already noted. Josephus agrees with the

Epistle to the Ephesians in identifying the commandments of Jewish Law as a source of enmity with Gentiles.[13] His answer to unreasonable hostility among 'both us and them' is to stress that differences of custom are universal, but that what really matters is the attachment of a community to justice and honourable behaviour – virtues which in fact form the chief concern of the Jewish laws.[14] Corresponding Jewish contempt for Gentile rites was also a known irritant, and internal attempts to restrain it are probably already reflected in Exod. 22.28 (LXX), 'Thou shalt not revile the gods'.

Josephus' eloquence in the nineties reflects a long record of Jewish–Gentile strife in the cities. It continued after his time, notably in the Diaspora revolt of 115–8. The increase of the Christian population thereafter brought shifts in the pattern of disturbances involving Jews, who are described as co-operating with pagans or with one or other of the Christian parties, according to circumstances. Thus Jews and pagans appear together in Alexandria as riotous partisans of the bishop Gregory, who supplanted Athanasius in 339; and laws of 408–9 suggest that Jews supported the outlawed Donatists in attacks on Catholic churches in North Africa.

From the pre-Christian period onwards, Jewish–Gentile conflicts were accompanied by literary polemic. Anti-Semitic accounts of the Exodus and the Jewish polity and worship are reproduced, with a fine reply, in Josephus, *Against Apion*. He views Egyptians as inveterately anti-Jewish, but also exposes the hostility of influential Greek writers like the philosopher–historian Posidonius of Apamea and the Carian rhetor Apollonius Molo, both teachers of Cicero.

The record of disturbances and literary polemic stands side by side with substantial evidence for settled Jewish life and for relatively favourable attitudes to Judaism. Josephus effectively ends his reply by stressing that Gentiles everywhere admire the Jewish laws, a claim on which the Aphrodisias list of godfearers over a hundred years later forms a supportive comment. It was in its appeal to Gentiles inclined to sympathize with Judaism that Christianity initially complicated an already delicate Jewish–Gentile relationship.

JEWISH RELIGION

The Judaism which impinged on Christians in the Roman Empire is difficult to reconstruct. Jewish literature is unevenly distributed geographically, and presents Judaism under strikingly different aspects. Other more fragmentary evidence comes from Jewish inscriptions and papyri, from archaeological finds, from laws, and from non-Jewish authors, including abundant patristic material. This additional evidence is vividly informative, but it sharpens the questions on the nature of the Judaism of the period already raised by the disparate Jewish literary sources.

Talmud and *Midrash*, in Hebrew and Aramaic, represent the Rabbinic movement in Palestine and Babylonia. Their formal concentration on the *Mishnah* and the Bible, respectively, has already been noted, but in both the religious emphasis falls on observance – *halakhah* [walking], the subject of legal discussion and exegesis – although important teachings on Judaism appear concurrently in the refreshing *haggadah* [telling] of anecdote or legend or non-legal exegesis. The Hebrew Bible is expounded practically, with acute discussion of the Rabbinic legal tradition – envisaged as an oral law inherited from Sinai together with the written law – with a homiletic use of *haggadah*, but with very little that a Greek would readily recognize as history or philosophy.

Philo of Alexandria and Josephus, on the other hand, wrote in Greek, and represent the Roman Diaspora at the time of Christian origins (and Josephus was born in Jerusalem). They too emphasize Jewish observance, but in the idiom of late Greek moral philosophy, especially Stoicism. They are acquainted with a legal tradition, but it has a less developed and independent form than it has in Rabbinic texts. The Greek Bible is expounded, with special reference to philosophy in Philo, and to history in Josephus; both assume, in Josephus' words, that Moses spoke in solemn allegories, as Homer was understood to do by pagan contemporaries; and both have many points of contact with Acts, Paul, Hebrews and the Apologists. Philo's allegorical interpretation of the Pentateuch unites Scripture with the theology and ethics of the Greek philosophers, Plato above all, and in Greek fashion it describes intellectual illumination (here, by the law of Moses) in terms of initiation into the secrets of the mystery religions. Moses and the patriarchs become exemplars of the truly philosophical way of life. The few remains of Greek Jewish literature after Josephus indicate that there continued to be Jews in the Philonic tradition.

The contrast between these two great bodies of Jewish literary evidence, Rabbinic on the one hand and Greek on the other, immediately suggests an inner-Jewish form of the famous contrast between Judaism and Hellenism. Were there two different types of Jewish religion, one centred on native Jewish traditions and more tenacious in attachment to Hebrew, the other far more fully assimilated to Greek culture and thought; one associated primarily with Palestine, the other with the Diaspora? There is some truth in this suggestion, but clearly no neat linguistic or geographical distinction can be drawn between types of religion. Further, the bodies of literature which suggested their differentiation have one great common feature, their focus on the law of Moses, understood as including the prophetic hopes, and their conviction that Jewish observance is of prime importance. Consequently, although the rich but fragmentary additional evidence from the Roman Diaspora often indicates diversity and assimilation, and needs continuous reassessment as new archaeological finds are made, it should not be taken to mean that there was no corporate unity in adherence to Jewish customs and convictions. Patriarchal government drew on an existing intercommunion between homeland and Diaspora, and the separation of the early Christians from the Jewish body underlines the communal loyalty of Jews as well as Christians.

JEWISH–CHRISTIAN LINKS

Christians nevertheless continued to have much more in common with Jews than with pagans. Perhaps the single most important Jewish–Christian common factor is the Septuagint. To describe it as the Old Testament in Greek is not inaccurate, but hardly does justice to its significance. A translation made in the third and second centuries BC, it achieved classical status among Greek-speaking Jews, was read in the synagogues, and had formed the holy book of the first Christians before the writings eventually known as the New Testament were added to it. As seen already, it incorporated developments in the ideas of Judaism, sometimes bringing the Greek world into the Bible, but often also anticipating Rabbinic exegesis. The distinctive Christian tenets were linked to the Septuagint both intrinsically and by interpretation, and it constituted the basis of Christian teaching and thought. A major Jewish influence on Christianity was that of the Septuagint as interpreted by Philo, to whom Clement of

Alexandria, Origen and Ambrose of Milan were all indebted; but the direct influence of the Septuagint itself was all-pervasive.

This meant a Christian cultural dependence on the Jewish community. Christians gladly accepted Jewish views of the translators as inspired, but they also had to come to terms with Jewish revisions or replacements of the Septuagint, notably Aquila's rabbinically oriented Greek version, with Jewish definitions of the canon, and with the importance of a Hebrew original which for the most part they could not read. The great landmarks of some Christian independence in these matters, the works of Origen and Jerome, are also great monuments to Christian dependence on Jewish biblical knowledge.

A comparable dependence is likely in Christian art, which is attested from about the year 200 onwards, and based to a large extent on Old Testament scenes. Surviving public Jewish art on a large scale comes from the same period, notably at Dura Europos and in the Roman catacombs, but probably it was already traditional in some circles, despite the opposition to it evinced in zealous interpretation of the Second Commandment. At the end of the first century BC the Jews of Berenice in Cyrenaica had an 'amphitheatre', probably a meeting-hall, decorated with murals. Eudoxius the *zōgraphos* (painter) could have had Jewish as well as Gentile trade.

Judaism therefore shared a family likeness with Christianity rather more obviously than is now the case. The synagogues with their Greek Scriptures, Greek prayers (the *Mishnah* allows the *Shema*' and the *Eighteen Benedictions* to be recited in Greek), their often elaborate buildings and decorations and their Gentile adherents clearly and authoritatively embodied the tradition to which the Christian Scriptures, prayers, art and institutions also belonged, and which Christians persistently claimed as their own. If the Christian body was in many ways like a nation, the Jewish nation resembled a church, especially in unity, catholicity, and custody of the holy Scriptures.

JEWISH–CHRISTIAN CONTROVERSY

The Christian claim to the biblical inheritance forms the keynote of the many treatises 'against the Jews'. These seek to show from the Scriptures that Christ, though crucified, was the Messiah, that the (ceremonial) Law was symbolic or has been abrogated, and that the Christians rather than the Jews are now the elect people of God. The skeleton of such argument is exhibited in Cyprian's *Testimonies*, a collection of biblical extracts which will have had many predecessors.

These books often reflect the need to confirm Christian waverers and to put a credible case to pagans, in the face of an established Jewish community with substantial Gentile adherence; proselytes were known to present the argument for Judaism. The hope that Jews might be won over is not wholly given up in Justin Martyr's *Dialogue with Trypho the Jew*, about the year 155, when there were still many Jews in the Christian body,[15] and it reappears in the inclusive outlook of the Christian Empire, but defence and Gentile-oriented apologetic often seem paramount. Church and Synagogue vied for proselytes, it was not unknown for Christians to adopt Judaism, and many other Christians, without going so far, attended synagogue as well as church services. Chrysostom's sermons against Judaizing in Antioch are the best-known evidence for a widely-attested practice. As they show, the situation did not immediately change with Constantine, but some indications of increased Christian influence appear. Thus the conversion of the Jews becomes more prominent as a topic in the fifth-century West, for example in the sermons of Leo I (compare the slightly earlier mosaics of 'the church from the circumcision' and 'the church from the Gentiles' in S. Sabina, Rome). The changed political situation is reflected on a large scale on the Jewish side, Jacob Neusner has suggested, in the convergence of the themes of Rabbinic documents representing fourth-century Palestine, including the *Jerusalem Talmud*, with the themes of major Christian writers of the same period.

Christians believed that the Jews as a body were hostile, although individual Jews and Christians clearly conversed amicably. The fragmentary evidence for the Jewish side of the argument before Constantine, exemplified in Origen,[16] and the *Babylonian Talmud*,[17] suggests forthright critical comment on the life of Christ, with the claim that he was rightly condemned as a deceiver.[18] The New Testament and Josephus, after all allowance for distortion, suggest that Jewish authorities repressed Christianity from an early date, but that Jewish opinion was sometimes divided (as over the execution of James the Lord's brother in AD 62, according to Josephus).[19] Patristic remarks on Jewish hostility sometimes relate primarily to these antecedents, but sometimes, as in Justin Martyr, seem genuinely to attest contemporary anti-Christian measures.

The bitterness of some anti-Jewish polemic is consistent with this situation, but the same tone can persist under the Christian empire. Pagan anti-Semitic attacks on the Pentateuch were not taken over by Christians, because the Jewish Scriptures were regarded as the Christians' own inheritance, but the more general pagan invective was used, and harsh anti-Jewish accusations clustered round the gospel passion narrative. A standard charge from the second century onwards is provided by Isa. 1.15–16, 'your hands are full of blood', since Pilate washed his hands. Sometimes, but not always, there is the sequel, 'Wash you, make you clean', in baptism. Patristic assertions that Israel's hands are always unclean[20] were read as authorities in the Middle Ages, and so contributed to the blood libel. In the early Church they were part of a dispute which was forthright on both sides, and their rhetorical character was less likely to be misunderstood; but they can still be called expressions of a Christian anti-Semitism. This sombre conclusion should not obscure the *éclat* of the Jewish community in the Roman Empire, or the profound significance for the Church, in its own life and thinking as well as in its outward circumstances, of the Jewish dimension.

NOTES

1 AD 66–70 in Judaea, AD 115–8 in the Diaspora, and AD 132–5 under Bar Cochba in Judaea.
2 See especially chaps. xviii–xxi.
3 Deut. 30.3–4, etc.
4 Greek *diasporā*, Deut. 30.4 (in LXX = Septuagint, see below).
5 Isa. 27.13; Hos. 11.11, etc.
6 *Babylonian Talmud*, Pesaḥim 87b; Baba Bathra 158b.
7 John 7.35.
8 *Babylonian Talmud*, Sukkah 51b.
9 See Tertullian, *Apology*, xviii. 8; xxi. 1.
10 Acts 16.1–3.
11 Acts 18.7.
12 *Babylonian Talmud*, Sotah 49b.
13 Eph. 2.15.
14 Josephus, *Antiquities*, xvi, 175–78.
15 *Dialogue with Trypho*, 47, 3.
16 *Against Celsus*, i, 28.32; ii, 9.
17 *Sanhedrin*, 43a.

18   cf. Deut. 13.1–15.
19   *Antiquities*, xx, 200–3.
20   So Tertullian, *On Prayer*, 14.

BIBLIOGRAPHY

Levine, L I, ed., *The Synagogue in Late Antiquity*. Philadelphia, The American Schools of Oriental Research, 1987.

Neusner, J, *Judaism and Christianity in the Age of Constantine*. Chicago and London, University of Chicago Press, 1987.

Reynolds, J, and Tannenbaum, R, *Jews and Godfearers at Aphrodisias*. Cambridge, The Cambridge Philological Society, 1987.

Schürer, E, Vermes, G, Millar, F, Goodman, M, Black, M, and Vermes, P, *The History of the Jewish People in the Age of Jesus Christ (175 B.C.–A.D. 135)* (Edinburgh, T & T Clark, i [1973], ii [1979], iii.1 [1986], iii.2 [1987]), includes introduction to primary sources.

Simon, M, (ET) *Verus Israel: A study of the relations between Christians and Jews in the Roman Empire (135–425)*. Oxford and New York, Oxford University Press, 1986.

Williams, A L, *Justin Martyr, The Dialogue with Trypho: Translation, Introduction and Notes*. London, SPCK; New York and Toronto, Macmillan, 1930.

5

The Pagan Religious Background

LUTHER H MARTIN

The story of Christianity's diverse origins, its formative travails of collective identity, its final emergence to cultural dominance following the celebrated conversion of Emperor Constantine in AD 313 and the subsequent anti-pagan legislation of Emperor Theodosius at the end of the fourth century AD, remains one of the most consequential and well-documented instances of religious change in the history of religions. As with any new cultural system, Christianity began with the legacy of its past. Its background, and, for some four hundred years its context, was Graeco-Roman culture, which Christians called 'pagan'.[1]

Pagan religions in the Graeco-Roman period were 'Hellenistic'. They participated in political and cultural developments associated with the internationalization of Greek culture following the conquests of Alexander the Great at the end of the fourth century BC, were shaped by scientific assumptions about a universal order of things objectified in the 'Ptolemaic' cosmological revolution, and gave expression to ethical concerns about relationships within the immensely expanded sense of space afforded by these new political and cosmological structures. Christian origins belong to the history and phenomenology of these Hellenistic religions.

HELLENISTIC CULTURAL CONDITIONS

POLITICAL TRANSFORMATION

The son of Philip of Macedon (d. 336 BC), Alexander (356–323 BC) inherited his assassinated father's aborted challenge to Persian hegemony. Whether by the charismatic genius of his bold generalship, so romanticized in antiquity as in modernity, or as the consequence of a more complex network of historical explanations, much of the western world, and some beyond, had succumbed to Alexander's

military advances by the time of his death at the age of thirty-three. From the Aegean Sea in the west to the Indus River in the east, from the Danube River in the north to the Sahara Desert in the south, Persian, Semitic, and Egyptian civilizations conquered by Alexander received the political impress of his ecumenical ideal for Hellenistic culture.

Though largely successful if measured in terms of the international acceptance of Greek language, Alexander's ideal of Greek cultural homogeneity was otherwise as often resisted as welcomed by conquered peoples, as had been the internationalism imposed by the Persian Empire two hundred years earlier. In fact, sixth-century Persian conquests under Cyrus had become the occasion for a renewal of local loyalties. It was the Persian imperial threat to national identity that had stimulated the Greek 'patriotic' histories of Herodotus, as well as those of the Jewish Deuteronomic historians. These first historians organized against the threat of Persian dominance by focusing upon those collective memories that established a corporate identity distinct from others: for Jews, the commemoration of their covenant tradition as embodied by the Jerusalem Temple; for Greeks, their 'kinship ... in blood and speech' and 'the likeness of [their] way of life' as embodied by 'the shrines of gods and the sacrifices that [they] have in common' (Herodotus, 8.144).[2] Similarly, concessions to and conflicts with Alexander's ecumenical ideal, were focused by such native traditions as those of the Hellenic Dionysus, the Egyptian Isis, the Syrian Atargatis, the Phrygian Cybele, or the Hebrew Yahweh, resulting in a profound enrichment of cultural possibilities during the Graeco-Roman period.

Following his death, Alexander's legacy of world ecumenicity remained a shattered ideal of three warring dynasties that had inherited his empire: the Ptolemies of Egypt, the Seleucids of Syria, and the Antigonids of Macedonia, until the reality of international empire was successfully revived by Caesar Augustus. A Hellenistic period of political history is usually dated to 31 BC when Augustus defeated Egypt at the Battle of Actium and incorporated the last of Alexander's former kingdom into the Roman Empire.

Cultural periodization, however, rarely conforms to political change. Rome had long been enamoured of Greek culture, and Augustus modelled his reign and person upon that of Alexander. As opposed to the ancient Greek and Jewish historiographies that had defined an identifying allegiance in antagonism towards others, a technique of collective identity still exemplified in the Augustan period by the Jewish historian Josephus, Roman historiographers produced comprehensive histories of all peoples as they related to the new internationalism centred in Rome, the founding of which was traced by such writers of the Augustan era as Livy and Vergil to the Aeneas of Homeric epic.

A distinctively Hellenistic period of cultural – and religious – history, that included contributions from all those cultures incorporated into the Alexandrian as well as Augustan Empires, must be dated as extending from the end of the fourth century BC until the formalization of a catholic Christian culture by the beginning of the fifth century AD.

COSMOLOGICAL REVOLUTION

Greek assumptions about a naturally given order of things, already apparent in the writings of Homer and Hesiod, became a focus of cosmological thought among the sixth-century BC Ionian philosophers. By the Hellenistic period this order had become objectified in a 'scientific' image of the physical cosmos that bears the name of its second-century AD systematizer, Ptolemy Claudius.

In contrast to the traditional 'three-storied' cosmic image of antiquity, in which an overarching heaven and a corresponding underworld defined a geocentric locale, the Ptolemaic cosmology differentiated an universal system of seven planetary spheres that surrounded the globe. A terrestrial realm, a cosmological correlate to political internationalism, was distinguished from the planetary realm of celestial order, the whole contained within a finite sphere of fixed stars. Western culture imagined its physical universe in terms of this cosmology until the 'Copernican' revolution in the sixteenth century.

As virtually all mythic expression is cast in terms of cosmic imagery, the Hellenistic cosmological framework described by Ptolemy is at least as significant for an understanding of Hellenistic religious expression as the political and cultural transformations initiated by Alexander's conquests. This new cosmic topography shared with its political contemporary a protracted conquest of space that revealed the parochial character of traditional, locally defined images of divine, as of political, power. Native deities either became

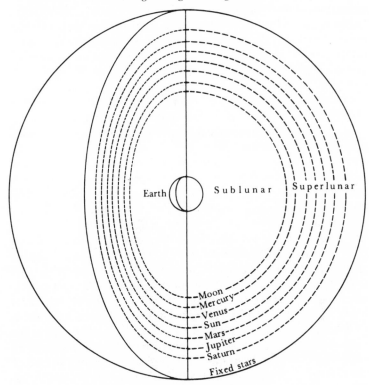

The Ptolemaic Cosmos

repositioned in terms of this new cosmopolitanism, or they declined into poetic memory.

ETHICAL CONCERNS

As did the earlier threat of Persian power, the internationalized and universalized order that characterized Hellenistic culture challenged traditional parameters of local identity (Greek *ethos* = the customs or habits of a particular people). This 'ethical' problem of identity occupied the Hellenistic Stoic and Epicurean philosophers for whom the classical cosmological speculations of Plato and Aristotle, Alexander's teacher, gave way to reflections on the nature of 'self'. This problem of the self was epitomized for popular consumption by the aimless wanderings of the asinine Lucius, hero of Apuleius' delightful second-century AD romance, *The Golden Ass*, for example, or by the question posed by the curious crowds to Jesus: 'What must we do . . . ?' (John 6.28).

The issue of self was formulated most sharply in Pseudo [?]-Plato's *Alcibiades* II. Questions of authenticity aside, this dialogue, in which Alcibiades poses the question of self and self-knowledge to Socrates, was widely influential in Hellenistic philosophical circles. In contrast to modern views of individuality, Socrates defines the self always in relationship, and links knowledge of this self (*gnōthi seauton*), thereby, to social practices of 'taking care of one's self' (*epimelēsthai seautou*). This philosophical admonition concerning self involved practical teachings about the conduct of everyday life, about relationships to the material, political, and divine world, about health, diet, and education. Hellenistic religions during the Graeco-Roman period gave ritualized expression to such ethical strategies, which in turn became the basis for Christian monastic practices in the fourth and fifth centuries.[3]

In summary, three conditions for knowledge, expressed both in popular practices and in philosophical and religious thought, were characteristic of Hellenistic culture. The first was the political reality of an internationalism imposed by Alexander's conquests, and a consequent cultural and religious pluralism. This Hellenistic internationalism was reinforced by cosmological revolution. More than the system of concessions and conflicts that resulted from an imposed imperialism, the universalism of nature represented by cosmic image structured a framework for the shared possibilities of Hellenistic life and culture. Finally, political internationalism with its problems of cultural interaction and identity, together with cosmological universalism, structured local and ecumenical possibilities of collective identity, an identity focused by those social practices associated with self-knowledge.

HELLENISTIC RELIGIOUS SYSTEM

In the first century AD, Josephus differentiated for his Roman audience various schools of Judaism by their views on the relationship of human affairs to fate (*Antiquities*, 13.171–3; 18.12–22; *Jewish War*, 2.162–6). Perhaps it is not too great a simplification to suggest that the varieties of Hellenistic religions might be similarly characterized.[4]

The classical Greek notion of fate, the manifestation of cosmic order in human affairs, was revived in Hellenistic culture to provide a comprehensive explanation for variously perceived possibilities of self within the newly expanded but still contained and containing political and cosmic orders. The cartography of fate charted various views of deficiency within the formal cosmic system in terms of which a solution (Greek *sōtēria* = salvation) might be offered. Three 'loci of deficiency' may be located on the Ptolemaic cosmological map, each with its distinctive rule of fate; and three types of response, associated by modernity with the category 'religion': piety, mysteries, gnosis, characterized Hellenistic alternatives to the play of fate.

PIETY

A traditional view of things continued to assume the harmonious nature of the cosmos. Any perceptions of disorder suggested, therefore, some deficiency of the knowing self. The soteriological response to this deficiency was twofold. Because the fated order of things was generally considered to be knowable, philosophy countered a 'deficiency of mind' with an epistemological response of self-knowledge, whereby the exercise of rational free will negated any misperceptions concerning the random effect of fate (e.g., the Neoplatonism of Plutarch), or with self-reflective techniques whereby the exercise of self-discipline re-established self in harmony with the 'fated' natural order (e.g., Stoicism). Piety, on the other hand, those popular practices associated with local tradition, countered the 'deficiency of self' with practical rites of relationship that might necessitate either the knowledge of specialists or the received gestures of folk wisdom. Hellenistic piety shared with philosophy, thereby, the assumption of an ordered cosmos; they differed on overlapping strategies for knowing, or achieving equilibrium with this order.

Piety (Greek *eusebeia*, Latin *pietas*) means 'right relationship'. The word was used in antiquity to designate relationships between husband and wife, parents and children, masters and slaves, officers and soldiers, rulers and subjects, and, by extension, gods and mortals, in which the 'rightness' of the relationship was socially prescribed, i.e., 'fated'. The corpus of piety, in other words, represented a social system; its practices 'properly' constituted the selves of their practitioners in terms of the accepted social (local), political (international), and cosmic (universal) order of things assumed in Hellenistic culture generally.

Family rites, for example, ensured harmony within the family unit, while agricultural rites maintained productive relationship with the land itself. The use of amulets warded off malevolent forces and persons by allying their wearers with like-minded neighbours. The science of dreams did not involve interpretation in any modern sense, but represented a social taxonomy in which 'true' dreams differentiated conventional and desirable associations from those deemed questionable or inappropriate. Similarly, the incubation oracles of those deities who would reveal a 'cure' (Greek *sōtēria* = salvation) through dreams to those who spent the night in their shrine, established, or re-established, right relationship between self and the gods. Votive offerings bore witness to such relationships.

Although structurally similar practices of piety are attested by historians of religion in all cultures, their particular significance is always specified with respect to this family or group and not others, with respect to this place or locale and not that. Already Herodotus had described problems encountered by non-Greek 'others' when they improperly or inappropriately consulted such distinctively pan-Hellenic oracles as that at Delphi (see esp. Herodotus, 1.46–7; 2.174; 8.133).

The theoretical problem that confronted piety during the changing conditions of the Graeco-Roman period was the increasing isolation of these locally defined practices from a growing international and universal culture. Some pietistic practices, however, were able to adapt to these new conditions. The much-misinterpreted Roman emperor cult must be understood in the pietistic sense of maintaining a 'proper' socio-politically prescribed relationship between an imperial ruler and his multinational subjects, a practice that today would be addressed under the complex rubric of patriotism with its components of legitimate instruments and agencies of power, collective nationalistic identity, and associated religious sanctions and practices.

Most successful in its adaptation to the new conditions of Hellenistic culture was the ability of popular astrology to incorporate Greek mathematical precision and cosmological advance. This attempt to relate a perception and system of universal 'natural law' to the conditions of Hellenistic cultural pluralism became the most important and widespread Hellenistic system of piety. In this 'scientific' system, perceptions of disorder attributed to a capricious play of fate in the terrestrial realm might be corrected by exact observation of the obviously orderly movements of the celestial spheres and the application of this order to mundane events and life, a cultural system analogous to that of the mystery cults.

MYSTERIES

Similar to astrology, a second Hellenistic view emphasized the operation of an unpredictable randomness of fate in human affairs in contrast to celestial order. This cosmological topography directly refracted the new internationalism that was beyond the comprehension of local understanding by locating deficiency within the entire terrestrial sphere. This alternative view, further, mythologized the ill as well as the good character of fate's effect, thereby personifying the Hellenistic concern with ethics. This strategy was associated primarily with the 'mystery cults' which repositioned traditional deities in the celestial realm of order, thereby providing them a privileged perspective over the shifting fortunes occasioned by terrestrial internationalism. Through cult initiation (Greek *mystēria* = Latin *initia*), the mysteries offered a harmonious relationship with these celestial deities, now explicitly identified with 'good fortune'. These deities might intervene in the lives of their devotees to provide a remedy (*sōtēria*, salvation) for their 'bad fortune', invariably cast as political or social adversity.

The following typology for the variety of Hellenistic mystery cults may be suggested. A distinction may be made between cults that retained a localized focus, exemplified pre-eminently by the famous mysteries of Demeter celebrated exclusively at Eleusis, and those cults that, although still identified with their native origins, spread throughout the Graeco-Roman world, such as the Greek mysteries of Dionysus, or the celebrated mysteries of the Egyptian goddess, Isis.

Eleusis, the only fortified city-state incorporated by Athens into Attica, had preserved its own identity by maintaining its ancient privilege of the mysteries. Under later conditions of pan-Hellenism, eligibility for initiation was extended to all Greeks, and with Hellenistic internationalism, this eligibility was extended to any who would come. The Eleusinian mysteries not only provided an early example for the internationalization of once local cults but a Hellenizing paradigm of cultural inclusion, for the sole prerequisite for prospective initiates was their ability to speak Greek (which the Greek word *hellenismos* in fact means).

The mysteries of Isis, on the other hand, were a Hellenized development of her ancient Egyptian cult. Rather than opening her native cult to all who would come, as was the case with Demeter, the goddess of this Roman client nation became universalized by being identified as a lunar goddess, a strategy adopted by various other native deities threatened with neglect as a result of international shifts in the centres of power. From her newly elevated celestial throne, this universalized Queen of Heaven could counteract bad fortune throughout all nations, and her temples could be distributed throughout the world (Apuleius, *Metamorphoses*, 11.5). Although Isis continued to be identified with the ancient wisdom of Egypt and books of hieroglyphics were displayed in her cult, her widespread mysteries were conducted in Greek.

Secondly, we may distinguish mysteries of Greek origin from those of non-Greek origin. Under the impress of Hellenistic culture, the ancient Greek mysteries, and especially those of Demeter, seemed to provide the paradigm for the redefinition of native cults as Hellenized mysteries. Lucian, for example, explicitly states that Alexander borrowed from the Eleusinian cult in establishing the mysteries of Glycon (*Alexander*, 38), and the Eleusinian model is implicit in Plutarch's account of the Isaic mysteries (*On Isis and Osiris*, 12–19).

Finally, we may distinguish traditional native cults that were internationalized under the conditions of Hellenistic culture from those newly created out of these cultural conditions. The widespread Roman mysteries of Mithras are the primary example of religious innovation during the Graeco-Roman period, along with the mysteries of Glycon invented by Alexander of Abonoteichus, and, of course, Christianity.

Although a 'mystery' in the sense of requiring initiation, the enigmatic cult of Mithras differed in important ways from the other Hellenistic mysteries. Whereas the deities of the other mysteries were chthonic, devoted to goddesses or to the effeminately imaged Dionysus, Mithras was a strikingly masculine, celestial deity associated with the sun and with astrological imagery. And while initiation into the other mysteries was open to all, that into the mysteries of Mithras was restricted to males. Originating during the first century BC, probably in the eastern empire (Plutarch, *Life of Pompey*, 24) and spreading rapidly throughout the west during the second century AD, Mithraism assumed the pre-eminence of a natively Roman cultural identity now antagonistic to Greek influence, as suggested by its claim on a Persian deity and its use of Latin. The presence of Mithraists especially among the petty bureaucracy in Rome and among the military along the borders of the Western Empire indicates the role of this cult in maintaining and disseminating a Roman cultural influence.

As opposed to those who would romanticize the mysteries as primarily secret societies and elaborate their role with ethnographic parallels from other cultures, the mysteries represented a Hellenistic strategy of cultural inclusion in face of the social dislocation imposed by an internationalized culture, and articulated as a capricious cosmic play of fate. If their ritualized formation of self was perceived to be in some sense socially 'improper', they were not tolerated, as suppression of the Dionysian mysteries by Roman senatorial decree in 186 BC (Livy, Bk 39) and the case of early Christianity indicates.

GNOSIS

A sense began to grow from the first century BC that the entire cosmos was deficient, ruled by an oppressive fate exemplified politically by the very success of the Augustan *pax Romana*, and cosmically by the virtually universal acceptance of an ordering but deterministic astrological system or by the removed sovereignty of distant celestial deities. This anticosmism resulted in a rejection of any this-worldly techniques for 'salvation' in favour of 'redemption', or escape from cosmic limit itself. This other-worldly goal was exemplified by the redemptive strategies especially of Gnostic traditions. Associated with this anticosmism was a rejection by this new religious expression of any self-knowledge arrived at by practical or initiatory techniques for 'taking care of one's self', whether 'religious' or philosophical, as governed by this-worldly concerns. It emphasized, rather, self-knowledge as a transcendent or spiritual content (*gnōsis*).

The Gnostic rejection of this-worldly concerns extended to Hellenistic notions of a natural order of things and cosmic structure, to its explanatory system of fate, to the traditional deities, and to philosophical thought, all of which were held to be deterministic and oppressive, that is, bound to the finite totality of cosmic deficiency. This late-antique rejection of the very conditions for Hellenistic thought and expression anticipated the 'desacralization of the world' by Renaissance/Enlightenment thought, and its religious face, Protestantism.

Representing differing valuations of a common culture system, these three distinct but related types of religious expression: piety, mysteries, and gnosis, characterized religions during the Graeco-Roman period. Historically considered, early Christianity was but another Hellenistic religion cast in terms of one or another of these expressions of its contemporary culture.

CHRISTIANITY'S PAGAN LEGACY

Early Christian alternatives shared in the rich possibilities of Hellenistic religious culture, from Christianized examples of pietistic soteriology to the redemptive claims of the Gnostic traditions. As the heterogeneous spectrum of Christianity became welded into homogeneous orthodoxy, however, it became impatient to establish a catholic identity, not only over against paganism, but what it increasingly considered to be 'heretical'. In its early rejection of the widespread Christian-Gnostic tendencies as heresy, an 'official' Christianity implicitly allied itself with characteristics associated with piety and the mysteries.

Pietistic practices tend to persist from one religious system to the next. It was no different with the rise of Christianity. Sheltered now by an umbrella of orthodox formulations, the Christianized practices retained their largely local character. Incubation, for example, was practised continuously until modern times in certain churches of Greece and southern Italy.[5] Letters of supplication addressed to the 'Bambino' in the Church of the Aracoeli on the Campidoglio in Rome recall the letter oracles of old, sealed epistles miraculously answered in writing by the addressed deity. But such practices as votive offerings spread throughout Christianity and are commonly practised today through announcements in the 'Personal' column of newpapers.

Since the setting of an apologetic agenda by the church Fathers, the mysteries, on the other hand, have been much studied as a background and context for Christian origins since their overall structures, institutions, and teachings were perceived to be similar to those of the developing Church. For Christianity shares with one or another of the mystery cults soteriological goals often expressed in the symbolism of death and rebirth and focused upon a saviour deity. Both practised such cult rituals as initiation, baptism or purification, and fellowship or sacramental meals. They shared a central terminology of cult expression such as 'mystery', 'perfection', 'spiritual'. And both embodied similar ethical concerns. Rather than understanding these religious themes as borrowed from the mysteries, however, they are better understood as parallel religious expressions generated by a shared cultural system.

Although Christianity and the mysteries shared common religious expressions, they must finally be judged as incommensurable. Associated with one another by pagan apologist and Christian polemicist alike, the mysteries as a group were a loose collection of cosmic religious expressions, such as the chthonic cults of Demeter, Dionysus, and Isis, on the one hand, with the celestial, such as those of Mithras and Helios, on the other. With such traditional Roman cults as those of Jupiter and Liber Pater, these 'foreign' or Roman 'client' cults together represented an attempt at cosmic federation, as it were, to negate the ravages of a cosmic fate in the context of, and in support of, ecumenical culture and imperial internationalism.

An emerging Christian 'orthodoxy', on the other hand, represented a 'catholic' internationalism as the 'providential' outcome of historical development and progressive expansion. This historically structured cultural system was modelled not only upon Jewish salvation history, the immediate background of Christianity, but also upon the Roman paradigm for the development of Rome from Greek origins popularized, for example, by Vergil's *Aeneid*, a text specifically evoked in the late fourth century by Prudentius in his own argument (*Peristephanon*) for the inevitable emergence and greatness of a Christian Rome.

In addition to this historicized ideology of universalism, Christians were able to construct, on the basis of 'kinship in Christ', a practical network of relationships and communication that successfully spanned the decentralized distribution of pagan cult centres as well as the crumbling political structures of empire. It was this new Christian cultural system that finally was able to effect the failed dream of Alexander, as well as the temporary successes of Augustus from whose era Christians trace their own beginnings.

NOTES

1   Jacques Le Goff, *The Medieval Imagination*, tr. Arthur Goldhammer (Chicago and London, University of Chicago Press, 1988), p. 193.
2   Luther H Martin, 'Fate and Futurity in the Greco-Roman World', in *Proceedings of the Boston Area Colloquium on Ancient Philosophy*, eds John J Cleary and David Konstan, vol. 5. Latham, MD, University Press of America, 1990.
3   Luther H Martin, Huck Gutman, Patrick H Hutton, eds, *Technologies of the Self: A Seminar with Michel Foucault* (Amherst, The University of Massachusetts Press, London, Tavistock, 1988), pp. 16–40.
4   Apuleius so characterized the Mysteries of Isis (*Metamorphoses*, 11. 15); and W Anz so defined Gnosticism (*Zur Frage nach dem Ursprung des Gnostizismus* (Leipzig, J C Hinrich, 1898)), p. 13.
5   See the classic study by Mary Hamilton, *Incubation or The Cure of Disease in Pagan Temples and Christian Churches*. St Andrews, W C Henderson, 1906.

BIBLIOGRAPHY

Although there is a great number of specialized studies of pietistic practices during the Graeco-Roman period, there is no systematic treatment of Hellenistic piety. One might begin, however, with:

A J Festugière, *Personal Religion Among the Greeks*. London, Cambridge University Press; Berkeley, University of California Press, 1954.
Martin P Nilsson, *Greek Piety*. Oxford, Oxford University Press; New York, Norton, 1969.
E R Dodds, *Pagan and Christian in an Age of Anxiety*. Cambridge, Cambridge University Press, 1965; New York, Norton, 1970.

On the mysteries, see:

Burkert, W, *Ancient Mystery Cults*. Cambridge, Mass., and London, Harvard University Press, 1987.
Meyer, M W, ed., *The Ancient Mysteries: A Sourcebook*. New York, Harper & Row, 1987.

On Gnosticism, see:

Rudolph, K, *Gnosis, The Nature and History of Gnosticism*, tr. Robert McLachlan Wilson. Edinburgh, T & T Clark; New York, Harper & Row, 1983.

A more extensive treatment of these themes and a more comprehensive bibliography organized around them may be found in my book, *Hellenistic Religions: An Introduction*. New York and Oxford, Oxford University Press, 1987.

6

Christian Mission and Expansion

KNUT SCHÄFERDIEK

The earliest Christian communities developed within the Jewish communion. They were based on the belief that Jesus by his resurrection had brought about the beginnings of final salvation. Thus the primitive Christian Church gathered in Jerusalem as the true Israel. Its message found its way into other Jewish communities in Palestine as well, though to what extent remains unknown. It also reached synagogues of the Diaspora at a very early date, as is shown by the example of Damascus, where Christians could be found as early as the date of St Paul's conversion (AD 32/33). Within the sphere of hellenized Judaism of the Diaspora, Christianity however soon ceased to be an internal Jewish movement. According to Acts, this development was initiated by members of the Jerusalem community, that is to say St Peter[1] and some of the so-called Hellenists.[2] But also St Paul, who did not belong to the Jerusalem community and preferred to stress his independence from it, considers his own early missionary activity a mission to the Gentiles.[3] This mission, not mentioned in Acts, was carried out in the Nabataean kingdom, south of Damascus, as well as in Syria and St Paul's native province of Cilicia in south-eastern Asia Minor. Moreover, St Paul gave mission to the Gentiles its proper theological justification based on the distinction between Law and Gospel.

Hellenized Jewish communities offered conditions favourable to such tendencies. In many of them an informal circle of so-called God-fearing Gentiles had arisen. They were fascinated by the 'reasonable worship'[4] of the Synagogue with its ethical orientation. They hesitated, however, to submit to the ceremonial legislation of the Mosaic Law, including circumcision. Therefore, according to strict Jewish standards, they were regarded as Gentiles. From these groups the first Christian believers of Gentile origin were recruited, achieving full membership on the sole condition of Christian baptism. According to Acts, the first community including Gentile Christian members was the church of Antioch in Syria. This development inevitably caused disagreement. Opposition arose among Jewish Christians who considered unconditional admission of Gentiles an intolerable disregard of God's Law. As a result, a separate Jewish Christianity emerged. At the same time, Jewish resistance to Christian infiltration increased, and mutual separation of Jewish and Christian communities was rapidly enforced. In this situation, the name 'Christians' itself, meaning followers of Christ, came into use in Antioch.[5] Before, Christians had been called 'Nazarenes',[6] which remained the designation for them in Semitic languages. About two generations later, they considered themselves a third 'race' beside Jews and Gentiles.

The further progress of early mission cannot be traced. Only the Pauline mission can be outlined to some degree, though the evidence of St Paul's letters and the account of Acts do not totally agree with each other. From Antioch, after his early activity already mentioned, St Paul visited Cyprus and parts of south-western Asia Minor together with Barnabas. Afterwards, he worked again on his own behalf, travelling across the interior of Asia Minor to Greece, and founding churches in Galatia, a region south and east of Ankara, and in Philippi, Thessalonica and Corinth. Subsequently, he was active for some time in Ephesus and western parts of Asia Minor. St Paul also developed the idea of a world-wide mission, intending to establish Christian churches in centres all over the Mediterranean world, but he did not have the opportunity to implement his plans. Alongside the Pauline mission, other successful missionary efforts were made as well. The Christian church in Rome, for instance, was founded before AD 49, and Christianity is considered to have penetrated into Egypt at an early date, though there is a total lack of evidence. On the other hand, Jewish Christianity too advanced, obliging its converts to keep the Mosaic Law and developing traditions of its own. Thus various Jewish Christian churches arose, at least in East Jordanian Palestine and in Syria.

The paths followed by early Christian mission were prepared by the spread of hellenized Jewish communities. The God-fearing Gentiles attached to the synagogues showed themselves especially receptive to the Christian message. This offered a starting point, which to a large extent accounts for the surprisingly rapid advance of early Christianity, but at the same time also determined its character.

The Greek lingua franca became the Christian language. This meant an opportunity as well as a limitation. Christian preaching did not make use of Latin prior to the second century, probably beginning in North Africa. Christianity also spread as an urban religion among largely cosmopolitan groups of population. It was not at all restricted to the lower classes. From the beginning, its communities also included members of the middle and upper classes, who often played an important part in community life and administration. Among them women apparently formed a considerable majority.

In the early period, Christianity was spread by the ministry of apostles, itinerant charismatics forming a loose, not precisely defined, group. From the very beginning, however, spontaneous mission played an important part as well. It spread the Christian message through everyday relationships. During the first two centuries, favourable travel conditions and great mobility, especially among those social groups which were susceptible to the Christian appeal, made this kind of evangelization quite effective. It grew even more important when the charismatic element lost its strength by the late first century. Itinerant charismatics were replaced by teachers, though their main concern was apologetic rather than missionary. Adopting current philosophical ideas they tried to propagate Christian faith as 'true philosophy'. Examples of this attitude are found in Justin Martyr (died 165) and – on a higher level, both intellectual and spiritual – in Clement of Alexandria (died before 215). A concept of missionary strategy was not developed. Christian expansion did not take place on the basis of planned ecclesiastical activities, but was essentially an incidental result of social interchange.

The effect of Christianity on its environment was ambivalent. Its claim to religious exclusivity, its rejection of traditional religious manifestations, the 'in-group' mentality of Christian communities, provoked suspicion and disgust. The devotion of Christian martyrs was regarded by some as fanaticism. On the other hand, Christianity responded to an existing demand for religious and ethical direction and spiritual guidance. Thus it successfully competed with other religious manifestations of the time as, for instance, mystery cults, but also with contemporary philosophy. Christian communities offered to their members a well-defined identity and religious self-consciousness. Christian charity was, at least according to

Christian opinion, appreciated also by non-Christians. In the event, Christians did continuously gain ground within the Roman Empire, though they had to face a widespread animosity, being regarded as hostile to traditional values of human society.

Christianity had never been a homogeneous unity, and its early extension meant diversification as well. The question of the Mosaic Law and its value had aroused disagreement. Non-theological factors also as, for instance, different cultural backgrounds, may well have resulted in different developments. By the end of the second century, however, the outlines of a 'catholic' church appeared. It did not form a comprehensive ecclesiastical organization, but it was marked by common features: the rule of faith, which means an elementary consensus of doctrinal tradition, an established order of ministry based on the episcopate, and the scriptural canon of the New Testament[7].

At this time Christian communities were especially numerous in the interior and western parts of Asia Minor, where they had even been able to gain ground in rural areas. There was only slow progress in the former Pauline mission area of Greece, though in the meantime Christianity had advanced to Crete. It had extended its position in Syria. In Palestine, Greek Gentile Christianity replaced the former Palestinian Jewish Christian communities after the suppression of the Jewish Bar-Cochba revolt (132–135). In eastern Syria, east of the Euphrates, in the kingdom of Osroene with its Capital Edessa,[8] which did not fall under Roman domination before 214, a particular Syriac-speaking Christianity with features related to Gnostic thought had developed. It is represented by the Syrian theologian Bar Daisan.[9] Catholic Christianity did not begin to gain ground in this region before the third century. In Egypt, different Christian groups and schools, among them also Gnostic ones, seem to have existed in Alexandria and at other places. From Alexandria, Egyptian Christianity was organized as a catholic church from the late second century. It is not unlikely, though not provable, that Greek Egyptian Christianity had also advanced to south India through trade relations as early as the second century. During the third century, however, these relations were broken off.

In the West, Christianity was largely confined to scattered centres at the end of the second century. Its originally Greek character is still reflected by numerous Greek loan words in ecclesiastical Latin. Until well into the third century, the important church of Rome remained mostly Greek. At the end of the second century, there were also other churches in Italy, though clear evidence is lacking. The origin of Christianity in Roman North Africa remains obscure. Here also, the earliest Christian influence – either from the East or from Rome – was certainly Greek. Clear evidence of Christian life, however, does not occur before the late second century. By this time, African Christianity had adopted a Latin character, and apparently had even reached smaller rural settlements. Nothing is known about the beginnings of Christianity in Spain. In Gaul, Christian penetration followed the old trade route along the river Rhone. About AD 180 churches of primarily Greek character were found in Vienne and Lyon. At this time, further diffusion seems to have already begun from Lyon.

The preaching of the gospel from Jerusalem 'unto the uttermost part of the earth'[10] is the leading subject of Acts. About AD 200, Tertullian considered the gospel to have been proclaimed all over the world, from Egypt to Morocco, from Iran to Spain, from the south Russian steppe to Britain.[11] This view, however, does not really reflect an actual state of Christian expansion. It is rather an idealization, expressing Tertullian's belief in the universal concern of the gospel. In the East, the same conviction gave rise to the legend that the apostles divided the world between themselves in order to 'teach all nations'.[12] Now the apostles are understood to have formed a well-defined group of authentic witnesses to the truth (the 'Twelve Apostles'). They were entrusted by the Lord with the task of preaching the gospel to all nations, and they were considered to have fulfilled their duty. According to this view, the Church only needed to maintain and to improve a position already held.

This improvement did rapidly occur during the third century. On the other hand, it also provoked anti-Christian reactions. Severe steps to suppress Christianity were taken by the emperors Decius (249–51) and Valerian (253–60). But in spite of some temporary setbacks, they did not succeed in preventing further Christian advance. By an increasing number of community houses, cemeteries, and epitaphs, Christianity manifested itself in public. The agents of mission remain unknown. About 250, Origen speaks of Christians who entirely devoted themselves to the spreading of their belief.[13] In addition, local or regional missionary activity was carried out by bishops and their clergy, and spontaneous transmission of Christian belief through everyday relationships was still effective.

Christianity continued to be particularly widespread in Asia Minor, not only in urban, but also in rural, districts. In some parts, cities with a Christian majority seem to have existed by the end of the third century. It is even reported that an unnamed Phrygian town was completely Christian, and was therefore destroyed during the great persecution (303–11) of Diocletian.[14] Systematic missionary activity has been ascribed to the bishop of Neocaesarea in Pontus[15] in northern Asia Minor, Gregory the Wonderworker (died *c.* 270). He is said to have travelled across the country, discrediting pagan priests, and substituting feasts in honour of Christian martyrs for pagan festivals. But his life, which relates these details, is largely legendary. There was steady advance of Christianity in Syria, in the west as well as in the east, Antioch and Edessa being the respective centres. In east Syria, a majority of the population seems to have been Christian at the end of the third century, and Syriac developed as a language of Christian learning. In the Roman frontier fortress of Dura Europos on the Euphrates[16] the oldest known Christian community house, dating from *c.* 240, has been excavated. It was used by Greek-speaking Christians. In Phoenicia (Lebanon and adjoining regions of Syria) and Palestine, Christian communities remained confined to the hellenized cities, but they formed a close network of bishoprics. Communities were also found in the northern part of the Roman border province of Arabia, on the southwestern edge of modern Syria. At the same time, Egypt emerged as one of the most important regions of the ancient Church. The steady Christian penetration of the country was accompanied by a centralized hierarchical organization of the Egyptian church, with the bishop of Alexandria as its head. The beginnings of a Coptic Bible translation indicate that Christianity was not restricted to the hellenized classes of Egyptian population.

In the West, Christianity substantially increased in Roman North Africa, particularly in the provinces of Africa *proconsularis* and Numidia,[17] with Carthage[18] as its centre. In these parts of North Africa, Christians formed a considerable minority of the population at the end of the third century. Whether this development might be regarded as an expression of a distinct African identity opposed to Rome, remains doubtful. In any case, North African Christianity permanently remained a Latin one, and thus was a means of

Romanization for the Punic- or Berber-speaking classes. In Italy, the Roman church had a clergy of more than one hundred and fifty persons at the middle of the third century. In the central and southern regions, a network of episcopal sees had emerged, but there was only slow progress in the north, with Milan and Aquileia as centres. Spain had churches in nearly all parts of the country, especially in the south at the beginning of the fourth century. Little can be said about the further advance in Gaul. A group of bishoprics had been established in the south-east, in Provence. From its early foothold in Lyon, Christianity had also spread towards the north, and via Trier on the river Moselle advanced to Cologne on the Rhine. This advance left a peculiar mark of the original Greek character of ancient Gaulish Christianity. The English word 'church' (Old English *circe*), like the German *Kirche*, and Scots *Kirk*, derives from the Graeco-Latin *cyrica*, which in its turn is based on the vernacular Greek *kurikon*, belonging to the Lord. It is assumed that *cyrica* came to the Moselle with the Church as a special Christian term, was adopted by the Franks at a later time, and was eventually transmitted to England by Frankish intermediaries. Altogether, the number and strength of Christian communities seem to have remained rather modest in the Gaulish provinces except in the south-east. Nevertheless, Christianity had even reached Britain. The martyrdom of St Alban at Verulamium[19] might already have taken place during the persecution of Decius (249–51). At the beginning of the fourth century, at least three episcopal sees were established: York, London, and *Lindum*, probably Lincoln. In south-eastern Europe Christianity had begun to penetrate the Roman border provinces of the middle and lower Danube.

In the east Syrian region of Edessa, Christianity already had been firmly established in pre-Roman times. It also gained ground in the Mesopotamian region under Persian domination and even beyond the Tigris at an early date. This position was strengthened during the 250s, when the Persian king Sapor I, after military expeditions into Roman provinces, had groups of captives displaced from Roman Syria into his own domain, among them many Christians. Thus, in Mesopotamia and adjoining Iranian districts, an important Syriac-speaking Christian church began to develop. It was to represent Christianity in Asia for centuries. During the late third century, it probably first appeared in the south-east Indian region of the Malabar coast.

In the kingdom of Armenia, extending from the upper Euphrates to Lake Urmia and the Caspian Sea, early East Syrian and Greek Christian influences overlapped. About 300, Christianity was officially adopted as a result of the conversion of King Trdat (Tiridates) III, and thus, for the first time in its history, achieved the status of an official religion. The church was organized under Greek influence from Asia Minor by Gregory the Illuminator. Gradually, however, it assumed national features, and Christianity came to be an expression of national identity. Armenian became ecclesiastical language by the effort of the monk Mesrop (died 440) in the fifth century, and a Christian national literature developed. In the sixth century, the Armenian church adopted Monophysitism as its creed.

About 300, a Gothic national church also emerged north of the Roman frontier on the lower Danube in parts of what is now Romania. It originated from Greek Christians of Asia Minor, displaced by Gothic invaders in the 250s. Their gothicized descendants were able to maintain their forebears' belief, and established a bishopric before 325. A Gothic ecclesiastical language was developed by the Gothic bishop Ulfila in the fourth century.

On the eve of the great persecution, instigated by the emperor Diocletian (284–305) in 303, Christians formed a firmly established minority within the Roman empire, though there were considerable differences between its various regions. The persecution did not effectively alter this situation. As a result, the Christian religion was legalized by Diocletian's successor Galerius and his co-rulers in 311. The steady expansion of Christianity continued until the end of late Antiquity and even beyond it. The adoption of the Christian faith by Constantine (306–37) did not mark any major watershed, though external conditions for Christian activity did improve. Non-catholic Christian groups, like the Marcionites or the Novatians, were marginalized. But as a result of the doctrinal controversies which permanently disturbed the Church as well as the Empire from the fourth century, separate churches emerged. They were stamped by the officially recognized Catholics as Arian, Nestorian or Monophysite respectively. All of them contributed considerably to the expansion of Christianity.

Ecclesiastical organization advanced into barely or non-christianized regions. In many parts of the Empire, as on the Balkan Peninsula, in Italy, or in the provinces of western Europe, Christian penetration of rural areas only began at this time; in others it continued. To a large extent it was initiated and advanced by the bishops. They now were increasingly supported by monks, at first in the East and later also in the West. In North Africa, the separate Church of the Donatists seems to have been especially successful in integrating rural populations. The reason for this success is disputed, but notwithstanding its rural support, the Donatist Church, like the western Church in general, remained a Latin church. On the other hand, in Syria and Egypt, non-hellenized rural populations formed the national basis of the indigenous Monophysite Churches, established in the sixth century, the Jacobite Church of Syria, and the Coptic Church of Egypt.

The expansion of Christianity beyond the borders of the Roman Empire continued to depend on spontaneous mission. But from the sixth century at latest, Christian mission also became a political instrument of the Byzantine (East Roman) emperors. At the time of Constantine, the kingdom of Georgia, south of the Caucasus, halfway between the Black Sea and the Caspian Sea, adopted Christianity as its official religion. A captive Christian virgin called Nino is said to have converted the royal family. Armenian influence was crucial in the shaping of early Georgian Christianity, and, in the fifth century, it contributed even to the development of the Georgian ecclesiastical language. Before the middle of the fourth century, king Ezana of the Ethiopian kingdom of Aksum[20] accepted the Christian faith. Two Syrian merchants, Frumentius and Aedesius, who unintentionally came to the court of Aksum, are said to have played an important part in his conversion. Ezana might also have been interested in relations with the Byzantine Empire. In any case, Frumentius was ordained bishop of Aksum by archbishop Athanasius of Alexandria about 350, while on the other hand, the Ethiopian Church owed much of its distinctive character, including its monophysite doctrine, to Syrian traditions. North Ethiopian Ge'ez, the official language of Aksum, also came to be used in the Church. Different Christian influences affected pre-Islamic Arabia. Christianity probably advanced to southern Arabia[21] as early as the middle of the fourth century. Here, East Roman, Ethiopian, and East Syrian influences succeeded one another. Among the tribes of northern Arabia, Christianity constantly gained ground during the fifth and sixth century. It was advanced by the West Syrian Monophysite Church, operating from Byzantine territory, and the East Syrian Nestorian Church with its base in Persian Mesopotamia. In the seventh century, all Christian progress in Arabia was brought to a sudden end by the rise of Islam. In Nubia, on the upper Nile, extending from Aswan to Khartoum, three native kingdoms had arisen in the early Byzantine period. Influenced by Egyptian church and imperial Byzantine missions, all of them officially adopted Christianity during the sixth century. Earlier Christian penetration from Egypt and, in the south, also from Aksum had probably taken place. Nubian Christianity derived its distinct character from the Monophysite Coptic Church of Egypt, and developed its own ecclesiastical language.

Since Constantine, the Christians under Persian domination were suspected of subversive attitudes, and had to face a long persecution (341–79) during the reign of Sapor II (309–79). Afterwards, their relations to the Church within the Roman Empire loosened, and the East Syrian Church of Persia formed a Christian communion of its own under the bishop of the capital, Seleucia–Ctesiphon[22] as its head (*katholikos*). In the fifth century, it also cut doctrinal ties with the Byzantine Church by adopting the Nestorian creed. Its diaspora communities spread all over Iran, and as far as Transoxania[23] and Bactria.[24] An important centre emerged in the oasis town of Merw,[25] in the Kara Kum desert. From the sixth century it became the starting-point of an extensive Nestorian mission in Central Asia and China. Up to the sixth century new communities were also founded in India, at Kalyan and Thana[26] on the north-west coast, and in Meliapore[27] on the south-east coast as well as in Sri Lanka.

An episode on its own was the brief history of Gothic Arianism. It arose out of earlier Gothic Christianity after the middle of the fourth century, and preserved the Arian creed officially accepted by the East Roman Church of this time. Between about 374 and 560/570, it was adopted by a group of Germanic peoples, Burgundians, Vandals and Sueves in the West, Visigoths, Ostrogoths, Gepids and Lombards in the East. At the time of their official Christianization, most of them had settled within the Roman borders, and all of them underwent social and political restructuring or at least political reorientation. They were apparently attracted not by the doctrine of Gothic Arianism, but by its independence from Roman hierarchy. As a result of the political disintegration of some of these peoples and the cultural assimilation of the others to their Roman environment, Gothic Arianism vanished during the sixth century or, in the case of the Lombards in northern Italy, in the seventh century.

Outside the sphere of Roman domination, development in the West was not at all comparable with that in the East. Western theologians tended to look on the barbarians and their openness to Christian preaching with scepticism. This attitude, questioned by St Augustine, certainly does not account for the particular western situation, but it might reflect it to some degree. This situation is illustrated by the statement of an anonymous fifth century author: 'In the land of the Franks and the Saxons, and in any barbarian land, there is God, but there are no worshippers of God'.[28] Only in the far north-west, in Britain, did Christianity advance beyond the Roman frontiers, and it did not do so before the sub-Roman period. Roman domination over Britain actually came to an end at the beginning of the fifth century. Nevertheless Romano-British Christianity had gained ground even north (in later Scotland) of Hadrian's Wall, the former Roman frontier, by the middle of the century. The British bishop St Ninian was active in Whithorn (Wigtownshire) probably in the first half of the fifth century. The British Christian king Coroticus reprimanded by St Patrick may well have been a ruler of the kingdom of Strathclyde in western Scotland. During the first decades of the fifth century at the latest, Romano-British Christianity advanced to Ireland. In 431 Pope Celestine I sent a certain Palladius as bishop to the 'Christians among the Irish'. Probably during the second third of the century, the Briton St Patrick worked as a missionary and bishop in Ireland. Afterwards, Irish Christianity in its turn assumed missionary responsibilities. In 563, Irish mission in Scotland started with the foundation of a monastery on the isle of Iona in the Inner Hebrides by the Irish monk Columba. It was to continue with Aidan in England in the seventh century.

In Central Europe, Roman frontier security on the Rhine and the Danube finally broke down during the fifth century. The border provinces from the Channel coast to Pannonia[29] were occupied by Germanic invaders. They did not suppress Christian religion, but considerable diminution of the romanized population as a result of a long period of war and misery was to weaken the position of the Church substantially in these regions. In Britain, Romano-British civilization and with it Christianity retreated from the advancing Jutes, Saxons, and Angles westwards from the second half of the century.

On the other hand, two events indicate a turning-point: the baptism of the Frankish king Clovis in 499, and the official adoption of Christianity by the Jutish kingdom of Kent a century later. To Clovis, Christianity meant a new religious legitimation of his royal position at a time when he was about to establish the Frankish kingdom. In 598, King Ethelbert of Kent followed the Frankish example. His conversion was the result of an action of planned church mission unprecedented in the West. It was carried out by the Roman prior Augustine and a group of monks, who had been sent to southern England as missionaries by Pope Gregory the Great (590–604). Both events, the baptism of Clovis and Gregory's mission, mark the beginning of a new, the mediaeval, period in the history of western Christianity.

NOTES

1   Acts 10.
2   Acts 8.26ff.; 11.19f.
3   Gal. 1.15–21.
4   cf. Rom. 12.1.
5   cf. Acts 11.26.
6   cf. Acts 24.5.
7   cf. Chapter 9 below.
8   Urfa, south-eastern Turkey.
9   Bardesanes, died *c.* 222.
10 Acts 1.8.
11 *Against the Jews*, 7.
12 Matt. 28.19.
13 *Against Celsus*, 3.9.
14 Eusebius, *Ecclesiastical History*, 3.11.1.
15 Niksar, Turkey.
16 Qalat es Sālīhiye, Syria.
17 Northern Tunisia and north-eastern Algeria.
18 Near present-day Tunis.
19 St Alban's.
20 Northern Ethiopia.
21 Yemen.
22 Ruins on the river Tigris, south-east of Baghdad, Iraq.
23 Uzbekistan.
24 Afghanistan.
25 Ruins east of Mary, Turkmen Soviet Republic.
26 Near Bombay.
27 Near Madras.
28 *Epistula Honorificentiae tuae.* PL Suppl. 1.1687.
29 Hungary.

BIBLIOGRAPHY

Atiya, A S, *A History of Eastern Christianity*. London, Methuen, 1968; enlarged and updated edn: Millwood, NY, Kraus Reprint, 1980.

Frend, W H C, *The Rise of Christianity*. London, Darton, Longman & Todd, 1984.

Hillgarth, J N, ed., *Christianity and Paganism, 350–700. The Conversion of Western Europe*, Rev. edn, Philadelphia, University of Pennsylvania, 1986.

Latourette, K S, *A History of the Expansion of Christianity, vol. i: The First Five Centuries*. New York and London, Harper & Brothers, 1937; reprint: South Pasadena, Cal., 1970.

Meer, F van der, and Mohrmann, Ch, *Atlas of the Early Christian World*, London and Edinburgh, Nelson, 1958.

Harnack, A von, *The Mission and Expansion of Christianity in the First Three Centuries*. London, Williams & Norgate, 1908; reprint: Gloucester, Mass., Peter Smith, 1963.

PART THREE

Evolution of Christian Norms

7

The Bible

ROWAN WILLIAMS

WHAT COUNTS AS SCRIPTURE?

The first Christian generations did not have *a* Bible in our sense of the word – a single volume, its contents more or less identical in every edition, divided into two unequal parts. What they possessed was a collection of *graphai*, 'writings': in the first place, the writings that constituted the sacred and authoritative books of the Jewish people, and then, taking shape very gradually in the first two Christian centuries, an assortment of books by members of the Christian community. From early in the third century after Christ, we begin to find lists of the books generally agreed to be properly part of these two collections, along with notices of the works about which there is disagreement and books generally agreed *not* to belong in the authorized list. This process mirrors what had been going on in the Jewish world during and after the lifetime of Jesus: some books – the five books of the Law, the Torah were by that time fixed in form and accepted by all; others – the prophets (including the historical books) and the miscellaneous works known collectively as 'Writings', *Kethubhim* – were widely read but not uniformly accepted as having the same authority as Torah. It looks as though, by the middle of the first century AD, there was a standard collection of prophets and 'Writings' regarded as authoritative by the lay teachers of Palestine (the 'scribes and Pharisees' of the Gospels) and probably read aloud in the worship service of the synagogue, a semi-formal gathering of devout Jews that had begun in the Jewish communities outside Palestine and spread into the Holy Land itself during the first century. The Gospels show Jesus reading from the prophet Isaiah at such a gathering, and quoting texts from sources other than Torah in his debates with other teachers.

81

In Alexandria, the comprehensive translation of Jewish sacred texts into Greek (which came to be known as the Septuagint, the 'work of the Seventy', because of the legend that seventy scholars working independently had miraculously produced a single identical version) was establishing a slightly larger range of books as normative, though the Torah continued to occupy a special position. By the end of the first century, the Jews of Palestine had established a normative collection including most of the current non-Torah material that was regarded as fit for public reading and study; though certain 'Writings', such as Esther and the Song of Songs, were still considered doubtful for some time afterwards. But this still excluded books or portions of books, by now surviving only in Greek, which formed part of the Alexandrian collection – the literature that Protestants know as the Apocrypha. The great majority of early Christians (and Jews outside Palestine) took the Alexandrian collection as authoritative, since they were practically all part of a Greek-speaking culture: Origen, in the third century, knew about the Palestinian list, the shorter collection of works in Hebrew, but used the Alexandrian collection in his own exposition and argument. Only with Jerome, late in the fourth century, do we find any tendency to prefer the Hebrew texts to the Greek, any hint that the Septuagint is of less authority than the Hebrew Scriptures.

So we can assume that by AD 100, most Christian communities would have shared with their Jewish neighbours a 'canon' of sacred books in Greek, consisting of the books of our Old Testament, along with the extra material of the Septuagint. The word *kanōn*, which originally meant a measuring stick, had acquired the sense of a standard of virtue and purity, a touchstone of excellence. It does *not* seem to have been used (as was once widely believed) for collections of books setting the standard for Greek grammar in the Alexandrian schools, and it was Christians who first used it (from about 300 onwards) as the designation of the books which provided the source and norm for true teaching; they had long used it to refer to the standard summaries of Christian faith current in the churches, and as a general term for the sound teaching to which Christians must be obedient. But even without a special word for it, the authorized collection of holy writings, *graphai*, is a plainly visible phenomenon in the first Christian communities. Paul in his letters refers frequently to 'the writing', *hē graphē*, as the source material for illustration and argument, and takes it for granted that his readers will know what he is talking about. Early Christianity is a faith which gives an authoritative, though not exactly central, place to sacred writing; and its reflection and speculation, as we see this at work in the letters of Paul and other works, is grounded in and to some extent controlled by this sacred text.

Two questions thus arise immediately. First, how did the notion of holy writing come to be applied to books written by Christians? And second, how did Christians set about defining *their* canon, as the Jews had defined theirs? 2 Pet. 3.16 strongly suggests that Paul's letters, or some of them, were included in a Christian collection of sacred writings by the time this epistle was written: the author speaks of the problems people have in interpreting Paul's work, and of the way in which unscrupulous folk distort Paul's theology, 'just as they do with the rest of the *graphai*'. 2 Peter is most unlikely to be earlier than AD 100, but it can hardly be much later than 125; so this is probably the earliest evidence we have for a collection of Christian 'Scripture'. The anonymous sermon long known as the 'Second Letter of Clement', written between 130 and 150, refers to Matthew's Gospel as *graphē*; so that it looks as if one or more Gospels and at least some of Paul's letters formed the nucleus of a Christian canon by the middle of the second century. Obviously, this did not happen overnight; and indeed, if we look through the surviving Christian literature of the early second century, we can see that, even before the idea of a new Christian canon appears, there is already a certain degree of consensus about the status of some writings: they are quoted, or at least echoed, in works from all around the Mediterranean. They may not yet be regarded as holy or inspired by God in the same way as the Jewish Scriptures, but they have a 'classical' standing, they express the foundational truths of Christian belief in a way recognizable to a wide variety of people. They have begun to shape a common language for Christians.

This is especially clear in the letters of Ignatius, bishop of the Christians of Antioch at the very beginning of the second century. The letters were written to churches in Asia Minor and to the church in Rome, as Ignatius was being taken to Rome for trial and martyrdom, and so they tell us something about Christian communities spread over quite a wide area. Ignatius never quotes directly from the Gospels or the Pauline epistles, in the sense of reproducing a whole sentence or passage; but he repeatedly echoes single phrases or idioms in a way which makes it clear that he was familiar with a largish number of books from our New Testament, and expected his readers to share this familiarity. He knows Matthew, probably John and perhaps Luke, 1 Corinthians (a great favourite), Ephesians (another favourite), Romans, Galatians, Philippians, Colossians and 1 Thessalonians. He does not speak of any Christian texts as holy or inspired: for him, the contrast is not between Jewish and Christian *graphē* but between the writings of (Jewish) Scripture and the facts of the birth, cross and resurrection of Jesus. But in his own witness to that history, he instinctively treats his Christian texts as a proper source for the moulding of his own idiom and imagination, and as a common frame of reference within which to exhort and dispute with other believers.

Several other second-century texts tell a similar story: allusion and reminiscence rather than quotation, but a clearly discernible body of literature underlying these echoes. Matthew, 1 Corinthians and Ephesians are evidently widely known; the other Pauline letters are echoed fairly often, though reference to the Pastorals is rare; James, Hebrews and 1 Peter are familiar in more than one area. The other Gospels are not much in evidence, though we find a few allusions to Luke and John (and papyrological discovery has established that John was known in Egypt before the middle of the second century). We know that Mark was not regarded all that highly before 200; but by the last quarter of the second century, the Western Churches at least were taking for granted the existence of four 'canonical' Gospels.

The writings of Justin Martyr in the middle of the century tell us that the Gospels were read during the eucharistic worship of the Church, along with the Jewish Scriptures; and this is our best clue as to how Christian *graphē* came to be treated in the same way as Jewish. The earliest Christian worship is likely to have occurred in two different contexts: the synagogue, where Christians would hear Jewish *graphē* read, explained and discussed by the community's teachers; and the Christian fellowship meeting with its ritual meal. Letters from senior figures like Paul, addressing themselves to a whole group of believers, were written to be read at such meetings; and the fact that they were copied and preserved and passed from one community to another (Col. 4.16) shows that they were not read only once. Again, it is likely, though not certain, that sayings of Jesus were used in public teaching, along with the stories that set the scene for them, and that narratives like that of the Last Supper and the crucifixion played some part in worship – following the Jewish practice of telling the story which lies at the origins of the ritual now being performed. When Christians had generally became separated from the synagogue (no doubt at different times in different places), they had to construct their own 'synagogue service': they went on reading Jewish Scripture (and singing Jewish psalms), but now read it alongside Christian literature – letters, stories of Jesus. Teaching in the worship meeting would inevitably use these resources in the same sort of way, as texts that could be appealed to because everyone knew them. It is a very short step to the idea of Christian Scripture.

The pressure to decide on canonical limits to Christian *graphē* was acute by the end of the second century. The Christian churches had never been monolithic; but the growth of groups, within and on the margin of the churches, which took an exceptionally radical line on the Church's relation to Jewish Scripture, prompted the question of acceptable limits to diversity. For some decades at least, there had been Christian teachers using the books of our New Testament to support various sorts of 'Gnostic' theology: world-views emphasizing the corruption or godlessness of the visible and tangible world, the divine dignity of the soul, and the centrality of enlightenment, knowledge (*gnōsis*), in attaining salvation. Increasingly, they produced not only their own glosses on existing texts (there was a major commentary on John by the Valentinian Gnostic Heracleon), but fresh writings of their own. And although they were not particularly interested in the idea of a fixed canon, they evidently treated these texts as having some authority in debate and practice. The new development in mid-century was the coming to prominence of an Asian Christian who had settled in Rome, Marcion, who argued for the complete irreconcilability of Jewish and Christian Scripture, and was the first to propose a specifically and exclusively Christian canon. Since the God of Jewish Scripture, the creator of the world, was in Marcion's eyes tyrannical and immoral, anything in Christian writing that suggested a positive understanding of this God and the material world he had created had to be rejected. Marcion accepted only Luke's Gospel (stripped of the stories of the nativity and the resurrection) and heavily edited versions of ten letters of Paul (not the Pastorals). His followers produced a set of 'prologues' to some of the epistles, explaining the corruption and interpolation of the supposed 'originals' by pro-Jewish hands, and underlining Paul's hostility to the Jewish God.

Marcion's work forced the churches to define the nature of their *graphē* more closely, to provide a rationale for reading Jewish and Christian Scripture alongside each other. Since much of Christian Scripture took it for granted that the events of Jesus' life and death fulfilled the hope of the Jewish people and had been foretold or foreshadowed in Jewish Scripture, there was already a strong assumption of continuity. A work like Justin Martyr's *Dialogue with Trypho* (*c.* AD 160) shows how some Christians argued over the right interpretation of Jewish Scripture with those whose sacred text it was. By 200 or thereabouts, Christians are beginning to produce fuller, more detailed discussions of the 'Old Testament' (the term begins to appear in Christian writing about this time); and the summary 'rules of faith' of the major churches often include reference to God as creator and to the work of God's spirit in 'the law and the prophets'. In the closing decades of the second century, we find authors like Irenaeus of Lyon defending the acceptance of four Gospels, and the Mesopotamian Tatian producing a harmony of the gospel texts, the *Diatessaron* or 'Fourfold Chord'. Recognition of the Acts of the Apostles and, less universally, the letters and Revelation of John was spreading. In short, by the year 200, something quite close to our Bible has taken shape, thanks partly to the internal development of Christian practice and partly to the specific challenge of marginal and radical groups. By the early to mid-fourth century, writers like Athanasius and Eusebius can refer confidently to a scriptural canon accepted in the same form in all the major churches.

TEACHING THE SCRIPTURES

Texts from outside the canon were still widely read and treated with respect by some authors; isolated communities might go on reading suspect works when these had been abandoned by the larger urban churches (Eusebius' *History* tells us of one such case not far from Antioch around 200); and non-canonical Jewish texts, of an apocalyptic and visionary nature, held great fascination for theologians, especially in the lively atmosphere of Alexandria. But the ground rules were now fixed: public teaching would rely only on *these* books. The condemnation in the late second century of the charismatic movement called Montanism had carried with it the implicit denial that there could be any further authoritative divine communications once the apostles had left the scene (hence some of the unease about New Testament texts not firmly attached to the name of an apostle – particularly Hebrews – and the widespread tendency to circulate new compositions under apostolic names: the Gnostic gospels associated with Peter, Philip, and others). Authority lay firmly with a *limited* set of texts, and, more practically, a set of texts interpreted by a limited group of people: not self-appointed visionaries and prophets, but the bishops of the churches, those who could present themselves as standing in unbroken succession of teaching and hearing from the apostles.

To an outsider, Christian worship would have had a lot in common with the activity of the lecture-hall where a *grammaticus*, a teacher of literary style, would sit among his pupils, explaining the finer points of an approved text, setting out good examples; though the bishop's good examples would be examples of right conduct, not good style. He would be mixing the work of the grammar teacher with that of the true philosopher, who would teach you the wisdom you needed for the moral life. But here was a source of conflict: a grammar teacher would have clear and identifiable qualifications in a set of skills; the philosopher's authority certainly depended on 'qualifications', standing in a succession of wise teachers, but would also have to establish itself by the teacher's individual virtue and insight. What if a bishop was *less* qualified in virtue and insight than some other teacher in the Church? Who had the higher authority?

The great theological disagreements of the third and fourth centuries were often not only about the correct interpretation of Scripture, but about *who* could tell you what this correct interpretation was. Bishops became more cautious about delegating their responsibilities to more than a few authorized assistants. In Alexandria in the early third century, the bishop forbade laymen to expound the Bible in church. This was his task, or that of the official aides, the 'presbyters' or ordained elders. A layman might teach privately, in a study group, or even prepare candidates for baptism, but he could not speak to and for the whole community as it reflected together on its *graphē*. Slowly, other churches came to adopt similar policies; though this did not entirely solve the problem, since there could just as easily come to be conflicts of this sort between bishop and presbyter. The case of Alexandria is of special interest, since the bishop's policy there seems to have had a good deal to do with the influence and authority of one particular lay teacher, Origen (*c.* 185–*c.* 253/4), the foremost biblical scholar and expositor of the early Christian centuries. Origen had been involved in private teaching and instructing converts; but when he was asked to preach in church on a trip to Palestine, his bishop objected, and cited the ruling by which he worked in Alexandria. The bishops in Palestine were evidently surprised at his strictness, and found it hard to believe that this was really a matter of long-established custom. It is likely enough that it represented an attempt to unify the discipline of the Alexandrian church after a damaging period of persecution.

But Origen was controversial in what he taught as well as where he taught. He followed a venerable Alexandrian tradition in treating the sacred text as a sort of code, conveying mysteries not at once apparent to the reader. Alexandrian scholars had used the works of Homer and Hesiod in this way, as symbolic statements about the divine, and the great Jewish exegete Philo, writing in the first century AD, had applied this strategy to the Torah. The crudities, the anthropomorphic language and the moral contradictions of the sacred narrative, the grotesque elaboration of ritual and dietary laws, all the things which the educated Greek would find repellent in Jewish Scripture, were explained as symbol, *allegory*. The text was an invitation to the spiritually and intellectually mature to explore, to penetrate to the hidden depths. Origen applied this to the whole of the Bible, and, justifying his method by appealing to the Septuagint version of Prov. 22.20 ('write these things down in a threefold way'), he proposed that every part of the text worked at three levels: the literal, the moral and the spiritual, corresponding to the three levels of human existence, body, soul and spirit or intelligence (*nous*). Contemplation and asceticism, the spiritual life, were a necessary condition for grasping the hidden meaning of Scripture; not all rose to these heights, but even the simplest would gain some benefit from the surface meanings. The Bible was a testimony to God's providence and generosity: inspired in every detail (Origen again echoes Philo and pagan Alexandrians in believing that the text is *wholly* controlled by divine agency, a view present in some earlier Christian writers, but here given unprecedently clear and systematic expression), the text offers God's wisdom to all – to the simple, who read and are touched by the stories, to those advancing in maturity who see the moral lessons to be learned, and to the truly spiritual, who learn the mysteries of the divine nature from these symbols.

Scripture is thus an open book, a sign of God's love for all; but it lays special responsibilities on the spiritually advanced. Here are the roots of some of the difficulties Origen experienced in his career, the apparent risk of a self-selected spiritual élite taking authority. But he was also criticized on two other counts. His philosophical assumptions about human nature entailed a sharp soul–body disjunction, uncongenial to many traditional Christians; and his conviction that the literal sense of certain biblical passages (especially the beginning of Genesis) did not represent historical fact caused much offence. Even those who followed him in using the tools of allegorical interpretation rejected much of what he said on these points. Yet he continued to exercise vast influence; and his work as a textual critic of the Septuagint remained unsurpassed. He produced the first 'scientific' edition of the Old Testament text: six parallel columns, giving the Hebrew text and a variety of Greek translations; and this alone would have secured his reputation as the greatest biblical scholar of the patristic age.

Nearly a century after Origen, Lucian of Antioch (martyred *c.* 311) made a further edition of the Septuagint. This seems to have been a single text, without critical apparatus, based on the versions of Septuagintal translations current in Syria and Palestine, and aiming to smooth out difficulties and contradictions; it became the standard edition for most of the eastern Church, though Jerome was very critical of it. The world of biblical interpretation in Syria, however, had taken a different course from Alexandria in more than merely textual matters. Interest centred on the literal, historical (i.e. narrative) sense, and exposition of the Bible was less a matter of philosophical meditation on mysteries than the commendation, in traditional style, of examples of good behaviour. The foremost exegete of this school, Theodore of Mopsuestia (died *c.* 428), was hostile not only to allegory but to typology, the technique used by practically all earlier writers of identifying Old Testament persons and events as symbolic foreshadowings of Christ; but not all the Syrian writers (the 'school of Antioch', as they are rather misleadingly called) shared his extreme position, even if they used allegory sparingly.

Various translations into Latin of books from the Septuagint had been made, especially in North Africa, between the second and the fourth centuries. If Origen and others had to work hard in the Greek-speaking world to convince educated Hellenes that the Bible was worth reading despite its archaic, clumsy and unliterary Greek, the problem was far worse in the Latin-speaking regions. The 'Old Latin' versions were often grotesquely literal and almost unintelligible: one of the things which St Augustine often recurs to is the temptation of the cultivated person to mock or despise the Bible, as he had done when he was a clever and sceptical young man. The 'humble' style of Scripture, he insists, can only be appreciated by the humble reader: style itself becomes a means of spiritual teaching. The work of St Jerome (*c.* 347–419/20) on what was to become the 'Vulgate' text of western Christendom brought some order into the chaos of Latin translations. What was new in Jerome, however, was his belief that inspiration belonged in the first instance to the Hebrew originals, not the Septuagint; so that his version utilized authorities other than the Greek translations, resulting in an interestingly hybrid text.

By the mid-fifth century, there were versions of the Bible, more or less complete, in Gothic and Syriac, as well as the languages of official life in the Roman Empire; the same books were studied and read aloud from the Severn to the Euphrates, and a common ground for doctrinal debate was firmly established. Such debate, up to and including the Donatist controversy in North Africa and the great christological disputes of the first half of the fifth century, continued to turn on the interpretation of scriptural passages. Doctrinal education, before and after baptism, was education in the proper reading of the Bible – what St Athanasius called the 'ecclesiastical sense' of Scripture, as opposed to the interpretations offered by particular groups or individuals. But, although Christianity had become definitively a 'religion of the Book', its Bible never quite became a book of holy law, sufficient of itself to settle all dispute. Its sacredness was from the first rooted in the quest of the believing communities to maintain integrity and continuity; its place was always first and foremost *within* the worshipping assembly, as something which both interpreted and was interpreted by the activity of Christians at prayer together.

BIBLIOGRAPHY

Davies, W D, 'Canon and Christology', in L D Hurst and N T Wright, eds, *The Glory of Christ in the New Testament. Studies in Christology in Memory of George Bradford Caird* (Oxford, Clarendon Press, 1987), pp. 19–36.

Lampe, G W H, ed., *The Cambridge History of the Bible, vol. 2: The West from the Fathers to the Reformation* (Cambridge University Press 1969), chaps. 1 to 4, 6.1 and 9.1.

Metzger, B M, *The Canon of the New Testament: Its Origin, Development, and Significance*. Oxford, Clarendon Press, 1988^2.

Hennecke, E, and Schneemelcher, W, *New Testament Apocrypha*. Vol. 1 (London, SCM, 1963), esp. pp. 19–84.

Trigg, J W, *Origen. The Bible and Philosophy in the Third-century Church*. Atlanta, John Knox Press, 1983; London, SCM, 1985.

Young, F, 'The rhetorical schools and their influence on patristic exegesis', in R Williams, ed.,- *The Making of Orthodoxy: Essays in Honour of Henry Chadwick* (Cambridge Unversity Press, 1989), pp. 182–99.

8
Creeds

CREDAL ELEMENTS IN THE NEW TESTAMENT

The creed, understood as confession of faith, is said to be as old as the Church, or indeed as the people of God. It is believed to have developed continuously from very simple forms, such as 'The Lord is God' in the Old Testament, and *Kyrios Iēsous* ('Jesus is the Lord') or *Iēsous Christos* ('Jesus is the Messiah') in the New Testament. From the outset it served to demarcate orthodoxy from heresy (the 'right' from the 'wrong' expression or form of faith) as well as to recapitulate now and then what Christians believed to be fundamental and indispensable. If this understanding is true, then there is every good chance of distilling something approaching an original or archetypal Apostles' Creed (*Urapostolicum*), deriving probably from the second century; this can be done, it is claimed, by means of a regressive analysis, starting with the classical credal formularies of the fourth and fifth centuries, viz. the *Nicene Creed* (AD 325), the *Constantinopolitan Creed* (AD 382) and the *Old Roman Creed* (fourth century), as the most important preliminary stage in the evolution of the *Apostles' Creed* (eighth century).

Theories of this kind were in vogue during the great flowering of credal studies between 1860 and 1914.[1] Typical of this approach is the attempt to detect everywhere in the texts of the first centuries baptismal creeds, or at least vestiges and paraphrases of them. However, modern investigations on credal elements in the New Testament, or on the 'rule of faith', have in the meantime made these previous (and legitimately) renowned theories obsolete.[2]

According to the New Testament, to 'confess' is equivalent to *homologein*. The noun derived from it, *homologia* (confession), does not mean an enumeration of diverse *credenda* (things to be believed), rather the acknowledgement of the divine One, the person of Jesus Christ; acceptance of him suffices to distinguish a Christian from a non-Christian. Towards the end of the New Testament period, however, the confession came to serve a different purpose. When differences emerged which were seen as not just errors and offences within the Christian community, but as a total undermining of it, the confession was then used for 'intra-mural' delimitation and assembly. Apart from the Johannine Epistles,[3] the earliest manifestations of this tendency are to be found in the *Corpus Ignatianum*,[4] and one or two decades later in the letter(s) of bishop Polycarp of Smyrna *to the Philippians*.[5] In his letter *to the Trallians*,[6] Ignatius wrote:

> Be deaf when anyone speaks to you apart from Jesus Christ, who was of the stock of David, who was from Mary, who was truly born, ate and drank, was truly persecuted under Pontius Pilate, was truly crucified and died in the sight of beings heavenly, earthly and under the earth, who also was truly raised from the dead, His Father raising Him . . .[7]

The same tendency was apparently partly responsible for some other significant changes. Thus in the end it was no longer *homologein* (to confess), together with its derivatives, which functioned as the key term in credal contexts (as well as for introducing creeds!), but *pisteuein* (to believe).

THE REGULA FIDEI (RULE OF FAITH)

Even in first-rate credal studies, much confusion arose, since people did not appreciate the difference between *symbolum* (creed) and *regula* (rule, or standard). In its turn, this vagueness resulted from uncertainties as to the relationship between *regula fidei* and Scripture on the one hand, and ministry on the other. For example, Irenaeus of Lyon (born *c.* AD 140/150) and Tertullian of Carthage (*c.* AD 150–225) certainly did not understand this 'rule' as a norm higher than the Bible On the contrary, both regarded Bible and 'rule' as sharing the same source in the original apostolic preaching – the foundation of the Church (Eph. 2.20) – and were therefore in substantial agreement. And for them, it was all the more out of the question that bishops should possess a monopoly of exegesis, restricting free access to Scripture; therefore Scripture continues to be the highest and surest, though certainly not the unique dogmatic and ethical norm of the 'orthodox' Church. Certainly by the same token, Scripture never displaces or substitutes living, public preaching which is bound in turn to the original 'rule' or 'canon of truth'. This 'rule' or 'canon' highlights the main aspects and consequences of faith, responding and corresponding to particular challenges. Below is an example (in wording somewhat suggestive of the Apostles' Creed, the best known and most used early Christian creed in the West):

> The Christian faith is addressed to and follows *one* God, the Father almighty, Who made the heaven and the earth and the seas and all things in them; and *one* Christ Jesus, the Son of God, Who was made flesh for our salvation; and the Holy Spirit, Who through the prophets proclaimed the saving dispensations [of God] and [the two] advents and the birth from the Virgin, and the suffering, and the rising again from the dead and the taking-up, in the flesh, into the heavens of the beloved Christ Jesus our Lord, and His second coming from the heavens in the glory of the Father to sum up all things and to raise up all flesh of all humanity, so that . . . He may make a just judgment among all men . . .'[8]

But what has to be underlined emphatically is that the 'rule of faith' is a free résumé, fixed in outline, yet almost wholly flexible in detail as well as in form. In other words, the Church of the first two centuries AD was quite satisfied with agreement on the substance of the faith, the basis of belief, without a normative, fixed formula or *symbolum* (symbol), binding in detail as well as in its entirety.

CREEDS AND BAPTISM

As Kelly's copious account shows, it took a long time before things changed noticeably and moved towards fixity. Just as much time was to pass before it became customary everywhere to use 'declaratory creeds' in baptismal services, i.e. formularies beginning with 'I believe' or 'We believe', and then 'declare' the faith, or at least its main aspects (especially in the matter of the Trinity and christology).

We do not possess any unequivocal testimony of such a 'declaratory creed' before the middle of the fourth century. But there are some plausible reasons for believing that the infancy of the imperial Church was just the right moment for the emergence, or at least the spread of this new custom: (a) the new situation for the Church (after the 'Constantinian turning-point') called for a restructuring of Christian public services and their ritual, until then extremely meagre; (b) the rush of *competentes* (candidates for baptism) now made *cathechesis* (instruction) a lifelong task, far beyond baptism; (c) the outbreak of the Arian controversy may have persuaded the church authorities of the advisability of imposing from now on a well-defined and dogmatically unobjectionable *symbolum* on every candidate for baptism, on whom it was to be impressed word for word in order to protect him from seduction.

During the previous hundred years or so we encounter 'interrogatory creeds' or baptismal interrogations. It looks as if it had soon become fairly usual to address certain questions to the candidates just before the triple immersion or submersion, by now conventional, such as:

> Dost thou believe in God the Father almighty? ... Dost thou believe in Christ Jesus, the Son of God, Who was born by the Holy Spirit from the Virgin Mary, Who was crucified under Pontius Pilate and died, and rose again on the third day living from the dead, and ascended into the heavens and sat down on the right hand of the Father and will come to judge the living and the dead? ... Dost thou believe in the Holy Spirit [or: in the Holy Spirit also], in the holy Church and the resurrection of the flesh?

And in answer to the candidate's threefold 'I believe', immersion or submersion took place.[9]

The earliest clear evidence for 'declaratory creeds' is to be found in the *Catechetical Lectures* of St Cyril of Jerusalem, written *c*. 350, and in St Augustine's *Confessions*. In the latter, and in connection with the spectacular conversion shortly after 354 of the famous rhetorician and philosopher, Marius Victorinus, we read:

> So came the time for rendering the creed. In Rome it is the custom [and so not elsewhere, as in Africa, (yet)!] that [the creed] is recited by those on the point of Your [God's] grace [i.e. of being baptized], in a set form of words which they had memorized, from a lofty position in full view of the faithful.[10]

Cyril of Jerusalem is also our first clear witness for the (a) *traditio* and (b) *redditio symboli*. The first was the custom of 'delivering' or 'passing on' the creed orally – for reasons of *disciplina arcani* (enjoined secrecy) – to the *photizomenoi*, catechumens on the point of being 'enlightened', in order to be memorized by them.[11] The catechist recites the creed phrase for phrase, and the catechumens repeat it.[12] The second refers to the 'rendering' or 'profession' of the creed, possibly several times, during the last stages of the catechumenate, or at the end of it, or in connection with the imminent baptismal preparations at the Easter vigil.

The most famous and influential western creed of this type used in a catechetical context is the *Apostles' Creed*. Its current text, usually referred to in scholarly circles as the *textus receptus* (TR, received text), emerges for the first time, at least in its entirety, in St Pirmin of Reichenau's *Compendium of each of the Canonical Books*,[13] composed between 710 and 724. An earlier version is found in a sermon of St Caesarius of Arles (*c.* 470–524). But nowadays it is unanimously held that this *textus receptus* developed from the *Old Roman Creed* or *Romanum* (usually called R). As far as we know, this was the first to have the title 'Apostles' Creed'. Its wording is known to us from a *Commentary on the Apostles' Creed*,[14] written about 404 by the Aquileian priest Tyrannius Rufinus. A similar, but not wholly identical version is also known to us in a letter of Marcellus of Ancyra to bishop Julius I of Rome. This must have been written *c.* 340 and has been preserved by Epiphanius of Salamis (310/320–402/3) in his famous *Medicine-Chest*.[15] Following Rufinus, the wording of the text runs:

> I believe in God the Father almighty; and in Christ Jesus, his only Son, our Lord, who was born from the Holy Spirit and the Virgin Mary, Who under Pontius Pilate was crucified and buried, on the third day rose again from the dead, ascended into heaven, sits at the right hand of the Father, whence he will come to judge the living and the dead; and in the Holy Spirit, the holy Church, the remission of sins, the resurrection of the flesh.[16]

PRIVATE CREEDS

In G L Hahn's *Library of the Symbols and Rules of Faith of the Ancient Church*, the fifth and last section, entitled 'Private Symbols', is by far the most extensive, though in this respect it is far from being exhaustive. Developed from the 'rule of faith', the first paradigm may well be that confession with which Heracleides, an otherwise unknown bishop, opens his 'conference' with the great Greek theologian Origen (*c.* 185–254). This was in fact a solemn public disputation.[17] And it looks indeed as if there were certain links between the emergence of 'private creeds' and the noticeable theological development associated with, and mainly represented by, Origen. From the beginning of the Arian controversy (from *c.* 318) the practice of clarifying one's theological position by a statement of faith seems to have been established and quite common. It is indeed Arius himself who starts things moving.[18]

Closely related to these 'private symbols' in respect of their theological character are the numerous synodical creeds or credal statements which also came into fashion from the time of the Arian crisis. An example of these was the creed appended to the circular letter sent out by the Synod of Antioch in 324/325.[19]

NICAEA AS THE TURNING-POINT

The council of the '318 Fathers of Nicaea' in 325, convened to overcome doctrinal disputes, took an existing 'declaratory' creed of Syro-Palestinian provenance and inserted a number of qualifying phrases, e.g.: 'that is, from the substance of the Father'; 'true God from true God, begotten, not made, of one substance with the Father'.[20] At the end, the following anathemas were added:

> But as for those who say 'There was a [time] when He was not', and 'Before being born he was not', and that 'He came into existence out of nothing', or who assert that 'the Son of God is of a different hypostasis or substance' or 'is subject to alteration or change', these the Catholic and apostolic Church anathematizes.[21]

To all intents and purposes, this revised formulary was intended to be used henceforth as a test of orthodoxy. In this respect, the Council of Nicaea does represent a turning-point or 'great revolution'.[22] However, if the Nicene fathers really did have the intention to establish a fixed formulary as a test of orthodoxy, success was denied to them, at least for the time being. If in the end *one* creed became universally obligatory, and if it superseded the plurality of local creeds including those in the liturgies of Mass and baptism, this was very much only the outcome of a long process.

It was the *Creed of Constantinople*[23] (=C, or NC), which was destined to assume this role in the East.[24] An old tradition attributes it to the synod of the 'one hundred and fifty Fathers' of the Council of Constantinople in 381, the second Ecumenical Council. And modern studies have proved that there are no valid reasons at all for refuting this. It seems that the 'Constantinopolitan Creed' served originally as a basis for certain peace-making efforts between those who were 'orthodox' and the 'Macedonians'.[25] Hence its cautious wording, especially in the third article, or more precisely, in its pneumatological passages, for the doctrine of the Holy Spirit was the most disputed area of belief towards the end of the Arian Controversy. This 'pneumatological' third article in C runs as follows:

And in the Holy Spirit, Who is lord and life-giver, Who proceeds from the Father, Who with the Father and the Son is together worshipped and together glorified [NB not: Who is God and of one substance with the Father and the Son!], Who spoke through the prophets; in one holy Catholic and apostolic Church . . .[26]

All things considered, one still hesitates to call even the theologians and bishops of the fourth century credal fetishists. It was only after the end of the 'golden age' of patristic literature[27] that things began to change. This could be demonstrated in regard to the development of eastern theology between the Councils of Chalcedon (451) and Constantinople III (680/681). Yet to a certain extent it is also true of the older Athanasius of Alexandria, the great champion of Nicene orthodoxy. About 350 he began to insist more and more on the 'sufficiency' of the Nicene Creed; for him it encapsulated the 'one faith' of Christians, an agreed basis as the criterion of true doctrine.

This development of a certain stiffness and fossilization is also to be observed in the West. The so-called 'Athanasian Creed',[28] presumably of fifth- or sixth-century Spanish provenance, supplies the most concrete evidence. For according to this Creed, the criterion on which salvation depends is nothing else than scrupulous adhesion to the Christian faith as defined by the contents of the

Athanasian Creed, and especially its trinitarian and christological elements. The Creed begins as follows:

> Whoever desires to be saved must above all hold the Catholic faith. Unless a man keeps it in its entirety inviolate, he will assuredly perish eternally. Now this is the Catholic faith, that we worship one God in Trinity and Trinity in unity ... It is necessary, however, to eternal salvation that he should also faithfully believe in the Incarnation of our Lord Jesus Christ.[29]

Yet previously, to use a fine formulation by the late R P C Hanson:

> The theologians who were most responsible for fixing these dogmas in their traditional form had an undoctrinaire and flexible attitude to formulae, were well aware of the inadequacy and limitations of language in expressing propositions about God, and were more concerned with the doctrine expressed by the language than the language itself.[30]

NOTES

The English translation of this chapter was prepared in collaboration with Ian Hazlett.

1 e.g. A E Burn, C P Caspari, A von Harnack, F J A Hort, F Katten-busch, C H Turner.
2 cf. the studies of J N D Kelly, E Flesseman-van Leer, B. Hägglund, R P C Hanson, H von Campenhausen, etc.
3 1 John 4.3; 2 John 7.
4 The corpus of letters written by the bishop and martyr, Ignatius of Antioch, early in the second century.
5 ch. 7.1. cf. Kelly, *Creeds*, p. 70.
6 ch. 9.
7 After Kelly, *Creeds*, p. 68.
8 Irenaeus, *Against Heresies*, 1, 10.1, after Kelly, op. cit., p. 79 (altered); cf. Tertullian, *On the Prescription of Heretics 13*; *Against Praxeas 1*; *On the Veiling of Young Women 1*.
9 See Hippolytus of Rome, *Apostolic Tradition*, (early third century AD), according to the reconstruction of B Botte, and translation of Kelly, *Creeds*, p. 46. cf. also Tertullian, *Against Marcion*, 3.1; *On Spectacles*, 4.1; *On Baptism*, 2.1; *On the Crown*, 3.3; *Against Praxeas*, 26.9; also Cyprian, *Epistle*, 69.7, etc.
10 *Confessions*, 8, 2.5.
11 *Catechetical Lectures*, 5.12; 6.36; 15.2; 18.32.

12 ibid., 18.32.
13 *De Singulis Libris Canonicis Scarapsus.*
14 *Commentarius in symbolum apostolorum.*
15 *Panarion.*
16 ibid., 72, 3.1, after Kelly, *Creeds*, p. 102.
17 cf. *Dialogue of Origen with Heracleides and his episcopal colleagues on Father, Son, and Soul*, ed. J. Scherer. Sources Chrétiennes, vol. 67, Paris 1960.
18 cf. H G Opitz, *Urkunde* 6 and 33 (=Hahn, *Bibliothek*, 186.187), also NE, pp. 353–4.
19 =H G Opitz, op. cit., 18; cf. Kelly, *Creeds*, pp. 209f., along with the improvements of L. Abramowski, *Zeitschrift für Kirchengeschichte*, vol. 86 (1975), pp. 356–66. Also NE, pp. 334–7.
20 Homoousion tō patri.
21 After Kelly, *Creeds*, pp. 215f; cf. NE, 345.
22 Kelly, *Creeds.*
23 *Constantinopolitanum* or *Nicaeno-Constantinopolitanum*, AD 381.
24 cf. Kelly, *Creeds*, pp. 344ff.
25 A name for those who doubted the full divinity of the Holy Spirit. [Ed.]
26 After Kelly, *Creeds*, p. 298 (altered); cf. CCC, p. 115.
27 J. Quasten.
28 *Athanasianum* or *Symbolum 'quicumque'*, after its initial word: 'Who-ever'.
29 After Kelly, *The Athanasian Creed*, pp. 17ff.
30 *Dogma and Formula in the Fathers.* Studia Patristica 13,2 (Berlin 1975), p. 183.

BIBLIOGRAPHY

Campenhausen, H von, *Urchristliches und Altkirchliches* (Tübingen, Mohr, 1979), pp. 217–72. 278–99.

Flesseman-van Leer, E, *Tradition and Scripture in the Early Church.* Assen, van Gorcum, 1954.

Hahn, A and G L, *Bibliothek der Symbole und Glaubensregeln der Alten Kirche*[3]. Breslau, 1897; repr. Hildesheim, Olms, 1962. (Most comprehensive collection of original texts).

Hanson, R P C, *Tradition in the Early Church.* London, SCM, 1962.

Kelly, J N D, *Early Christian Creeds*[3]. London and New York, Longman, 1972 (fundamental).

——, *The Athanasian Creed.* London, A & C Black, 1964.

9

Ministry, Worship and Christian Life

STUART G HALL

When the gospel was first preached by travelling apostles, it was in Jewish synagogues that the message was heard. Sometimes a whole congregation might turn to faith in Jesus Christ. In that case its existing organization would continue, but with adaptations. That meant different things in different places. But generally it meant that it was governed by a body of older males, who would be called Elders, in Greek *presbyteroi*, who would form a council to take decisions. One of them would preside, the 'ruler of the synagogue' (*archisynagōgos*), but would not necessarily hold the office for life. Among the elders would be teachers and readers, responsible for reading and expounding the Law and other books of Scripture and for training young people and any proselytes (converts), and more menial servants for various functions like door-keeping and cleaning.

Christians formed synagogues too; *synagōgē* means 'a gathering', and continued to be used by Christians for some centuries alongside the commoner *ekklēsía*, 'assembly' or 'church'. But the gospel brought with it new features. The travelling apostle (*apostolos* means 'messenger' or 'deputy', of Christ) would leave with his young church several things. First and foremost he left people baptized in the Holy Spirit. This manifested itself in various ways: the worship of God in Christ; a tradition of bible interpretation; principles of conduct towards each other and the world. Each of these was immediately found to need some organizaton for its ordering, control and perpetuation. Where, as often happened after the first wave of preaching, congregations were formed predominantly of pagan converts who were not used to synagogue life, these needs were more urgent than ever.

WORSHIP IN THE EARLY PERIOD

The worship of God in Christ was at first quite different from what went on in the world around. In the second century the anonymous writer of the *Letter to Diognetus* describes the error of pagan worship in offering sacrifice to false gods, and of Judaism in offering sacrifice to the true God. His answer to the question, 'How do Christians worship?', is to describe their way of life, a third people, neither idolaters nor Jews, who have received the truth through the Word of God and live as the soul of the world, pure in morals, chaste in sexual living, generous and longsuffering. There is no question of an alternative cult in the ordinary sense. In this respect they resemble both the synagogue and the Greek philosophic ideal. The synagogue was not a cult-centre where sacrificial worship was offered: to the Jew that could happen only in the Temple in Jerusalem. It was a school for living according to God's Law; prayer was also offered, and the discipline of the community and its judicial relation to other synagogues and (while it survived) to the Temple played a part, but the reading and interpretation of Scripture was the predominant concern. It could be presented by Philo of Alexandria, Jesus' contemporary, as a school of philosophic living.

And so the Christian religion too resembled philosophy. A widespread philosophic opinion regarded sacrifice as not in itself pleasing to God, but rather prayer from a pure heart. Rabbis and philosophers alike regarded the outward forms of sacrifice as expressing such a spiritual disposition, and pleasing to God for that reason. The Christians went further, and rejected the sacrifices altogether. They inherited from Judaism a hatred of idols and their worship: the gods of the heathen were non-existent, or were demons with limited power prescribed by the true God, who deceived mankind and fed on animal blood. God had himself abolished the sacrificial system of the Law of Moses: it was either a temporary expedient (the usual Christian explanation) until the true meaning was made clear, or its meaning had always been mystical and non-literal, so that the Jews were mistaken to take it literally, or even (among radical Marcionite and Gnostic groups) it all came from an inferior, legalistic creator God and was not binding on those liberated by the truly spiritual supreme being above him.

Because the Christians deliberately rejected the central act of

Graeco-Roman religion, and most of them were not Jews, they were accused of atheism, 'godlessness'. Their defenders ('apologists') in the second century repeatedly argue against this charge.[1] But rejecting pagan religion remains the foremost feature of the ceremony which made a Christian, the ceremonial bath of baptism, commonly called 'enlightenment' (*phōtismos*). A classic pattern of baptismal ceremony is visible in Hippolytus,[2] a pattern widely known in both West and East. It begins with a renunciation: 'I renounce you, Satan, and all your service, and all your works', and as a sign of cleansing from the foul evil of idolatry the candidate was anointed with 'oil of exorcism' specially prepared by the bishop. Thus freed from the demonic power, the candidate stands in a bath and is washed down three times, preferably in running water. Each washing recalls the name of one of the Trinity, and the candidate professes that faith before each bathing. So the washing, originally the token of cleansing, becomes the means of professing true faith; an unorthodox formula betrays false teaching and may be repudiated by the main Church.[3] After bathing, the candidate is anointed with 'oil of thanksgiving', an oil scented and blessed for the purpose, dried and clothed in clean robes, and taken to the bishop in the presence of the congregation. The bishop anoints the candidate again, signs him with the cross, and blesses and kisses him; a eucharistic meal follows, at which the newly baptized have a privileged place.

Some things are worth noting. First, the baptism is chiefly private. Surviving ancient church sites have a separate room for the bathing, away from the *ekklēsía* or church assembly, or often a totally separate building. This is partly because the bath is taken naked by both sexes. But also, until they are enlightened, they are not fit to enter the congregation of those sanctified by the Spirit. Secondly, what we have described is a typical mainstream rite. Among some groups baptism might be simply 'in the name of Jesus Christ', and accomplished by a single dipping, a practice still recognized, even among groups which followed the trinitarian ritual, in the third century. Thirdly, almost universally baptism was associated with oil; the ancients would no more wash without oil than modern people without soap. The oil rapidly took on symbolic meaning: th pre-baptismal oiling corresponded to the cleansing oil used at *t*e Roman bathhouse, and was seen as purging out demonic influ*e*; the post-baptismal corresponded to the perfume applied after *ath*, and could symbolize light, Holy Spirit, anointing as proph*e riest*

103

and king, and becoming like Christ (whose name means 'Anointed').
Fourthly, the oriental Syriac-speaking churches, until they came
into line with their more westerly partners, anointed once and then
washed once in water, both parts being regarded as symbolic.
Finally, the whole procedure came at the end of a rigorous period of
preparation. For two or three years a candidate would be instructed
in the Scriptures and correct conduct. Many of Origen's homilies
probably originated as daily bible readings, which candidates for
baptism would be expected to attend.[4] For a much shorter period
(classically, forty days) more intense preparation, including instruction in the Gospels, was carried out. Then there was special teaching
and testing about the creed, and a period of fasting, intense for two
days, immediately before baptism. This preparation of candidates
for baptism went with the development of the Easter festival,
which was the normal time for baptism and for reconciling lapsed
Christians to the Church.

Those baptized were accustomed to meet regularly, chiefly on
Sundays, but also on some other days. The features of such meetings
included prayer and thanksgiving, various forms of teaching and
preaching, discipline and judgement, a collection, and a common
meal.[5] The prayer was originally offered by various members of the
congregation, especially those gifted with prophecy,[6] and a strong
corporate sense remains about the urgent pleading with God. The
petitions and intercessions were later integrated, or partly so, in the
bishop's eucharistic prayer. In Justin they were still separate at least
on special occasions.[7] Teaching, preaching and prophesying went
on. This included the reading of Scripture and its moral and spiritual
explanation. But it could mean simple divinely inspired directions,
like providing a meal for the poorer members.[8] This process passed
over into the disciplinary and judicial one. Christian congregations,
like synagogues, had some of the features of a court, where decisions
had to be made about who was fit to participate in the prayers (which
would prove futile if tainted with sin), where the erring were
rebuked, the penitent reconciled, and messages from other
churches, sometimes controversial or divisive, heard, discussed and
answered. Originally the founding apostles might take such decisions; after they were gone, synagogue-style elders, or divinely
inspired prophets, had to pronounce judgement. They would also
decide whom to appoint, or rather, who it was that God had chosen,
to fill church offices, and a variety of means were available.[9]

The importance of such decisions was heightened, and controversy exacerbated, because belonging to the clergy or congregation entitled one to material benefits. Each church kept a chest, into which regular offerings were made, and from which the clergy received their living, as did various church dependants, like widows, orphans, elderly and outcast slaves, abandoned babies picked up from the street, and people forced to abandon their craft on conversion (like prostitutes, idol-makers, and actors): in AD 251 the Roman church had 153 clergy and over 1500 widows and paupers, 'supported by the grace and loving kindness of the Master'.[10] The idealized account of Acts 2.43–47, in which goods are all surrendered on conversion, and meals regularly shared, gives way to regular giving to the common chest, or to some form of tithing for the clergy and the poor,[11] and eucharistic meals take place on fixed occasions, not when the prophets decree it.[12] The practice of the charitable meal, given by the rich for the poor, continued intermittently, and is usually referred to as the *agapē* or 'love-feast'. But the idea of feeding on the Body of Christ by sharing gifts with the members of that Body (being sustained 'by the grace and loving kindness of the Master') weakened, as the Eucharist became a formal, religious act of intense divine significance.

That divine significance appeared in more than one form. It could celebrate the gift of divine knowledge imparted through the Son of David, and look forward to the consummation when all is gathered into one in his Kingdom.[13] It could commemorate the death of the Messiah.[14] It was the Bread of Life in John's Gospel, and the medicine of immortality in Ignatius of Antioch: a means by which divine life is conveyed to the souls and bodies of human beings. But as time passed another view developed, that of sacrifice. But to understand it aright, we must first consider another topic, that of the organization and officers of the churches.

MINISTRY

We have already referred to the ministry of the earliest churches in various ways. There were the original apostles – not just the 'Twelve', some of whom are obscure characters, but also others raised up in the first generation, like Paul (Saul of Tarsus), and his associate in the Gentile mission, Barnabas. We have serious record only of Paul and indirectly of Peter, James and John in Jerusalem.

105

They clearly exercised great authority among their converts. But in the Pauline churches there were other officers, persons with special gifts.[15] In 1 Cor. 12.28 the first leaders named are apostles, prophets and teachers; the same groups appear in *Didache* 11–13, where (despite some problems of interpretation) the apostles seem to be travelling agents between churches, the prophets take precedence in leading the preaching and prayers, and the teachers are responsible for the tradition of moral and liturgical teaching. Apostles disappear after the earliest period, being increasingly identified as exclusively those appointed by Christ personally. Prophets lingered on, and were still claimed among the orthodox late in the second century; but perhaps that was merely a riposte to the emphatic claims of spiritual gifts and prophecy among the Montanists of Phrygia.[16]

But by the third century the right to see visions and dream dreams is increasingly limited to bishops, who take over the whole *charisma* of the prophets. This includes their status as 'high priest' attributed to them by *Didache* 13, which is first attributed to bishops by Hippolytus of Rome about 200. The primitive office of teacher lingers much longer. In the second century we find teachers common. Some wear philosophic attire, like Justin and Tertullian; some end up as presbyters, like Origen. Some are highly critical of the growing power of the bishops and deacons who dominate the main church, and we meet such criticisms explicitly in some of the Gnostic writers and in Origen. The tradition of divinely inspired theologians, independently teaching and interpreting the Scriptures both to believers and unbelievers, was one of the sources of division which caused the rise of the bishops in power.

From early times bishops and deacons were known.[17] *Episkopos* (bishop) means 'supervisor' or 'inspector', and became the name of the chief officer in each congregation. Ignatius (not after AD 115) was bishop of Antioch, and argues strongly that the unity of the congregation depends on the one bishop, without whom assemblies and actions are not valid.[18] Irenaeus about 180 takes this further, seeing the bishops of the great cities as succeeding each other in a recorded line from the time of the apostles, and the assured trustees of the original apostolic doctrine.[19] Cyprian in 251 regards the bishops of the churches throughout the world as the glue which holds the Church together, the structure by which the Church is one in time and space.[20] In practice this unity was achieved by the mutual recognition by one bishop of another, and by the ordination of each bishop by at least three neighbouring bishops. But not every bishop could possibly be in correspondence with every other: there were now hundreds of Christian congregations huge distances apart.

In fact a system grew up in parallel with the Roman administrative order, so that the bishop of a local city (*metropolis*) would be regarded as the superior of his local district, and the bishop of a major city as superior to him. Alexandria after about 200 increasingly led in Egypt and Libya; Antioch in Syria and Cilicia; Ephesus in Asia (that is, western Asia Minor) and Phrygia; Carthage in Africa (approximately modern Tunisia) and Numidia; and Rome in Italy, Sardinia and Sicily. The influence could extend further, and Spain could look for support to Carthage, Gaul to Rome. The Council of Nicaea in 325 began defining such powers,[21] and the rise of Constantinople as a new capital after that time raised a host of problems for the traditionally-minded Church; the patriarchal powers were defined by the Councils of Constantinople in 381[22] and Chalcedon in 451,[23] but rejected by Rome and Alexandria.[24] By then the supremacy of the bishop of Rome over all others was being claimed, not on the basis of the city's status as capital, but on the theological grounds of the primacy of Peter among the apostles and the powers inherited from him. But all that came later.

In the earliest phase the bishop's powers were not even necessarily that of the Jewish *archisynagōgos*. The term could be interchanged with *presbyteros* or 'elder'.[25] The expression 'bishops and deacons'[26] thus comprehends a whole body of bishops who are also elders, the council of the church inheriting the synagogue structure; Luke thus sees the authorities of the dominant Jerusalem church as 'apostles and elders'.[27] His supervisory role was exercised either corporately as appears to have happened at Rome in the early phase, or as a superior to all others, as in Ignatius and in all churches later. It seems to have arisen partly directly from Jewish models, partly from the felt inadequacy of the informal charismatic government by prophetic decisions.[28] A final judge was needed of the correctness of traditional teaching, the true inspiration of the prophet, the claim of individuals to be Christians, and the requests for help and recognition from other congregations; someone had to make the decisions. This touched very deeply when it came to claims on the common purse, whether from members of doubtful standing, from clergy, from members in prison, or from other churches. A bishop had to be 'proven' and 'not covetous'. This judicial control affected also the central work of prayer. To admit sinners to the prayers of the church, or worse still to lead that prayer with hands soiled by sin, was to anger God and make the prayer ineffectual. Thus the strong emphasis grew on the bishop as the leader in offering prayer and sacrifice acceptable to God. He was a priest, a function emphasized in the prayers of Polycarp before his martyrdom in 156(?).[29]

Churches like other households employed servants of both sexes. Their functions were originally menial, like serving the food at sacred meals, taking portions to absent members, and helping the candidates with clothes at baptisms. The word 'servant' (*diakonos*) became 'deacon', and the role of the male deacon became quite important. From the time of Clement of Rome (95?) it was regarded as of divine as well as apostolic institution. Male deacons, especially those attached to important bishops, acting as secretary or registrar, could become more powerful than bishops in lesser churches and presbyters in their own, and not infrequently succeeded the bishop in office. In later times the singing of the gospel of the Eucharist was assigned them as the highest dignity next to offering the eucharistic prayer. The female deacons (or deaconesses) remained confined to menial tasks, such as teaching children and assisting female candidates at baptism.

The presbyter or elder not only had a name which was for long interchangeable with that of bishop, but shared and sustained his ministry. Jerome was not alone in arguing the dignity of presbyters against the presumption of ambitious deacons.[30] These elders shared the bishop's ministry, including laying on hands when other presbyters were ordained; but they could act only on the bishop's authority. In a large church there could be many presbyters (Rome had forty-six in 251). They advised the bishop on disciplinary matters and all judgements, examined and instructed candidates for baptism or readmission after lapse, and led liturgical prayers and conducted sacraments (like domestic baptism of dying persons) in the absence of the bishop.

THE IMPERIAL CHURCH

We have already seen how a hierarchy developed, shadowing that of the Empire. It made the Church conveniently adaptable to the purposes of Christian emperors after the rise of Constantine. But there were other important changes in the way the Church functioned, which have deeply affected it ever since. The bishop's office came to be likened to that of the Aaronic priests of the Old Testament, and at the same time their public function replaced that of pagan sacrificing priesthoods. The term for priest (Greek *hiereus*, Latin *sacerdos*) was regularly used for bishops from the third century; in later ages, when the principal liturgical ministry was conducted by presbyters, it was applied to them as distinct from bishops. The bishop's ministry was seen as the offering of sacrifice. This was no longer a metaphor for the pure prayer of the Church,[31] but referred directly to the offering of bread and wine with thanksgiving in imitation of the dying prayer of Christ: it availed with God for the forgiveness of sins and the welfare of the Church and mankind. Ambrose uses language about the Eucharist in his conversation with the Emperor in 388, which well illustrates this change: 'Let me offer for you with a clear conscience . . . , so I went to the altar.'[32] It became customary to think of the presence of the bread and wine, after it had been converted into the Body and Blood of Christ, as a 'bloodless sacrifice' which made the prayers of the faithful particularly potent. Cyril of Jerusalem (*c*. 313-*c*. 386) was a good example of this. Some of these ideas remain with us to this day.

The baptismal ceremonial, which had long ago been assimilated to the practice of Roman baths, was now likened to the pagan mystery cults. In these, for a fee, suitably qualified persons were initiated with rites kept secret from the uninitiated: words, prayers and titles were received, and there were varying degrees of initiation. The purpose was in some sense to unite with the life of the god, and images of death and resurrection, birth and rebirth, were prominent. The primitive Christian initiation into wisdom with the forgiveness of sins was deliberately made an initiation into secrets not otherwise known, with even the meaning of the Eucharist held back till after baptism. But this effort was too late. Ironically, the very documents from which we know it, such as the *Mystagogical Catecheses* attributed to Cyril of Jerusalem, show by their existence that the secrets were out. The Church had become part of the ordinary life of the Empire, and indifferent Christians being baptized for conventional or practical reasons, rather than from converted conviction, were increasingly the norm. There was no martyrdom at the end of the road, and priestly hype about mystagogical initiation was no substitute.

One substitute, however, was found. If there were no martyrs, there were martyrs' bones and other relics. These were now discovered in large numbers, usually as a result of miraculous revelations, and were related to miraculous healings. Ambrose is a good example of a well-educated upper-class Roman believing in and encouraging the cult.[33] Round martyr shrines and martyrs' anniversaries multitudes gathered to celebrate with pious ceremony and irreligious parties; other saints, biblical and monastic, were soon added. That cycle of festivity formed one element in a growing Christian calendar. And the martyr shrines stood alongside the other church buildings (though relics could also be introduced and venerated in others), which became the focus of the new imperial cult from Constantine's time onwards. From the third century we know of the existence of Christian 'prayer-houses', where the principal synagogal gatherings were held for teaching, prayer and eucharistic worship – and where the bishop held his court. They were usually of 'basilica' shape, that is, like the imperial public buildings. The existence of such buildings, and the need for public cult, meant that these churches were filled with ceremonial from week to week and day to day. Monastic choirs came to be introduced, adding piety and habituation, and greatly filling the hours of day and night with psalm-singing and Scripture-reading.

From the old centre of Passover, the Christian Holy Week and Easter, developed the wide routine of Lenten preparation and Pentecostal celebration. Beside it, from the time of Constantine, pagan midwinter festivals were adapted to celebrate the birth and miracles of Christ, producing Christmas and Epiphany and eventually a wider cycle including Advent and the birth of John the Baptist at midsummer. So the whole imperial year was in theory sanctified. All this stamped on the face of the Church, its ministry and worship, characteristics which have become more or less permanent. How far the Church should regard such features as essential to its life is an open question.

NOTES

1 So Justin, *Apology*, 1.5–6; Athenagoras, *Legation*, NE, pp. 60, 66–7.
2 *Apostolic Tradition*, 21–22, NE, pp. 141–3.
3 Compare Irenaeus, *Against Heresies*, 1.21.3, NE, p. 91 and Canon 9 of the Synod of Arles, NE, p. 294.
4 Origen's own obscure description of the procedures of training and testing is in *Against Celsus*, 3.51, NE, pp. 209–10.

5 Compare Tertullian's summary in *Apology*, 39, NE, pp. 163–4.
6 1 Cor. 14.26; *Didache*, 10.7, NE, p. 10.
7 *Apology*, 1.65, NE, pp. 63–4.
8 *Didache*, 11.8, NE, p. 11.
9 In Acts already there are idealized accounts reflecting what Luke knew in other places: 1.23–26; 6.1–6; 13.1–3.
10 Cornelius in Eusebius, *Ecclesiastical History*, 6.43.11, p. 232.
11 1 Cor. 16.1–2; *Didache*, 13, NE, pp. 11–12.
12 *Didache*, 14, NE, p. 12.
13 *Didache*, 9–10, NE, p. 10.
14 1 Cor. 11.26.
15 See especially 1 Cor. 12.4–11 and 12.28–30.
16 See extracts from Eusebius, *Ecclesiastical History* 5.16 and Epiphanius, *Heresies*, 48, 49 in NE, pp. 102, 106–7.
17 Phil. 1.1; 1 Tim. 3.1–13.
18 See for instance *To the Smyrnaeans*, 8, NE, pp. 15–16.
19 *Against Heresies*, 3.3, NE pp. 114–16.
20 *On the Unity of the Catholic Church*, 5, NE, pp. 229–30.
21 Canon, 6, NE, p. 340.
22 Canon 3, CCC, p. 117.
23 Especially Canon 28, CCC, p. 362.
24 See especially Pope Leo's repudiation in *Letter* 105, CCC, pp. 365–7.
25 As in Acts 20.17,28; Titus 1.5–7; 1 Clement, 44.4–5, NE, pp. 8–9.
26 Phil 1.1; 1 Clement, 42.4, NE, p. 8 *Didache*, 15.1, Ne, p. 12.
27 Acts 15.28.
28 See the problems of false prophets and the recommendation to appoint and honour bishops and deacons in *Didache*, 11–12 and 15, NE, pp. 11, 12.
29 *Martyrdom of Polycarp*, 5.1; 7.3; 14, NE, pp. 24, 25, 27.
30 *Letter* 146, NE, pp. 356–7.
31 As in 1 Clement, 44.4, and *Didache*, 14, NE, pp. 9, 12.
32 Ambrose, *Letter* 41.28, CCC, p. 137.
33 *Letter* 22, CCC, pp. 132–4.

BIBLIOGRAPHY

Aune, D E, *Prophecy in Early Christianity and the Ancient World*. Grand Rapids, Eerdmans, 1983.
Campenhausen, H von, *Ecclesiastical Authority and Spiritual Power*. London, A & C Black; Stanford University Press, 1969.
Jungmann, J A, *The Early Liturgy to the Time of Gregory the Great*. Notre Dame University Press, 1959; London, Darton, Longman & Todd, 1960.
Swete, H B, ed, *Essays on the Early History of the Church and the Ministry*. London, Macmillan, 1918.
Theological Dictionary of the New Testament (Grand Rapids, Eerdmans, 1964 etc.), relevant articles.

10

Christian Asceticism and the Early Monks

PHILIP ROUSSEAU

A history of Christian asceticism, especially in its more organized forms, seems easy to construct. Familiar patterns assert themselves in book after book.

Almost every survey starts with some account of Antony the Egyptian hermit, who was born around 250 and probably lived for more than a hundred years. His ascetic career, described for us mainly in the famous *Life*, saw him moving gradually but steadily away from the centres of habitation on the Nile itself. His final place of settlement was in wild country near the western shore of the Red Sea. Yet even as a recluse he maintained contact with groups of disciples. The *Life* contains long if artificial addresses to such followers. Some of them shared for a while his distant retreat; others contented themselves with periods of instruction at those times when their 'father' came down from his 'inner mountain'. Antony, therefore, was never completely isolated. If we can trust the *Life*, we may interpret his teaching as marked by keen psychological insight into the mechanics of temptation and self-control, and by a firm attachment to the dignity and potential of human nature, in its bodily as well as in its spiritual aspects.

The story not unusually continues with Pachomius, a contemporary of Antony, though younger and shorter-lived. The two men are traditionally contrasted because, whereas Antony is thought of predominantly as a hermit, Pachomius is famous for having initiated a more communal or 'coenobitic' style of asceticism. Before his death in 346, he had helped to found seven communities in the Nile valley; and by the end of the fourth century his disciples and imitators had founded many more. The essential characteristics of a Pachomian monastery were carefully organized collaboration, both in material practicalities and in spiritual development; a high degree of economic self-sufficiency, through both agricultural endeavour and simple manufacture and trade; and loyalty to an abbot and other monastic officials, and to a growing body of traditions and regulations.

This initial concentration on Egypt is probably justified. Organized asceticism was in a very real sense an Egyptian invention. But the story has to take account also of similar developments in other parts of the eastern Roman Empire. In Cappadocia, Basil of Caesarea (d. 379), with relatives and friends, developed a style of organized asceticism closely interwoven with the pastoral and broader social development of church life generally, and inspired both by the memory of Origen (on whom more below) and, for a time, by the teachings of Eustathius of Sebaste (d. *c.* 377). In Palestine and Syria, evidence is much less readily available and much less easily interpreted, but one finds the same variety – hermits on the one hand, community asceticism on the other. The Syrian church reached during the fourth century an important peak in its development, symbolized by the career and fame of Ephraem (d. 373); and an ascetic emphasis lay at its heart. Ascetic practice in Palestine (which was not unaffected by the experiments under way in Egypt) was of particular importance from a western point of view, because of the impact it had on Jerome (d. 420) and his friend Rufinus (d. 410). They both spent many years in the province, living as monks, and sent back to friends and patrons, in Italy especially, a stream of letters, commentaries, and translations. These, influential in many other respects, affected in their turn the progress of the ascetic movement in the West. Finally, both Palestinian and Syrian asceticism, the latter in particular, hint at longstanding antecedents reaching back perhaps to the New Testament period itself.

Once they have described these developments, and shown how they gained some institutional sophistication and a sense of rootedness and tradition, historians customarily turn their attention to their impact upon the western, Latin-speaking provinces of the Roman Empire. The increasing mobility of bishops and other churchmen, not least (travelling from council to council) in the cause of ecclesiastical controversy, and a growing enthusiasm for pilgrimage – for travel from Spain and Gaul, for example, to the lands and cities of the biblical narrative – meant that more and more potential enthusiasts began to hear about, and perhaps even to see, the quality of ascetic life undertaken in Egypt and other parts of the eastern Mediterranean world. Such impressions were quickly reinforced by a proliferation of texts translated into Latin, most famously the *Life* of Antony (two surprisingly different versions appeared in quick succession scarcely ten years after his death). In Italy and Gaul, and very soon in Spain and North Africa, men and women began to imitate the pioneers and heroes of Egypt. The generation of Martin of Tours (d. 397) and of Sulpicius Severus (d. *c.* 420) in Gaul, of Ambrose (d. 397) in Italy, and later of Augustine (d. 430) in North Africa, began to lay firm foundations for a growing movement. Although they never legislated for monastic communities in detailed written form, as had Pachomius and his associates, these men left a collection of documents – the *Dialogues* of Sulpicius, for example; Ambrose, *On Virginity*; and Augustine's skeletal precepts – which lie at the root of western monasticism, and which point forward (though the links are still not wholly clear) to the life and *Rule* of Benedict in the sixth century. They had as contemporaries, and indeed at times opponents, more shadowy figures, who undoubtedly made a contribution nevertheless to the same tradition: one thinks of the eccentric Paulinus of Nola (d. 431), of the obscure extravagances of Priscillian of Avila (executed 386), and above all of the enduring seriousness of Pelagius (d. after 420).

All of this prevents us from exaggerating both the singularity of western asceticism's thrust and character and of the immediate influence of Benedict himself (d. *c.* 550). The latter's *Rule* acquired dominant authority only with time; and his reputation owed a great deal to the skilful hagiography of Gregory the Great (d. 604). Other traditions, in Gaul especially, remained independent. A fertile and constant relationship between northern Gaul and the long-established Christian community in Britain, together with the expansion of Christianity into Ireland in the fifth century, made of those three territories a lively and important alternative to patterns of the ascetic life set in place in southern Gaul and Italy; and they found their own Benedict perhaps in the figure of Columbanus (d. 615). Only later and with some pain, and under the influence of papal pressure and patronage, would those two great traditions coalesce, or at least contribute to one another's future; and in that achievement the hegemony established by the Franks in the eighth century played a not insignificant role.

In addition to these stages of institutional growth, the survey attends also to spiritual development, to the emergence of ascetic theory. The New Testament itself was of paramount importance, together with sections of the Old. Ascetic literature is full of commentary on Scripture, seeking not only moral precepts and associated exhortations but also examples of behaviour that seemed either conducive to ascetic achievement or the fruits of that success. With time, the writings of the commentators themselves acquired canonical status within the ascetic world. Chief among them was Origen, the great theologian of Alexandria (d. 254). His view of human nature and destiny was in theory universal; and its moral implications were intended to affect all Christians. But the cast of Origen's mind, inspired above all by his view of Scripture, lent itself more readily to ascetic enthusiasm than to compromised moral struggle in the mundane circumstances of secular life. Of central value in a person's makeup was, according to Origen, the element of spirit; and cultivation of that God-like force would carry one away from the realm of bodily experience, from subjection to passion, and help to focus one's energies on contemplation, a constant and unsullied attention to all signs of the power and presence of God.

The pioneers of the ascetic movement were instructed at the most detailed level by this great thinker. Other influences, of course, were brought to bear – the Stoic, the Pythagorean – as we shall see. But Origen enjoyed a primacy. The two greatest theoreticians of the ascetic life, Evagrius of Pontus in the East (d. 399) and Cassian in the West (d. 435), regarded themselves as his disciples. In their descriptions of human virtue and of human destiny, and in their analysis of temptation and of self-improvement, they applied his insights and his vocabulary to the expectations and requirements of an ascetic audience. Cassian appears more reserved in his allegiance; but this makes his Origenism tactful rather than ambiguous. His remained the single most important corpus of spiritual theology in the western Church, regarded by Benedict as second in value only to the Bible itself.

Other theorists followed to some degree the same path. Basil imbibed his Origen less directly perhaps than did Evagrius, and less extensively than did his own brother Gregory of Nyssa (d. *c.* 395); but Origen's ideas were an essential component of his thought, and coloured his own crucial impact on the later development of monasticism in the eastern Church. Jerome tried to repudiate in himself the influence of Origen, but not with complete conviction or success. Several of the works that contributed to his own influence on the development of western asceticism continued to carry the infection, as he might have seen it, of his youthful admiration. Certainly his one-time friend Rufinus was not ashamed to admit dependence; and he also had an important role to play in the development of western spirituality, especially through his translations of Origen's own writings and of Greek theologians influenced by him.

Such is the familiar history: largely a chain of famous names, implying a development essentially unbroken. But grave misgivings are easily aroused, once we ask where this history comes from. What are the primary materials upon which it is based? We face serious questions, not just about the reliability but also about the very nature and purpose of ascetic literature.

The first feature to notice is its variety. We have already mentioned biography. Almost every figure we have listed attracted the attention of a biographer. Then there are collections of rules, ranging from formal prescriptions, such as those issued in Pachomian circles and (less extensively) by Augustine, to more loosely structured exhortations, such as we find in the *Moralia* of Basil and the *Letters* of Jerome. And beyond that there are the broader treatises of an Evagrius or a Cassian (by no means the only examples). Lastly, we have a whole range of other works, not necessarily directed at an ascetic audience, but inspired by the ideals and practices of the ascetic life, and used by ascetics themselves as sources of encouragement and instruction: the sermons and exegetical works of almost any Father of the Church would fall into this category.

What this variety implies is that ascetic literature was inspired by many different styles and models, and addressed itself to many different types of audience. It is a mistake to suppose that it originated and circulated only within a milieu that we could call specifically 'monastic'. Ascetic behaviour and reflection sprang from and operated within many different levels of Christian society. Even more important, the literature strives to defend or impose this or that attitude, this or that pattern of behaviour. It is, in that sense, propaganda.

In the first place, it often addresses the question of whether asceticism can be written down at all; whether, that is, ascetic ideas and practices can usefully be understood and acted upon via the process of reading (as opposed, for example, to the study of a living spiritual master); whether asceticism can be handed on, can be inherited, in that way. Anxiety of this kind is probably nowhere more vividly demonstrated than in the *Sayings of the Fathers*, which attempt to bring the reader face to face, so to speak, with the great pioneers of Egyptian asceticism. Many of the *Sayings* date from the fourth century. Much of Cassian's work was in fact preoccupied with the same issue, and adopted the same model. It cannot, then, be taken simply at face value; and nor can other similar treatises.

Then there comes the question of which achieves better results: the life of a hermit, or the discipline of an ascetic community? The history outlined above may suggest that hermits came first, and that monasteries in the modern sense were a later development. But when we recognize more fully the propagandist character of the literature, it becomes clear that those two ways of life existed in parallel and indeed competed with one another for a long time. Many a biography and many a treatise revolve around this very problem. A degree of compromise was achieved; one which, for practical reasons, largely favoured community life, and suggested that more solitary asceticism was either the choice of dead heroes, and no longer attainable, or a goal towards which just a few might aspire on the basis of long-term success within a community. That compromise was achieved, however, only with time; and its forceful defence in written form did not signify its immediate acceptance.

Another issue debated in the sources was whether ascetics should or should not maintain contact with secular society. This was partly a response to temptation and backsliding; but it also had much to do with economics. In the period following the reign of Constantine (d. 337), the Church had grown accustomed to the administration, and indeed the enjoyment, of wealth. That, undoubtedly, was a development some ascetics wished to reject or escape from. Yet the scrumpulous use of property, government exemptions, and popular generosity by donation or bequest could benefit the poor or the disadvantaged. Other ascetics saw no reason why they should not engage in such merciful enterprise. One had to ensure also that religious enthusiasm did not become a burden to others. Self-sufficiency, therefore (which implied property, work, income, and trade), could be seen as an obligation upon ascetics, drawing them into the broader economic structures of society precisely in order to avoid too heavy or too selfish a dependence upon it.

A further topic of debate was the ascetic's relation to the Church as an institution. To what extent, for example, did the ascetic endeavour depend for its authenticity and its vigour upon the sacramental life of the Church? The assertion of close and enduring dependence (and most ascetics thought in those terms) inevitably demanded the presence of priests within the ascetic community, either drawn from its own members (and that became more often than not the case) or from nearby villages and towns. Once one has clergy among the ascetic groups, one immediately faces a second problem: to what extent should ascetics allow themselves to be drawn into the clerical body more generally? That gave rise to a great deal of anxiety. Pachomius, for example, was most insistent upon avoiding such involvement. Basil, on the other hand, was famous for advocating a very close association between the ascetic community and the Church at large. Certainly, many ascetics undertook pastoral roles within local communities, and even became bishops. Basil and Augustine were merely outstanding examples of a widespread, if contested, development.

Finally, there was the question of the past. The fourth century was fascinated by history; and among Christians this took the form of a question: where was history, the history that God controlled, leading Roman society? Constantine, in the eyes of some, had given new meaning to the very flow of time, to that human progress governed by the providence of God; and surely, they said, the new freedom, the expansion, the very dignity and prosperity of the Church was part of that divine plan. That was what 'Church' and 'Christian society' were destined to mean. Ascetics, on the other hand, often saw God's purposes and the thrust of history in quite different terms; and they saw within their own society, with its disciplines, its abnegation, its withdrawal, its new sense of community and authority, the true fulfilment of the New Testament ideal, the true demonstration of what 'Church' should mean.

Such considerations lead us to acknowledge that the early history of Christian asceticism was not one of smooth development, least of all development from a period of eccentric and lonely pioneers to a period of corporate endeavour fully integrated into the life of the Church and dominated by its episcopal leadership. On the contrary, it was a history of intense debate: debate about the mechanics of inheritance and tradition, about the relative merits of the solitary and the community life, about one's proper distance from secular society, about one's relationship with sacrament and priesthood, and

118

about the future (not least, the social future) envisaged for Christians by their God. At the beginning of our history, during the years when Antony and Pachomius were conducting their experiments, not one of those questions had been answered in a definitive way. Indeed, some of them had not even been raised. The answers with which we are now familiar, and which so much of the literature was designed to defend (probably in the face of so much practice to the contrary), found their clearest form not when they were written but some way in the future.

Armed, therefore, against the tendentious character of the sources themselves, and conscious that practices were not so much described as either championed or undermined, we come to see that the situation during the lifetime of those pioneers was much more fluid than we had supposed. Many different types of ascetic behaviour were both pursued and tolerated. Some of the earliest examples of ascetic vocation seem to have affected individuals who remained surprisingly close to their secular communities. They lived at times with their families (this was especially true of women), they took at least some less regular part in the economic life of their villages and towns (as part-time labourers, for example), and they were recognized by others as a familiar feature of the religious scene – 'wanderers', 'enthusiasts', 'single-minded', 'loners'; all those terms occur, and vague enough they are. Both Antony and Pachomius, in their early years, were precisely such persons; even their much later biographies fail to disguise the fact. It is possible, therefore, that both the communal *and* the solitary life were both *later* developments; reactions, perhaps, to earlier custom. They competed with one another, in fact and, most importantly, in writing, for the allegiance of a new generation.

The earlier situation was fluid also in relation to its own ascetic tradition. Although a simplistic history of asceticism, reaching back to the New Testament and to even older biblical exemplars, came to characterize later ascetic literature, the 'freelance' ascetics of the Constantinian period were drawing upon a much broader range of ideas and practices; and not all of them were Christian. Here we meet with what is, perhaps, the most interesting set of questions facing the student of early ascetic history today. Anyone in the late third century intent upon becoming a serious-minded religious enthusiast in pursuit of virtue and self-improvement (and that would have been the kind of description most likely to spring to mind) had available a wide variety of traditions and models to choose from. As a result, even among Christians (for there were pagan ascetics also), the range of ascetic styles touting for custom in the fourth-century Church was broader than subsequent literature might lead us to suppose. Ascetic experiment took more forms than were later allowed by orthodoxy or encouraged by experience.

Inquiry into the antecedents, say, of Antony and Pachomius can quickly lead us into all sorts of areas; but three main sources of inspiration demand particular attention. The first is paganism. The term covers, of course, an enormous variety of practice and belief. The Platonist view of matter and spirit, the Epicurean delight in secluded comradeship, the Stoic emphasis on interior detachment and tranquillity: all had their part to play in the formation of the Christian ascetic. There is some point, too, in exploring attitudes to miracle, to enthusiasm, and to self-denial among the cultic confraternities of pagan religious centres. But the most important tradition was that labelled Pythagorean, which advocated a life of physical simplicity, detachment from homeland, indifference to sacrifice and other rituals, prayerful intimacy with the divine, and the development of verbal skills in the service of practical wisdom, encouraging not only imitation by other devotees but also proper conduct in public life. That vocation would have been long familiar to anyone in the Roman world. We see it enshrined in such texts as the *Life of Apollonius of Tyana* by Philostratus (fl. 220) and the *Life of Pythagoras* by Iamblichus (d. *c.* 330). Christian biographers, no less than Christian imitators, were conscious of the model.

There was a specifically Christian tradition commonly described as 'heterodox'. One does not wish to imply (for it certainly was not true) that the ascetic life either started or ended up at odds with the 'orthodox' Church. But dedication to ascetic ideals was one of the ways in which Christians tested the authenticity of their own traditions, and searched for a common form of religious practice that could honestly claim descent from, and loyalty to, the community of Jesus' time. That testing took place at institutional levels and, perhaps more famously, at theological levels also. At whatever level of inquiry and criticism, it was some time before an authentic tradition was confidently identified. Take the ascetic component of Montanism, for example, championed by Tertullian (d. *c.* 225), or

120

those swayed by the dualistic teaching of Mani (d. 276?), or those Christian groups that we label vaguely 'Gnostic', or the teachings of the great Origen himself: each in their time encouraged what others came to regard as falsity; and each led some up blind alleys for a while. But they were not mere flashes in the pan, threats identified and defeated once and for all in their own age. They exemplified longstanding features of the late Roman religious climate within which Christians had to operate. The decision to abandon or to modify certain emphases, certain ways of defining and pursuing virtue, was often postponed for longer than the literature might suggest. 'Orthodoxy', in written form, is often little more than energetic optimism or wisdom after the event.

Finally, the historian of Christianity must more and more take account of the Jewish past. As far as asceticism is concerned, Christians have always paid attention to the hints dropped by Eusebius of Caesarea (d. *c.* 340) in his *Ecclesiastical History*: hints that the first-century Essenes and the slightly later so-called *therapeutai* of Alexandria were remarkably like groups of Christian ascetics in his own time – so much so, indeed, that he believed the *therapeutai* were Christians also. But those 'proto-monks' were, of course, Jews. The discovery of the Dead Sea Scrolls and archaeological work at Qumran have helped us to fill out the picture. Continuous connections, however, between those Jewish ascetics (if that was what they were) and the communities familiar to Antony and Pachomius have been very difficult to establish. There are, in any case, more interesting connections to be made. The very notion that virtue can be acquired by following a rule of life has a certain Jewish complexion. Some Christians, of course, falsified and diminished for their own purposes the breadth and humanity of Jewish understanding, and used 'law' as a term of theological disparagement. Consequently, attachment to regular discipline became precisely an accusation some Christian ascetic communities felt forced to resist, lest they be branded 'Judaizer'. But of course the antecedent was unavoidable, as well as a source of honour. Syrian ascetics, in particular, used a vocabulary of brotherhood based on covenant, which hints strongly at a Jewish past. Traces of the same concept can be found in Egypt, especially in Pachomian texts. Then the notion of purity of heart and the cult of virginity, although in many ways reconcilable with a Platonist emphasis, have many parallels in the teachings of the rabbis. Indeed, it is the rabbis themselves who emerge as the most attractive claimants to the status of proto-abbot! Their firm attachment to Scripture, their emphasis on a tradition of discipleship from generation to generation, and above all their enforced independence (following the loss of the Temple in 70) from the religious economy of sacrifice and priesthood, should force us to examine in a new light the strikingly analogous attitudes and conduct of many ascetic leaders in the Christian world.

Realizing, therefore, that there can be no straightforward account of Christian asceticism and of the emergence of the monastic life, we end with two consoling emphases. First, we must sharpen our skills in relation to the texts. The texts are tendentious. Their apparent reportage is an illusion. We must let them hint more loudly at the variety they attempt to deny or undermine. Second, we must investigate a wealth of antecedent: pagan, of course; but heterodox also; and above all, Jewish. These are the areas of inquiry that should stimulate the history student today. They remind us forcibly of the fragility, as well as the diversity, of the ascetic enterprise, even as we see it practised by the vocal and apparently confident aristocrats of Christian history. And thus we shall acknowledge that it was far from inevitable that monastic history turned out the way it did. We may discover in the process unexpected freshness, and perhaps even clearer relevance to our own lives, in its less enduring ventures.

BIBLIOGRAPHY

Brown, Peter, *The Body and Society*. New York, Columbia University Press; London, Forbes, 1988.

Cassian, John, *Conferences and Institutes*, tr. E C S Gibson. In *The Works of Sulpitius Severus*, etc. A Select Library of Nicene and Post-Nicene Fathers, n.s. no. 11. Oxford, Parker, 1984.

Chitty, Derwas J, *The Desert a City*. Oxford, Blackwell, 1966; repr. Oxford, Mowbray, 1977.

The Desert Christian: Sayings of the Desert Fathers: the Alphabetical Collection. tr. with a foreword by Benedicta Ward. New York, Cistercian Publications, 1975.

The Life of Saint Antony, tr. R C Gregg. New York, Paulist Press, 1980.

Pachomian Koinonia: The Lives, Rules, and other Writings of Saint Pachomius and his Disciples, tr. Armand Veilleux. 3 vols. Kalamazoo, Cistercian Publications, 1980–2.

Rousseau, Philip. *Ascetics, Authority, and the Church in the Age of Jerome and Cassian*. Oxford University Press 1978.

11

Church Councils and Synods

JAMES ALEXANDER

For over a century the Church in Roman Africa was split into two halves, Catholic and Donatist (so-called after Donatus, rival bishop of Carthage to Caecilian, whose contested appointment to the chief African see remained the ostensible cause of the schism). In a final effort to heal the breach, in 411 the contending parties, each represented by not far short of three hundred bishops, met in the great hall of the Gargilian baths in the African capital to submit their case to the adjudication of a specially-appointed imperial commissioner, Marcellinus. Although seven speakers were chosen by either side, Augustine (for the Catholics) and Petilian (for the Donatists) did most of the talking.

Marcellinus, of illustrious rank, tribune and notary: 'Let his previous statement be read out again so that it can be clearly shown that Caecilian was neither his "father" nor "mother".'
Petilian: 'You don't half defend them, by God!'
Augustine: 'Look, I say it – as often as they wish, I say it: Caecilian is not my "father", for my Lord says: "Call no man on earth your father; you have only one father, God (Matt. 23.9)." I call Caecilian "brother", a good "brother" if he was good, a bad "brother" if bad, because he is my "brother" in the sense we share the same sacraments . . .'
Petilian: 'Will he now at long last clearly tell us whether they regard Caecilian as the "father" whose offspring they are by descent? For nothing can be born without a progenitor, begin to flow without a fountain-head, or grow without a root. Your Lordship, then, sees how [Augustine] has often declared himself to have no beginning. But to have no beginning makes him all the more a heretic, since he has no "father", since by his own judgement he has condemned the "father" he had. Let it be laid

down therefore that if it is established his "father" is guilty, he too is implicated in that guilt . . .'
Augustine: 'I have a Head, namely, Christ, whose Apostle [Paul] I recall –'
Petilian (interrupting): 'Who ordained you bishop?'
Montanus (Donatist bishop): 'And what of the Apostle Paul's dictum: "Even if you had ten thousand tutors in Christ, you do not have many fathers, for, through Christ, it is I who have given birth to you, through the preaching of the Gospel (1 Cor. 4.15)"?'
At this [the Donatists] applauded noisily.
Alypius [Catholic bishop]: 'Let it be placed on record that they created a disturbance.'[1]

It is rather like switching on a tape-recording of the proceedings. As distinct from the impression we often get from the formal writings of the early Fathers it is in such scenes as this, preserved for posterity in that very small proportion of the recorded minutes of the early councils which has come down to us, that they suddenly spring most vividly to life, as here in the cut and thrust of a spirited, if somewhat tortuous, debate. We see Petilian losing his temper with the presiding judge in his eagerness to catch an extremely evasive St Augustine in his trap as he tries to forge an incriminating link between him and his fellow-bishops of the Catholic party on the one hand and on the other Caecilian, from whom ultimately they derived their ordination. Appropriately, in this volume of essays, it is a debate on which William Frend has himself made some typically astute comments about the material the Donatists had at their disposal had they wished to attempt a character-assassination of Augustine as by far their most redoubtable adversary on the Catholic side.

Councils, which we may perhaps broadly define as meetings attended by representatives of a number of individual churches to resolve problems in common, first appear in our sources in the latter part of the second century in connection with issues of more than merely local interest which had come to a head, namely, the dating of Easter and the validity of ecstatic prophecy. So in evolving a rudimentary form of conciliar government the Church seems to have been stimulated by the need to find an effective instrument for wider consultation and, if possible, agreement. Already in the second century, as we learn from the letters of Ignatius of Antioch, neighbouring communities often associated themselves through elected representatives in the appointment of a new bishop to his church. It is not therefore surprising to find a similar system of representation in operation in the case of councils. Local disputes could often be resolved at a congregational meeting of clergy and laity. Councils thus began as congregational meetings expanded by the inclusion of visiting members, usually bishops or other clergy, from churches round about. How widely representative such councils were depended on the geographical grouping of churches in the area, and no doubt also on how far local agitation sent out ripples of concern. The decisions of a council were regarded as binding upon the participants, but were often circulated more widely by letter, in an 'official communiqué', by way of information and in the hope of securing further adhesion. Thus the decision to reject ecstatic prophecy, agreed by councils in Asia Minor (modern Turkey) where the problem originated, gained further confirmation by the concurrence, after initial hesitation, of the Church in Rome. Harmony over the Easter date proved harder to achieve, though, once again, the Church in both halves of the Empire, East and West, was drawn into the debate. The impetus towards universalism, which eventually found expression in the first council which could claim to represent the Church as a whole, held at Nicaea in 325, is already discernible.

Within this general framework councils varied considerably in character, as we can see from two examples from the middle of the third century. One, which probably met in Roman Arabia (Jordan) to consider the controversial theological opinions of bishop Heracleides, invited Origen, the distinguished Alexandrian scholar then living in Palestine, to take the leading part, though he was only a presbyter. The neighbouring bishops who attended played little more than a supporting role in the high-level theological discussion staged in the presence of the local congregation, which, it may be inferred from what survives of the council minutes, was called upon to witness the agreement reached at the end of the debate, thereby, it was hoped, putting a stop to any further trouble. But all were free to ask awkward questions and argue the point if they wished or could. With this central emphasis on rational inquiry and free discussion we may contrast a council attended not long afterwards by bishops from Roman Africa at Carthage under the presidency of its bishop, Cyprian. The main item on the agenda – should baptism administered by breakaway groups of Christians be recognized as genuine by

125

the main body of the Church? – raised theological issues which Cyprian had already fully aired in correspondence, but at the meeting itself the decision was taken by balloting the bishops. Each of the eighty-five present spoke up in support of Cyprian's 'official' line rejecting baptism 'outside' the Church. The meeting has something of the flavour of a session of the Roman Senate, with the bishops passing a motion proposed by the presiding magistrate, thus giving it the force of 'law'. The laity of the local congregation was again present as well as clergy other than bishops. But the decision-making process is clearly monopolized by the bishops. This was no doubt a natural development from the fact that the bishop had by now emerged as the acknowledged leader of his local church, a focal point of unity and authoritative teaching for the community over which he exercised responsibility-in-chief.

So far we have been considering councils mainly as 'crisis meetings', summoned only when the need arose in a particular area. But by the third century in Asia Minor and North Africa councils met also on a regular, annual or twice-yearly, basis. They were, in short, becoming a built-in feature of the way the Church governed itself.

The earliest lists of conciliar decisions to survive date from the first part of the fourth century. In effect these canons throw a window wide open onto the life of the Church in the Roman world. A small sample will perhaps convey some idea of the range of issues which preoccupied the bishops in their deliberations. Understandably, residual difficulties from the recent persecution of the Church under the emperor Diocletian stood high on the agenda at the Council of Ancyra (Ankara) which met sometime between 314 and 319, as they did also at the Council of Arles in 314. The bishops at Ancyra show considerable discrimination in regulating the return to the Church of those who had lapsed during the persecution. It had fallen to local magistrates to implement the imperial order that Christian clergy should make a public gesture of compliance with the rites of Roman religion by offering sacrifice to the gods. To most Christians this was idolatry. But it had apparently been possible for certain Christians to bribe local officials only to pretend to torture them after they had duly performed public sacrifice, so that they could then pose as heroes in spite of their lapse. The council therefore stipulated that, in the case of lapsed presbyters, they should be restored to the Church provided only they were innocent of such subterfuge, but that they should nevertheless be debarred from preaching and priestly functions. Further, Christians who had disappeared into hiding to avoid the persecution, only to be given away by their slaves, or who had suffered torture, loss of property, or imprisonment, or had actually been compelled by physical force to offer incense or eat sacrificial meat, were to be reassured of their innocence and encouraged to return, provided they had during the persecution confessed themselves Christians and now repented their involuntary compliance. Indeed, laity in this category were not thereby disqualified from ordination. But there were also Christians who, having willingly complied in the persecution, simply did not bother to apply for readmission to the Church; then illness struck and they asked for communion. The bishops assembled at Arles said 'No': their only hope was to get better and give proof of repentance. At the Council of Elvira (near Granada), as at that of Neocaesarea (in north-eastern Turkey), both probably to be dated a little later in the century, concerns other than those arising from the persecution predominate. Neocaesarea ruled that presbyters who married after ordination should give up their clerical status; if they committed adultery, they should be excommunicated and submit to the normal procedures of penitential discipline before readmission. Emergency baptism in time of illness was deemed a bar to ordination to the presbyterate, since those who received baptism under such circumstances did so from 'necessity', not 'spontaneous resolve'. The canons of Elvira are of special interest in showing how successfully Christianity was ceasing to represent a 'ghetto society' and was gradually achieving 'integration'. But not without compromise. As one might expect, the sexual mores of both clergy and laity often fell short of the Christian ideal. It is perhaps more surprising to find Christians resorting to the uncanny, esoteric art of black magic. Perpetual excommunication is decreed for those who contrive the death of another by such means. A comparatively paltry penalty, on the other hand, is prescribed for the Christian lady who subjects her slave-girl to such a severe flogging that she dies: seven years' penance if it was done on purpose, otherwise only five. If however the lady meantime falls ill, she may be restored to communion forthwith. The promise of eventual restoration is even held out to Christian laymen who receive the hereditary office of a pagan priesthood, provided they manage to dissociate themselves personally from pagan sacrifice, murderous gladiatorial contests, and lewd plays, for all of which the job normally involved responsibility.

The conversion of the emperor Constantine opened a new chapter in the development of church councils, as in so much else. Constantine's victory in 324 over Licinius, his erstwhile colleague in the eastern half of the Empire, made him sole ruler of the whole Roman world. That enabled him in 325 to summon the first 'world council' of the Church to meet at Nicaea in Asia Minor, not far from his eastern capital, Nicomedia. Already, in the second half of the third century, a series of councils at Antioch in Syria had drawn wide representation throughout the eastern provinces from the Black Sea to Egypt. It was now at Antioch that, early in 325, to prepare the way for Nicaea, a preliminary gathering of eastern bishops occurred under the presidency of the western bishop, Ossius of Cordova, acting as the emperor's special envoy for church affairs. By far the most contentious issue due to come up at Nicaea involved an abstruse point of theological speculation which had nevertheless become a cause of serious discord in the eastern Church and so a threat to the new imperial ideology of 'one God, one Church, one Empire.' Arius, a presbyter of the Church in Alexandria in Egypt, had maintained there was an essential difference between God the Father and the divine Word, his Son, in that the Father alone was without beginning, the one unoriginate source of all that is. The Son could therefore be quite properly described as a 'creature', who took his origin from the Father. Some felt that to emphasize the difference between Father and Son in this way was equivalent to saying the Son was less than truly God. The opinions of Arius became controversial when he clashed with his bishop, Alexander. But Arius won many distinguished supporters among the eastern bishops, including Eusebius of Caesarea in Palestine, the church historian, whose personal involvement in the affair is particularly instructive for the history of conciliar diplomacy. At the preliminary meeting at Antioch, Ossius managed to secure the condemnation of Arianism and thus set the tone for the forthcoming council. Eusebius and others of similar persuasion found themselves under provisional sentence of excommunication pending the decision reached at Nicaea. In a fascinating letter to his congregation at Caesarea written shortly after that council we find Eusebius trying to justify the highly embarrassing fact that at Nicaea he had, along with virtually everyone else, duly signed the approved version of the creed, which contained the statement that the Son is of the 'same essence' (*homoousios*) as the Father. This had been intended to rule out the Arian view that Father and Son were essentially different, but, as Eusebius clearly demonstrates, this key clause could be given more than one interpretation. It could be explained away and therefore Eusebius' apparent volte-face excused. A similar attitude was no doubt true of the other Arian sympathizers who also signed and so goes some way to account for the astonishing degree of unanimity achieved at Nicaea: only two out of a total attendance of about two hundred and twenty bishops refused to sign.

Unfortunately, the minutes of Nicaea have not survived, so we know little of what went on. Constantine's role at the council however was symbolically important for Eusebius, when, soon after the emperor's death in 337, he wrote his 'propagandist' *Life of Constantine*. The main theme of the work is the Christian emperor's providential role in world history, which also included his acting through the Church, most notably at Nicaea. Eusebius describes the opening scene as the bishops assembled in the council chamber in opposite rows, rising to greet Constantine as he entered clad in his imperial finery. After some hesitation as to who should sit first, all took their seats, the emperor on a humble stool instead of his usual throne. In a brief response to a speech of welcome from one of the bishops he stressed above all the need for agreement. Ossius may have chaired most of the debates, but the emperor himself regularly attended the council's many sessions, intervening personally as he thought fit. Eusebius passes swiftly over the Arian affair, not surprisingly. Harmonious agreement achieved by the council over the date of Easter seemed to him a more suitable symbol of Christian unity. When the time came to endorse the council's anti-Arian creed, as we learn from the pro-Arian church historian Philostorgius, the high-ranking imperial secretary Philumenos took round the book for the bishops to sign, with exile the alternative for those who refused.

It is possible however that Constantine employed the carrot as well as the stick. Indeed it may even have been on this occasion that the expression 'ecumenical council' (*oikoumenikē synodos*) was used for the first time in an ecclesiastical context. Athanasius of Alexandria and Eusebius of Caesarea both use it of Nicaea some years after the council. But precisely the same phrase was already in current use to denote the 'universal association' which actors and atheletes had formed to obtain tax concessions and other privileges for their members. We know that in the course of the fourth century

Christian clergy came to enjoy similar financial privileges and so it seems very much a possibility that, to secure the agreement to which he attached so much importance, such concessions were part of the bargain Constantine offered the bishops. And it may have been in the more traditional sense as a 'universal association', assembled at Nicaea, that they asked for and got generous tax relief, although of course the expression later acquired other levels of meaning.

The canons of Nicaea show the bishops legislating to transform regional into provincial councils, drawing together bishops whose sees lay within a Roman province under the chairmanship of the capital's bishop. Thus the Church's system of conciliar self-government, as this had developed from earlier times, was now restructured on the basis of civil service boundaries. Following earlier precedent, Nicaea laid down that there should be two such provincial meetings a year, before Lent and in the autumn, and further that from the decision of a provincial council there should be no appeal. It was also recognized, although at this stage only in the most general terms, that certain sees, namely, Rome, Antioch, and Alexandria, exercised a wider jurisdiction than that of a mere provincial capital. But it was the provincial councils which provided the basic structure of church government. Over and above these, however, there were further councils which met only as occasion demanded and which were, on the model of Nicaea, summoned, supervised and endorsed by imperial authority. Of those which met before the year 600 five such councils (all in western Turkey), Nicaea (325), Constantinople (381), Ephesus (431), Chalcedon (451), and Constantinople (553), came to be looked on as having a special status and so to merit distinction from the rest by conferment of the title 'ecumenical'. Why are they ascribed this special status?

The most obvious answer, admittedly given with the benefit of hindsight, is that, with their pronouncements on the Trinity and the person of Christ, these councils defined the doctrinal foundations of the church. But while acknowledging that their authority to do so rested ultimately on fidelity to the traditional teaching of the Church as derived from Scripture, the bishops at these councils were in fact attempting to clarify what the Church's teaching on such highly controversial points should be. It was only after the second Council of Constantinople (553), which found it necessary to condemn certain theologians who had won approval at Chalcedon (451), but whose teaching did not explicitly form part of that council's credal definition, that it came to be recognized that the authority of a council in matters of doctrine was restricted to its official formulation of the faith.

Yet in the years between Nicaea and Constantinople (553) many councils to all appearances similar to those known as 'ecumenical' were held, as at Sardica (342/3), at Seleucia and Ariminum (359), and that at Ephesus (449) which Pope Leo the Great in a famous phrase dismissed as a piece of daylight robbery.

It was not just a matter of how widely representative of the Church a council might be. A sizeable section of eastern opinion represented at Antioch in 341 abandoned the credal formula agreed at Nicaea. On the other hand, the Council of Constantinople (381) itself was purely a regional affair, not a universal gathering, yet along with Nicaea it was recognized as authoritative at Chalcedon. Nicaea itself was in theory a meeting of the universal Church. In practice the vast majority of its bishops came from the eastern provinces, with only a 'token' representation from the West, Pope Sylvester's legates and a few others. This remained true of western participation in other councils such as Ephesus (431), where however, because western opinion had already found expression through a preliminary council in Rome, the papal legates could perhaps be said to have exercised a 'block vote'. They were by no means uninfluential. At Ephesus they allied themselves closely with Cyril of Alexandria against Nestorius of Constantinople to secure the latter's condemnation for propounding an inadequate doctrine of Christ's person.

The degree of unanimity achieved by a council in arriving at a decision was another consideration. The unanimity of Cyprian's Council at Carthage (256) was for him a sign of the Holy Spirit's operation, confirming its authority. The Council of Ariminum (359) spoke of Nicaea's doctrinal formulation as similarly inspired, as did Basil of Caesarea. Yet unanimity could be engineered. At Constantinople (381) acceptance of the Nicene formula was made a condition of attendance at the council, so that those who disagreed were automatically excluded.

The idea of endorsement or reception by the Church as a whole of the decisions taken on its behalf at a particular council was one on which Athanasius of Alexandria, in the course of his long struggle against Arianism, came to lay great stress, when the general consensus of opinion began to look back more favourably on Nicaea. But of course Nicaea would not have passed this test if it had been applied during the ascendancy of the Arian party which lasted well into the second half of the fourth century.

Indeed the history of the Arian controversy illustrates only too clearly how important it was for an ecclesiastical party, whether pro-Arian or pro-Nicene, to win the ear of the emperor. Because, for much of the fourth century, it was the Arian supporters who enjoyed this privilege, it was they, not the diehard adherents of an apparently outdated Nicene formula, who represented the official orthodoxy of the day. And it was equally vital that Nicene orthodoxy, reaffirmed at Constantinople (381), in its turn received unwavering imperial support.

To sum up, in answer to the question why some councils eventually came to be seen as more authoritative than others we may perhaps list among influential factors the extent to which a council could be held to represent the Church generally, the degree of unanimity it expressed, whether its decisions were widely received by the Church, particularly by its leading sees, Rome in the West, Antioch, Alexandria, and Constantinople in the East, and, last but not least, whether its decisions had the backing of the emperor.

NOTE

1   *Acts of Carthage Conference*, 3.233–240 (slightly abridged), PL 11.1404–5.

BIBLIOGRAPHY

Dvornik, F, *The General Councils of the Church*, Faith and Fact Books 83. London, Burns & Oates, 1961.

Councils and the Ecumenical Movement, World Council Studies 5. Geneva, World Council of Churches, 1968.

Chadwick, H, *History and Thought of the Early Church*, chaps. X, XI, and XII. London, Variorum Reprints, 1982.

Grillmeier, A, (ET) *Christ in Christian Tradition*. London, Mowbray; John Knox, Atlanta, 1965, 2nd edn 1975.

Hefele, C J, (ET) *A History of the Christian Councils to AD 451*, 3 vols. Edinburgh, T & T Clark, 1872–83.

Sieben, H J, *Die Konzilsidee der Alten Kirche* (*Konziliengeschichte*, ed. Brandmüller, Reihe B: Untersuchungen). Paderborn and Zurich, Ferdinand Schöningh, 1979.

PART FOUR

Work and Writings of the Church Fathers

12

The Greek Fathers

FRANCES YOUNG

The title suggests that the subject of this chapter is straightforward, but problems of definition soon become apparent. What is a 'Father'? What period do we include in the 'patristic' age?

W H C Frend, in whose honour this volume appears, wrote of 'Saints and Sinners in the Early Church', and he would be the first to insist that the evidence for understanding the early centuries must include the work and writings of heretics and others who were scarcely 'Doctors of the Church', as well as non-literary remains such as archaeological finds. Yet the term 'Father' goes on being used. We can see how it arose. Sociologically, the nearest analogy in ancient society to the earliest churches seems to have been the 'household', and family language was natural; they called each other 'brother' and 'sister', and Paul claimed to be the 'father' of the Corinthian church which he had founded. As time went on, bishops and patriarchs were addressed as 'Father'. The term carried the overtones of a figure accorded authority and affection, and increasingly one from the past who conveyed the authoritative interpretation of the tradition.

For the Orthodox Churches of eastern Christendom, the Fathers are the great church leaders and authors right up to the time of Gregory Palamas (1296–1359), and it is believed that all theology is contained in the patristic literature. For the western Churches things are less clear, some using the term to refer to important figures in the period up to the time of the mediaeval Schoolmen, others, particularly in the Protestant tradition, accepting the date of the Council of Chalcedon (451) as the effective terminus.

We cover the period up to about AD 600: for it is important to recognize that Chalcedon did not represent in the East the satisfactory conclusion it appeared to be for the western Church. We also adopt a wider interpretation than the term 'Father' suggests: for it is impossible to exclude one such as Origen, the profoundly influential scholar of the third century, despite the fact that he was never a bishop, and was condemned as a heretic a couple of centuries after his lifetime. Some may hope that 'mothers' too might be included – certainly there were some very powerful women around in the period, martyrs, ascetics, patrons, and the mothers and sisters of great men, such as Macrina, sister of Basil and Gregory (see below), or Monica, mother to Augustine; but on the whole they were written about rather than writing, and it is the literature which primarily concerns us here, particularly literature which forwarded the development of the doctrine and practices of the Church.

For if we are to speak of the 'work' of the Greek Fathers, it must surely be about their contribution as authoritative theologians for the future, rather than their immediate influence, political or otherwise; and their significance in this respect is inevitably more apparent by hindsight, by the selection of literature the Church chose to refer to and preserve, than by their immediate activity.

THE SECOND CENTURY

Greek was the language of the earliest churches as the New Testament makes clear, and in fact Greek remained the language of the Church, even in the West, well into the third century. The work and writings of the Greek Fathers therefore begin with the immediate post-biblical writings, some almost certainly predating the later epistles which were eventually incorporated into the canon, and dealing with issues that are hinted at already within the pages of the New Testament.

THE LITERATURE

The Apostolic Fathers

The Apostolic Fathers include the earliest non-scriptural writings, some indeed regarded as canonical by some early scholars such as Origen. The chief documents are:

1 Clement, a letter to the Corinthian church written from Rome round about AD 96, endeavouring to sort out problems of leadership and authority in that turbulent church. Clement appears to act as secretary to the Roman presbyters, but tradition soon suggested he was the third pope in a direct line from Peter. It is interesting that the Roman church already felt it should be responsible for what was going on in churches elsewhere. This letter heads a considerable Clementine literature, but is now recognized as the only authentic writing, the rest of the corpus being attributed later to this early authoritative figure despite being later compilations from very different contexts. *2 Clement* is usually included still among the Apostolic Fathers, being a second century homily of some interest.

The Shepherd of Hermas, a prophetic and visionary work emanating from Rome in the early second century. It had a great deal of influence and is found listed as scriptural from time to time.

The *Letters* of *Ignatius*, a small authentic corpus which also 'grew' over time, modern scholarship identifying seven as genuine. Ignatius was bishop of Antioch, and round about AD 110 he was conveyed from Antioch to Rome where he was to be martyred. En route he wrote letters to the churches he would pass by. In the face of doctrinal conflicts in those churches he recommends that the authority of the bishop be the defence, likening the monepiscopate to the one God known in Jesus Christ. It would appear that this does not so much reflect the existence of the monepiscopate as the movement towards that form of church government, there previously having been a college of presbyters giving local churches their leadership structure. Ignatius also allows us to see the attraction of martyrdom as fulfilling the Christian ideal of following Christ even unto death.

The *Didache*, or the *Teaching of the Twelve Apostles*, was again highly regarded in the early Church, but over the centuries it disappeared, to be rediscovered in 1875. It is a compendium of church practice, with ethical and liturgical advice, some rules and regulations. The contents would appear to belong to various different dates and stages in the development of the early Church, the whole compilation coming from the second century. This first 'Church Order' would itself be incorporated in later Church Orders as this type of literature expanded over the centuries.

Some other writings are usually classed in this category: such as the fragments of Papias, the letter of Polycarp and the account of his martyrdom, *The Epistle of Barnabas*, and *The Epistle to Diognetus*, really an apologetic work.

The Apologists

The Apologists include a number of second-century writers who attempted to explain Christianity to the Graeco-Roman world, and in the process began to give a rational account of Christian theology. There were many later Fathers who also undertook the apologetic enterprise, finding new issues to handle in a new situation, but the second-century apologists initiated the tradition and set the fundamental patterns of defence against criticism and slander. The most important are:

Justin Martyr, who donned the philosopher's garb and set up as a teacher in Rome, seeing Christianity as the fulfilment of the philosophical quest for truth. He wrote two *Apologies*, and a work known as the *Dialogue with Trypho*, a debate with a Jew, largely about the meaning of the prophecies. The latter work would seem to have an apologetic motif also, in that the rejection of the Christian claims by the parent Jewish community was a serious problem in commending the faith.

Aristides, whose work was rediscovered in Armenian and Syriac translation in the late nineteenth century, and also *Athenagoras*, addressed *Apologies* to the Emperor like Justin, and like him acted as Christian philosophers. *Theophilus* was bishop of Antioch towards the end of the second century, and wrote three books of *Apology* to one Autolycus. The works of other apologists are referred to in other literature like Eusebius' *Ecclesiastical History* (see below), but little has survived. One such, Melito, bishop of Sardis, is better known as the author of a *Homily on the Pasch*, which again was rediscovered in comparatively recent times. *Tatian* the apologist is also known for having compiled the *Diatesseron*, a Harmony of the Four Gospels, and for going as missionary to the east: the Syriac-speaking churches used the *Diatesseron* as Scripture well into the fifth century, but the Greek tradition rejected Tatian as a heretic.

Irenaeus and the Gnostics

Irenaeus and the growing corpus of Gnostic literature reflect the most crucial second-century issues internal to the Church.

Irenaeus was bishop of Lyon in Gaul (France). His originally Greek writings survive in Latin and Armenian translation. He came from Asia Minor, claimed to have known Polycarp the famous bishop and martyr, and through him to have access to the apostolic tradition of John. In the face of the threat of Gnosticism and other groups he regarded as deviant, he defended the ecclesiastical tradition, shaped the canon of Scripture, and outlined what many regard as the first systematic theology.

Marcion and the Gnostics were once known chiefly through the literature written against them, but the discovery of the Nag Hammadi library now gives us access to heretical texts from groups like those Irenaeus opposed. The texts date physically from the fourth century, but include documents from much earlier, one being the Gospel of Truth, plausibly identified as the work of Valentinus whose influence Irenaeus was most anxious to neutralize.

THE ISSUES

Reconstructing exactly what was going on is not easy, but clearly the little Christian community began to map out its identity in relation both to the pagan world and the Jewish matrix from which it had sprung, and the surviving writings are the deposit from that process to which these people made a key contribution.

Christianity inherited much from the Jews, their Scriptures, their identity as God's chosen people, their loyalty to the one true God. They believed that the Christian community constituted the true fulfilment of what God intended his people to be, and that the Scriptures pointed to Christ. But how was it that they could compromise their inherited monotheism by proclaiming Christ as Son of God, especially as they took on the Jewish mantle of opposing idolatry and polytheism, utilizing the ethical monotheism of the best of Greek philosophy to commend an essentially Jewish position?

The philosophical solution of the apologists exploited the concept of the Logos, drawn from the Stoic–Platonic rapprochement of the past century or so. With Jews and Platonists they accepted the transcendence of God; with Stoics they affirmed the pervading immanence of the Divine Reason in the universe. The Logos became the Mind of God, his inner Wisdom containing his purposes and ideas, but then expressed in creation and revelation, ultimately to be embodied in the person of Jesus, the Word become flesh. This was what the prophecies all pointed to, and Christ was already present in the Word of Scripture. Such a concept set the parameters in which all subsequent Christian theology was to develop, though not without challenge in the third century.

But the problems were not simply external to the community. Christians were themselves subject to influences from various quarters as they tried to establish their identity, and internal pressures were considerable. Marcion found it difficult to reconcile the God of mercy and love revealed in Jesus and the God of wrath and judgement who appears in the Jewish Scriptures. He advocated cutting the Jewish connection, suggesting that Christians had received a new revelation of a higher God, different from the Jewish God. Gnostics made a similar move, though probably on different grounds. They were alienated from the material world, regarding it as a prison from which the soul or spirit needed to escape and return to the spiritual world from which it had come. This kind of outlook seems to have been fairly widespread, and Gnosticism is found in Jewish and pagan forms, not just Christian ones. But Christianity experienced it as an internal threat, Valentinus and other Christian Gnostics providing an attractive 'existential' interpretation of Christianity which suggested that the Demiurge or Creator God was evil, and that Christ brought spiritual salvation, the knowledge (*gnōsis*) necessary to achieve escape from his clutches.

Coupled with such notions was a tendency to regard Christ as a spiritual being who only appeared as a man (docetism) and did not really suffer and die on the cross. Ignatius was already confronting such ideas at the beginning of the century. By the end of the century, Irenaeus was developing a strong doctrine of the goodness of creation, and understanding redemption not as escape but as the re-creation of a world that was not created wrong but went wrong through the sin of Adam. Christ 'recapitulated' Adam's story and reversed the Fall, so creating a humanity redeemed and renewed in him. This theology was reinforced by stress on the unity of the Scriptures, both old and new, and of the one God of whom they spoke. Together with the Logos theology of the apologists, these developments established the fundamental shape of Christian theology, though 'otherworldliness' and ambivalence about what we now call the Old Testament have remained persistent problems.

THE THIRD CENTURY

The second century is tantalizingly difficult to get to grips with, but nevertheless it set the patterns: the third century can be called the period of scholarship. Christianity began to develop a scholarly literature concerned with exposition of its literary heritage (the Scriptures) and modelled on the techniques of textual and literary scholarship found in the schools of the Graeco-Roman educational tradition. Much of the older prophetic and typological use of the Jewish Scriptures was incorporated into an allegorical approach to exegesis which facilitated the recognition of the unity and value of the Scriptures and constituted a rejection of Marcion's travesty.

Irenaeus' work *Against Heresies* was developed in new compendia, while Christian philosophy became more sophisticated, tackling the standard philosophical questions about 'first principles' from a Christian standpoint. Apologetic undertook the larger task of answering pagan anti-Christian works point by point; and internal debate reaffirmed the Logos doctrine against various forms of monarchianism, that is, attempts to reassert monotheism by suggesting that Christ's divinity was by 'adoption', or by denying any distinction between Father and Son and affirming one God known in different 'modes'. The Logos tradition was then further refined by the activity of a sophisticated Christian intellectual like Origen. By the end of the century, the scholarly traditions pioneered by Origen reached a flowering in the first drafts of Eusebius' great works, to which we owe much of our ability to piece together the history of the preceding centuries and place the extant literature in context.

THE LITERATURE

Hippolytus represents the last great western thinker to write in Greek. He was opposed to monarchianism, indeed he became 'anti-pope' in protest against current tendencies in Roman theology. He composed a vast anti-heretical encyclopedia, and a number of important documents like the rediscovered *Apostolic Tradition* have been attributed to him by modern scholars (though not with universal agreement).

The Alexandrians represent the principal flowering of Greek patristic literature in this century. Tradition says that a Catechetical School was founded, which was headed by Pantaenus, then Clement, then Origen, but this tradition is difficult to substantiate, not least because Origen's activities seem less catechetical and more like an advanced 'university' education in Christian philosophy.

Clement of Alexandria has left us a number of 'scattered thoughts' in several books which reveal him as highly philosophical, as 'mystical' in tendency (though what the ancients meant by mystical is not exactly the same as what it has come to mean), and ready to pursue a Christian *gnōsis* without the dualistic theology of Gnosticism as sketched above. His reflections are Logos-centred, and highly allegorical: for in his view, all religious language is symbolic and 'riddling', speaking of a higher reality beyond human expression, but constituting the fundamental rationality of the universe. The material and literal are 'sacramental', communicating deeper truths. His principal writings are the *Protreptikos*, the *Paedagogus* and the *Stromateis*, but his little work, *The Rich Man's Salvation (Quis dives salvetur?)*, is also much referred to as evidence of Christianity accommodating to the world. All philosophy was in this period deeply imbued with ethical and ascetical interests.

From *Origen* we have much more extant material, though often through the medium of translation into Latin, and an enormous amount of his work has been lost or destroyed. In *Homilies* and *Commentaries* he seems to have covered the bulk of the Greek Bible, being the first systematic commentator. A good deal survives, but mostly in excerpts or translation. He compiled what is known as the *Hexapla*, which placed different versions of the Jewish Scriptures in columns side by side for critical comparison: this work disappeared, perhaps was never copied for its sheer bulk, and is known only through the reports of ancient users in succeeding centuries. It reposed in the library at Caesarea; Origen had moved there from Alexandria after differences with his bishop.

Despite this range of biblical scholarship, Origen is regarded primarily as a Christian Platonist, and certainly his philosophical understanding affected his biblical exegesis, which followed the ancient allegorical approach to interpretation. His thought is usually discussed on the basis of two important works: *De Principiis (On First Principles)* and *Against Celsus*. The *De Principiis* was probably an early work, following the standard questions of philosophical schools and providing Christian answers, but it has often been treated as a kind of systematic theology. Because some of Origen's hypotheses became questionable in the light of later doctrinal development, this work no longer exists in the original: Greek fragments can be placed in context by comparison with a tendentious and defensive translation into Latin by Rufinus. The state of the evidence leaves a number of questions about Origen's teaching unsettlable. The *Against Celsus* works through an anti-Christian treatise written a generation or so earlier, answering it point by point and clarifying the difference between Celsus' Platonism and Origen's Platonic Christianity.

Eusebius of Caesarea bridges the third and fourth Century. By the time the final persecution was over he was an old man of sixty who became an elder statesman in the Constantinian Church. But his viewpoint remains essentially third-century. He inherited Origen's library at Caesarea, and developed Christian scholarship in massive apologetic treatises, the *Praeparatio Evangelica (Preparation for the Gospel)* and the *Demonstratio Evangelica (Proof of the Gospel)*, showing how Christianity fulfilled not only the Jewish Scriptures but pagan aspirations to discover the truth. He is best known, however, for his *Ecclesiastical History*, the first attempt to give an account of the rise of Christianity. Eusebius believed that all had happened under the guidance of providence, and saw the conversion of Constantine as fulfilling the prophecies of the Kingdom of God on earth. Much of his work consists of vast extracts from other writings proving his points, and so his works are a quarry for fragments of missing literature, Jewish, pagan and Christian.

THE FOURTH AND EARLY FIFTH CENTURIES

THE ISSUES

After the conversion of Constantine, internal pressures towards uniformity of belief and structure were reinforced by the state's demand for a united Church upholding a united Empire. Internal controversy became more bitter as external pressures eased. We enter the age of the conciliar creeds and definitions, and the great literary figures were involved in ecumenical politics as well as usually exercising the office of bishop. The period has often been referred to as the Golden Age of patristic literature, and there is a great wealth of material available. The literary forms of classical culture were taken over and Christianized, sermons becoming orations such as panegyrics on saints and martyrs, the conventions of 'consolation literature' being adopted, correspondence being published, encyclopedias and histories being compiled. Alongside this we find further development of commentaries, apologetics, homilies, and the literature of controversy, treatise and counter-treatise.

During the century and a half which primarily concerns us, the Arian controversy forced clarification of the relationship between the Logos or Son of God and the Father by the Arians' defining the divine in such a way that only the Father could truly be God. After the Council of Nicaea, the more traditional Logos theology with its tendency to subordinate the Son to the Father, reasserted itself, the Nicene definition 'of one substance with the Father' being rejected as modalist (see above). Partly but not wholly for political reasons, it took until 381 and the Council of Constantinople for views subsequently labelled neo-Arian or semi-Arian to be suppressed.

Meanwhile the relationship between the incarnate Logos and humanity became an issue. Apollinaris in particular insisted that the Logos replaced the human mind or soul in the Christ, while others attempted to undercut Arian arguments and preserve the transcendent divinity of the Logos by attributing the weakness and fallibility of the incarnate one to the human nature he had assumed. Two approaches to this christological problem developed, loosely associated with Antioch and Alexandria. These traditions came into collision in the Nestorian Controversy, and eventually led to the formulation of the Chalcedonian definition in 451. The western Church treats this as the culmination of patristic doctrinal formulation, but it remained controversial in the East, eventually producing the Monophysite schism, and the still persisting division between the Chalcedonian (Orthodox) churches and the anti-Chalcedonian (Coptic and Syrian Jacobite) Churches.

THE LITERATURE

The following introduction can only be a rapid and superficial summary of a great deal of material. The reader is referred to a patrology to obtain a fuller picture.

Athanasius, patriarch of Alexandria, is supposed to have had a hand in the Nicene decisions, but at that stage he was merely a deacon. More definite is his lifelong defence of the Nicene formula during the succeeding reaction against it. He was sent into exile five times, and composed a range of controversial literature, against the Arians in particular but also later dealing with controversy about the Holy Spirit and Christology. He became the great Nicene authority appealed to by both sides in the subsequent christological controversies. He is also known for his classic two-volume work *Contra Gentes – De Incarnatione (Against the Pagans – On the Incarnation)*, the first engaging in the apologetic task, and the second taking the argument further by explaining and justifying the Christian doctrine of incarnation. In ancient times he was highly regarded as the author of the *Life of St Antony*, a work which did much to create the monastic movement, particularly in the West, but recent scholarship is increasingly questioning the attribution. The Athanasian corpus was certainly subject to accretion.

Cyril of Jerusalem represents the many conservative churchmen who barely contrived to escape condemnation for surviving the years of Arian ascendency. He is best known for his *Catechetical Lectures*, delivered during Lent to prepare candidates for baptism. The *Mystagogical Catecheses* attributed to him deal with the sacraments and are of particular interest to liturgiologists.

The Cappadocians, *Basil the Great, Gregory of Nazianzus* and *Gregory of Nyssa*, effectively ensured the reassertion of the Nicene formula at the Council of Constantinople by developing an exposition of trinitarian doctrine which was recognizably not modalist but expressed in Nicene terms. Basil and his brother, Gregory of Nyssa, wrote a series of treatises against Eunomius, their extreme Arian contemporary, and Basil's university friend, Gregory of Nazianzus, preached a crucial series of *Five Theological Orations* in Constantinople, for which later Orthodoxy has accorded him the title, 'The Theologian'. But the Cappadocians were also important for the development of a Christianized culture and philosophy in this period of rapid adjustment to being the 'established' religion of the Empire, and the range of their writings, orations, exegetical treatises, letters, etc., reflects this. Basil is also important for his activity in founding monasteries and drafting monastic rules.

Christian scholarship continued, and is represented in the figures of *Didymus the Blind*, an Origenist exegete (whose remains have been much increased by papyrus discoveries at the end of the last war), and *Epiphanius*, the great collector and analyser of 'heresies'.

John Chrysostom (the Golden-Mouth) has left a vast library of *Homilies* and *Sermons*, mostly collections preaching through particular books of the Bible. He became the classic popular preacher, renowned for his rhetorical skill and crowd-pulling powers. He was not so successful as a politician, and ended his life in disgrace and exile, but rapidly his name was restored, his literary remains were treasured (and expanded), and remain the highlight of patristic literature for the Greek Orthodox tradition.

A lot of the most interesting material from this period is extant only in fragments or ancient translations as a result of the controversies in which the chief actors were involved: the Antiochenes, *Diodore of Tarsus* and *Theodore of Mopsuestia* are a case in point, as is *Nestorius*, whose work known as the *Bazaar of Heraclides* turned up round about the turn of the century in Syriac. But *Theodoret of Cyrus* fared better, probably because of his acceptance of the decisions taken at the Council of Chalcedon. His *Letters* are a fascinating collection giving a range of insights into the period; and apart from controversial literature he wrote apologetic works, a series of lives of great ascetics known as the *Historia Religiosa*, and a *Church History*. Other accounts of famous monks and collections of anecdotes begin to make their appearance in this period, and other historians were also active in the early fifth century, *Socrates Scholasticus* and *Sozomen*.

Cyril of Alexandria's literary remains are considerable, mostly controversial letters, pamphlets and treatises, but also interesting exegetical works, and a great work against the apostate emperor Julian. It was not simply the Nestorian controversy which occupied his mind, but the defence of Christianity against Jews and pagans.

AFTER CHALCEDON: FROM 451 TO 600

It was Cyril's heritage which many felt had been betrayed at Chalcedon, and the political story of this next period is as complicated as in the earlier post-Constantinian struggles. The leading literary defenders of Cyril's doctrine, known as Monophysites by the Chalcedonians, included *Severus of Antioch*, *John Philoponus* and

Julian of Halicarnassus: generally speaking their works survive, if at all, in Syriac, or in fragments. They were opposed by certain neo-Chalcedonian theologians, notably *John of Scythopolis* and *Leontius of Byzantium.*

This period began the process of 'conservation' rather than being creative. Extensive catena commentaries were compiled, consisting of extracts from the great commentators of the past. But in the realm of spirituality there was not just the process of collecting the *Apophthegmata*, the sayings and stories of important and outstanding ascetics: there was the remarkable collection of works purported to be by Dionysius the Areopagite (Acts 17.34), pseudonymous works which must date from the turn of the fifth and sixth centuries, and which exercised an enormous influence on mediaeval thought; and the writings of ascetics like Dorotheus of Gaza and John Climacus.

To end on that note is a salutary reminder that it was not just dogmatic theology that the 'work' of the Greek Fathers produced. As the survey of literature should have indicated, it was in this period that the traditions of preaching and biblical scholarship had their origins, that the lasting shape of church government and of liturgies was established, and the fundamental ideals of ethics and spirituality formulated.

BIBLIOGRAPHY

To give detailed bibliographical guidance or substantive footnotes is beyond the scope of this introduction. Readers are referred to the following for further reading and for precise references:

Kelly, J N D, *Early Christian Doctrines*. London, A & C Black, 1960.
Quasten, J, *Patrology*. 3 vols., Utrecht and Antwerp, Spectrum; Westminster, Maryland, Newman Press, 1962–4.
Boniface Ramsey, *Beginning to Read the Fathers*. London, Darton, Longman & Todd, 1986.
Wiles, M F, *The Christian Fathers*. London, Hodder, 1968.
Young, Frances, *From Nicaea to Chalcedon*. London, SCM; Philadelphia, Fortress, 1983.

13

The Latin Fathers

DAVID WRIGHT

The beginnings of Christian writing in Latin are lost in obscurity. The earliest datable work is a brief record of some martyrs' trial at Carthage (near modern Tunis) on 17 July 180 (*Acts of the Scillitan Martyrs*). By then some Gospels and Pauline letters had been translated, the first parts of the 'Old Latin' Bible (as all Latin versions before Jerome's are known). Other Greek Christian works had been Latinized by 200, including 1 Clement and Irenaeus' *Against Heresies*.

Christianity had come to the western, Latin-speaking world from the Greek East. (The linguistic dividing-line ran roughly along the Danube, cutting southwards across Yugoslavia and the foot of Italy into western Libya.) Greek remained in use in the leading churches in the West – Rome, Carthage, Lyon – until at least 200. Tertullian, the brilliant Carthaginian 'creator of Christian Latin', also wrote Greek, perhaps for the Greek-speaking Christians glimpsed in the *Passion of Perpetua*. This vivid account of a group martyrdom at Carthage in 203/4 displays astonishing feminine sensitivity, incorporating Perpetua's prison diary, the earliest writing by a Christian woman.

Constantine's reign and the barbarians' takeover of the western Roman Empire are convenient dividing points within the period under review here – roughly 200–600. A broadly geographical framework will be followed within each section. Brief biographical details will help to set writers and writings in context, in a survey that, while inevitably selective, aims to portray the range of the Latin Fathers' work.

FROM TERTULLIAN TO CONSTANTINE: 200–330

Little is known of Tertullian's life. He was a lay teacher, author of over thirty books (*c.* 195–215) and exponent of an uncompromisingly rigorous Christianity. In mid-career he welcomed the 'New Prophecy' of Montanism from Asia Minor (modern Turkey), and became the mouthpiece of critical protest within the Carthaginian church.

Tertullian was highly educated, a master of rhetoric, which he deployed best in defending Christianity against persecution and misinformation. His *Apology* exposes with biting irony the illogicalities of persecution; its combative tone differs markedly from the philosophical discussions of Greek apologists like Justin. Refutation of error also preoccupied Tertullian, both specifically (e.g., *Against Marcion*, who had set the OT God over against the Father of Jesus) and comprehensively, in *The Prescription of Heretics*, which casts all heretics as latter-day corrupters of the original faith, inspired by pagan philosophies. Christianity is God-given revelation, to be believed, not discovered by human enquiry. This contrasts sharply with the Christian Hellenism of Alexandria; but Tertullian was no anti-intellectual obscurantist. His own debt to Stoicism is explicitly acknowledged, and his formidable intellect is everywhere evident: e.g. in *Against Praxeas*, which sets the framework of western trinitarianism, supplying the language of 'Trinity', 'person' and 'substance'.

Many works regulate Christian life in pagan society. *Idolatry* places many areas of activity off limits to scrupulous Christians, and other writings cover entertainments, military service, marriage and women's dress. Montanism made him tougher still. His early *Penitence* allowed penance after baptism, but later *Purity* (or *Modesty*) excluded it.

Tertullian's importance in laying the foundations of Christian Latin theology is immense. Almost at a stroke he gave it a forceful identity in the Latin-speaking world.

Roman North Africa (chiefly modern Tunisia and Algeria) retained the intellectual leadership of Latin Christianity throughout 'the age of the martyrs'. Cyprian was heavily indebted to Tertullian. He was a late convert who rapidly became bishop of Carthage *c.* 248. Martyrdom (258) capped an energetic episcopate, to which he brought high social standing, professional experience as a rhetorician and total dedication. His writings concern the Church's domestic affairs in some critical years.

Some eighty letters deal mostly with two controversies: the readmission of Christians who 'lapsed' during the Decian persecution, giving rise to schisms in Carthage (and Rome) over disputed disciplinary policies; and a quarrel with Stephen, bishop of Rome, about the need for (Catholic re)baptism of those baptized in schism. *The Unity of the Catholic Church* sets out Cyprian's basic convictions: a firm doctrine of apostolic succession, communion with the bishop as the boundary of the Church, schism as spiritual death, and the total unavailability of salvation outside the Church. *The Lapsed* insisted on episcopal control of discipline (against the claims of Spirit-filled martyrs and confessors). Rebaptism was essential, despite Stephen's disagreement. When Stephen misread *The Unity*'s references to Peter (who for Cyprian stood for unity and priority, not primacy), he revised the text. Stephen cited Matthew 16.18f. – the first to do so – in favour of the authority of Rome.

Cyprian's prestige reinforced some dubious theology. He applied OT priestly and sacrificial categories to the ministry and sacraments, and in *Work and Almsgiving* spoke crudely of purchasing salvation. His distinction lay in crisp episcopal leadership.

In African Christianity persecution repeatedly had an energizing effect. During the Great Persecution, begun in 303–4, an eminent rhetorician named Arnobius was converted to Christianity in Sicca Veneria. To convince the bishop of his genuineness (according to Jerome's account), he wrote *Against the Pagans*, which says little about Christianity but very much about pagan religions. In part it was a response to anti-Christian propaganda inspired by the Neoplatonist Porphyry.

Lactantius' roots were African (Arnobius taught him rhetoric), but his teaching career was spent in imperial courts in East and West. His *Death of the Persecutors* is an indispensable source on the Great Persecution – although harbinger of a new Christian triumphalism on the condign fate of the Church's oppressors. Other works argue for the reality of providence, as do the *Divine Institutes* (*c.* 304–13), which aim at a comprehensive exposure of pagan religion and philosophy and a rounded exposition of Christianity – almost the first Latin systematics. Its elegant style, modelled on Cicero, made Lactantius popular in the Renaissance, but its theology is heavily moralistic. Its conflicting tendencies (primitive millenarianism and a rigorism that outdoes Tertullian, alongside the humane moderation of a 'university Christian') reflect an era of transition.

Rome's most prolific writer in this period, Hippolytus, wrote still in Greek. Probably contemporary with him was Minucius Felix, author of a stylish apologetic dialogue, *Octavius*. The setting is Ostia, the port of Rome, but its connections are strongly African. Its dependence on Tertullian's *Apology*, and hence a date *c.* 235, are now accepted by most scholars. Its obvious indebtedness to Cicero and Seneca, without a single biblical quotation, points to its intended readership.

Victor (d. 198) was perhaps the first to be rightly called 'the bishop of Rome', and perhaps the first to write in Latin – but again he was an African. From later bishops before Constantine little remains. The sole substantial Roman author was Novatian (martyred 258), schismatic counter-bishop, who stood for strict discipline and a holy Church like Tertullian. But *The Trinity* (a word he did not himself use) is a mature exposition which marks an advance on Tertullian's understanding (e.g., on the eternity of the Son). He insists strongly on the unity of God (a characteristic western emphasis), with a clear subordination of the Son and more so of the Spirit, and had a firm grasp on the union of divine and human natures in Christ. He thus anticipates later developments in trinitarianism. Like many Latin Fathers, his thought betrays Stoic influence.

Finally among pre-Constantinians falls Victorinus, bishop of Pettau (now in northern Yugoslavia), a martyr in the Great Persecution, a writer less at home in Latin than Greek but a pioneer of Latin biblical exposition. Only his work on the Revelation of John is extant; it is in many respects (chiliasm, language, thought-forms) a relic of an earlier era.

THE GOLDEN AGE: 330–450

Although in volume the Latin Fathers' output by no means equals the Greek Fathers', the fourth and fifth centuries, roughly from Constantine to the terminal decline of the westen Empire, produced a galaxy of outstanding figures, including Ambrose, Jerome and Augustine, who with Gregory the Great became the four

'Doctors' (teachers) of the Latin Church. This survey can only outline their distinguished achievements.

The Arian controversy was largely an eastern affair. Hilary, bishop of Poitiers (350–67), was an important mediator of Greek biblical and theological thought, and whose versatile opposition to Arianism earned him the title 'Athanasius of the West'. A handful of works, especially *The Synods*, are historically valuable for the dispute, but none equals *The Trinity*, one of the finest fourth-century defences of the Son's full deity, marred, however, by a docetic notion of his body as heavenly in origin. Hilary distinguished three stages of Christ's existence: pre-incarnate, incarnate (with some kind of *kenōsis*, self-'emptying'), and glorified. He endeavoured to write as nobly as his subject deserved. He was also the first known Latin hymn-writer, and more of a commentator in the modern sense than any predecessor (on Matthew and the Psalms, not without allegorism).

Marius Victorinus from Africa was an eminent rhetor at Rome before his conversion *c.* 350 (celebrated in Augustine's *Confessions*). His extant Christian works, anti-Arian treatises, Pauline commentaries, and three hymns, are complex exercises in Christian Neoplatonism (he translated Neoplatonic texts read later by Augustine). His highly metaphysical trinitarianism also used psychological analogies – also taken up by Augustine.

North Italy produced a galaxy of Fathers in the later fourth century. Zeno, bishop of Verona (363–71/2), another African, left a major collection of sermons, revealing a faithful teacher particularly interested in Mary. Ambrose of Milan (*c.* 339–97) was already provincial governor when in 374, still unbaptized, he was chosen bishop by popular acclamation. He became an outstanding preacher (as Augustine's *Confessions* attest), and successfully defended not only orthodoxy but also the Church's independence of, and even ascendancy over, Christian emperors. Against Rome's pagan senators he vindicated the removal of the altar to the goddess Victory from the Senate house. He promoted monasticism, and adapted antiphonal Psalm singing and Greek hymn tunes for Latin use. Some twelve to fifteen of the hymns ascribed to him are genuine.

Ambrose was supremely a man of speech and action, and most of his works derive from oral delivery. He was not a creatively original thinker, although he spoke more clearly than any earlier westerners on original sin, the transformation of the eucharistic elements, and

152

the holy war. He was an important mediator of Greek Christian thought, with a Neoplatonic flavour. Numerous treatises interpret OT passages or subjects allegorically, the most dazzling being the *Hexaëmeron* (the 'six days' of creation). Several works advocate virginity, while *The Duties of Ministers* is the first manual of Christian ethics, modelled on Cicero and deeply marked by Stoicism, like much early Christian ethical teaching. Arianism is the target of some books written for the emperor Gratian, including the first Latin treatise on *The Holy Spirit*. *The Mysteries* and *The Sacraments* are expositions for the newly initiated, and important for liturgical developments. Over ninety of Ambrose's letters are extant.

The identity of Ambrosiaster (pseudo-Ambrose) is still unknown. He composed at Rome around Ambrose's time a very fine commentary on Paul's Epistles, and two or three other works. Their exegesis is largely literal and historical rather than allegorical, and a major witness to western understanding of Paul before Augustine.

From the northern Adriatic region came Rufinus and Jerome, whose long friendship dissolved in the bitter Origenist controversy. They were fellow-students at Rome and fellow-monks at Aquileia. Rufinus (345–410) travelled to monastic centres in Egypt, and founded a monastery and became a presbyter in Jerusalem before returning to Italy. His written contribution lay largely in Latin translations of many Greek Fathers, including Eusebius' *Ecclesiastical History*, Basil's *Monastic Rule* and above all Origen's biblical expositions and *First Principles* (*De Principiis*). This last, however, he purged of heterodox elements; whereupon Jerome, once an admirer of Origen but now, disenchanted by Epiphanius' exposures, a harsh critic, produced a literal version (now lost). Apart from a couple of salvos in the pamphlet war over Origen, Rufinus' only extant independent work is a *Commentary on the Apostles' Creed*, which gives its earliest Latin text.

Jerome's career was not dissimilar. From Rome he travelled widely in the East, associated with leading churchmen, was ordained presbyter at Antioch and started translating Origen. Back in Rome (382–5) Pope Damasus commissioned him to revise the Latin texts of the Bible. Thereafter biblical study remained his main preoccupation, and he became the most learned of all the Latin Fathers, almost alone in his mastery of Hebrew as well as Greek. Yet his angular temperament, given to sarcasm and invective, littered his path with ruptured relationships. Fleeing unpopularity in Rome, he settled eventually in Bethlehem, where his biblical labours were dogged with repeated controversies.

Nevertheless Jerome's work on the biblical text was epoch-making. He revised the text of the Gospels but moved on to a fresh translation of the Hebrew OT. This displacement of the Septuagint proved provocative, eliciting a sharp correspondence with Augustine. Not until the ninth century did the Vulgate, incorporating Jerome's versions, become the standard text.

Accompanying translation went exegesis of much of the OT (Psalms, Genesis, Prophets) and some of the NT, and translations or adaptations of others' writings, including Eusebius' *Chronicle* and biblical gazetteer and Didymus the Blind's *The Holy Spirit* (otherwise lost). Controversial treatises defended Mary's perpetual virginity, denigrated marriage in extolling virginity, gave a nasty taste to the Origenist quarrels, and attacked the Pelagians (with little perception of the deeper issues). To major collections of homilies and letters – written for publication and often treatise-length – were added works of history and biography, supremely his *Catalogue of Ecclesiastical Writers*, known as *Famous Men*; this surveys one hundred and thirty-five authors and began the science of patrology.

Jerome was no philosopher or theologian, but a giant of scholarship – one in whom Christianity's Hebraic inheritance partly came into its own, in the teeth of dominant Hellenism.

Some lesser figures merit a mention. Niceta of Remesiana (*c.* 335–414) was a missionary bishop among the Goths on the Danube frontier. Author of an important explanation of the Apostles' Creed and of *The Usefulness of Psalmody (Hymnody)*, he is often credited with the Te Deum. Maximus, bishop of Turin (d. *c.* 410–20), is elusive biographically, but his many sermons (of great interest for liturgy and paganism) reveal a vigorous popular preacher. Much the same goes for Peter Chrysologus (d. *c.* 450), bishop of Ravenna – obscure historically but author of an extensive body of sermons.

Christian poetry flourished almost wholly in the Latin West, and especially in the fourth and fifth centuries. It is a field where the interplay between secular (classical) and Christian sometimes frustrates easy classification. The early efforts were mostly biblical paraphrases, like the Vergilian portrayal of redemptive history by Proba, a distinguished Roman matron (*c.* 360). Ausonius of Bordeaux (*c.* 310–95) was a rhetorician whose gifted verse presents ostensibly orthodox sentiments with a nominal Christian's lack of personal engagement. The *Paschal Poem* of Sedulius, a presbyter of uncertain origin, is a lively account of salvation history, but not until the Spaniard Prudentius (348–*c.* 410), who attained high civil office before devoting himself to piety, do we meet a fluent poet of profound Christian inspiration and versatile imagination. *Peristephanon* praises martyrs, *Battle for the Soul* is the first allegorical Christian poem in Latin and *Apotheosis* a defence of the doctrine of the Trinity, while *Against Symmachus* opposes the paganism of a prominent senatorial leader. A master of many poetic forms, Prudentius was very popular among medieval churchmen. The Christmas hymn 'Of the Father's love begotten' is his work.

Paulinus (353–431), a pupil of Ausonius from Bordeaux, similarly enjoyed exalted office and leisure before adopting asceticism and becoming bishop of Nola (south of Rome). His letters reflect a wide friendship with leading Christians and throw much light on piety and liturgy. Many of his poems, cultured and refined rather than creatively inspired, are dedicated to his patron, St Felix.

The African church in the fourth and fifth centuries was rent asunder by Donatism, and almost all the literature surviving before Augustine is taken up with it. Few Donatist texts remain, but some can be partly reconstructed from refutations, like *Against Parmenian the Donatist* by Optatus, bishop of Milevis (fl. 370). Of great historical value for Donatism's origins, this work provides a theological response that significantly anticipates Augustine's. The ablest Donatist thinker was the layman Tyconius (fl. 370–90), whose *Books of Rules* was the earliest Latin essay in biblical hermeneutics, its substance being reproduced in Augustine's *Christian Instruction*. His spiritualizing *Commentary on the Apocalypse* had an immense influence on later western commentators, from whom it may with difficulty be partly recoverable. Tyconius made other significant contributions to Augustine's intellectual formation.

Augustine himself (354–430) towers over all subsequent western theology, at least until the Reformation. His much-praised *Confessions* interpret his religious development with mature hindsight and almost lyrical sensibility. The son (physically and later spiritually) of the pious Monica, Augustine was long estranged from the Church until his baptism by Ambrose in Milan in 387. While teaching at Carthage he had espoused Manichaeism, a late-Gnostic ascetic religion from Persia, which despite increasing disaffection he did not abandon until he reached Milan (384). There he was finally won to Catholic Christianity by Ambrose's intellectual weight and allegorical exegesis, the challenge of Christian asceticism and Neo-platonism's vision of spiritual reality.

The new convert pursued the life of a contemplative philosopher in Italy and Africa, until in 391 he was unwillingly ordained presbyter at Hippo (modern Annaba, on the Algerian coast), becoming bishop in 395. Major controversies preoccupied him. Against the Manichaeans he vindicated the OT (with the first Christian defence of the 'just war'), fixed the relation between faith and reason, clarified the nature of evil as the absence of good and emphasized free will. The Donatists, who were strong in and around Hippo, drew from Augustine lasting contributions to western understanding of the Church and sacraments. Against their obsession with personal holiness, Augustine made Christ the author of sacramental gifts, however unworthy the human minister, thus undermining the Donatists' grounds for rebaptism (inherited from Cyprian!). The Church was inescapably a mixed body in this life. Augustine was unhappily provoked into justifying the coercion of dissidents like the Donatists, and he led the Catholic case against them at an imperial conference at Carthage in 411, which led to a decisive clamp-down on their activities.

The same year the Pelagian issue surfaced in Africa. Pelagius had enjoyed success in Rome (his British origin is irrelevant) as a champion of an uncompromising ascetic Christianity undergirded by the conviction that God had made us inviolably capable of fulfilling his will. He composed *Expositions of the Thirteen Epistles of Paul*, an ascetic manifesto to Demetrias and some other treatises, including lost works on *Free Will* and *Nature*. (The authorship of many Pelagian writings remains disputed.)

Augustine's response to the teachings of Pelagius and his associate Caelestius started coolly, with defences of original sin and the necessity of infant baptism, but moved into higher gear with their exoneration in Palestine and their claim to represent the Church's traditional position. In writing, in synods and through pressure on Rome, Augustine campaigned relentlessly, eventually securing the Pelagians' condemnation by Pope Zosimus in 418. Augustine's teaching became ever sharper on the necessity of inward grace, given gratuitously by God to the elect alone, to free the human will from captivity to sin.

Some Italian bishops led by Julian of Eclanum dissented from the papal verdict, and for the rest of his life Augustine waged an increasingly bitter paper war with Julian, Pelagianism's most systematic exponent. Only commentaries on Job and some minor prophets can confidently be credited to Julian, but his theology is easily read off Augustine's refutations, with their hardening accents on the link between transmission of sin and sexual intercourse, and on human helplessness apart from the grace of predestination and perseverance.

Such teachings appeared to monastic groups in Africa and around Marseilles in Gaul to be incompatible with human responsibility before God. Their protest, misleadingly known as semi-Pelagianism, insisted that the unaided will was capable of the initial response to God. Augustine replied, but the controversy continued long after his death.

Augustine's enormous corpus extends far beyond these controversies: hundreds of sermons, including full expositions of the Psalms and John; numerous letters, often minor treatises themselves, with another two dozen only newly discovered: *The Trinity* (399–419), his pre-eminent non-controversial work, as much contemplative exploration as dogmatics, stressing 'relations' within the Godhead rather than 'persons' and seeking illustrations of God's trinitarian being in the inward life of his human image; and the massive *City of God* (413–26), embodying wide-ranging reflections on the interaction between God's essentially other-worldly purposes and human history and society. In his last years Augustine reviewed his writings in his *Revisions (Retractationes)*; of more than a hundred this survey has mentioned a mere handful.

Other writers were inevitably caught up on Augustine's coat-tails. The Spanish priest Orosius brought him his exposé of Priscillianists and Origenists. (Priscillian was the bishop of Avila in Spain who in 386 became the first Christian to be executed for heresy – a bizarre mix of ascetic extremism, magic and flamboyant fervour. A body of Priscillianist texts survives, of which some probably belong to Priscillian or his associate Instantius.) Orosius was enlisted as Augustine's agent against the Pelagians in Palestine (producing another exposé), and in supplementing the *City of God*. Unfortunately his *History Against the Pagans* adopted a quite different, triumphalist, reading of history and misled medieval readers of Augustine's magnum opus.

Prosper of Aquitaine (d. *c.* 463) took up Augustine's cause against (semi-Pelagian) criticism in Gaul. His works included compilations from Augustine's writings, but long before his death (while secretary to Leo the Great) he tempered his Augustinianism with an acceptance of God's universal saving will. Augustine's critics included John Cassian (*c.* 360–*c.* 435), who founded monasteries at Marseilles and wrote for them the *Institutes* (regulating monastic life) and the *Conferences* (on monastic spirituality). These collections distilled the essence of eastern monasticism for western churchmen. *Conference* 13 insists on the co-operation of human freedom and divine grace – the core of 'semi-Pelagianism'. Another exponent was Vincent (fl. *c.* 434), a presbyter-monk on Lerins, an island near Marseilles, famous for the 'Vincentian canon' advanced in his *Commonitorium*. This defined Catholic teaching as what has been believed 'everywhere, always, by all'. Intended to debar Augustine's doctrines of grace, it would of course have excluded much else as well.

The supreme model of monasticism in Gaul was the missionary bishop Martin of Tours (d. 397) – as packaged by his disciple, Sulpicius Severus (d. *c.* 420), whose hagiographic *Life*, as popular as the *Life of Antony*, depicts him as more than a match for the eastern desert fathers. Sulpicius' *Chronicle* reveals a more discerning mind; it is indispensable on the Priscillianist saga.

None of the bishops of Rome before Leo was a writer of note. Most left merely a handful of letters or documents. Damasus (366–84) also wrote inscriptions for martyrs' tombs in the catacombs – among other measures to enhance the aura of the Roman church. A letter by Siricius (384–99) is often labelled the first papal 'decretal', a ruling modelled on the emperors' decrees. Papal contributions to current controversies often boosted the papacy's own pretensions, and Leo the Great (440–61) was no exception, but with him the words had substance. By his generalship in the turmoil of barbarian invasions, intervention in the East's christological disputes (summed up in his dogmatic *Tome*, a mediating statement canonized at Chalcedon in 451), and unrestrained advocacy of the Petrine basis of papal authority, he elevated it to new heights. Many of his ninety-six sermons deal with the Petrine office, and over a hundred letters display a mind acute theologically and sharp and lucid administratively.

FROM THE BARBARIAN TAKEOVER TO THE END OF THE PATRISTIC ERA: 450–600

With Leo we are moving towards post-imperial Europe. The Latin Fathers' concerns increasingly lay with conservation and transmission; creative figures are rare.

Although Italy holds centre stage, few popes deserve inclusion here. Gelasius (492–6) enunciated the influential theory of the 'two swords', the priestly and the royal, that independently rule the world under God. The *Gelasian Decree*, listing approved and rejected books, reflects Roman opinion but is not his work. Later popes were caught up in the eastern 'Three Chapters' controversy. Pelagius had written *In Defence of the Three Chapters* (554) but as pope (555–61) changed sides, despite widespread western opposition.

Gregory the Great, 'the founder of the medieval papacy' (590–604), held high office in Rome before becoming a monk and serving as papal agent in Constantinople. His financial, diplomatic and administrative skills, revealed in over 850 letters, strengthened the papacy religiously and politically, in its dealings with Europe's new rulers. His *Pastoral Rule* became the standard handbook for medieval clergy, while the *Moralia* on Job was a massive manual of spirituality and moral guidance. Collections of homilies on the Gospels and Ezekiel, reform of the liturgy (the *Gregorian Sacramentary*) and innovations in church music (Gregorian chant and a choir school) further exemplify his versatile practical bent. The crude miracle-mongering *Dialogues*, on Benedict and other saints, are most unlikely to be his work.

To Benedict of Nursia (north of Rome) belongs authorship of the monastic *Rule* (*c.* 520) which later dominated western monasticism. Knowledge of Benedict's life is minimal, but the *Rule*, written for his foundations at Monte Cassino and elsewhere, attests his practical and humane genius. Although it draws on many sources, in East and West, it is a very Roman document, capable of development to accommodate the scholarly and missionary activities Benedict scarcely envisaged.

Unlike Benedict, Boethius was excellently educated, with years at Alexandria. He entered political service under the Ostrogoths in Italy, but was executed in 524 after falling foul of Theodoric. His best-known work, *The Consolation of Philosophy*, written in prison, contains nothing specifically Christian, expressing an attractive philosophical faith of Neoplatonic inspiration. Yet his writings on the Trinity, the person of Christ and *The Catholic Faith* put his Christianity beyond doubt. For Boethius Greek philosophy was invaluable for articulating Christian beliefs; hence his translation and commentary on Aristotle's *Categories* and Neoplatonic texts, his own works on logic and his manuals on arithmetic and music. For centuries the West knew only Boethius' Aristotle.

Cassiodorus (d. *c.* 583) also served Theodoric, helping to reconcile Roman and Goth, before founding a monastery at Vivarium in the far south of Italy. He arranged for a translation of Greek church histories in a combined *Tripartite History*, and compiled extensive biblical expositions based on Augustine and an expurgated Pelagius. But most important were his educational programmes: *Orthography* (written when he was 92!), and *Introduction to Divine and Human Learning*, which promoted the study of both Scripture and theology and the traditional secular disciplines, the seven 'liberal arts'. The work foreshadowed the learned culture of 'the monastic centuries' in the West.

On Augustine's death Roman Africa was about to fall under Vandal rule. Bishop Victor of Vita (south of Carthage) wrote a history of the Vandal persecution (488/9). Among leading churchmen to be exiled were Quodvultdeus, briefly bishop of Carthage, author of some sermons and a major treatise on *The Promises and Predictions of God*, and Fulgentius (467–533), bishop of Ruspe, who was exiled to Sardinia, and wrote against the Vandals' Arianism and in defence of Augustinianism. After the Byzantines had recovered Africa from the Vandals, African churchmen vigorously opposed the East's condemnation of the 'Three Chapters' (see above). Their ablest spokesman was Facundus of Hermiane, with an extended *Defence of the Three Chapters* (*c.* 550). However, Primasius of Hadrumetum (modern Sousse) accepted the ban. He compiled a commentary on the Apocalypse, from which Tyconius' lost work can be partly recovered.

In Gaul a presbyter-monk at Marseilles named Salvian (*c.* 400–80) defended *The Government of God* by contrasting the barbarians' discipline with decadent Roman-Christian civilization. A valuable historical source, it shows unusual insight into the significance of the Germanic conquests. Augustinianism remained controversial, being harshly criticized by Faustus (*c.* 408–90), bishop of Riez in

Provence, in *The Grace of God*. Many of his highly esteemed sermons were heavily used in a collection circulating under the name of Eusebius of Emesa in Syria. Gennadius was another presbyter of Marseilles (fl. 470–80), of similar semi-Pelagian sympathies. His *Famous Men* continues Jerome's catalogue of Christian writers.

Sidonius Apollinaris was a statesman and orator who in 469 reluctantly became bishop of Clermont-Ferrand. His poems are based on the best classical models but have no Christian inspiration. His epistles are likewise richer in form than content, although valuable evidence for social, cultural and religious life. Venantius Fortunatus (d. *c.* 600) settled at Poitiers and became its bishop late in life. He was perhaps the most gifted Christian Latin poet of the patristic era. Over three hundred poems cover innumerable subjects, such as the saints (e.g., Martin of Tours) and the cross (including the hymns 'The royal banners forward go' and 'Sing, my tongue, the glorious battle'). He displayed 'the first poetic view of nature penetrated by religious Christian feeling'.

Caesarius, bishop of Arles (502–42), had been a monk at Lerins. Effectively patriarch of the Gallic church, he presided over the second Council of Orange (529) which condemned semi-Pelagianism while endorsing only a qualified Augustinianism. His writings are heavily dependent on Augustine and other predecessors. Gregory, bishop of Tours (573–94), came from a distinguished clerical family and interacted prominently with Frankish rulers. His prolific writings include the *History of the Franks*, the first national history written by a Christian, and eight uncritical *Books of Miracles* about saints and martyrs.

Ireland (but not Britain) just squeezes into the picture. Patrick, 'the apostle of the Irish' (d. 461), left scanty remains, a *Confession*, a letter and a couple of hymns; but they are of great value when evidence is so scarce. The (Irish) 'apostle of the Scots', Columba (d. 597), bequeathed but one hymn, but Columbanus (*c.* 543–615), scholar-monk turned missionary who founded famous monasteries on the continent, composed monastic and penitential writings, letters of interest for relations between the Celtic church and Rome, and poems.

Spanish writers also call for note only late in the day. Martin (d. 580) ended as bishop of Braga in Portugal after travelling widely. His wide-ranging writings exemplify the learned pastoral bishop of late antiquity. Isidore, bishop of Seville (600–36), fittingly closes this survey, as the 'last of the Latin Fathers'. His *Etymologies* (or *Origins*) is an encyclopaedia of religious and secular knowledge, beginning in most cases with an etymology. Its derivative character did not limit its wide popularity. Isidore wrote, unoriginally, on many other topics, including a continuation of Jerome-Gennadius' *Famous Men*, thus maintaining the tradition of patrology.

BIBLIOGRAPHY

Campenhausen, H von, *The Fathers of the Latin Church*. London, A & C Black, 1964.

Dekkers, E, *Clavis Patrum Latinorum* (Sacris Erudiri III). Steenbrugge, St Peter's Abbey, 1961.

Greenslade, S L, *Early Latin Theology*, Library of Christian Classics, 5. London, SCM; Philadelphia, Westminster, 1956.

Labriolle, P de, *The History and Literature of Christianity from Tertullian to Boethius*. London, Kegan Paul; Trench, Trübner, 1924.

Rusch, W C, *The Later Latin Fathers*. London, Duckworth, 1977.

Wright, F A, *Fathers of the Church: Selected Writings of the Latin Fathers*. London, Routledge, 1928.

14

The Oriental Fathers[1]

SEBASTIAN BROCK

It is often forgotten that, besides early Christian literature in Greek and Latin, there are also extensive specifically Christian literatures in the various oriental languages in the easterly part of the Roman Empire, or just beyond its borders: Syriac, Coptic, Armenian, Georgian, Arabic and Ethiopic. All of these still survive today in some form as liturgical languages of the different Eastern and Oriental Orthodox Churches, and each of these communities has its own 'Fathers' whose teaching is revered alongside that of the familiar Fathers of the Greek- and Latin-speaking Church. If these oriental Fathers are very little known to Western Christians, this is due, not to any intrinsic inferiority on their part, but to the heavily Eurocentric character of the academic study of church history and doctrine. The early Syriac Fathers in particular deserve more attention than they customarily receive, since they represent the unique phenomenon of a genuinely Semitic form of Christianity that has, prior to about the fifth century, only a modest overlay of Hellenization, and whose theological discourse remains essentially symbolic, and has not yet been dominated by the agenda and thought categories of the Greek-speaking world. The significance of this should not be hard to grasp at a time when Christianity is shrinking in the Western world, but expanding in parts of the rest of the world where there is often an understandable desire to throw off some of the European cultural baggage of a form of Christianity introduced during a colonial past.

From the point of view of the student of the early Church, the Oriental Fathers are of interest from two different points of view. In the first place they provide primary evidence for the life and history of the Church, not only in the important eastern provinces of the Roman Empire, but also in territory actually outside the Empire's bounds – thus at once enlarging on the narrow but extremely influential perspective on church history set by Eusebius. Secondly, the literature in these oriental languages includes massive numbers of translations from Greek of patristic writings, many of which no longer survive in Greek. (This applies above all to writers like Theodore of Mopsuestia who subsequently came to be regarded as heretical by the Greek Church).

Although one customarily thinks of the Greek and Latin Fathers as coming to an end with the advent of the Dark Ages, the Greek Church has always had a wider perspective and includes among the Fathers writers like Gregory Palamas who belong to the later Middle Ages. Similarly the time span of the Oriental Fathers also extends into the Middle Ages, for chronologically these oriental Christian literatures fall into one or more of three main periods, (1) fourth – seventh century (advent of Islam), (2) mid seventh – end thirteenth century, and (3) fourteenth century and later. Diagramatically this can be set out as follows, where an asterisk denotes the occurrence of both original literature and translations (where a period is represented predominantly by translations, rather than original writings, this is marked by T; an asterisk in brackets signifies that the surviving literature is much less extensive):

	4th–7th cent.	7th–13th cent.	14th cent.–
Syriac	*	*	(*)
Coptic	*	(*)	–
Armenian	*	*	*
Georgian	T	*	*
Arabic	–	* (from 8/9th cent.)	*
Ethiopic	T	(*)	*

Ecclesiastically the Oriental Fathers represent all three theological positions which emerged as a result of the christological controversies of the fifth century: (1) the Church of the East, which rejects the Council of Ephesus 431 (often misleadingly referred to as 'Nestorians'); (2) Churches accepting both the Council of Ephesus and that of Chalcedon 451 (i.e. in doctrinal agreement with the Greek and Latin Churches); (3) the Oriental Orthodox Churches (Armenian, Coptic, Ethiopian and Syrian Orthodox), which reject the Council of Chalcedon (often misleadingly referred to as 'Monophysites' or 'Jacobites'). In tabular form we thus have:

The Christian Oriental Languages

	(1)	(2)	(3)
Syriac	*	(*)	*
Coptic	–	–	*
Armenian	–	–	*
Georgian	–	*	–
Arabic	*	*	*
Ethiopic	–	–	*

THE SYRIAC FATHERS

Syriac is the local Aramaic dialect of Edessa (modern Urfa, SE Turkey) which from about the second century became the literary language of Aramaic-speaking Christianity in the Eastern provinces of the Roman Empire and in the Persian Empire further east. Hardly any literature prior to the fourth century survives, but to that century two great Fathers belong, Aphrahat 'the Persian Sage', author of twenty-three fine theological *Demonstrations*, and the poet-theologian Ephrem (d. 373, Edessa). Contemporary of Athanasius and the Cappadocian Fathers, Ephrem offers through the unexpected (but entirely appropriate) medium of poetry an exciting and all-embracing theological vision which, though in outward expression very different from, at a profound level of understanding is often astonishingly close to, the insights of these Greek Fathers.

The tradition of using poetry as a vehicle for theology was continued in the next century and a half by two writers who, after Ephrem, are much revered in Syriac tradition. Narsai, head of two famous theological schools, first that of Edessa, and then that of Nisibis (in the Persian Empire), was an exponent of the distinctively Syriac genre of verse homily. Although he was an ardent proponent of the Antiochene tradition of Christology, as expounded above all by Theodore of Mopsuestia, only a few of his homilies are strictly theological, the rest being primarily exegetical. His younger contemporary, Jacob of Serugh (d. 521), though a supporter of the opposite christological tradition, disliked controversy and his eirenic approach (exceptional for his times) has resulted in his acceptance as a 'Teacher' or 'Doctor' in both Chalcedonian and anti-Chalcedonian Syriac communities. His vast output of verse homilies, like Narsai's, mainly exegetical, offer wonderfully imaginative insights into the spiritual senses of the biblical text.

Also belonging to Syrian Orthodox tradition (for which he was an active protagonist), Philoxenus, metropolitan of Mabbugh (d. 523), was one of the most original theologians of his time, providing a synthesis which drew both on his native Syriac and upon Greek theological tradition. At the same time he was author of a number of fine monastic writings, one of which was surprisingly translated into Greek and found its way into editions of works by St Isaac the Syrian.

Philoxenus' counterpart as theologian par excellence of the Church of the East, Babai the Great, flourished a century later (d. 628), and he too combined the same interests, in both Christology and monastic spirituality. The late sixth to ninth centuries witnessed an astonishing flowering of the monastic life, producing an extensive and very fine literature on the spiritual life. Among these writers best known and most influential (thanks to early translations into Greek, Latin, Arabic and other languages), is Isaac of Nineveh (Isaac the Syrian), but it is important to realize that he was by no means an isolated phenomenon.

As was the case in both the Greek Church and the Muslim world, the period from mid seventh to the late thirteenth century was one of consolidation more than of creativity among the Syriac Fathers, and from the ninth century onwards their writings became increasingly encyclopaedic in approach. In the seventh and eighth centuries Syrian Orthodox Fathers, such as the polymath Jacob of Edessa (d. 708), provided an essential link in the chain of transmission of Greek philosophical and scientific learning which was ultimately to reach the Arabic-speaking world in the ninth century. The earliest translators of these works into Arabic (made either directly from Greek, or by way of Syriac versions) were largely writers belonging to one or other of the Syriac Churches, several of whom were important theologians in their own right (see below). It was thus thanks to this initial work by scholars of the Syriac Churches that writings of Aristotle and others ultimately reached the Latin West in the twelfth century, travelling by way of North Africa and Spain.

Belonging to the Arab period one might single out as the most respected of the Syriac Fathers the following names: from the Syrian Orthodox tradition, besides Jacob of Edessa (already mentioned), Moshe bar Kepha (d. 903), Dionysius bar Ṣalibi (d. 1171) and Bar Hebraeus (Gregory Abu 'l-Faraj, d. 1286), all bishops whose extensive writings cover a remarkably wide range of subjects (though predominantly theological). Bar Hebraeus' large theological compendium entitled *The Lamp of the Sanctuary*, in particular, has played a role in the Syrian Orthodox Church analogous to that of Thomas Aquinas' *Summa Theologiae* in the West.

In the Church of the East similar theological compendia were composed by 'Abdisho' (Ebedjesu) of Nisibis (d. 1318) and Timothy II (d. 1353). Among earlier Fathers who have left important writings are the Patriarch and liturgical reformer Isho'yahb III (d. 659), Timothy I (d. 823), and Isho'dad of Merv (ninth cent.) whose extensive commentary on the whole Bible is a repository for a large number of earlier traditions.

Finally, attention should be drawn to a number of Greek Fathers whose writings survive only, or primarily, in Syriac translation. Since Theodore of Mopsuestia is the 'Interpreter/Exegete' par excellence of the Church of the East, it is no surprise that many of his works (condemned by Justinian in the mid sixth century) survive only in Syriac versions. Syrian Orthodox tradition, on the other hand, has preserved numerous works by Severus of Antioch (d. 538), the finest Greek theologian of his time and a notable exponent of Cyril of Alexandria's christology. Syriac translations are also a prime source of our knowledge of the writings of the influential monastic author, Evagrius of Pontus (d. 399), since his works were condemned for their alleged Origenism in the Greek Church in the sixth century.

THE COPTIC FATHERS[2]

Coptic is the descendant of ancient Egyptian, written in Greek script. Though the earliest biblical translations into Coptic probably belong to the third century, most Coptic literature belongs to the fourth to seventh centuries. Pride of place among the Coptic Fathers is taken of course by the great monastic founders Pachomius (d. *c.* 348) and Antony (d. 356). Pachomius's *Rules* are the earliest piece of original literature in Coptic, and were soon to be translated into Greek, Latin, and other languages. This early Egyptian monasticism gave birth to a new type of literature, the collections of *Apophthegmata*, or *Sayings, of the Desert Fathers*, which circulated in Coptic as well as in Greek.

Almost all the best known Coptic Fathers of the next few centuries, such as Shenuti (Sinuthius, d. 466), belong to the monastic world. Shenuti (who is the most important surviving writer in

Coptic) was famous for his stirring sermons, several of which are extant. The sermon was in fact a favourite genre, alongside hagiography, among the Coptic Fathers, and other notable homilists include Besa (late fifth century) and Constantine of Siout (late sixth century), while exegetical literature is represented best by Rufus of Shotep (also sixth century, a period of considerable literary activity in Coptic).

Numerous translations of the Greek Fathers were made into Coptic in the course of the fourth to seventh centuries.

THE ARMENIAN FATHERS

The Armenian script was invented in the early fifth century specifically so that Armenian (an Indo-European language most closely related to Greek) might serve as a literary language for Christians in Armenia (which uncomfortably straddled the Roman and Persian Empires).

Mesrop, to whom the Armenian alphabet is traditionally ascribed, may have been the author of *The Teaching of Gregory* (the Illuminator, who established the Armenian church, d. *c.* 325), a work transmitted under the name of Agathangelos. Also belonging to the 'Golden Age' of Armenian literature (first half of fifth cent.) is Eznik, author of an important theological work entitled *Against the Sects*.

The best-known writers of the next few centuries are mostly historians: Faustus of Byzand, Lazar of Pharp, Elishe, Moses of Khorene (who belongs to the eighth century, even though he purports to be writing in the fifth!). Important theological writers from this period include John Mandakuni (fifth cent.) and John of Odzun 'the Philosopher' (d. 729).

Some of the most famous Armenian Fathers belong to the early Middle Ages, especially the period of the Kingdom of Lesser Armenia (*c.* 1080–1375, in Cilicia). Notable among these are Gregory of Narek (d. 1003), author of *The Book of Prayers* consisting of ninety-five meditative 'Sacred Elegies' (sometimes translated 'Lamentations'), and the poet-theologian Nerses the Graceful (Shnorhali, d. 1173).

A vast number of Greek patristic (and philosophical) writings were translated into Armenian, and in several cases such works survive only in Armenian translation.

THE GEORGIAN FATHERS

The Georgian alphabet, like the Armenian, was devised specifically so that this Caucasian language could become a vehicle for a Christian literature. Although this took place in the fifth century, rather little literature – largely hagiography – survives from the fifth to ninth centuries, apart from translations. During the earlier part of this period the Georgian church was under Syriac and Armenian influence, but from the seventh century onwards it came under increasingly strong Byzantine influence. The Golden Age of Georgian literature belongs to the period from the late tenth to the mid thirteenth century, during which time there were flourishing monastic centres near Antioch, in Palestine, and on Mount Athos, as well as in Georgia (Iberia). Georgian theological writing is especially rich in hagiography, liturgical poetry, canon law and history.

Again, a large number of Greek texts were translated into Georgian, both in the earlier period (fifth-ninth cent.) and later on, from the tenth to the twelfth century; in the latter period the names of Euthymius (d. 1028) and Ephrem 'the Small' (Mcire, eleventh cent.) are especially famous. From the early period several translations of Greek liturgical texts from Palestine are of particular importance since the originals do not survive.

THE ARABIC FATHERS

Although the two Arab buffer kingdoms between the Roman and Persian Empires (the Ghassanids on the Roman side, the Lakhmids on the Persian) were both largely Christian by the mid sixth century, there is no clear evidence of any translation of the Bible into Arabic until the Islamic period, and the earliest extant Christian Arabic literature belongs to the eighth century. The first Christian community to adopt Arabic as a literary language was the Chalcedonian Orthodox ('Melkites') of Palestine; there, monks of the Monastery of St Saba (in the Judaean desert) were particularly active, both in producing several original works and (above all) in translating from Greek. In the ninth century Arabic was adopted by many writers belonging to the Syrian Orthodox and the Church of the East as well.

Over the course of the ninth to thirteenth centuries a number of important (and often still influential) theological compendia, heavily influenced (like John of Damascus' writings in Greek) by Aristotle's logical writings, were produced, notably by Theodore Abu Qurra (Melkite, d. *c.* 820), Yaḥya ibn 'Adi (Syrian Orthodox, d. 974), and 'Abdallah ibn aṭ-Ṭaiyib (Church of the East, d. 1043). The thirteenth century witnessed a number of encyclopaedic theological works in Arabic by Coptic Orthodox writers.

A very large number of translations into Arabic of the Greek and Syriac Fathers were made between the eighth and thirteenth centuries, and quite a number of these then found their way into Ethiopic.

THE ETHIOPIC FATHERS

Ethiopic (properly called Ge'ez) is, along with Arabic, a South Semitic language. According to Rufinus' *Church History* the Ethiopian royal house was converted in the mid fourth century by Frumentius (Abba Salama) and Aedesius, but practically no literature apart from translations (mostly from Greek) survives from the Axumite period (fourth–seventh cent.) or the succeeding centuries, prior to the advent of the 'Solomonic' dynasty in 1270. The fourteenth and fifteenth centuries, however, were extremely productive, both in original literature (hagiography, liturgical poetry, chronicles, etc., much of it anonymous), and in translations from Arabic (notably by the Metropolitan Abba Salama, d. *c.* 1388). Many of the indigenous Fathers revered in Ethiopian tradition are monastic figures such as Takla Haymanot (d. 1313), known as the founder of a famous and influential monastery (Dabra Libanos); most of these left no writings and so are only known from often much later hagiographical tradition.

Among the translations of the Axumite period the theological anthology known as the Qerellos ('Cyril') is of especially importance, though Cyril of Alexandria is by no means the only author represented. The translations of the fourteenth/fifteenth centuries include works written originally in both Syriac and Latin.

NOTES

1 This summary survey is confined to those Oriental Fathers who have left writings. Though there were certainly some Oriental Mothers, virtually no literature by them has been transmitted and they are known only through hagiography (thus Georgian tradition greatly venerates St Nino, a slave woman from Cappadocia, who converted the royal house in the early fourth century).

2 'Coptic Fathers' here refers to Egyptian Fathers who wrote in Coptic; many other Egyptian Fathers, like Athanasius and Cyril, of course wrote in Greek.

BIBLIOGRAPHY

No general introduction to the Oriental Fathers is available in English. Reliable guides, with the basic bibliography, to all the oriental Christian literatures can, however, be found in German, in:

Assfalg, J, and Krüger, P, *Kleines Wörterbuch des Christlichen Orients*. Wiesbaden, Harrasssowitz, 1975

Also in French, in:

Guillaumont, A, and others, *Introduction aux littératures chrétiennes orientales*. Paris, forthcoming.

In English the following may be mentioned for the individual literatures:

Syriac: Brock, S P, 'An introduction to Syriac studies', in Eaton, J H, ed., *Horizons in Semitic Studies* (University of Birmingham 1980), pp. 1–33.

Coptic: Orlandi, T, 'Coptic literature', in Pearson, B A, and Goehring, J E, eds, *The Roots of Egyptian Christianity* (Philadelphia, Fortress, 1986), pp. 51–81.

Armenian: Sarkissian, K, *A Brief Introduction to Armenian Christian Literature*. London, Faith Press, 1960.

Ethiopic: Ullendorff, E, *The Ethiopians* (1965 2nd edn), pp. 131–51. Oxford University Press.

PART FIVE

Shaping of Faith, Doctrine and Spirituality

15

Greek Influence on Christian Thought

CHRISTOPHER STEAD

Christianity was first preached as an invitation to accept Jesus as Lord; his coming was seen as the fulfilment of God's purpose for the human race. But the earliest preachers could take for granted a belief in God's existence and his providence, already well recognized in Judaism. When the Church began to expand into non-Jewish societies, it met with enquirers who doubted or denied such beliefs, and was forced to defend them by argument; St Luke presents an early stage of this development in Acts 17.16ff., where St Paul encounters Epicurean and Stoic philosophers. By the second century, Christian writers had begun to restate their faith as a coherent theology, drawing largely upon Greek thought, which was by far the most important intellectual influence on the Roman Empire, and indeed since the Renaissance has reinvigorated our own art, science and philosophy.

The Greeks' most creative period can be roughly defined as 500–200 BC. By early Christian times they had become less bold and experimental, more accustomed to imitate classical models, and more inclined towards religion; atheism and scepticism were still taught, but were less popular in a society which sought reassurance. Nevertheless Greek culture retained an attraction and power which cannot be appreciated without some understanding of its great classical masterpieces.

Among the Greeks the visual arts were better developed than their music, which remained very simple; and their sculpture was far more impressive than their painting. Early Christian monuments echo contemporary Graeco-Roman styles, influenced by the great Greek masterpieces of the fourth century BC; thus the earliest portraits of Christ depict him as a handsome youth not unlike the Greek Apollo. The severe lines of the later Byzantine portraits, however, owe something to Graeco-Roman paintings like those discovered at

Pompeii. Greek architecture also made its contribution; the earliest large Christian churches were rectangular pillared halls, resembling the secular 'basilica' (law-court and commercial exchange). Later examples adopted the distinctive Roman use of arches and domes, which was finely exploited in the Byzantine period.

Greek literature did not always appeal to Christian writers. They often profess to despise fine writing; and of course the Greeks had produced, *inter alia*, bawdy comedies and erotic lyrics which were offensive to serious men. Christians made use of the Greek orators for training preachers, and of the historians, to supplement the biblical narratives; but the great Greek dramatists were undervalued, as presenting the gods in human guise. The attitude of St Cyprian is instructive; on becoming a bishop he threw away his pagan books, and professed that he owed nothing to paganism, while continuing to write the impeccable formal prose which he had learnt from his pagan schoolmasters. Tertullian, Jerome and others show a similar combination of affected disdain with actual indebtedness.

But such attitudes were not unknown in the pagan world. Pagan teachers would introduce their charges to the great Greek classics, especially the poetry of Homer; but they approached them in the serious, questioning frame of mind that was common in late antiquity, treating the Homeric poems as instructive works, indeed as actually intended to convey lessons about human life and destiny which the careful student could detect. The philosophers also were of course consulted for moral and religious guidance; but whereas Plato, for example, wrote many of his dialogues in a vein of light-hearted, tentative enquiry, his followers usually regard them as an authoritative text in which apparent inconsistencies must be explained away. One reason for this was the importance which pagan educators attached to rhetoric, the art of persuasion and public speaking, where self-contradiction is a fault to be avoided at any cost. Christians accordingly made strenuous efforts to present the Bible as an inspired book, consistent and harmonious in all its parts. What we regard as crude and primitive ideas expressed in the Old Testament could be defused by spiritualizing interpretations like those invented by high-minded expositors of Homer.

One favourite method among others was to treat the offending passage as an allegory. Thus Homer describes the high god Zeus reminding his consort Hera of her adultery with the fire-god Hephaestus, for which she was bound in golden chains (*Iliad*

15.18ff.). A first-century commentator explains that 'the words of Zeus to Hera are the words of God to matter'; he transforms the wronged husband into a supreme creator who imposes restraints on matter to produce an orderly world. The method of allegory grew up at Alexandria and was already applied to Scripture by the Greek-speaking Jewish aristocrat Philo, who died *c.* AD 50. Origen, who records the interpretation of Zeus and Hera, (*Against Celsus* 6.42, written *c.* AD 250) uses similar methods to explain puzzling or objectionable passages of Scripture; many examples are given in his *On First Principles*, 4.3.

But it was Greek philosophy to which Christian thought was chiefly indebted. 'Philosophy' means 'the love of wisdom'; in ancient times it included a great variety of subjects which are nowadays regarded as separate disciplines. In early Christian times it was conventionally divided into three departments: logic, ethics, and physics. 'Logic' and 'ethics' meant roughly what they mean today, despite dramatic developments in both subjects in the last hundred years. Ethics in Aristotle's day had included political science and the germ of economics, but these had little interest for later thinkers. 'Physics' was a general term for the study of the universe; it included all that was then known of physics proper, cosmology, astronomy, geography, biology, psychology, and theology too, for those who believed in divine action affecting the world. We should also notice two studies closely allied to philosophy, but not normally reckoned as belonging to it, namely medicine and mathematics. These had little direct influence on Christian thought, but the sheer brilliance of Greek mathematics in particular compels our attention.

Logic was virtually the creation of Aristotle, who was also accepted as the primary authority until well on in the nineteenth century. Christian writers tended to criticize his *minutiloquium*, his obsession with exact detail; and it is certainly true that the minority of theologians who did try to adopt his methods, by expressing their teaching as a series of syllogisms, make notably dismal reading. The reason is not that Christian teaching is necessarily illogical, but rather that logical method requires exact definition and consistent use of terms; and this is hard to achieve where religious truths have been expressed in poetic language or in metaphors drawn from everyday life. It is especially misleading if, on a pretext of exact definition, one represents ancient writers as arguing for or against a proposition defined in contemporary terms. The better course was to pay attention to the uses of metaphor; and here the Greek literary critics and their Latin imitators could offer valuable guidance. But the way was constantly blocked by the assumption that the Bible must be a wholly consistent and uniformly uplifting text, rather than the legacy of many different writers of different periods and different levels of culture, as we tend to see it today.

Greek ethics, in early Christian times, usually assumes a distinctive theory of human nature. Most philosophers, Pythagoreans, Platonists and many Stoics, held that consciousness arises within the soul, a personal being which can function independently of the body and survives its death (whereas for the Hebrews the so-called 'soul' is an impersonal animating principle, and consciousness can only arise within an animated body). Yet Plato suggested two distinctly different pictures of the soul. The *Phaedo* sees it as essentially concerned with higher truths, in contrast with the distracted pleasure-loving body; but the *Republic* describes it as having three parts, of which only the highest, the mind or intellect, is capable of real virtue; it is the directive principle which our emotions and impulses ought to obey.

Plato's strongly idealized view of the intellect will hardly convince us moderns; we see too clearly that the intellect itself can be misused or corrupted. Moreover it distorted the Christian moral tradition. St Paul, though he spoke of antagonism between flesh and spirit (Gal. 5.17), accepted self-denial for the sake of his mission (Phil. 4.12) without condemning bodily satisfactions; but later Christians, like many pagans, often assumed that the first step towards moral improvement was to neglect the body and cultivate the mind. Charity, if it meant concern for the *bodily* needs of others, was thus often undervalued.

Christians made only a rather selective use of the Greek moralists. Plato was widely praised, for reasons which will soon appear; even so, his *Republic* caused offence by its eccentric programme for women in society, as mere child-bearers without attachments either to husbands or children; while his *Symposium*, a magnificent defence of physical love as a gateway to higher affections, presupposed the Greek acceptance of homosexuality. Aristotle, who wrote important treatises on ethics, was criticized for what seemed an unheroic view, that perfect happiness requires some degree of outward prosperity; also, less fairly, for his concept of virtue as a middle course between two opposite failings (e.g. cowardice and rashness); this 'doctrine of the mean' was often misconstrued as implying only a moderate enthusiasm for virtue. The Stoics were often tedious to read, and moreover changed their ground; the earlier Stoics preached a fierce and exclusive morality; perfect wisdom was demanded, and the slightest occasional lapse condemned; all other supposed goods were considered worthless. But the later Stoics took a more moderate view: our nature, they said, prompts us to seek certain advantages, such as bodily health and tranquillity; these were not good in the absolute sense, yet it was 'preferable' to seek them, at least for other people. It is this later phase of Stoic ethics, with its stress on common duties, which influenced St Paul's teaching.

There was thus no universally approved authority; the most convenient handbooks were probably Cicero's popularizing Latin adaptations, which set various systems side by side. And the further difficulty of amalgamating Greek and biblical teaching meant that Christian ethics was slow to develop a coherent framework. The Bible provided simple folk with divine laws and virtuous examples. These were supplemented by the doctrine, derived from the Stoics, of a 'natural law', which implied that all men have the same perception of basic moral duties (1 Cor. 11.14); this ignored the actual evidence of diversity among different races, and even suggested, absurdly, that wrongdoers are adequately punished by the agonies of conscience that they are bound to feel. But Christian Platonists tended to define goodness as a right choice of objectives; our affections must be fixed on the eternal rewards. Indeed Augustine, for instance, tends to suggest that all our feelings are forms of affection; fear, e.g. of robbery, is really a bye-form of the love of riches and ease.

Moreover the clash between Platonic and biblical views of the soul confused the Christian teaching on the afterlife. The Hebrews looked forward to a resurrection of the body; only so could consciousness be restored; and it would take place on a day of judgement after a period of absolute non-existence. But Christians tended (as many still do) to accept also the survival of the soul as Plato conceived it, so that consciousness continues without interruption beyond the moment of death (cf. Luke 23.43). But granted the promise of a fully surviving consciousness, it is hard to see the point of a subsequent resurrection of the body, which Christians were bound to accept in accordance with their Creeds.

Before coming to the central topics of Greek philosophy, something should be said about their mathematics. The Greeks excelled here through their intense interest in solving problems for their own sake, irrespective of any practical value. Their geometry, as formulated by Euclid (*c.* 300 BC) held the field until the nineteenth century, and is still acceptable as a basic discipline. In arithmetic they achieved remarkable results despite the handicap of a clumsy system of numeration, using thirty letters of the alphabet to denote units, tens and hundreds up to 1000, where the system began to repeat. Consequently, to know that twice three is six did not at once indicate how to multiply twenty by thirty; it was as if we wrote the two sums as 'b × c = f' and 'k × l = x'.

The Bible, in 1 Kings 7.23, states that Solomon made a 'sea', or ceremonial water-tank, ten cubits in diameter and thirty cubits round, thus implying that the constant we know as π is 3.0. The Greeks not only knew that it was not an exact whole number, but that it was not expressible by any ratio of whole numbers: Archimedes (*c.* 287–212 BC) computed it by approximation as between $3\frac{1}{7}$ and $3\frac{10}{71}$, i.e. roughly between 3.142857 and 3.140845. Many further examples could be given, if space allowed.

On the other hand, the Greeks did not solve the much more difficult problem of the nature of number itself, which was elucidated by Bertrand Russell some time ago. If I understand him right, the primary function of numbers is that by which (e.g.) we 'number off' the houses in a street; cardinal numbers, which we use to quantify a group, depend on the further operation of 'summing up' how many houses we have passed. The Greeks, however, assumed that the cardinal numbers were primary, and that the whole system of numbers originated from the 'monad', the number one; their arithmetic lacking a zero. Mathematically minded philosophers such as Pythagoras and his followers could thus suppose that the Monad was the source of all rational order in the universe; or, put conversely, that the creative power behind it had the characteristics of the Monad. This prompted Christians to think that God must be completely simple and strictly immutable, a view which still remains the official orthodoxy, though it has recently come in for vigorous attacks.

This doctrine of God was combined, rather awkwardly, with the biblical picture of God as a creator and loving Father of the world and mankind. Plato, moreover, gave support to this theology through an influential dialogue, the *Timaeus*, which pictures the creation of the world by a divine 'craftsman' or 'artificer'. It was never clear whether this divinity was meant to be the source of all perfection (as in Christianity), or merely to imitate some reality higher than himself. But Plato's work was valued by Christians as confirming the biblical account of the creation. Yet when God came to be described in mathematical terms as simple and immutable, it became less easy to understand his providential care of the world; this must, it would seem, require a divine mind which can attend to many different concerns. Christians tended to solve the problem by developing St John's concept of the divine Word or Logos in a manner already foreshadowed by the Stoics; God the Father was seen as wholly transcendent; he exercised his providential care not directly, but through his Logos; who is sometimes described, e.g. by Athanasius, as actually pervading the physical world, and indeed inherits the Father's title of 'Craftsman', *demiourgos*.

Greek philosophy affected Christianity most directly through the department of 'physics' together with the very abstract study which came to be called metaphysics. The early history of this subject is far too complex to be summarized here; but we may notice two philosophers earlier than Plato who left their mark on all subsequent thought.

Parmenides (*c.* 515–450) attempted to deduce the nature of the universe, by purely logical methods, from the nature of being as such. He treated 'being' as a simple concept, a view which logicians have now discarded; for it can indicate both passing states ('he is ill') and invariable facts ('he is a man'); or again, mere existence, as opposed to fantasy; or again truth, as opposed to falsehood ('that is so'). But for Parmenides these concepts were indistinguishable; thus the necessities of logic required that the world, despite appearances, must be unchanging, simple and compact (for empty space would imply the contradiction that 'not-being *is*').

In sharp contrast Heraclitus (*c.* 544–484) saw the world as a perpetual process of change; but farsightedly perceived that this need not make it unintelligible, since its changes take place in an orderly sequence and in principle can be measured. They were governed, he thought, by a 'logos', a controlling agency diffused throughout the universe; Heraclitus' obscure language does not make it clear whether this logos should be considered simply as a mathematical measure or ratio, or as a controlling mind.

Plato (*c.* 429–347) was not impressed by Heraclitus' claim that change can be measured. He sought not only mathematical but moral truths, where it is harder to distinguish objective changes from changes and uncertainties in human judgement. He therefore saw reality or being (*ousia*) as twofold; an eternal world of perfect Forms, perceived only by the mind, and the confused and changeable world of perceptible things, which become real and definite only in so far as they imitate those eternal prototypes. This view is known as 'Plato's Theory of Ideas'; but it is important to note that these are objective realities, not just products of our thinking; Plato calls them both *ideai*, Ideas, and *eidē*, Forms.

Plato never made it clear what kinds of Forms there are; it sometimes appears that there is a Form for every class of natural phenomena (e.g. even for diseases!); but sometimes only where perfection is possible. Some later Platonists regarded the Forms not only as 'thinkable' (*noēta*) but as thinking beings (*noera*), playing down the original emphasis on their unchanging character; thus Christians could easily regard them not only as moral ideals but as equivalent to the biblical angels. This was a drastic departure. Plato had pictured the Forms as a hierarchy, such that the more inclusive Forms are nobler and better. But there can be no society between beings of different logical levels; Socrates may converse with a nobler and better man, say Parmenides; but not with ideal manhood itself, any more than a woman can marry the average man. *A fortiori* the all-inclusive Form, pure Being itself, could have no contact with human beings. Nevertheless Christian writers adopted 'pure Being' as an appropriate symbol of God's supremacy and unchanging power.

Aristotle (384-322) raised logical objections to Plato's doctrine of transcendent Forms, but retained the notion of form as an immanent principle which, e.g., guides the development of living things. The form (small 'f' now better!) belongs to the species; individual beings exhibit the same form in a separate bit of matter; and the word 'being' (*ousia*) can denote either the form, or the matter, or the compound individual which results from their union. But this relatively clear picture is confused by two other developments. First, Aristotle modifies the sense of 'being' by recognizing a special sense which came to be known as 'substance'. A thing's 'substance' is the character which it must have and can never lose (contrast the sense of 'being' in 'he is a man' and 'he is here'); and 'substances' are things which retain their identity despite changes of size, condition, etc. Secondly, despite his emphasis on form and species, Aristotle asserted, in the *Categories*, that the individual, not the species, is the primary form of being, or 'primary substance'.

The notion of substance became a battle-ground for later Christian theologians; but before describing this, we must introduce a related term, 'hypostasis', which owes its popularity to the Stoics, beginning in the century after Aristotle (Zeno, *c.* 332–262; Chrysippus, *c.* 280–207 BC). The Stoics wholeheartedly accepted Heraclitus' picture of the universe as a process of perpetual change (whereas Aristotle saw it as basically unchanging, and indeed eternal). They held that matter is the only true reality; thoughts and concepts arise in men's material organ of thought. But they also held that every kind of matter exhibits some degree of order; this increases as we pass to plants, to animals and human beings, and finally to the universe itself, which is pervaded by a supremely rational principle or Logos, who can appropriately be honoured as a god.

'Hypostasis' literally means 'that which underlies or supports', e.g. the legs of an animal, the base of a statue. The word took on many different meanings; but we have to mention two, which, strangely, have almost exactly opposite implications. 'Hypostasis' can mean the 'underlying reality' of a thing, which probably it will share with other things; or it can mean the 'emergent perceptible reality', which is more likely to be taken as individual. The former meaning is suggested, e.g., by a counterfeit coin; the coin 'really is' lead, the base metal underlying its gilded surface. The second meaning stems from the use of 'hypostasis' to mean a 'sediment'. The Stoics pictured the universe as evolving from a primary condition of pure fire, which by degrees produces solid matter, like a sediment or precipitate deposited by a liquid, and so gives rise to persistent individual things.

The natural Latin equivalent for 'hypostasis' was *substantia*; but this latter word was used to translate the Greek *ousia*; a better Latin equivalent here would have been *essentia* (cf. 'essence'); but this word sounded artificial to the Latins, and was not much used before Augustine's time, though it became popular later with the medieval philosophers.

Greek theologians came to describe the Father, Son and Holy Spirit as a triad, or Trinity, of divine beings. They often spoke of three hypostases, i.e. three distinct individual beings; to acknowledge only one divine hypostasis might suggest, e.g., that only the Father is divine. But the Latins, following Tertullian, spoke of them as three persons proceeding from a *single* 'substance', as having a common origin in the Father and a common divinity; and some Greeks agreed to accept the idea of 'one hypostasis', taking that word in its larger sense. The Latins disliked 'three hypostases', which to them suggested three gods.

The tension and misunderstanding came to a head when Arius (*c.* 265–337) began to affirm that the Son and Spirit were subordinate and hence inferior to the Father. The Council of Nicaea, AD 325, ruled that they were 'the same in being' (or 'consubstantial', or 'coessential'); and the position was clarified by the Cappadocian Fathers, half a century later, who argued that the recognition of one 'being' or 'substance' did not conflict with 'three hypostases', which they now clearly defined as *individual* realities, or 'persons'.

Much ink has been wasted in discussing the precise meaning which the Council of Nicaea gave to 'consubstantial'; did it imply 'same individual being', or merely 'same species', or something else. It must be emphasized that the Nicene Fathers were not trained philosophers; in particular, Aristotle's distinction of *ousia*, 'substance', as *either* individual or generic, was quite unfamiliar to them. *All* the terms they had available at this stage carried a variety of senses which their users only half understood. Thus modern scholars who have debated whether such-and-such a term was used 'in the sense of Person', or the like, give us an impression of clearly defined alternatives which is completely unhistorical.

Something more should be said of 'Person', none the less. Latin usage was largely based on legal convention; a 'person' was anyone competent to plead in a law-court, excluding slaves and minors. The corresponding Greek word *prosōpon* suggested rather a character in a play (cf. our phrase *dramatis personae*). Neither word strongly emphasized the qualities we associate with 'personality', viz. originality, enterprise, leadership. Moreover, as first used, neither word *necessarily* implied an individual; a party to a law-suit could be a group of people acting jointly, and in a play a chorus of actors could take a single part. But later Christian usage followed the Cappadocians' clear distinction between (individual) Person and (common) Substance; other kinds of individuals, e.g. individual islands or stars, were left out of account.

Christians were disappointingly slow to realize that the same distinction applied to the word *phusis*, 'nature'; and this led to bitter disputes concerning the doctrine of Christ which should have been avoided. It should have been clear that Christ existed 'in two *phuseis*', *provided* that this was clearly understood as indicating two states or conditions, his eternal fellowship with the Father, and his incarnate life as man. But devout eastern Christians were haunted by the suspicion that 'two *phuseis*' must imply two distinct individual beings, a divine Christ and a human Jesus, and consequently withdrew to form the Monophysite communities. The orthodox faith, as defined by the Council of Chalcedon, AD 451 agreed with the Latins that Christ exhibits two *phuseis*, two manners of being, divine and human, united in this one unique individual, or in a single hypostasis.

In conclusion: Christianity developed out of a Jewish sect into a world religion through the use of its Greek inheritance, by moulding its beliefs into a coherent system which could appeal to thoughtful men and leaders of society, without losing the element of faith and personal commitment exhibited by simpler believers. If we have learnt to appreciate the distinctive genius of Hebrew religious thought, this has come about through the gradual development of scholarly methods which were initiated by Greek literary critics. It remains a live question whether a Christian theology expressed in Greek concepts is still serviceable for a Church faced with the challenge of further expansion, e.g. in Africa and Latin America. What can be said with assurance is that such questions could not even be raised, let alone considered, without the arts of accurate statement and rational debate which the Church absorbed from its Greek-speaking adherents.

BIBLIOGRAPHY

Readers unfamiliar with Greek literature can gain a lively impression from Livingstone, R, *The Pageant of Greece* (Oxford University Press, 1923). He also edited *The Legacy of Greece* (Oxford University Press, 1921), a collection of essays dealing with all aspects of Greek culture.

There are numerous histories of Greek philosophy; Armstrong, A H, *An Introduction to Ancient Philosophy* (London, Methuen, 1965[4]; Totowa, Rowman, N J, and Allanheld, repr. of 3rd edn, 1983), has the advantage of giving generous space to philosophers of early Christian times.

Hatch, E, *The Influence of Greek Ideas and Usages upon the Christian Church* (London, Williams and Norgate, 7th edn 1898 and repr.), is still well worth consulting. Look in libraries or second-hand bookshops for a spine lettered 'The Hibbert Lectures 1888'. The faint-hearted may prefer to begin with Lecture II. See also: Jaeger, W, *Early Christianity and Greek Paideia* (Cambridge, Mass. Harvard University Press, 1962); Chadwick, H, *Early Christian Thought and the Classical Tradition* (Oxford University Press, 1966); Markus, R A, *Christianity in the Roman World*, (London, Thames and Hudson, 1975), with excellent illustrations.

16

Gnosticism

KURT RUDOLPH

The writing of history is dependent on many hypotheses. This makes it difficult to achieve the enduring ideal of objectivity. One of the vital questions is the state of the sources. As regards 'gnosis' or 'Gnosticism' – as this religious stream in late antiquity has been known since the eighteenth century – this question can be illustrated especially clearly.

The increase in new, and above all, original sources and monuments has altered fundamentally the state of research in the last few decades. Consequently, older notions must, and should, be abandoned. Accompanying progress in the critical analysis of sources there has been a change in the formulation of questions. This was brought about largely by the *Religionsgeschichtliche Schule* ('History of Religion School') of Protestant historical theology at the turn of the century. This situation reveals another aspect of historiography – the standpoint of the investigation.

In the nineteenth century, the Gnostic sects were still generally seen as early Christian heresies. Scholarly presentations followed the Church Fathers, who were responsible for this view. However, all this changes with the approach adopted by the History of Religion school. Influential church-historical research of the kind conducted by A von Harnack in particular was replaced by religio-historical research as practised notably by W Bossuet and R Reitzenstein. A regional perspective was replaced by one more universal; a theological perspective by a religio-historical one. This change in standpoint extended even further. Questions were formulated so as to include the new approaches of sociology, social science, economic and social history. The aim was to place gnosis into the context of the history of ideas of the Hellenistic world and late antiquity. Gnosis was seen as part of a religio-philosophical protest movement – manifesting the dissolution of the ancient world-view. It was also

186

seen as a partial attempt to master social, political, and intellectual problems by opposing 'lower' and 'higher', between East and West (Rome), as was done by other religions and groups. The inclusion of gnosis within a universal, ecumenical compass strongly shapes research in the present day, at least to the extent that this research is devoted to more than the requisite processing and analysis of sources.

When speaking of 'gnosis', one is just introducing into modern research and modes of thought a notion pertaining to early Christian history and its historical context. It originates in theologians, principally Church historians and New Testament scholars. Early Christian authors already used the designation; the first certain reference is 1 Tim. 6.20. It was employed to cover groups of people who were not content with the statements of faith and modes of behaviour which had been handed down and widely accepted. On the problem of evil, its origin and development, and that of humanity's place and destiny in the cosmos, these groups went their own way. Their thinking was dominated by dualism, which in the ancient world was found in Platonism, in Iranian and Zoroastrian religions. It also penetrated early Judaism, as at Qumran and in apocalyptic writings. It explained the miserable state of the world. Conquered peoples could grasp the true nature of the situation in the world – in Near Eastern politics going back to Alexander the Great and again with the activities of the Romans – as originating in primeval times (*Urzeit*) when the cosmos was created.

Such a view was certainly not new, but it was perceived by the Gnostics in a very radical and significant manner. Beginning with the biblical account of creation, and faith in an absolute, transcendent God, most of them advocated the knowledge (*gnōsis*) that this world is the product of a foolish creator, an inferior 'demiurge', who set to work without the permission of the 'unknown God' (*agnōstos theos*). He was assisted in the creation of the world by a lower angel or planetary being. In order to terminate the process of creation once it had begun, the supreme God had only one choice: to employ cunning counter-measures. He initiated these among human beings as the centre of creation. Without the knowledge or consent of the demiurge, he provided humans with an other-worldly, divine substance called either 'Spirit' or 'Soul' or 'Spark'. This substance enabled humanity (that is, the ideal Adam) to see through the work of the inferior creator and to perceive the true goal of humanity as the return to the realm of the supreme God – often depicted as the Kingdom of Light.

In the Gnostic view, the *telos* ('end') of history was the ultimate dissolution of the cosmos. The 'knowledge' (*gnōsis*) of these cosmological and anthropological correlations is, of course, supernatural. It is mediated to the 'knowers' (*gnōstikoi*) through revelation. This could be either through messengers who acted on instructions from the supreme God, or through the traditional form of the myth (that is, the sacred narrative) concerning the events of primeval times, which determine the present state of the world and humanity.

The Gnostics understood themselves as a 'chosen people', as an élite that, in opposition to the 'worldly-minded', has perceived the strong connection between world, humanity and salvation. With the help of 'insight' (*gnōsis*), the objective of Gnostic teaching is to free the elect from the fetters of this world; that is the meaning of 'salvation' in this context. It is not a matter of liberation from sin and guilt, but of releasing the soul or the spirit from the body and matter (*hylē*). The entire apparatus which the Gnostics created in the course of time out of their myths as well as out of their ethical and devotional practice worked to that end. It involved an 'exegetical protest' against the older traditions, that is, the interpretation of older traditions in a manner contrary to their original sense. The area of activity involved two things. First, their customary world-denying ascetical ethos. Second, an ideologically inevitable curtailing of sacramental rites in favour of a salvation achieved only through 'insight' (*gnōsis*). The libertine traits, which arose from the same desire to conquer the world as is found in asceticism, are as yet attested only in heresiological accounts. Moreover, the attitude towards sacramental ritual did not exclude the continuation, reinterpretation, or re-establishing of older religious ceremonies. Gnosis was not devoid of formal worship! That the Gnostic community, with the exception of the Manichaeans, was established in the form of a 'school of doctrine' or a 'mystery-club' with at most only a rudimentary organization, has the outward appearance of the ancient manner of association.

The above characterization of Gnostic belief and practice is, of course, only a broad outline. There are marked variations, and their relative importance differs a great deal in texts accessible to us. Despite much borrowing from older and contemporary religions of Hellenism and the imperial world (*c*. the second century BC to the third century AD), it forms a relatively autonomous religious structure. This can be reconstructed from Hellenistic, early Jewish, and early Christian sources. Until 1945, scholars lacked original Gnostic texts for all branches of gnosis except Manichaeism. For the latter, findings from 1902 to 1914 and again in 1930 had unearthed original sources. In a polemical guise, naturally, the Church Fathers from the second to the fourth centuries provide us with several accounts, including abstracts from texts. Among them may be mentioned Justin (*d.* 165), Irenaeus of Lyon (*c.* 140–200), Hippolytus of Rome (died *c.* 235), Tertullian (*c.* 150–223/5), Clement of Alexandria (*c.* 140/50–211/215), Origen (died *c.* 253/4) and Epiphanius of Salamis (315–403).

The difficulties in using this literature lie partly in the standpoint of the writers – they saw in the Gnostic schools only deviations from pure doctrine which were spawned by the devil and partly in the interdependence of the sources. That is, the later authors copied the older accounts, adding only a few new bits of information to them. Moreover, the heresiologists have different theories about the historical origin of gnosis in this world. These theories determine the way they present their materials. Justin and Irenaeus opt for a Jewish origin. Hippolytus and Clement look to precursors in Greek philosophy. Epiphanius tries to trace back eighty heresies to Greek and Jewish schools or sects, but in a purely schematic way (cf. the 'eighty concubines' of the Song of Sol. 6.8). Nevertheless, older research (that is, from the time of F C Baur and A von Harnack) was able to construct a clear picture of its subject-matter, even if the church-historical perspective dominated, as previously.

Until recent times, very little original source material was available. Quotations found in the heresiologists comprised no more than fifty or sixty pages. The so-called *Corpus Hermeticum* (the 'Corpus of Hermetic (sealed, esoteric) Writings'), whose origin is still not entirely explained, contains a few Greek tracts whose tenor is obviously Gnostic. This is allowing for a strong influence of Hellenistic-Egyptian, that is, Alexandrian traits. The first text in the collection is an example, known in Europe since the fifteenth century as *Poimandres* (Shepherd of Men). The only extensive original works were two Coptic manuscripts brought to England in the eighteenth century, but not published until the end of the nineteenth. They contained the so-called *Pistis Sophia* (Faith and Wisdom), the two books of *Jeu*, and four fragments. Another

Gnostic codex was discovered in 1896 by the Berlin church historian, C Schmidt; this was the *Papyrus Beroliniensis 8502*, first published in 1955, and containing among other things two writings vital to research on Gnosis: the *Apocryphon of John* and the *Sophia Jesu Christi* (the Wisdom of Jesus Christ). Finally, amongst alleged Gnostic texts are the 'Odes of Solomon' from the Coptic and Syriac traditions, and the so-called 'Song of the Pearl' from the apocryphal Acts of the Apostle Thomas (chaps. 108–13). The largest amount of Gnostic literature has been transmitted to us through the small baptismal community of the Mandaeans, located in the region of the lower Tigris and Euphrates and the Iranian Karūn river (in Khuzistan). Detailed knowledge about this community, however, has only become available since the end of the nineteenth century.

A momentous event in Gnostic studies was the discovery in 1945 of thirteen Coptic books in Upper Egypt at a place called Nag Hammadi. The books are named the *Nag Hammadi codices*. Only recently has the discovery been recounted in detail, and it is almost as fantastic as the account of the discovery of the Dead Sea community (Qumran). It was even more clandestine, and political occurrences hindered the publication of these important texts for over a decade. An Egyptian camel-driver, who with his brothers was searching for richer land, discovered a jar containing the precious manuscripts. Since he was unable to find a purchaser for them, he sold them for a small price and left their further sale to Cairo antique dealers and various middlemen, who were chiefly Copts (Egyptian Christians). The sale of treasures is strictly controlled in Egypt. But since business with foreigners could be very lucrative, an agreement was reached whereby a section of the discovery was brought to Europe in 1947–8. This part is known as the *Jung Codex*, after the famous psychologist, Carl G Jung. It was to be two years (1946–8) before the remaining and larger part of the find finally made its way to the Coptic Museum in Old Cairo.

The first report of this discovery was published in 1948. Then in 1950 the first general survey was published by H-Ch Puech in Paris. In 1955 there appeared a detailed account of the *Jung Codex*, now known as *Nag Hammadi Codex I*, which was then in Switzerland. (In 1975, this was brought back to Cairo.) It took almost five years, from 1956 to 1961, to conserve and to make an inventory of the codices. At the end of this period, M Krause was able to provide a very precise account of the contents in 1962. Our understanding of the contents was repeatedly corrected due to further work, until finally – following an international cooperative venture led by the Institute for Antiquity and Christianity at Claremont, California, and funded by UNESCO – a large facsimile edition of the entire find was published in eleven volumes. All told, the volumes contain fifty-two writings, for the most part previously unknown, amounting to 1153 pages. About 90 per cent of the approximately 1257 original pages has been preserved.

This discovery is one of the most extensive manuscript finds of recent times. Editing, translating into modern languages (chiefly German, English, and French), commenting and analysis began early on, where texts were available to individuals. After H-Ch Puech, J Doresse has made an enormous contribution to the effort. In the German-speaking world, the texts became known through the editions and translations of A Böhlig, M Krause, etc. A handy English translation of all the text appeared in 1977 (a third revised edition in 1988). There is a study series of publications about the texts (Nag Hammadi Studies, beginning in 1971), and in which the Coptic-English edition appeared. A Coptic-French edition has been issued in Quebec since 1977.

The great importance of these new sources is transparently obvious. Even if no precise explanation has yet been given of how the collection came into being, and of the circles in which particular writings were transmitted, the bulk is still of Gnostic origin, amounting to at least forty of the fifty-two writings. At all events the entire corpus seems to have been collected and used by Christian Gnostics. From the documents, which had been placed in a case for protection, we can establish that their place of discovery is not far from where they were drafted in antiquity. This was in the area of the Egyptian monastic settlements at Chenoboskion, or rather Diospolis Magna (Thebes) and Parva. We can also firmly establish by palaeography that the date of the documents can have been no earlier than the middle of the fourth century AD.

It would appear that we are dealing here with a collection of documents made by heretical monks, against whom polemics were being aimed from Alexandria, the spiritual centre of orthodox Christianity in Egypt at the time. The dominant ascetic and encratite (that is, abstemious and continent) character of the texts makes this thesis even more plausible. Upper Egypt was a very frequent meeting place or haven for heretical groups, such as the Manichaeans; further, forms of Coptic language are often referred to as *Ketzerdialekt* ('the dialect of heretics'). Especially on Alexandria's loss of some of its importance under Roman rule, cultural centres shifted to Middle and Upper Egypt. Evidence for this cultural diffusion is provided not only by Gnostic and Manichaean texts, but also by the discovery of classical and Greek texts (e.g. Menander). The Neoplatonist Plotinus also comes from Upper Egypt.

Thus the collection of original Gnostic source material has been extended considerably, placing research on an entirely new footing. Since the texts are almost completely translations from Greek originals (e.g. the Gospel of Thomas), and several derive ultimately from Syriac originals, the actual date of composition can of course be put earlier than the drafting date of the discovered texts. On the whole, the majority of the writings are now dated in the second and third centuries. Some of them, such as the Apocryphon of John, are also mentioned by name in the heresiological sources (e.g. Irenaeus of Lyon).

Apart from their basically Gnostic content, the texts possess no uniformity of approach. But they can be arranged according to various Gnostic divisions based on heresiological classifications of sects. Accordingly, they present us with quite a broad spectrum of Gnostic authors. Apart from the Hermetic and decidedly Valentinian texts, the so-called 'Barbelognostic' and 'Sethianic' schools are most prominent (I cannot discuss any further here these heresiological designations for sects, since they are very controversial). Thus the multiplicity of Gnostic modes of thought and action is very clear. Here we also have an unexpected glimpse into the development of Gnostic systems and piety.

The great significance of the discovery is that it presents us with both Christian and non-Christian writings. The former were subjected to some minor editing from a Christian standpoint. In other words, the writings demonstrate the independence of Gnostic writers from Christians. This corroborates the thesis of the non-Christian origin of Gnostic teaching. At the same time, a strong connection with Jewish apocalyptic and extra-biblical traditions is visible. Hence, the older and popular view, that gnosis germinated on the fringes of early Judaism, can no longer be dismissed.

On the other hand, we can now see in the intertwining of Gnostic and early Christian ideas in the Christian-Gnostic texts the principal background for the polemic of the mainstream Church's heresiologists. They recognized, in my judgement, the danger that an alien thought-world might provoke losses for Christianity. Nevertheless, the Gnostics often contributed to christological, trinitarian and cosmological teachings. They were often the first to bring up such questions for discussion, thereby forcing the mainstream Church to take a stand. In this respect, their activity was of positive value. Moreover, the new texts occasionally exhibit very clearly the role of Greek philosophy in gnosis; they were especially helpful in the question of the role of gnosis in the formation of Neoplatonism. So the discovery of the Nag Hammadi codices has provided us with many new insights. It has also fixed the agenda for future research on gnosis in an unexpected manner.

Importantly, new light has been cast on the 'history of effects' (*Wirkungsgeschichte*) of Gnostic thought because of availability of new sources. On many points there have been corrections of what early Christian historiography had taught. The relationship of the 'official (orthodox) Church' to Gnostic groups and theologians must be seen as extremely manifold. Further, the significance of Gnostic ideas and practices for the understanding of many writings which to-day are within the canon of the New Testament – a significance which the History of Religion school was already aware of – has again become very topical. We need always to bear in mind that the New Testament canon contains writings from 50–140 AD. This means that there was a long period during which the Gnostic movement influenced not only anti-heretical polemics, but also Christian teaching. To some extent, theological problems arose through the encounter with Gnostic concepts.

The after-effects of gnosis as well as organized Gnosticism are part of the religious history of late antiquity, the Middle Ages, and the ideas and philosophy of the modern period. Earlier, J G Herder (1744–1803) saw in gnosis the 'first religious philosophy in Christendom'. And he realized that the shaping of Christian theology since the second century is unintelligible when divorced from questions raised by Gnostics. The theological efforts of Irenaeus, Clement of Alexandria, Origen, Lactantius, and Augustine (due to his ten-year adherence to Manichaeism) were to a large extent determined by their opponents. The state of the world, the problems of creation and salvation, the status of Christ the Saviour in relation to God and to the man Jesus of Nazareth, the relationship between faith and knowledge, death and resurrection, good and evil, tradition and interpretation – all are subjects which the Gnostics set for discussion. Since their position often diverged widely from official Christian tradition, they provoked a response.

The Gnostic models are reflected not only negatively, through attempts to distance oneself from them, but also often quite positively in the counter-programmes of the heresiologists. Also, in practical and sociological spheres, Gnostic foundations were of direct and tangible importance for the development of the Church, e.g. polity and church order (the episcopal system), the exclusion of women from community leadership (advocated especially by Tertullian), and forcing the laity into the legal and hierarchical institution of a state Church.

The Church just barely escaped from the 'Gnostic danger'. As the Gnostic systems of the second and third centuries (especially Valentinianism and Marcionism which also belonged to gnosis) declined in influence, a Gnostic world-religion emerged in Mesopotamia, which was Persian at the time. This was Manichaeism. Its founder, the gifted Persian, Mani (216–77) created an adaptable system in the spirit of Gnostic dualism. Furthermore, he set up a well-organized church of the Elect and the Catechumens with a proselytizing missionary outreach. In this form it spread from the third to the fourteenth centuries over almost the whole of the then 'civilized world' through Syria, Egypt, North Africa, Spain, and Rome in the West, through Iran, North India, Central Asia (where it was recognized as the state religion in the ninth century) and China in the East. The documents from this wholly independent religion – it is wrong to consider it as a Christian heresy, as Byzantine theologians later considered Islam – have been rediscovered in this century in various languages in Egypt (Coptic) as well as in Central Asia (Turfan/Mongolia).

In addition to Manichaeism, Gnostic influences extended into the Christian and Islamic Middle Ages. In the West, the Bogomils and the Cathars (or Albigensians) provoked conflict with the Catholic Church from the tenth to the thirteenth centuries, showing clearly that the Church had not escaped from the 'shadow of gnosis'. The most effective instrument of power which the Christian Church possessed, the Inquisition, was created initially to root out these movements. After the elimination of the Cathars, the last great movement with the stamp of the Gnostic-Manichaean momentum, elements of more or less distinctive Gnostic systems were preserved in the West. Ideas and practices often accommodated themselves to changing historical circumstances, thereby altering or metamorphosing. Among these elements were cosmological, dualistic, anthropological, and mythological ideas, libertine or ascetic practices, and an esotericism or élitist awareness.

Radical world-denying, mystical, and cabbalistic groups are, to be sure, not always motivated by Gnostic thought; but they may at least be linked to Gnosis in the history of ideas. This is also true for the spokesmen of later religious philosophies such as J Boehme, F W J Schelling, and G W F Hegel, who may be regarded as heirs of Gnostic speculation about the spirit. In this connection, one can also point to more recent theosophical, anthroposophical, 'existential', and 'syncretic' movements (all found in the contemporary 'New Age' movement).

Making such connections is not always justified for two reasons. First, too often the true character of Gnosis in late antiquity, with its hostility to the cosmos, is misunderstood. Second, magic, mysticism, and esotericism are carelessly passed off as typically 'Gnostic'. The latter would encounter opposition today. Future research, now shored up with better material, will have the task of exposing many more false inferences in the history of ideas, before it will be able to embark on an exact and historically verifiable account of the bearers of the Gnostic and Manichaean legacy. In recent times, some have begun this endeavour with reference to the Renaissance. But they have been more concerned with the after-effects of late Platonic and Hermetic literature.

The East, the ancient seed-bed of gnosis and Manichaeanism, is today the home of the last Gnostic community. This is the Mandaeans, a baptismal sect in south Iraq and south-western Iran. The sect still possesses an extensive literature in its own language and script, in which its unequivocal connection with gnosis can be seen. Because the Mandaeans were confined to fringe areas until the last few decades, their effect has been limited.

Manichaeism and Hermeticism have had more influential effects in the history of Islamic heresies. In early Islam, the 'Dualists' (*zanādiqa*) and the Sabians were very concerned with the life of the spirit. Like the Christian Gnostics, they provoked a polemical literature. This fertilized theological and philosophical thought, beginning with the concept of 'knowledge' itself. Islamic mysticism, too, carried on Gnostic ideas, such as the idea of the 'cosmic man'. In the thought of Muhammad himself, the Manichaean world view can be seen in the cyclical notions of revelation, to which other elements are added.

But ancient gnosis had marked effects particularly in a group of heretical Shi'ite movements, of which accurate knowledge has only become available in recent times. In the eighth century, there arose precisely in the old heresy centres of Syria and Mesopotamia the first advocates of Shi'ite extremism. They exhibit clearly Gnostic theologoumena (that is, speculation on divinity) and their present-day successors are to be found in the 'Alawis or Nuṣayris. In the middle of the ninth century there emerged in Iraq the Isma'ilis, Carmathians or 'Seveners', in whose older traditions a Gnostic heritage is at hand. The feared Assassins from the time of the Crusades belong to them. So also does the sect of the Druze, which came into being at the beginning of the eleventh century and is now found in Syria, Lebanon and Israel. Also belonging to the Isma'ilis are the Indian Khojas, together with their leader, the Aga Khan, and the Bohras.

There are striking parallels between the old, main, traditional teaching of a cosmological and soteriological myth and Gnostic mythology. Furthermore, the external and literary history repeats itself here in a noteworthy way. Apocalyptic and pseudepigraphical traditions are formed, reinterpreted in the course of time, and ultimately enter into larger systems dominated by philosophy, especially Neoplatonism. Teachings are traced back to earlier legendary figures, especially to 'Abdullāh ibn Sabā. The heresiologists make Ibn Sabā the ancestor of the Gnostic Shi'ites, just as the Church Fathers made Simon Magus the ancestor of the Gnostics.

The study of Islamic heresies has recently become very valuable to research on the after-effects of gnosis. It has demonstrated that Islam, the second post-Christian world-religion (Manichaeanism was the first), also possesses a 'Gnostic shadow'. This shadow has not only led a distinctive, independent existence. It has also kept up a thousand-year quest to answer the fundamental questions of cosmic and human existence dissociated from official theologies. And it has given limitless curiosity unobstructed room in the world of images and concepts.[7]

NOTE

1   The original German version of this chapter has been published in *Zeichen der Zeit* 38 (1984), 217–21. The English translation was prepared by Gregory D Alles and revised by Ian Hazlett.

BIBLIOGRAPHY

Foerster, W, ed., *Gnosis. A Selection of Gnostic Texts.* ET ed. R McL Wilson, vol. 1: *Patristic Evidence.* Oxford, Clarendon Press, 1972. vol. 2: *Coptic and Mandaic Sources.* Oxford, Clarendon Press, 1974.

Grant, R M, *Gnosticism. A Sourcebook of Heretical Writings from the Early Christian Period.* London and New York, Harper & Row, 1961.

Jonas, H, *The Gnostic Religion.* Boston, Beacon Press, 1958; 2nd enlarged edn 1963 (paperback).

Layton, B, *The Gnostic Scriptures.* Garden City, N.Y., Doubleday; London, SCM, 1987.

Robinson, J M, ed., *The Nag Hammadi Library in English.* 3rd, completely revised, edn. San Francisco, Harper & Row; Leiden, Brill, 1988.

Rudolph, K, *Gnosis. The Nature and History of Gnosticism.* Edinburgh, T & T Clark; San Francisco, Harper & Row, 1984, 1987 (paperback).

17

Orthodoxy and Heresy

MAURICE WILES

William Frend has not had an altogether wholesome influence on my own development as a patristic scholar. When in the 1960s I lectured on the development of early Christian doctrine at Cambridge, he used to lecture to the same students on the history of the early Church. So I knew that they would come to my lectures conversant with the findings of archaeology, alive to the importance of social factors in the life of the Church and fully aware of behind-the-scene intrigues at church councils and the eccentricities of some church leaders. I was fortunate enough to be able to take for granted a lively interest in the history of the early Church and a proper sense of its practical and human dimensions. So I could concentrate on my own particular interest in the development of Christian doctrine, knowing that my students could supply the appropriate historical context. But if subsequently, and in this chapter in particular, I have continued the habit and have dealt with questions of doctrine with less explicit reference to their historical setting than William Frend would think appropriate, some of the responsibility must be laid at the door of the verve and quality of his own teaching on the subject thirty years ago.

But my tendency to think somewhat too exclusively in terms of a history of conflicting doctrinal ideas is not only a result of that division of labour with William Frend at an early stage in my teaching career; it is also in part an outcome of the way in which the early Christian Fathers saw and presented themselves. It is as a result of that self-understanding, indeed, that the idea of heterodoxy or false belief has come to be integral to the meaning borne by the words 'heresy' and 'heretic' to-day. The root meaning of the Greek word, *hairesis*, is choice; it means a sect or school, for example of philosophers, who have chosen and follow a particular style of thought or interpretation. It is in itself a neutral term with no necessarily pejorative connotation. In Acts it is used to refer to the Sadducees and the Pharisees (5.17; 15.5) and also to Christians (24.5, 14). But a pejorative note is seldom far away; it is very likely to be lurking beneath the surface when the reference is to a sect or school, which has opted for a way other than one's own. It is clearly present in the one New Testament reference to a *hairetikos*, whom the author of the Pastorals says should be given two warnings before being written off (Titus 3.10). But in that instance it is probably more a matter of a factious individual, who is determined to go and to have his own way, than of someone explicitly committed to a divergent set of beliefs.

By the second century the pejorative sense of the word is clearly to the fore, and so is the intimate link with false doctrine. It is false teachers who are responsible for importing dangerous heresies according to the second-century author of 2 Peter (2.1). But it is not always easy to tell in such cases whether the underlying cause of division between a writer and those he dubs 'heretics' was a matter primarily of practice or of belief. Ignatius accuses his opponents of docetic and Judaizing tendencies, but in such general terms that scholars have been unable to agree as to whether it is one or two distinct heretical groups that he is attacking. It is possible that their root offence lay more in their challenge to his authority and to that of other emerging episcopal leaders gradually extending their authority over a number of separate local congregations. The Quartodeciman controversy between Rome and Asia Minor in the middle of the second century over the date for the celebration of Easter was probably sparked off by the practical embarrassment of Asiatic congregations in Rome celebrating Easter on a different day from indigenous Roman congregations in the same city. But it was tempting for those opposed to holding the feast on 14 Nisan, the date of the Jewish Passover, to suggest that those who did so had not properly freed themselves from Jewish beliefs. The issue was serious enough to prompt Victor, bishop of Rome, to try to excommunicate the Asiatic churches as unorthodox (Eusebius, *Eccl. Hist.*, V.24.9). The Novatianist schism in the next century centred on the practical question of how to deal with the needs of Christians who had lapsed under persecution. But in the attempts of each side to justify their preferred practice, the differences soon found expression in differing doctrines of Church and ministry. Whatever the initial cause of tension and conflict within the Church, it was natural enough to regard the real root of the problem as a matter of false belief.

Certainly that was the view that the Church came to adopt in the great majority of cases of conflict. And since the heart of the Christian gospel was salvation from God brought by Jesus Christ, it was in relation to the doctrines of God and of the person of Christ that true belief was regarded to be of crucial significance and in most need of careful safeguarding. But before we undertake a survey of how the orthodox doctrines of God and of christology emerged from a series of conflicts between 'orthodox' and 'heretics', it is important to distinguish two contrasting frameworks in terms of which Christian scholars have tended to interpret the evidence which we shall be surveying.

The traditional, 'orthodox' view of orthodoxy and heresy has assumed the essential homogeneity of Christian doctrine throughout its early history. Although the fully developed Christian doctrines of the Trinity and of christology are clearly not explicit in the early stages, they are, on this view, thought to constitute the implicit belief of the main body of Christians from earliest times. Their elaboration into more detailed formulations of belief was necessitated by the false teaching of the heretics, which were deviations from an already known truth, usually embarked on for reasons of personal ambition or intellectual pride. Orthodoxy is always in essence conservative; heresy is by definition innovative.

This way of viewing the general scene has come under increasing challenge. Underlying the older view is a conviction about the unity of teaching within the New Testament. And that conviction comes under great strain in the face of recent biblical studies. The emphasis of such studies is more on the diversity than on the unity of beliefs reflected in the New Testament writings. That there is a broad unity within the New Testament is not in question. Its books are, after all, the writings that were preserved and canonized by the later Church with its growing concern for a uniform orthodox belief. But do they represent the full range of early Christian life and thought? The claim that bona fide forms of Christianity were far more varied than even the acknowledged diversity of the New Testament suggests was vigorously presented by Walter Bauer in his *Orthodoxy and Heresy in Earliest Christianity* (first published in German in 1934; ET 1971). Not all of his controversial thesis has won agreement from other scholars. But his main contention, that early Christianity involved many differing styles of belief, is widely accepted. And if it is right, as I believe it to be in its broad outlines, it presents us with a very different framework for the understanding of orthodoxy and heresy. Heresy is not deviation from an already implicitly known truth, which orthodoxy preserves by the process of rendering it explicit at the points under challenge from heresy. Orthodox and heresy are rather alternative possible developments of an initially inchoate and variegated movement. Conflicting views can both expect to find support at differing points in the Christian past; and both will necessarily be innovative in developing the inchoate views of their predecessors in the face of changing circumstance and new experience. It is from this latter perspective that I shall be writing; but the former, as we shall see, is the way in which the Fathers themselves understood their own history.

Christian apologists were annoyed to find themselves accused of beliefs that they did not hold and had no desire to defend. They had to acknowledge that some people confessing faith in Christ did hold them, but they were the ravening wolves, the false Christs and false prophets of whom Matthew's Gospel had forewarned them (Justin, *Dialogue with Trypho*, 35: cf. Origen, *Against Celsus*, 2, 27). But despite such strong language of condemnation, Justin can still speak comparatively mildly of those who do not share his belief in the virgin birth of Christ as fellow-Christians, even if badly mistaken ones (*Dial.* 48). Such an attitude, however, was something of an exception and was certainly soon to disappear. No such note qualifies the all-out attack of Irenaeus in his five books entitled *Against Heresies*. The Gnostics were a more serious problem than a regrettable cause of confusion in the minds of pagan critics. They named the name of Christ, but did so in ways that did not require so sharp a break with the surrounding society and enabled them to avoid the persecution to which Irenaeus' Church was subject. Moreover their pretensions to a deeper, saving religious knowledge could serve to entice away members of Irenaeus' flock. The fact that they named the name of Christ did not imply that they were erring Christians. Rather it compounded their error into a form of blasphemy; they were the negation of Christianity, the Antichrist.

But Irenaeus does a good deal more than just pour vituperative scorn on his opponents, more indeed than outline their teachings about God, the world and Christ in a way designed to show their utterly mistaken character. He sets out to show the radical difference between their approach to determining belief and that which is followed by the true Church. As their title Gnostic (from the Greek word, *gnōsis*, meaning 'knowledge') suggests, their aim is to achieve knowledge by way of philosophical speculation; the true Church follows the contrasting route of faith by way of obedience to what has been revealed and handed down. The primary locus of that revelation is Scripture, which the true Church accepts in its straightforward sense, while the Gnostics read their own ideas into it by way of allegory. Irenaeus acknowledges that the true meaning of Scripture is not always self-evident; it contains, for example, parables whose sense is not immediately or unequivocally evident from the text. But the true Church allows its understanding to be guided by the rule of faith handed down under the guardianship of its public officers, the bishops, deriving in line of succession from the time of the apostles; any appeal to tradition on the part of the Gnostics, on the other hand, takes the form of an appeal to the esoteric teaching of a private succession of teachers in the particular Gnostic school.

The logic of Irenaeus' argument made a major contribution to the Church's understanding of orthodoxy and heresy. Orthodoxy is that which preserves the true sense of Scripture and the original teaching of the apostles. Heresy is a distortion of that teaching, following in the steps of some particular false teacher and deriving ultimately from undue deference to some particular form of philosophical reasoning. Justin (*Dialogue with Trypho* 35) had compared the way in which so many heresies (such as the Valentinians and Basilidians) were, like so many philosophical schools, known by the names of their founders. But Hippolytus, writing in Rome at the beginning of the third century, takes that kind of reflection a stage further. The heresiarchs, after whom the various heresies are named, were not original, creative thinkers. Each of them was dependent on some prior pagan philosopher. Let Christians recognize that link and they will see more clearly what an unchristian distortion of truth the teaching of the heretics is.

Not all those who saw themselves as belonging to the main body of the Church were as opposed in principle to speculation as Hippolytus. Origen, the great scholar of the Alexandrian church, also writing in the first half of the third century, was of a very different cast of mind. He was equally firm in his rejection of those same heretical schools that Hippolytus had denounced (see especially his commentary on Titus 3.10; PG 14, 1303b–1306C), but speculative thought, in partial and critical dependence on pagan philosophers, was meat and drink to him. He dealt with the problem by distinguishing between the core deposit of faith, which was handed down by tradition, and other issues, not directly given in that deposit of faith, on which speculative thought was not only permissible but desirable (*De Principiis*, preface).

But the spirit of Origen did not prevail. He himself indeed was to be condemned for heresy three centuries after his death at the second Council of Constantinople in AD 553. His ideas on some issues, such as the pre-existence of souls and the ultimate salvation of all, about which in his view the deposit of faith offered no explicit guidance, seemed to others to fall clearly within a spectrum of beliefs that needed to be rejected as heretical. Even more significantly, with the passage of time the degree of precision that was felt to be required on the central questions of the understanding of Father, Son and Holy Spirit and the relations between them, increased greatly. There too Origen's, often exploratory, ideas came to be regarded in retrospect in an increasingly hostile light.

It was on the topic of the nature of the Son and his relation to the Father that the most important controversy for the subsequent understanding both of orthodoxy and of heresy broke out in the early years of the fourth century. And it is in the context of that controversy, the Arian controversy, that the difference between the two competing frameworks for the understanding of the relation between orthodoxy and heresy is of the greatest importance.

An essay of this kind is not the place for a discussion of the substance of those long drawn out fourth-century debates. The fundamental issue was the nature of the divinity of the Son. That he was divine was not in dispute. But for Arius, and for many other churchmen of the time who did not see themselves as followers of Arius' teaching but who were regularly spoken of as Arians by their opponents, that divinity had to be of a secondary nature, compared with that of the Father. Only so could one avoid affirming two divine principles; only so could one be in a position to affirm a divine incarnation in the person of Jesus, who shared our human limitations and, above all, underwent the sufferings of the cross. For Athanasius and his allies, on the other hand, a secondary form of divinity was no divinity. There was only one divinity and one way of being divine; and if the Son was divine at all, he had to be divine in just the same sense as the Father was.

203

Athanasius saw the teaching of Arius, and other less extreme versions of a similar tendency, in the same light in which Irenaeus and Hippolytus had seen the Gnostics of their day. It was not a deviant form of the Christian gospel; it was the negation of it. It did not derive from a serious, even if misguided, reading of Scripture. Its inspiration lay in Judaism and in Greek philosophy, which for all their difference from one another had in common a monistic view of God, one quite incompatible with God's saving involvement with the world in Jesus Christ. It was an understanding, therefore, that orthodoxy had to repudiate absolutely and uncompromisingly. And so the creed adopted at the first Council of Constantinople in AD 381 (our Nicene Creed) made its point by insisting that the Son is not merely 'God' but 'very God' 'of one substance with the Father'. Athanasius was eminently successful in what he set out to do. For the Nicene Creed, shaped above all as a riposte to Arian heresy, has not only served throughout the Church's history as an official touchstone of orthodoxy, but also by its extensive use in eucharistic liturgy has moulded the Christian consciousness at the grass-roots level. And at the same time his perspective on the Arian heresy as a philosophically inspired undermining of the Christian gospel has been accepted, virtually unquestioned, by the vast majority of Christians, almost to the present day.

I say 'almost to the present day' because a very different perspective on Arianism, which has been put forward occasionally by rebel spirits in the past, is beginning to establish itself as the consensus view of modern scholars. This view acknowledges the Arians' motivation to have been as genuinely Christian as that of their opponents. The Arian appeal to Scripture was as basic as, and no more arbitrarily selective than, that of the orthodox. Philosophical influence had some part to play in determining the shape of their theology, but the same is true of their opponents. How would it have been possible to produce any coherent and intelligible account of God and his relation with the world without drawing on the best philosophical wisdom their world had on offer? And, above all, both sides of the controversy stood in the same relation to earlier Christian tradition. Earlier Christians had not raised explicitly the precise question which was now the issue of contention between the two sides. Traditional ways of speaking about the divinity of the Son were ambivalent at best; on balance they stood somewhat nearer to that of the Arians than of the orthodox. Either side could, and both sides did, claim with some plausibility that the witness of earlier tradition was in their own favour. But neither claim (particularly that of the orthodox) is as convincing or as decisive as they claimed it to be. Both sides were innovating in a way they were quite unprepared to admit. But on balance it was the Arian heretics who were the more conservative, the orthodox who were the more innovative.

Seeing the controversy this way does not necessarily imply that the Arians had the better case or that there was nothing to choose between the two sides theologically. Indeed some of those who fully accept the scholarly consensus, which acknowledges the responsible character of the Arian position, remain convinced that theological right was on the orthodox side – even to the extent of seeing that right as decisive for the truth of Christianity and properly enshrined in a normative, ecumenical creed. But it is not unreasonable to suggest that the changed historical understanding may in time give rise to a changed theological evaluation also.

But the Church's decision that the divinity of the Son was 'of one substance' with that of the Father was not the end of the historical struggle between orthodoxy and heresy. It was one thing to be clear that Christ was fully and unequivocally divine; it was another matter to be clear just how that full divinity was related to the human experiences of Jesus. Christians who were at one in their condemnation of Arianism answered that question differently, each side denying the creative novelty of its own view and claiming that its particular position was implicit in the earlier traditions of the Church, the only one compatible with the formulas about the person of the Son, already agreed at the Councils of Nicaea and Constantinople. Old attitudes died hard. Episcopal and archiepiscopal opponents might be heretics, but it became increasingly implausible to see them as Antichrist. But the strength of feeling was still there, for the proper resolution of the theological issue was seen as closely tied to the preservation and communication of saving truth. Yet it was closely tied also, as observers were aware then as well as now, to imperial support, and thereby to ecclesiastical influence and power.

The Council of Chalcedon (AD 451), which marked the end of one phase of these christological controversies by ruling out Nestorianism, Apollinarianism and Eutychianism, was nonetheless more of a compromise between competing forms of belief than the councils dealing with the Arian controversy had been. But even so its definition of Christ as one person but two natures failed to stem the continuation of the debate about the person of Christ. For reasons both politcal and theological large areas of Christendom refused to accept its 'two nature' doctrine and went their own monophysite way. And still further points of dispute arose. Even if Christ had two natures, did he have one or two wills? Monothelites and dyothelites denounced one another as heretics for giving the wrong answer to that question.

The earliest Christians had been taught to say 'Jesus is Lord' and, not surprisingly, to have nothing to do with anyone who said 'a curse on Jesus' (1 Cor. 12.2). But who was this Jesus? Some saw him as a purely spiritual being, unencumbered by a real human body. That was judged unacceptable; anyone failing to acknowledge that 'Jesus Christ has come in the flesh' was not of God (1 John 4.2–3). But who is the one who 'has come in the flesh'? The early baptismal creeds, forerunners of our Apostles' Creed, defined him as God's only Son. But again the question was asked: What is it to be God's only Son? The answer came back: It is one distinct from the Father, yet sharing in his full divinity without undermining the unity of God. Any lesser account of his divine status was to lie under the curse of the Church's anathema. But further questions were pressed: How was this fully divine Son united with the fleshly existence into which he came? And once again any suggested answer which called in question the reality of the integration of the two or qualified the fulness of either or implied a mixing of their distinctive characteristics was judged to put a person outside the true Church.

It was a natural enough process and it bears eloquent testimony to the intellectual vitality of early Christianity. But it is hard not to feel that the definition of orthodoxy, of beliefs required of the Church and of her teachers, was continually being extended beyond the bounds implicit in the fundamental nature of Christian faith itself. Every movement gives rise to 'heresies', different options which can take the form either of distinct but coexistent schools of thought and practice, or of rival, antagonistic groups each denying the other any rightful place in the continuing life of the original movement. Christianity soon chose the second road. Differences in the articulation of belief were too readily treated as denials of the faith itself. A natural tendency in that direction showed itself from earliest times as Christianity first marked out its own identity over against Judaism and other religious groups in the ancient world. But it was exacerbated by other factors – those personal, social, political and economic factors on which William Frend's work has shed so much light – and carried over to become the established pattern of handling intra-Christian disputes. The resultant legacy of a well thought out but over-defined concept of orthodoxy has given to the Church an intellectual vitality and toughness, but also a penchant for mutual vilification and the multiplication of division, together with a built-in resistance to change in the face of new circumstance.

BIBLIOGRAPHY

Prestige, G L, *Fathers and Heretics*. London, SPCK, 1940.
Frend, W H C, *Saints and Sinners in the Early Church*. London, Darton, Longman & Todd, 1985.
Lively presentations of particular orthodox and heretical figures.

Bauer, W, *Orthodoxy and Heresy in Earliest Christianity*. Philadelphia, Fortress 1971; London, SCM, 1972.
Turner, H E W, *The Pattern of Christian Truth*. London, Mowbray, 1954.
Walter Bauer's influential work discussed in the text and the main critical response to it from a British scholar.

Le Boulluec, A, *La notion d'hérésie dans la littérature grecque, IIe – IIIe siècles*. 2 vols., Paris, Etudes Augustiniennes, 1985.
Hanson, R P C, *The Search for the Christian Doctrine of God*. Edinburgh, T & T Clark, 1988.
Two very big books, embodying the best recent scholarship on the subject, the first dealing with the period up to the Arian controversy and the second with the Arian controversy itself.

18

Mysticism

ANDREW LOUTH

It is not possible to begin to say anything about mysticism without pointing out that the very definition and connotation of the word are hotly disputed, and, in the particular case of mysticism in the early Christian period, that the associations of the word in modern usage are likely to be highly misleading in the context of late antiquity. That said, a working definition is necessary, and the word 'mysticism' and its cognates will be used to refer to a relationship between men and women and God that is characterized as *union with God*, a union that is real, and therefore doubtless experienced, though the emphasis falls on the reality of the experience, rather than the experience itself.

Any Christian understanding of union with God will focus on the union between man and God established by God himself in the incarnation. Thus there are two foci in Christian mysticism (or better: mystical theology): the union between God and the believer who, through baptism, is 'in Christ', whose life is 'hid with Christ in God' (Col. 3.3), whose profoundest conviction it is, in St Paul's words, that 'I live, and yet not I, but Christ liveth in me' (Gal. 2.20); and the union with God expressed in and effected by the Eucharist, in which Christ is present to his Church, and men and women receive Christ's Body and Blood and are made one with him.

That this is true of early Christianity becomes evident if we look at the only thing that can be regarded as a 'peak experience' (as mysticism is commonly regarded) in the experience of the early Christians: that is martyrdom. From the beginning, the Christian Church experienced the threat of martyrdom; by the second century the martyr was regarded as the ideal Christian, and martyrdom as the ultimate test of one's faith. In part this was doubtless because Christ's death was readily seen as a martyr's death, and the Christian martyr thus most signally united with Christ, indeed united with

God: 'Allow me to be an imitator of the passion of my God,' says St Ignatius of Antioch (*Romans* 6.3). But, as Frend has insisted,[1] it was from Judaism that the early Christians inherited what one might call a 'spirituality' of martyrdom. The martyr stood on the brink of the age to come, his death atoned for the failings of those who lived in expectation of the coming age, and brought that age closer. The age to come would be Paradise, the restoration of God's original creation (it is worth noting that it is in reflection on the fate of the Maccabean martyrs that both the doctrine of creation out of nothing and, justified by that doctrine, belief in the resurrection of the body came to prominence within Judaism, and were thence bequeathed to Christianity: cf. 2 Macc. 7.23, 28). According to one tradition, which seeks to understand Christ's death in terms of martyrdom, Christ goes from the cross to Paradise, taking with him the repentant thief (Luke 23.43). The Christian martyrs, as they die, see the risen and glorified Christ: first, St Stephen (Acts 7.56) and then others, e.g. St Carpus (*Martyrdom of Carpus, Papylus and Agathonice* (Greek rec.), 39). Karl Holl was doubtless wrong in seeking the original meaning of the word *martus* in the fact that the martyr was a witness to the risen Christ (i.e., had literally seen him), but it was a profound insight that led to the mistake.[2] Some accounts of martyrdom, most notably the North African *Passion of Perpetua*, are full of items later associated with mysticism: visions, ecstasy, great intercessory power (availing even for the departed). But this literal following of Christ in martyrdom was not isolated from the other focus of Christian understanding of union with God, the Eucharist. Ignatius, in a clear eucharistic metaphor, sees himself as 'God's wheat, ground fine by the teeth of wild beasts, that I may be found Christ's pure bread' (*Romans* 4.1), and Saint Polycarp, as he prays before the pyre is lit, models his prayer of self-offering on the eucharistic prayer he offered week by week (*Martyrdom of Polycarp*, 14).

Martyrdom was not for everyone: the earliest of the Acts of the Martyrs – Polycarp's – contains a cautionary tale against voluntary martyrdom: one Quintus had given himself up voluntarily, but his courage failed him when he saw the wild beasts, and he recanted (*Mart. Pol.*, 4). Nonetheless, martyrdom was the ultimate test of faith and it was for steadfastness in the face of persecution that the Christian prepared himself (cf. Rom. 5.3–5). Very soon this is given systematic expression: for Clement and Origen, the great Alexandrian theologians, even if martyrdom in the literal sense is not the destiny of all, everyone may aspire to 'spiritual' martyrdom. Clement devotes a whole book of his *Stromateis* (book IV) to martyrdom, distinguishing between 'simple' martyrdom and what he calls 'Gnostic' martyrdom (IV.4.15.4). Simple martyrdom certainly achieves fulfilment or perfection (*teleiōsis*: a word often used, e.g. by Eusebius, to designate martyrdom), but achieves this not simply by death but because it displays the 'perfect work of love' (IV.4.14.3), and that 'perfect work of love' can be displayed by those who are not called to literal martyrdom. It is, in fact, displayed by those Clement calls 'Gnostics', men and women who have devoted themselves wholly to God, and who, like the martyrs, are close to God and able to bring blessings on others by the power of their intercession (see *The Rich Man's Salvation*, 34–41).

Clement's account of the Gnostic's perfection introduces two other themes into the 'mysticism' of the early Church. First of all, we find in him the use of those words that historically lie behind the word 'mysticism': words like *mystikos* and *mysterion*. *Mysterion* refers to the 'mystery of Christ' (cf. Col. 1.26), the secret that is revealed in Christ, which yet, because it is *God's* secret, remains a secret, though revealed. This mystery is revealed in a life lived close to Christ, in the Eucharist (though Clement himself does not emphasize this) and in the Scriptures: the word *mystikos* (hidden) can be applied in all these contexts. The 'unutterable mysteries' hidden 'in the depths of the mind' of the Gnostics (*Rich Man's Salvation*, 36) are nourished by their ever deeper understanding of the Scriptures.

> The Mosaic philosophy [= the understanding of the Scriptures] can be divided into four: (1) the historical and properly legislative, (2) that which belongs to ethical activity (*ethikēs pragmateias*), (3), the hierurgical, that is natural contemplation (*physikē theōrias*), and (4) the fourth theological kind that surpasses the others, contemplation (*epopteia*), which Plato said belonged to the mysteries that are truly great. (I.28.176.1f.)

In the three stages that go beyond the historical, we can see the beginnings of the three stages of the mystical life. This quotation also hints at the other theme Clement introduces into mystical theology: that is, the influence of classical philosophy, especially Plato. Clement's understanding of the ideal of the Gnostic owes a great deal to the philosophical ideal of the sage, especially in the way he characterizes this ideal as one of *apatheia* (dispassion): a detachment and serenity that frees the Gnostic from the disturbance of worldly matters and makes possible objectively loving activity in the world. But his understanding of the progress of the Christian towards *gnōsis* (knowledge) owes much to Plato: it demands *katharsis*, purification (cf. Plato's *Phaedo*) and this purification is most fundamentally a purification of *erōs*, love (cf. Plato's *Symposium*). Plato's statement in the *Theaetetus* that 'flight [from the world] is a likening to God (*homoiōsis theōi*) as far as possible' (176B) is one of Clement's favourite quotations: Clement identifies Plato's *homoiōsis theōi* with Moses' command to follow after God (Deut. 13.4: cf. *Stromateis* II.19.100.4). In this interpretation of the Old Testament in terms of Greek philosophy, Clement is evidently indebted to the Jewish Alexandrian philosopher, Philo, whose influence on this aspect of the Christian mystical tradition continued to be important into the fourth century, with St Gregory of Nyssa and St Ambrose (though Philo's interpretation of 'following God' is not identical with Clement's: cf. *De Migratione Abrahami (On the Migration of Abraham)* 127–31). Clement's fondness for Plato's *homoiōsis theōi* as a term for the goal of the Christian life is also related to his desire to see that life as the perfecting of the image of God in which man was created: a perfecting in which the image grows into the likeness (cf. Gen. 1.26, where the LXX translates 'likeness' as *homoiōsis*).

Whether or not Origen knew his great predecessor in Alexandria, Clement, his understanding of and contribution to mystical theology is very similar. There is the same shift of emphasis from literal martyrdom to a spiritual martyrdom of asceticism; even more than Clement he places Scripture and its understanding at the centre of the spiritual life; and the influence of Plato is also very palpable. But Origen systematically expounded Scripture in a way that Clement did not, and most of his contributions to the Christian mystical tradition are related to his interpretation of Scripture. Pre-eminent in this is the way he expounds the Song of Songs in relation to the mystical life. This celebration of human erotic love had already been interpreted by the Jews as referring to the love between God and Israel, and by the time of Hippolytus the Christian transposition of this to the love between Christ and the Church (cf. Eph. 5.25–32) had been made. For Origen, this interpretation remains of fundamental importance, but it is joined by an interpretation of the Song as concerned with the love between Christ and the individual Christian soul. Origen suggests two ways of seeing the Song as celebrating the consummation in union of the love between Christ and the soul. He sees the Song of Songs (a superlative in Hebrew, he notes) as the highest and greatest of the songs of the Old Testament which begin with Moses' song after the crossing of the Red Sea (Exod. 15), interpreted as celebrating baptism (cf. *Homily on the Song*, I.1; *Commentary on the Song*, prologue): 'mystical' union with God is therefore the fulfilment of what has already been initiated in baptism. Otherwise, Origen sees the Song of Songs as the last of the three books of Wisdom, and he draws a parallel between the three books of Wisdom and the three stages of philosophy: Proverbs corresponding to ethics, Ecclesiastes to physics, and the Song to 'enoptics' (presumably metaphysics, though comparison with Clement's triad above suggests that this should probably be read *epoptics*, i.e. contemplation); so there are three stages in the soul's ascent to God: *ethikē, physikē* and *epoptikē*. These three stages became canonized as *praktikē, physikē* and *theologia* by Evagrius and the monastic tradition dependent upon him. The three terms in this form, it will be noted, can be traced back to Clement as easily as Origen's triad: the soul is first purified by the practice of the virtues and struggle against temptation (*praktikē*: a stage that Origen treats rather cursorily, though Evagrius and the monastic tradition were to be much preoccupied with it), then it learns to contemplate the world, as God made it, and to realize its transience (*phusikē*), and finally the soul comes to the vision of God and union with him (*theologia*).

Another contribution Origen makes to the mystical tradition is his development of the notion of the spiritual senses. It is not clear that originally the notion of the spiritual senses was not much more than an attempt to explain such passages as Ps. 34.8 ('O taste and see how gracious the Lord is'), where, as bodily taste and sight can hardly be in question, recourse has to be had to *spiritual* sight and taste. But this leads on to the idea that, as the body has five senses, so analogously the soul has senses with which it perceives reality in the spiritual realm. These senses are dulled by sin, and can only be awakened by grace: it is often suggested that, as the bodily senses are mortified, so the spiritual senses come to life. The sensuous language of the Song of Songs – full of perfumes and gentle caressing (and sometimes not-so-gentle caressing), the soft sound of the voice of the Beloved and the sense of his presence – is interpreted in terms of the soul's growing awareness of the spiritual realm where Christ is to be found.

This suggests that 'mystical experience' is less some kind of inward 'altered state of consciousness' (as some later tradition suggests) than access to another realm, the paradise the martyrs beheld, the paradise to which St Paul was caught up (cf. 2 Cor. 12.2–4).[3] This sense that the soul is transformed by the awakening of its spiritual senses is taken by Origen a stage further. As with Clement, he sees the Christian's ascent to God in terms of the perfection of the image of God in which man was created, and which has been restored by baptism into Christ's victorious death and resurrection. This process of a growing assimilation to God Origen describes as deification (*theopoiēsis*): by perfecting its contemplation of God the mind 'is deified in what it contemplates' (*Comm. on John*, XXXII.27).

The fourth century saw the long-drawn-out Arian crisis culminating in the establishment of orthodox belief in a consubstantial, uncreated Trinity, in contrast with which all else is created 'out of nothing'. Underlying the Platonic understanding of the soul's ascent to the truth (the influence of which we have already alluded to) was the conviction of a fundamental kinship between the soul and the divine. This conviction was effectively embraced by Origen with his belief in an eternal spiritual realm forming a kind of pyramid, with the Father at the top, the rational spiritual beings (the *logikoi*) at the bottom and the Word and Spirit in between. But this conviction could not survive the orthodoxy of the fourth century and thereafter: when it surfaced in Evagrius and his disciples it attracted ecclesiastical censure. If the soul no longer enjoys kinship with God, if in fact there is an infinite gulf between the creature and the Creator, what kind of mystical theology is possible? Mystical theology, faithful to Nicene orthodoxy, manifests two features: first, an emphasis on the incarnation as bridging the gulf between Creator and creature, and secondly, a deepening insistence on the fundamental unknowability of God. St Athanasius is a convenient example of the first point (though it is affirmed by virtually all Orthodox theologians): the incarnation makes it possible for men and women to contemplate God by placing within the reach of their frail and fallen powers the true consubstantial image of God, that is the Son. By the incarnation man is drawn back to contemplation of God and deified: the Word of God 'became man that we might become God' (Athanasius, *On the Incarnation*, 54). (This theology of the Image, or Icon, can be seen to underlie the the logical justification of the veneration of icons in the eighth and ninth centuries.) The implications of the second point were most searchingly explored by St Gregory of Nyssa: if there is no natural kinship between the soul and God, then the closer the soul comes to God, the greater is its conviction of God's utter unknowability, the deeper the darkness it finds itself entering. The progress from purification, through contemplation of the world and God's activity within it, to contemplation of God himself, understood by Origen as a progress from darkness to ever increasing light, becomes for Gregory a movement from illumination, into the cloud, and finally into utterly impenetrable darkness. These three stages are symbolized in the life of Moses (like Philo, Gregory takes the life of Moses as an allegory of the soul's ascent to God) by the Burning Bush (Exod. 3.2–6), the ascent of Mount Sinai (Exod. 19.16–25) and his final experience of God in the cleft of the rock (Exod. 33.17–23). In this last episode, Moses is denied the vision of God face to face, but sees his back parts as he passes by: to see God is to be behind him, 'seeing God means following him' (*Comm. on the Song*, VI. 888A). The vision of God is inexhaustible, for God is beyond any human comprehension: the 'true vision of God consists in this, that the soul that looks up to God never ceases to desire him' (*Life of Moses*, II. 233). In the darkness God is experienced – Gregory makes signal use of the notion of the spiritual senses – but there is no final vision of God, in which he is comprehended.

Hitherto we have said nothing of the one who has been called the 'great philosopher of mysticism' (W R Inge). But, even though Plotinus flourished in the third century, his influence was hardly felt in Christian theology before the end of the fourth century. Two of the Fathers of the Church, one at the end of the fourth century, the other at the end of the fifth, were however influenced by Plotinus and the tradition of Neoplatonism that he inspired, and they both made profound contributions to the Christian mystical tradition. They were St Augustine in the West, and in the East the mysterious figure who veiled himself under the pseudonym of Denys (or Dionysius) the Areopagite.

Augustine was influenced by that tradition of Neoplatonism that flowed from Plotinus, through his disciple and biographer, Porphyry, and their Latin interpreter, Marius Victorinus, like Augustine an African and professor of rhetoric, who had converted to Christianity in Rome in the middle of the fourth century. What Augustine took from Plotinus was his *spirit*: his sense of the unity of everything, flowing out from the One and returning again, like the ebb and flow of the tide. His 'restless heart' (*cor inquietum*), in its inability to rest, manifested its remoteness from God and its longing to return to its Creator; for despite the influence of Plotinus, Augustine held to the Christian doctrine of creation out of nothing, not the Neoplatonic doctrine of emanation. The movement of return was a movement of unification and simplification. Augustine, however, soon became convinced that such 'being collected and bound up into unity' (which he called continence: cf. *Confessions*, X.29.40) was impossible for fallen man, save by the grace of God. With that realization he began to make much less of any ecstatic contact with the eternal Wisdom of God such as he had experienced in conversation with his mother shortly before her death (cf. *Confessions*, IX.10.23–6). That experience, however, despite the Plotinian language with which it is clothed, was distinctly un-Plotinian in that it was shared, and not solitary. Augustine's most important contribution to the mystical tradition, however, owes little directly to Plotinus. As he reflected on the implications of the notion of a co-equal, consubstantial Trinity, he came to reject the commonplace of Greek theology, according to which the Son is the Image of God and man created according to (*kata*) that Image. That seemed to Augustine to entail subordinationism, for an image must be inferior to the original; and instead Augustine came to see the spiritual part of man – the immaterial soul, the highest of creaturely beings – as directly an image of God, in fact an image of the trinitarian God. Such an image would itself be trinitarian; and Augustine sought, in his great work *On the Trinity*, to discover this trinitarian image in man, finding progressively more perfect forms of this image in the mind, knowing and loving itself (book IX), in memory, understanding and will (book X), and – the highest form ever found in this life – in the mind, remembering God, knowing him and loving him (XIV.12.15). The spiritual life – the mystical life – is to be understood as the gradual reforming of this image, a process begun in baptism, and perfected in slow and gradual struggle to respond to God's grace and be faithful to one's baptism. The journey of the trinitarian soul to the trinitarian God became a compelling image in western mysticism.

The indebtedness of Denys the Areopagite to Neoplatonism was rather different. It was a different tradition of Neoplatonism that attracted him: one that flowed through Iamblichus (probably a disciple of Porphyry's) and Proclus, the *diadochus* (or successor of Plato) in the Academy at Athens until his death in AD 485; and whereas Augustine was touched by the spirit of Plotinus, Denys was soaked in Iamblichean Neoplatonism. He shared its enthusiasm for elaborate metaphysical distinctions and constructions, usually triadic in form. But he was also well versed in Christian theology, especially that of the Cappadocian Fathers, profoundly moved by the rhythm and symbolism of the Christian liturgy, and deeply impressed by lives radiant with the glory of God (especially that of his mysterious mentor, Hierotheus). In the few short works that he composed at the end of the fifth or beginning of the sixth century, he sought to provide the richness of biblical symbolism as expressed in the Christian liturgy with a cosmic and metaphysical backdrop of matching splendour. For him, there are three levels of reality: the Uncreated God, the created, invisible, spiritual realm, and the created, visible world. Each level is triadic: God is Trinity; there are three ranks of angelic beings, each rank divided into three; at the visible level Denys is concerned only with the Church, which has three orders of clergy, three ranks of laity, and three sacramental rites. The cosmos, threefold rank on threefold rank, culminating in the Holy Triad, manifests and displays the glory and splendour that emanates from God (or the source of divinity, as he prefers to say, the *Thearchy*). The glory illuminates and draws all back to the source: this movement of alluring divine manifestation itself discloses a threefold character: of purification, illumination and perfection (*teleiōsis*) or union. Every creature is called both to manifest as purely and limpidly as possible the divine glory that it has received, and to trace that glory back to its source, by affirming its truth (what Denys calls affirmative, or kataphatic theology) and by denying its ultimacy (what Denys calls negative, or apophatic theology), thus purifying its love for the ultimate source of all, and in the end finding union with God in ecstasy. The sacraments play out this movement, and celebrate the divine works (*theougiai*), pre-eminently the incarnation, that make it all possible. The monk by 'a sacred folding together of all division into a God-like unity and the perfection of the love of God' (*Ecclesiastical Hierarchy*, VI.i.3: 533A) symbolizes the perfection of all striving to trace glory back to its source in the One God. By now, the transformation of the ideal of martyrdom begun by Clement of Alexandria was complete, and the monk had inherited the role of the martyr.[4] So in Denys' mystical theology, with its two *foci* in the union of all with God through Christ in the liturgy and in the martyrdom of (now) asceticism where the individual finds fulfilment or perfection in union with God, there can be heard an echo of that sub-apostolic period to which Denys so much wanted to be thought to belong.

NOTES

1 See *Martyrdom and Persecution in the Early Church* (Oxford, Blackwell, 1965), esp. ch. 2, 'Judaism and Martyrdom'.
2 Karl Holl, 'Die Vorstellung vom Märtyrer und die Märtyrerakte in ihrer geschichtlichen Entwicklung', in *Gesammelte Aufsätze zur Kirchengeschichte*, vol. 2 (Tübingen, Mohr, 1928), pp. 68–102.
3 See Anselme Stolz, OSB, *Théologie de la Mystique* (Chevetogne, éd. 2, 1947), esp. ch. 2, 'Le Paradis de Dieu', pp. 18–39, and pp. 231f.
4 See E E Malone, 'The Monk and the Martyr', in *Antonius Magnus Eremita 356–1956*, ed. B Steidle OSB (Studia Anselmiana 38; Rome 1956), pp. 201–28.

BIBLIOGRAPHY

Balthasar, H U von, *The Glory of the Lord*, vol. 2, Studies in Theological Style: Clerical Styles. Edinburgh, T & T Clark, 1984.

Lossky, V, *The Vision of God*, London, Faith Press, 1963.

Louth, A, *The Origins of the Christian Mystical Tradition: from Plato to Denys.* Oxford, Clarendon Press, 1981.

Plé, A OP and others, *Mystery and Mysticism. A Symposium* (London, Blackfriars Publications, 1956), esp. the articles by L. Bouyer: 'Mysterion', pp. 18–32, ' "Mysticism": An essay on the history of a Word', pp. 119–37.

Stolz, A OSB, *Théologie de la Mystique*. Chevetogne, Editions des Bénédictines d'Amay, éd.2, 1947.

19

Schism and Church Unity

GERALD BONNER

Schism may be defined as division within a Christian community, which may lead to external separation but does not involve disagreement over fundamental doctrines. It is this doctrinal element which essentially distinguishes schism from heresy; for heresy (at least in the opinion of the disputants, which may not be endorsed by later historians) involves radical disagreement over articles of faith essential for salvation. In the early Church, however, the boundaries between schism and heresy were not absolutely defined or clearly established. There was a tendency, particularly on the side which emerged as 'orthodox' and so set the pattern for later orthodox evaluation, to feel that schism contained within itself the seeds of heresy. Thus St Jerome (347[?]–420) declares that heresy involves perverse dogma, schism episcopal dissension, 'but, for the rest, there is no schism that does not devise a heresy for itself'.[1] In similar fashion St Augustine (354–430) could argue that while schism initially arises from disagreement over opinions, 'schism grown old becomes heresy'.[2] While both Jerome and Augustine had theological axes to grind, their declarations are a reminder that schism in the early Church did not result only from personal antagonisms, but frequently involved theological considerations whose full implications were only gradually appreciated. Thus, for example, a good many schisms in the early Church, such as Novatianism, arose initially from disciplinary considerations: should a penitent guilty of mortal sin be readmitted to communion, or ought he to spend his life in perpetual penance? But this disagreement over discipline had ecclesiological implications: Ought not the Church Militant to be a pure Church? Had she authority to pronounce absolution in God's name? In early Christian thought, heresy was concerned largely with belief about the doctrines of God and the creation of the world, with the Trinity, and with the incarnation. Ecclesiology was defined by

218

pastoral practice rather than by theological reflection; but in order to justify pastoral practice it was necessary to theorize, and so open lines of theological investigation which were to be increasingly developed in later centuries, until they came in practice to be deemed as much a test of right belief as the relation of the Son to the Father in the Trinity, or of the human to the divine in the person of Jesus Christ.

An example of such development is provided by the thought of St Cyprian, bishop of Carthage from 248/9 to 258. In the course of the disputes which arose in the wake of the Decian persecution of 250, Cyprian composed his treatise *On the Unity of the Catholic Church*, probably in support of his Roman colleague Cornelius, who was harassed at Rome by the antipope Novatian. Cyprian's argument, designed to have a profound influence on both African and later western theology, is rooted in the conviction that there can be no spiritual life outside the Catholic Church. Had there been safety from the waters of the Flood outside the Ark of Noah there might be salvation for the heretic or the schismatic; but there was none. Some years later, in 256, Cyprian found himself in dispute with Cornelius' successor, Stephen, on the question of the manner of receiving converts from heretical and schismatic churches. Cyprian followed a practice of rebaptizing them (in his view, baptizing them for the first time), which had been introduced into Africa by his predecessor Agrippinus in the early third century. Stephen maintained the Roman custom, in which the convert was not rebaptized, but received by the imposition of the bishop's hands. In the dispute between them, Stephen appealed to tradition to justify his practice: 'Let no innovation be made!'[3] Cyprian, despite his belief that a bishop enjoyed full autonomy in his diocese provided that he was orthodox in doctrine, nevertheless continued to press Stephen to adopt the African practice, apparently because he had been convinced by his own arguments, and wished to change Roman tradition on theological grounds. In the event, he failed; but his theorizing provides an illustration of the way in which pastoral practice could be questioned on theological grounds, and the distinction between schism and heresy effectively removed by an ecclesiology which regarded the one Catholic Church as the sole channel of divine grace.

Nevertheless, this narrowness of Cyprian's doctrine of the Church was the result of a passionate devotion to the ideal of

219

Christian unity, the natural development of St Paul's exhortation 'that there should be no schism in the body' (1 Cor. 12.25). The early Church normally recognized and respected local divergencies of practice, and St Ambrose of Milan (339–397) could say roundly to a questioner: 'When I am here, I do not fast on Saturday; and when I am at Rome, I do. If you do not wish to cause scandal, observe the local practice of any church which you may visit,'[4] and tell his congregation, when expounding the Milanese practice, not observed at Rome, of washing the feet of the newly baptized: 'We are well aware that the Roman church does not have this custom ... I say this, not to criticize others, but to commend my own practice. In general I desire to follow the Roman church; yet we too are not without common sense, and what other places have rightly retained, we also rightly maintain.'[5] Yet Ambrose did not hesitate to follow the example of the Roman church on all major issues so that, during the fourth-century schism in the church of Antioch, in common with the western Church as a whole and Alexandria in the East, he supported the minority Catholic congregation in that city led by bishop Paulinus, and refused to recognize Meletius, the bishop of the great majority of the Antiochene Catholics, who enjoyed the support of the bishops of Asia and Syria. The idea that the two congregations might be equally members of the one Catholic Church never occurred to him.

S L Greenslade, in his *Schism in the Early Church*, discussed the causes of schism under five headings: Personal; Nationalism, Social and Economic Influences; The Rivalry of Sees; Liturgical Disputes; and Problems of Discipline and the Puritan Idea of the Church. These divisions, which suited the pattern of Greenslade's book, are perhaps too refined, and are certainly controversial. Many scholars, following A H M Jones,[6] would regard the notion of a possible nationalistic element in early Christian schism as open to question, and Greenslade himself was constrained to admit that 'there was some tension between the opposing ideals of liturgical uniformity and liberty in the early Church ... but not much schism'.[7] Essentially, the causes of schism are personal and ideological, though it is to be doubted whether either of these factors ever wholly excluded the other. Any schismatic leader, however ambitious, is likely to urge some issue of principle as a justification of his actions, while on the other hand personalities may well render insoluble an issue which, left to other men, could be resolved with a little goodwill on both sides. Goodwill was not lacking in the early Church. During the late fourth century, a very small schismatic sect, known as the *Tertullianistae*, was quietly received back into the Catholic church of Carthage, apparently without account being taken of the belief of their alleged founder, the third-century African theologian Tertullian, that the human soul, and God himself, were bodies.[8] Here was a case when a minor theological error was not deemed to turn a schism into a heresy.

It will be helpful to consider certain well-known early schisms, in order to understand their origins and characteristics; and it is convenient to begin with that in the church of Corinth, which provoked the celebrated letter of the church of Rome, to be dated around AD 95, and written anonymously by Clement in the name of the Roman church. As the oldest non-biblical Christian writing that we possess (unless the *Didache* is older), Clement's letter is of particular interest.

Our knowledge of the Corinthian schism derives solely from Clement's letter. It appears that there had been 'an abominable and unholy sedition (*stasis*)'[9] in the church of Corinth, through which certain presbyters had been removed from their office. Since no motive other than *zēlos kai phthonos* (jealousy and envy) is given, it may be guessed that the issues were personal rather than ideological, and that the Corinthian church, after a period of peace and stability ('You were sincere and innocent, and bore no malice to one another. All sedition and all schism were abominable to you,' declares Clement),[10] was again manifesting the contentiousness which had formerly distressed St Paul (1 Cor. 1.11–13).

Clement's remedy is to commend mutual charity and submission to duly constituted authority. He likens the Church to an army, in which all serve within the military hierarchy. 'Not all are prefects, nor tribunes, nor centurions, nor in charge of fifty men, or the like; but each carries out in his own rank the commands of the emperor and the generals.'[11] We have no direct information about the effect of Clement's letter; but since it was apparently held in high esteem in the Corinthian church some seventy years later, being read in church as though it were a work of Scripture,[12] it may be concluded that it was successful in bringing about a reconciliation in the church to which it was addressed.

A feature of the Corinthian schism is that it involved factions within the Church, and not secession from it. With the Montanist movement of the second century, we have to do with a group which was eventually expelled and became a separate communion. Schism here led to separation, though only after attempts to obtain recognition by the Great Church had failed. Montanus, a Phrygian convert of the mid-second century, began after his baptism to speak in ecstasy, declaring that his utterances were the voice of God. He was shortly followed by two women, Prisca and Maximilla. Their prophecies, though not characterized by any particular profundity ('The Holy Spirit seemed to say nothing of any religious or intellectual value to his prophets'),[13] attracted many followers in Asia, and the movement subsequently spread to North Africa, where it made a notable convert in Tertullian.

However, although in itself the claim to speak with divine inspiration was not heretical, both the unbridled enthusiasm of Montanism, which was calculated deliberately to provoke the pagan authorities, and its ferocious asceticism, aroused opposition in the Asiatic church, with the result that two parties struggled for mastery, and at one time, in the reign of Pope Zephyrinus (199–217), Montanism came near to obtaining recognition by Rome. Eventually it failed; and at some later date, two Asiatic councils at Iconium (perhaps about 230) and Synnada (date unknown) decided not to recognize Montanist baptism. Thus a movement which began within the Church became an external schism and was eventually branded a heresy.

A curious feature of this progression is that it was the mood of Montanism – ecstatic, eschatological, and ascetic – rather than its doctrines, which gave offence. It appears to have been one of those revivalist movements which, from time to time, disturbed the life of the Church, and as such was rather a menace to order and established authority, than a deliberately secessionist sect.

With the Novatianist schism of the mid third century, we come to a movement which was determined both by personalities and principles. Novatian was a distinguished Roman presbyter, the author of a work on the Trinity. The Decian persecution of 250 left Church leaders everywhere with the pastoral problem of how to deal with penitent apostates who now sought reconciliation with the Church. Opinion on this matter was divided. Many Christians believed that with a mortal sin of such gravity as apostasy, no reconciliation was possible, and the repentant sinner ought to spend his remaining years in lifelong penance, in the hope that, at the last, God would give him the pardon which the Church Militant dared not pronounce. However, the great majority of the bishops decided that it was better to absolve such penitents, in order that they might be encouraged and sustained by the sacramental fellowship of the Catholic Church. From this policy Novatian vehemently dissented. He contrived to have himself consecrated bishop of Rome, in opposition to the reigning Pope, Cornelius, and so founded a schismatic Church which was to endure to the fifth century and enjoy a certain measure of respect, even from members of the Great Church.[14]

Novatian's character has naturally been unflatteringly depicted by his Catholic opponents; yet even allowing for bias, it is difficult not to feel that personal ambition, as well as zeal for a pure Church, played its part in leading him into schism.

With Donatism we come to what is probably the most famous schism of the early Church. Here again, the issue was one of ecclesiastical discipline, but one that was debated in a particular area – Roman North Africa – where rigorism enjoyed a great degree of popular support, to such an extent that some historians have interpreted Donatism as an expression of African national feeling in religious terms. The theological debate turned upon the status of those clerics who, in the Diocletianic persecution (300–11), had surrendered copies of the Scriptures for destruction to the secular authorities. Such surrender (*traditio*) was regarded by the Donatists as equivalent to apostasy and, in a tradition which looked back to the teaching of St Cyprian, these 'handers-over' (*traditores*) were deemed to have forfeited the power to administer valid sacraments. Accordingly, sacraments administered by *traditores* were not merely inefficacious but positively defiling, and anyone baptized in the Catholic Church needed Donatist baptism to cleanse him of his unremitted sins. Caecilian, the bishop of Carthage who initially provoked the controversy, was alleged to have had among his consecrators one Felix of Apthungi, an obscure bishop whose sole historical distinction is that he was alleged (untruly) to have been a *traditor*. The fact that Felix was acquitted by both ecclesiastical and secular enquiries made no difference to the enemies of Caecilian: in their eyes he had been consecrated by a *traditor*, and anyone who communicated with him, or with his successors, shared the taint of *traditio*.

Initially, the Donatist movement claimed to be a party within the

African Church, holding a common theology, but divided on a point of discipline. It also claimed – correctly – that it stood in the doctrinal tradition of St Cyprian, the great hero of African Christians. It was thus, technically, a schism; though its own claim, naturally, was to be the true African Church, and that its Catholic opponents were the schismatics. The fact that it attracted no support outside Africa, apart from a tenuous foothold at Rome, made no difference to its supporters, who were prepared to believe that true faith had perished in the Roman world and was preserved only in Africa. For that reason its fundamental principles made Donatism nearer to heresy than other early schismatic movements. But now secular considerations entered an ecclesiastical dispute. Since the conversion of the emperor Constantine, at the beginning of the fourth century, Christian emperors had shown a steadily increasing determination to enforce what they deemed to be right belief upon their subjects. This process had culminated in 392 by the law of Theodosius I against all heresies, which decreed that heretical clergy were to be fined ten pounds of gold (a huge sum) and the places where heretical rites were celebrated with the owner's consent were to be confiscated – a severe deterrent to lay patrons of heresy.[15] The question was: Were Donatists liable under this law? In the preceding decades, emperors had legislated spasmodically against rebaptism, but had not regarded Donatism as being in itself heretical. An action brought in 404 by Augustine of Hippo and his friend Possidius, bishop of Calama, against Crispinus, the Donatist bishop of that city, eventually procured a decision that the law was applicable, and so Donatism became legally liable as heretical.

The legal decision, although from the Catholic point of view a useful threat, did not involve an equivalent theological change of outlook. The Catholics passionately desired to see the Donatists restored to the universal Church. The Donatists were equally determined to remain apart. In consequence, both sides tended to minimize the theological differences between them, the one in order to forward the work of reconciliation, the other to avoid the operation of the imperial laws. Eventually the Catholics decided to have recourse to the secular arm, ostensibly – and perhaps sincerely – as a protection against Donatist terrorists; and after a conference between both churches at Carthage in 411, at which the imperial commissioner, Count Marcellinus, decided that the Catholics were the true Church of Africa, the work of forcible reintegration went ahead with considerable, though by no means complete, success, until the invasion of Africa by the Arian Vandals in 429 gave both disputants other matters to think about.

The history of Donatism is of an internal schism in a local Church which passed outside and soon became an independent Church, not only claiming to be theologically in the right, as did other schismatic Churches, but also seeking to be officially recognized as the lawful Church of Africa by the Roman government. The Donatist attitude to the secular world was a curious mixture of fundamental hostility and occasional opportunism. In essence, Donatist theology was based upon the ideal of a pure Church which, by its very character, would be persecuted by an inevitably pagan state, and Donatism was unable to adapt its thinking to the new conditions presented by a Christian Empire. It was therefore, by its very temperament, separated from the Catholic Church, which both could and did. It is here that there is a possibility, which by its very nature does not admit of proof, that the Donatist outlook made an especial appeal to the indigenous Berber population of North Africa.

This being said, it is also clear that personal factors played a part in initiating and consolidating the schism. Caecilian, whose consecration provided the pretext for Donatist opposition, seems to have been unpopular with a section of the Christian population of Carthage. Donatus the Great, the consolidator though not the founder of the schism, was accused by Augustine of having 'desired to obtain control of all Africa',[16] when he sought recognition as the legitimate bishop of Carthage from the emperor Constantine. Furthermore, throughout the controversy, individual Donatist leaders generally displayed a fundamentalistic hostility to any attempt at reconciliation.

Compared with Donatism the fourth-century schism in the Church of Antioch was a storm in a teacup; but it is important, in that it brought about a long-continued division among the great sees of Christendom. In 330 Eustathius, the bishop of Antioch, a strong supporter of Nicene trinitarian theology, was banished from his see, allegedly for political reasons. At his departure he urged his people to accept whoever should be set over them as their bishop. A small group, led by the presbyter Paulinus, showed its loyalty to Eustathius by disobeying his injunction and worshipping apart from the rest of the Christian congregation. A generation later, in 360, Meletius, bishop of Sebaste, was translated to Antioch, supposedly as an opponent of Nicaea. Once enthroned, he revealed that his theology was effectively Nicene, with the result that he was exiled and an uncompromising Arian named Euzoius put in his place. The majority of the Antiochene Christians, however, remained loyal to Meletius. In 364, on the accession of the Catholic emperor Jovian, Meletius and a group of Syrian bishops presented him with a statement of faith, declaring their adherence to the Creed of Nicaea of 325. Meletius then attempted to enter into communion with St Athanasius (*c*. 296–373), the great champion of Nicene trinitarian doctrine. The attempt failed, for reasons which are not clear, and Athanasius then communicated with Paulinus, who had recently been made a bishop by Bishop Lucifer of Cagliari (d. 370/1). Lucifer was himself later to found a schism, called the Luciferians, composed of those rigorist supporters of Nicaea who refused to be reconciled with penitent Arians. Thus from 364 onwards there were two Nicene bishops of Antioch: Paulinus, recognized by Alexandria and, subsequently, by Rome; and Meletius, recognized by the bishops of Asia and Syria. St Basil of Caesarea (*c*. 330–79), a friend of Meletius, laboured to have him accepted by Rome and Alexandria, and died embittered by the obstinate refusal of Pope Damasus (*c*. 304–84). Paradoxically, it was the defeat and death of the emperor Valens at Adrianople in 378 which helped to resolve the impasse, for it brought to the East the emperor Theodosius I who, when he discovered the strength of support for Meletius, accepted him as the legitimate bishop of Antioch. Meletius died unexpectedly at the Council of Constantinople of 381 and St Gregory of Nazianzus (329–89), who succeeded him as chairman, endeavoured to persuade the bishops to accept Paulinus as his successor. They refused, and nominated Flavian, thereby ensuring that the schism would continue. Paulinus continued to enjoy the support of Rome and the West, and before his death in 388 irregularly consecrated Evagrius as his successor. It was only in 393 that a council held at Caesarea in Palestine recognized Flavian, and Theophilus, the reigning bishop of Alexandria, then accepted him. Rome finally gave way some time before 398. It is sad to record that Flavian was ungenerous in his victory, and declined to recognize the orders of those whom Evagrius had ordained.

The Schism of Antioch is an excellent example of how personalities can affect the course of history. But for Paulinus' obstinacy in remaining loyal to Eustathius against the specific injunctions of the latter, it need never have arisen. If Lucifer of Cagliari had not consecrated Paulinus, or if Athanasius and Meletius had been able to agree in 364 (and the fault seems to have lain with Meletius), the division could have ended then. Again, had the bishops at Constantinople been willing in 381 to accept the urging of Gregory of Nazianzus to recognize Paulinus as Meletius' successor, the dispute would have ended. Finally, if Paulinus had not consecrated Evagrius uncanonically, the schism would have died with him. The whole story is a sad one, especially when we remember that, after 364, both Paulinus and Meletius subscribed to the Creed of Nicaea, with the result that there were two orthodox bishops in opposition in the same city, while the great sees of the Christian world, divided in their support, made little effort to bring the unhappy division to an end.

This survey of certain notable schisms in the early Church indicates the diversity of their origins. Some seem to have been essentially personal and internal, like that at Corinth, and to have been fairly easily resolved by a personal appeal. Others, like Montanism, were an expression of religious enthusiasm, innocent in itself, but distasteful to some Christians and a threat to any hope of toleration of Christianity by the Roman state,[17] so that an eventual break with the Great Church was almost inevitable. In Novatianism, and Donatism, disagreement on ecclesiastical discipline is the expression of deep underlying theological divergences about the nature and the powers of the Church which, in the case of Donatism, may have been exacerbated, though not actually caused, by social and psychological factors. Finally, the Schism of Antioch shows that, in an age of theological controversy, individual commitments and personal loyalties in a common cause could lead to deep and long-continued divisions among the great sees of Christendom, which lasted for many years and long resisted efforts to resolve them.

NOTES

1   Jerome, *On the Epistle to Titus*, 3, 11. PL 26.598.
2   Augustine, *Against Cresconius*, 2, 7, 9. PL 43.471.
3   In Cyprian, *Letters*, 74, 1. CSEL 3 (2), 799.
4   Augustine, *Letter* 36, 14, 32. PL 33.151.
5   Ambrose, *On the Sacraments*, 3, 5. PL 16.432–3.
6   'Were Ancient Heresies National or Social Movements in Disguise?',

    The Journal of Theological Studies, New Series x (1959), 280–98.
7   Greenslade, *Schism in the Early Church*, (London, SCM, 1964²) p. 98.
8   Augustine, *On Heresies*, 86. PL 42.46.
9   1 Clement, 1, 1. Text and trans. by Kirsopp Lake, *The Apostolic Fathers* (Loeb Classical Library edn), vol. 1, pp. 8–11.
10 ibid., 2, 5. Kirsopp Lake, pp. 12–13.
11 ibid., 37, 3. Kirsopp Lake, pp. 72–3.
12 Eusebius, *Ecclesiastical History*, IV, 23, 10–11. PG 20.388C–389A.
13 Greenslade, op. cit., p. 109.
14 One such was the fifth-century Church historian, Socrates Scholasticus.
15 *Theodosian Code*, XVI, 5, 21.
16 Augustine, *Psalmus contra Partem Donati* ('Psalm against the Party of Donatus'), lines 101–03 (ed. R. Anastasi, Padua 1957, p. 52).
17 'At the best the movement upheld important features of biblical Christianity; at its worst it was incredibly silly and its enthusiasm took pagan forms' (Greenslade, p. 223.).

BIBLIOGRAPHY

Cavallera, F, *Le Schisme d'Antioche*. Paris, 1905.

Evans, R F, *One and Holy. The Church in Latin Patristic Thought*. London, SPCK, 1972.

Frend, W H C, *The Donatist Church*. Oxford, Clarendon Press, 1971².

• Greenslade, S L, *Schism in the Early Church*. London, SCM, 1964².

Labriolle, P. de, *La crise montaniste*. Paris 1913.

Walker, G S M, *The Churchmanship of St Cyprian*. London, Lutterworth, 1968.

PART SIX

Church and Society

20

Pagan Perceptions of Christianity

TIMOTHY BARNES

'Blessed are ye when men shall revile you, and persecute you and shall say all manner of evil against you falsely, for my sake.'[1] Whether or not Jesus actually uttered these words, they accurately reflect what his followers in the second half of the first century believed to be their fate. When Nero needed to deflect blame from himself for the great fire of Rome in AD 64, he was able to find a scapegoat in the Christians of the city, because the general populace detested them as immoral enemies of the whole human race, so that the official story of Christian arson gained ready acceptance.[2] Three centuries later, one of the leading pagan aristocrats of Rome who died as consul-designate in December 384 was in the habit of saying to bishop Damasus: 'Make me Bishop of Rome and I will become a Christian at once'.[3]

The present chapter surveys pagan perceptions of Christianity between these two points. It has a different emphasis from Pierre de Labriolle's classic study *La réaction païenne*,[4] whose emphasis is reflected in its subtitle 'A Study of anti-Christian polemic from the first to the sixth century'. I have concentrated on social attitudes rather than explicit statements by members of the intellectual élite, and I have attempted, following the example of John Gager's *The Origins of Anti-Semitism*,[5] to capture the diversity of Graeco-Roman attitudes towards early Christianity as well as their development over the course of time. Perhaps the main novelty of my treatment is that it refrains from using the *Historia Augusta* (for example, for the private chapel of the emperor Severus Alexander), since I believe that all the references to Christianity in that work are inventions of the author, who was writing *c.* 395. My survey begins with the attitude of the ruling classes of the Roman Empire in the second century, then documents Christianity's gain of social status and intellectual respectability, and finally discusses anti-Christian polemics.

IGNORANCE, HOSTILITY AND CONTEMPT[6]

Most inhabitants of the Roman Empire in AD 100 were either unaware of or uninterested in the Christians in their midst. Even in Rome, where there had certainly been Christians since the reign of Claudius, the varied epigrams of Martial and the satires of Juvenal make no identifiable allusion to the new religion, though both authors deride Jews and Judaism. There is equally no hint of Christianity in the numerous speeches that Dio Chrysostom delivered in various cities throughout the East between *c.* 70 and *c.* 110, or in the voluminous and variegated ethical and theological writings of Plutarch of Chaeronea (*c.* 50–*c.* 120). Plutarch's silence is all the more significant since his work contains so many coincidences of thought and diction with early Christian literature.[7] Similarly, the guide to dreams which Artemidorus of Daldis composed in the middle decades of the second century has no Christians in its everyday world. Moreover, as late as the 230s Cassius Dio could complete a history of Rome down to 229 in eighty books without ever mentioning Christians. Dio's silence, however, betrays itself as both deliberate and forced when he makes Maecenas recommend the persecution of religious innovators[8] – a covert but undeniable allusion to the newly won respectability of the Church in the early third century.

Educated pagan attitudes at Rome can first be documented in three authors of the early second century. A letter of the younger Pliny, a successful orator and senator, whose correspondence reveals him as a man of relatively enlightened but conventional views, is devoted entirely to the Christians. The emperor Trajan sent Pliny as a specially appointed governor to the province of Bithynia–Pontus. There, probably in the autumn of 111, Pliny found himself sitting in judgement on people accused of being Christians. Although he had never been present at the trial of Christians, Pliny had no hesitation in punishing those who admitted that they were Christians, reasoning that their pertinacity and inflexible obstinacy deserved to be punished: the Roman citizens among them he sent to Rome, the rest he executed forthwith. Those who denied that they were Christians or ever had been, Pliny acquitted and released after they had performed a symbolic cult act and cursed Christ. But Pliny was puzzled by a third category of defendant – those who admitted that they had once been Christians but asserted that they now were no longer. He questioned them, using torture on those of servile status as was normal, and discovered only what he describes as 'a depraved and immodest superstition'. Pliny, therefore, held these apostates in prison while he consulted Trajan. The polished phrases in his letter to the emperor, with their subtle argument for clemency, mask an urgent practical question: were the prisoners still in custody to be executed or set free? In reply, Trajan laid down (or reaffirmed) the legal principle that Christianity was a capital crime, but of a unique type, in that anyone accused of Christianity would be acquitted if he performed an offering or libation to the pagan gods in court.[9]

Shortly after Pliny, his friends Tacitus and Suetonius expressed very similar opinions when describing Nero's burning of Christians in 64. Tacitus clearly believed that the Christians were innocent of the charge of setting fire to Rome: he informs his readers that, after Christ was executed by Pontius Pilate, the 'deadly superstition' spread from Judaea, 'the origin of that evil', to Rome where all the shameful excesses of the world flow together and are welcomed.[10] Suetonius for his part includes it among the neutral or praiseworthy actions of Nero that 'the Christians were punished with execution, a race of men belonging to a new and criminal superstition'.[11]

The stereotype of Christian immorality reappears in two Latin writers during the reign of Marcus Aurelius. Apuleius wrote in Carthage, but set his novel *The Golden Ass* (*Metamorphoses*), in contemporary Greece. One of its villains is unambiguously and unmistakeably depicted as a Christian. The wife of the baker who purchased the hero was the wickedest of women: she tortured her husband, she practised every vice, she was cruel, avaricious, a spendthrift and a nymphomaniac, she despised the gods in order to worship her own unique deity, and she used her devotions to deceive her husband, begin drinking at dawn and spend the whole day in an unbroken sexual orgy.[12] Fronto (100–66), the greatest Latin orator of the day and Marcus Aurelius' former tutor, is often credited with a formal 'speech against the Christians'. It seems more probable that he attacked Christianity in his lost forensic masterpiece *Against Pelops*, and that it was the mythological associations of his adversary's name that led him to associate Pelops with Christian ritual murder,

233

the cannibalism of infants and incestuous banqueting.[13] Christians had long been regarded as immoral as well as impious, but Fronto's charges of Thyestean feasts and Oedipodean intercourse added precision to the general distrust. The first Christian apologist to answer these specific charges is Athenagoras, who probably presented his *Legation on behalf of the Christians* to Marcus Aurelius in Athens in 176.[14] Moreover, Fronto's allegations appear to have been believed, at least for a time: in the pogrom at Lyon conventionally dated to 177, not only confessing Christians but also Christians who apostatized were executed.[15] This is the only known occasion when Christians who denied being Christians or performed a pagan cult act were executed: they were executed, therefore, not for being Christians, but for what Pliny called 'offences attached to the name'.[16]

A much more sympathetic attitude is exhibited by the satirist Lucian of Samosata, who mentions Christians in two works. In neither case are the Christians accused of any serious offence. On the contrary, they appear respectively as enemies and as dupes of Lucian's two main targets. Alexander of Abonuteichos, the 'false prophet', complained that Pontus was full of atheists and Christians who uttered terrible blasphemies against him and he ordered them to be driven away with stones. The festival of Alexander's new god began with the proclamation, 'If any atheist or Christian or Epicurean has come to spy on the rites, let him depart': Alexander led the expulsion of undesirables with the cry, 'Out with Christians'; to which the crowd replied, 'Out with Epicureans'.[17] This appears to be a factual report. Christians play a much larger role in Lucian's earlier account of Peregrinus who immolated himself at the Olympic Games of 165.

On Lucian's presentation, after adultery in Armenia, pederasty in Asia and rumoured parricide in his native Parium, Peregrinus went to Palestine and learned 'the wonderful wisdom of the Christians'. He soon excelled his teachers so that the Christians revered him as a god, treated him as a lawgiver and enrolled him as their official patron, all in due subordination to 'the man crucified in Palestine' whom they still worship. When Peregrinus was imprisoned for his beliefs, his co-religionists visited him, maintained him in luxury, and spent nights in prison with their 'new Socrates'. Christians even came from Asia with contributions, and Peregrinus rapidly amassed great wealth in prison. Lucian comments that Christians accept all the injunctions of 'that crucified sophist' without rational demonstration, including his command that they all be brothers and share everything: as a result any sharp operator can quickly make himself rich from them. In the sequel, Peregrinus was released by the governor of Syria, a friend of philosophy (conceivably to be identified with Bruttius Praesens, a friend of Pliny and probably an Epicurean, like Lucian himself), who saw that he sought only notoriety. Peregrinus returned to Parium, still a Christian but also now a Cynic philosopher, and publicly donated his estates to the city. He then left Parium again, supported in luxury by his fellow-Christians – until they expelled him for eating forbidden food.[18]

Lucian's picture reflects many facets of the reality described by Christian writers, but he consistently interprets what he knows only from a distance in terms of his own, Greek concepts. On an absolute scale, Lucian can hardly be characterized as favourable to Christianity, yet he avoids the customary wild allegations and presents Christians as nothing worse than credulous simpletons. An attitude intermediate between Lucian and Apuleius appears to surface in one passage in the vast output of the sophist Aelius Aristides (117–c. 185), who compares Cynic philosophers whom he is denouncing to 'those impious men of Palestine' who 'do not believe in the higher powers', and suggests that they resemble them because they too 'have defected from the Greek race, or rather from all that is higher'.[19]

The philosophers of the second century who mention Christianity do so with a mixture of intellectual contempt and moral admiration. The Stoic Epictetus, whose discourses are recorded by Arrian, who had studied with him at Nicopolis in the reign of Trajan, asked why philosophical reflection cannot remove men's fear of a tyrant when an individual can become fearless through madness and 'the Galileans from habit'.[20] Similarly, the emperor Marcus Aurelius approved of readiness for death, but recommended that it come from one's own dignified and unmelodramatic ratiocination, 'not from sheer contrariness like the Christians'.[21] Galen (c. 133–c. 200), who grew up in Asia Minor, criticized both Jews and Christians for appealing to divine authority and accepting everything on faith instead of using proper scientific methods, but he also expressed admiration for the Christians' steadfastness when facing death, for their sexual restraint, for their moderation in eating and drinking, and for their sense of justice – qualities which raised them to the level of genuine philosophers.[22]

SOCIAL AND INTELLECTUAL ACCEPTANCE

When Galen praised the Christians, probably *c.* 180, the general attitudes of society towards the Christians were already beginning to change. From the reign of Hadrian onwards a series of Greek apologists had attempted to disprove pagan calumnies. It is unlikely that many pagans ever listened to them. Yet a more confident tone can be detected in the *Apology* which Tertullian composed in Carthage in 197: he presents the Christian Church as a respectable corporation which conducts business as any Roman *curia* would, and he seeks throughout to make common cause with the cultured and educated classes of Carthage against the ignorant urban mob. Indeed, Tertullian claims that Christians already fill every stratum of Roman society, even the imperial palace and Senate.[23] In 197 he gave that boast no specific content, but fifteen years later his open letter to the proconsul Scapula reels off a list of senators, governors and imperial freedmen who are either Christians or sympathetic to Christianity, and warns the governor that if he continues to execute Christians he will decimate his own entourage.[24]

With Tertullian in Carthage, Clement and Origen in Alexandria, it became obvious to provincial pagans in the reign of Septimius Severus (193–211) that Christians could not any more be dismissed as uncultured simpletons. Hence Christian apologetic in the second century manner was no longer needed, though it finds an echo in the *Octavius* of Minucius Felix (probably composed *c.* 240), which documents the conversion to Christianity of leading citizens of the African colony of Cirta, the home town of Fronto. On the contrary, Christian intellectuals were now treated with respect. Origen was invited to an interview by a governor of Arabia; later, the empress Julia Mammaea summoned him to expound Christianity to her in Antioch; and later still, he corresponded with Octacilia Severa, wife of the emperor Philip (244–249), who had attended a Christian Easter service while a private citizen.[25]

After the first quarter of the third century, Christians were in practice rarely persecuted for their religion. Popular hostility towards them, however, may have continued to be widespread for a little longer. The attitudes of the inarticulate strata of any society are usually hard to measure, but the authentic *Acts* of the early martyrs provide an index of changing popular attitudes. In the second century, the crowd in the amphitheatre at Smyrna demanded the arrest of Polycarp, asked the Asiarch Philippus to set a lion on him, settled for burning the bishop and finally constructed a pyre themselves, while popular agitation was behind the executions at Lyon.[26] In this period it was plausible for Tertullian to claim that whenever disaster struck, the common people always reacted in the same way, by demanding 'the Christians to the lion'.[27] But the last attested outbreaks of popular fury against the Christians occurred in Cappadocia and Pontus in 235 and at Alexandria in 249.[28] It is true that the *Passion of Marianus and Jacobus* and the *Passion of Montanus and Lucius*, which appear to be contemporary accounts of the executions of Christians under Valerian in Africa in 257–9 still show the crowd jeering at Christians. But the *Acts of Fructuosus* present the bishop of Tarraco, who was martyred in January 259, as a figure loved by Christians and pagans alike, and the biographer of Cyprian claims that his hero was respected throughout Carthage and that the prospect of his execution in September 258 caused grief to pagans.[29] Fifty years later, neither the authentic *Acts* of the martyrs from the Diocletianic persecution nor Eusebius' contemporary memoir of the persecution in Palestine between 303 and 311 in his *Martyrs of Palestine* records any acts of pagan hostility towards the Christians; on the contrary, much of the local population was openly sympathetic to them and local magistrates often enforced the imperial edicts of persecution with great reluctance.

By the late third century, it is clear that the Christian church and its bishop were accepted as a normal part of the community in most cities of the Greek East and Roman Africa. The stages of this acceptance cannot be reconstructed in detail, but popular attitudes were decisively affected by the attempts of Decius in 250 and Valerian in 257/8 to compel all the inhabitants of the Roman Empire (except Jews) to sacrifice to the traditional gods for the welfare of the state. Since Christians and pagans shared a pragmatic or talismanic view of religion, the death of Decius on campaign against the Goths in 251 and the capture of Valerian by the Persians in 260 were widely interpreted as proof that the Christian God was more powerful than the traditional gods. Origen and Eusebius were typical of their age in their readiness to deduce the truth of Christianity from its observable worldly success.

ANTI-CHRISTIAN POLEMIC

The known literary polemics against Christianity share some common characteristics, but each was composed by an individual who had a specific motivation which can in principle be discovered. The first known large-scale polemic was Celsus' *True Word*, composed probably in the 160s and certainly in the East, possibly in Alexandria.[30] The greater part of the text survives as quotations in Origen's *Against Celsus*, but it cannot be assumed (as it often has been) that these quotations give an accurate overall impression of Celsus' work. On the contrary, Carl Andresen showed in 1955 that Origen largely omitted the non-philosophical parts of Celsus' work in which he had no great interest, but which were important for Celsus' general thesis. Andresen also explained in detail why Celsus wrote at all: he set out as a philosopher to refute Justin's claim that Platonism and Christianity were compatible.

Celsus presented the Church as an unpatriotic secret society whose typical members were 'wool-workers, cobblers, laundry-workers and bucolic yokels', who were able to convert 'the foolish, dishonourable and stupid, and only slaves, women and little children': Christianity was 'successful only among the uneducated because of its vulgarity and utter illiteracy'.[31] Celsus argued at length that the ancient 'true doctrine (*logos*)' had been perverted by the Jews and by the Christians, who were themselves no more than apostates from Judaism: in sum, what was intellectually acceptable in Christianity had been proved rationally by Greek thinkers, especially Plato, while what was new was irrational and usually also absurd.

More than a century after Celsus, the philosopher Porphyry composed fifteen books *Against the Christians*, the largest, most learned and most dangerous of all the ancient literary attacks on Christianity. Porphyry was dangerous because he wrote with a precise and detailed knowledge of the Bible (using a 'western text' for the New Testament), so that he could expose contradictions in the Scriptures and thus cause Christians to question their divine inspiration. He also deployed a vast scholarly knowledge of Greek literature and philosophy to criticize the Old Testament; for example, he

238

quoted Philo of Byblos to show that Hebrew religion derived from Phoenician, and he used his knowledge of Hellenistic history to construct a proof that the book of Daniel was written in the 160s BC, not in the sixth century to which it purports to belong. Porphyry attacked Origen, whom he had met in his youth, as an apostate from Greek culture, and he systematically substituted historical interpretations for Origen's allegorical exegesis of Scripture. It seems likely, therefore, that Porphyry's main target was Origen – just as that of Celsus had been Justin. Unlike Celsus, however, Porphyry could not be laughed off as an ignorant and ill-informed critic. His attack on Christianity dominated philosophical disputes between pagans and Christians until the focus of debate shifted to 'the fall of Rome' in the early fifth century.

Unfortunately, much is problematical about Porphyry's *Against the Christians*.[32] The standard edition of the fragments, by Adolf Harnack in 1916, needs complete revision. The fifty-three 'fragments' which Harnack included from the work by Macarius of Magnesia whose title is probably to be translated *'Answer-book, or the Only-begotten to the Pagans'* are not verbatim quotations of Porphyry, but Macarius' rewriting of him in the light of conditions in his own day a century later. On the other hand, new fragments have been discovered, and much more can probably be extracted from Eusebius' *Chronicle* and from his *Preparation for the Gospel* (*Praeparatio Evangelica*) and *Proof of the Gospel* (*Demonstratio Evangelica*), which together constitute a vast anonymous polemic against Porphyry; for Eusebius was writing before possession of Porphyry's work became a capital crime under Constantine. Modern estimates of the date of *Against the Christians* have ranged from 270 to *c.* 303, and it has been regarded on the one hand as a purely academic exercise and on the other as a politically motivated justification for the Diocletianic persecution. The arguments advanced in favour of a date as late as *c.* 300 lose their force if, as has recently been demonstrated, Porphyry never composed a *Chronicle* – a work which appears in all modern lists of his writings and in the standard collection of the fragments of the Greek historians. For, if Porphyry never wrote a *Chronicle*, then it follows that *Against the Christians* was used by Eusebius in the first edition of his *Chronicle*, which he probably completed before 300. However, Eusebius does not, as has universally been assumed, assert that Porphyry composed *Against the Christians* in Sicily.[33] All in all, it now seems more probable to me that Porphyry was writing in Rome between *c.* 275 and *c.* 290. Finally, the relationship of *Against the Christians* to Porphyry's fragmentary *Philosophy from Oracles* is also disputed: whereas most scholars regard the latter as an early work of Porphyry, composed before he went to Rome in 263 and hence before he met Plotinus, it has recently been argued that Porphyry wrote it in 303 'at the request of the emperor' to defend traditional religion against Christianity.

Lactantius describes two pamphleteers who attacked Christianity in Nicomedia in 303 when Diocletian initiated the 'Great Persecution'.[34] One was the magistrate Sossianus Hierocles, the other a philosopher who often dined with the emperor – and who has been identified with Porphyry himself. Hierocles ridiculed Jesus' low-class disciples and treated Jesus himself as a brigand who performed miracles inferior to those of Apollonius of Tyana, while the philosopher urged Christians to return to worship of the gods.

These two polemics had an obvious political motivation. So too did the savage attack on Christianity which the emperor Julian composed during the winter of 362/3 as he prepared to invade Persia. The content of the work, which bore the title *Against the Galileans*, is known only through quotations in the refutation which Cyril of Alexandria composed in the 430s, and of which only half survives. Hence the overall scope of Julian's work must be uncertain. However, three main themes can be disentangled: first, Julian ridiculed the notion of revelation as unnecessary and objectionable in itself; second, he attacked the Jewish concept of God and the biblical presentation of God as the protector of the Jews as crude and exclusive; and third, he criticized the 'Galileans' as Jewish apostates, and attempted to discredit the New Testament as a basis for Christian beliefs.

Julian composed *Against the Galileans* as part of a wholesale attempt to undo Constantine's establishment of Christianity as the official religion of the Roman Empire and to replace the Christian Church with what was in effect a pagan church.[35] He drew material and arguments from Celsus and Porphyry (whose work he doubtless put into circulation again): the unique feature of his attitude to Christianity was his visceral detestation of Constantine, Constantius and all that they represented in his mind. Brought up a Christian, losing his mother in infancy and most of his relatives in dynastic murders as a child, Julian came to regard Christianity as inherently evil. His most effective statement of this thesis, however, was not the open attack in *Against the Galileans*, but the covert one in his *Caesars*, also written in Antioch in the winter of 362/3. In this political satire, Constantine can find no model for his career among the gods, but when he sees Luxury and runs to her, she introduces him to Incontinence – next to whom is standing Jesus, who promises to purify seducers and murderers, the sacrilegious and unclean.[36]

After the disastrous defeat at Adrianople in 378, Julian's hints were taken up and developed into an interpretation of recent Roman history which blamed Constantine for destroying the Empire. This pagan historical apologetic, which we can see in the fragments of Eunapius, in Ammianus Marcellinus and most fully in Zosimus, equated Christianity with corruption, decadence and barbarism. Augustine answered the pagan case in his *City of God* by denying the traditional belief, common to pagans, Christians and Jews, that God rewards devotion with success in this life. But the pagan historical thesis was revived in a modified form during the sixteenth century, and it lies behind Edward Gibbon's presentation of the 'decline and fall of the Roman Empire' as the triumph of Christianity and barbarism. As a consequence, the continuing controversy over the 'conversion' of Constantine is to a large extent heir to ancient pagan perceptions of Christianity, and in particular of the first Christian emperor.

NOTES

1   Matt. 5.11 (AV), cf. Luke 6.22.
2   Tacitus, *Annals*, 15.44.
3   Jerome, *Against John of Jerusalem*, 8. PL 23.377.
4   Paris, L'Artisan du Livre, 1948[2].
5   Oxford and New York, Oxford University Press, 1983.
6   Translations of all the passages discussed in this section (and of some others too) are conveniently reproduced in S Benko, 'Pagan Criticism of Christianity during the first two centuries A.D.', *Aufstieg und Niedergang der römischen Welt* II.23.2 (Berlin and New York, De Gruyter, 1980), 1055–1118.
7   See H D Betz, ed., *Plutarch's Theological Writings and Early Christian Literature*. Studia ad Corpus Hellenisticum Novi Testamenti 3. Leiden, Brill, 1975; *Plutarch's Ethical Writings and Early Christian Literature*. Studia ad Corpus Hellenisticum Novi Testamenti 4. Leiden, Brill, 1978.

8   Dio, 52.36.
9   Pliny, *Letters*, 10.96, 97.
10 *Annals*, 15.44.
11 *Life of Nero*, 16.2, cf. 19.3.
12 *Metamorphoses*, 9.14.
13 Minucius Felix, *Octavius* 8.3–9.6; 30.2–31.2; cf. E Champlin, *Fronto and Antonine Rome* (Cambridge, Mass. and London, Harvard University Press, 1980), pp. 64–6.
14 *Legation*, 3.1, 31–32.
15 Eusebius, *Ecclesiastical History*, 5.1.14, 33.
16 *Letters*, 10.96.2.
17 *Alexander*, 25, 38: written after 180.
18 *Pereginus*, 11–16. For discussion, see H D Betz, 'Lucian von Samosata and das Christentum', *Novum Testamentum* 3 (1959), 226–37; C P Jones, *Culture and Society in Lucian* (Cambridge, Mass. and London, Harvard University Press, 1986), esp. pp. 121–3.
19 *Oration*, 3.671, Lenz-Behr: tr. from C A Behr, *P. Aelius Aristides: The Complete Works* 1 (Leiden, Brill, 1986), p. 275. Although some discussions quote much more of this passage as referring to the Christians, Aristides' use of the demonstrative pronoun 'these' after a 'those' referring to the people in Palestine seems to mark an immediate return to his main target, the Cynics.
20 *Discourses*, 4.7.6.
21 *Meditations*, 11.3. The last three words are rejected as an interpolation by P A Brunt, 'Marcus Aurelius and the Christians', *Studies in Latin Literature and Roman History* 1. *Collection Latomus* 164 (Brussels 1979), pp. 483–520.
22 R Walzer, *Galen on Jews and Christians* (London, Oxford University Press, 1949), esp. pp. 14–16.
23 *Apology*, 37.4.
24 *To Scapula*, 4.1–4; 5.1–3.
25 Eusebius, *Ecclesiastical History*, 6.19.15; 21.3–4; 36.3; 34.
26 *Martyrdom of Polycarp*, 3.2; 12–13; Eusebius, *Ecclesiastical History*, 5.1.7 ff.
27 *Apology*, 40.1–2.
28 Cyprian, *Letters*, 75.10; Eusebius, *Ecclesiastical History*, 6.41.1–9.
29 See, respectively, H Musurillo, *The Acts of the Christian Martyrs* (Oxford, Clarendon Press, 1972), nos. 14, 15, 12; Pontius, *Life of Cyprian*, 15.
30 For translations and recent studies of Celsus, see C Andresen, *Logos und Nomos. Die Polemik des Kelsos wider das Christentum* (Berlin, De Gruyter, 1955); H Chadwick, *Origen: Contra Celsum* (Cambridge, University Press, 1965[2]); R Wilken, *Christians* (1984), pp. 94–125; R J Hoffman, *Celsus: On the True Doctrine* (New York and Oxford, Oxford University Press, 1987).
31 Origen, *Against Celsus*, 1.1; 3.55, 44; 1.27.

32 Among relevant recent studies, note R M Grant, 'The Stromateis of Origen', *Epektasis*. Mélanges patristiques offerts à Cardinal Jean Daniélou (Paris, Beauchesne, 1972), pp. 285–92; T D Barnes, 'Porphyry *Against the Christians*: Date and the Attribution of Fragments', *Journal of Theological Studies* N.S. 24 (1973), pp. 424–42; R Goulet, 'Porphyre et la datation de Moïse', *Revue de l'histoire des religions* 184 (1977), pp. 137–64; A Meredith, 'Porphyry and Julian Against the Christians', *Aufstieg und Niedergang der römischen Welt* II.23.2 (Berlin and New York, De Gruyter, 1980), pp. 1119–49; B Croke, 'Porphyry's Anti-Christian Chronology', *Journal of Theological Studies* N.S. 34 (1983), pp. 168–85; R Wilken, *Christians* (1984), pp. 126–63; R Goulet, 'Porphyre et Macaire de Magnèse', *Studia Patristica* 15. *Texte und Untersuchungen* 128 (1984), pp. 448–52; B Croke, 'The Era of Porphyry's Anti-Christian Polemic', *Journal of Religious History* 13 (1984/5), pp. 1–14.

33 *Ecclesiastical History*, 6.19.2.

34 *Divine Institutes*, 5.2.3.–4.1.

35 On the historical context of the work, see G W Bowersock, *Julian the Apostate* (London, Duckworth, and Cambridge, Mass, Harvard University Press, 1978), pp. 94–105; R Wilken, *Christians* (1984), pp. 164–96. The fullest study is by W J Malley, *Hellenism and Christianity. The Conflict between Hellenic and Christian Wisdom in the* Contra Galilaeos *of Julian the Apostate and the* Contra Julianum *of St. Cyril of Alexandria.* Analecta Gregoriana 210 (Rome, Università Gregoriana, 1978).

36 *Caesars*, 336 A–B.

BIBLIOGRAPHY

Barnes, T D, *Constantine and Eusebius*. Cambridge, Mass., and London, Harvard University Press, 1981.

——, *Tertullian. A Historical and Literary Study*. Oxford, Clarendon Press, 1985².

Frend, W H C, 'Prelude to the Great Persecution: The Propaganda War', *Journal of Ecclesiastical History* 38 (1987), pp. 1–18.

Lane Fox, R, *Pagans and Christians*. Harmondsworth, Penguin, 1986; New York, Knopf, 1987.

Momigliano, A, ed., *The Conflict between Paganism and Christianity in the Fourth Century*. Oxford, Clarendon Press, 1963.

Wilken, R L, *The Christians as the Romans saw them*. New Haven and London, Yale University Press, 1984.

21

Church–State Relations

NOEL KING

THE FIRST CENTURIES

The Mothers and Fathers of the early Church, as well as their counterparts in the state, would undoubtedly have scratched their heads when asked questions about Church and State: the questions are ours.[1] Nonetheless, if we patiently study their thoughts and actions, 'the moments of encounter', they may present us with some answers.[2] There are many excellent ways of conducting the study, but it is perhaps appropriate to follow in outline the example of Eusebius, the father of Church History, and examine the sources and incidents reign by reign, drawing out general principles and understandings as they emerge.[3]

The Church in the person of her founder was born in the reign of Augustus, the inaugurator of the Roman Empire. In that same person she came face to face with the Roman power on a seat reserved by the Empire for non-citizen subjects. On Pilate's side, he was acting as a magistrate with the duty, and summary powers, to maintain the peace. As anyone who has served an imperial master knows, the first principles include 'Do something', then 'Let sleeping dogs lie'. There was also a strong Roman tradition that so long as the Roman gods received due honour and nothing was brought to the attention of the magistrates, people were free to worship as they liked. On the side of the Christians, we are able to follow the interplay of their fundamental attitudes by a study of the way in which they interpreted the Scriptures they had received and over the centuries made their own.[4] Definitive canon and method of use had to be worked out but there was always an agreed basis as community affected Scripture and Scripture community. From a very early incident and throughout, their tradition insisted that Christians

244

should give state-made things their due, but there was a point where the things of God overrode those of Caesar. At that juncture they had to refuse co-operation and receive the consequences (Matt. 22.17–21) and synoptic parallels, Rom. 12.1–3 with parallels in Tit. 3.1 and 1 Pet. 2.13–17). This is dominical and community material going back to the beginning, which they contextualized in the praxis of everyday life as well as of crucifixion and martyrdom. Beyond these basic principles the Christians discerned in Scripture a number of types and models which helped them as individuals and as corporate members of a body with a group consciousness of its own to know what was the will of God, the mind (*nous*) of Christ, the inspiration of Holy Spirit, for them in any situation involving the state. They could on the basis of the Pentateuch and other Jewish writings think of a theocracy. (Here one may pursue their exegesis of passages like Deut. 17.14–20 and Phil. 3.20). They could think of a king who was not of their community through whose Empire God had a cosmic plan in which they, exiled and suffering, were a vital part. (Passages like Isa. 44.24–45 were disproportionately important.) This kind of attitude was taken up strongly in Luke and Acts. There are unlucky episodes and finally we must put God first, but Church and Empire have much in common and can be useful to one another. At the opposite pole there could be a regime where evil had taken over and total resistance was necessary. The use of arms was a thinkable possibility. Here passages in Daniel are very influential especially as they are reinforced by 1 Maccabees and Revelation, and other such works which had some difficulties getting into the canon but exercised great influence. In the fourth century onwards the righteous king like David (1 Samuel and various Psalms) came into his own. He was an anointed member of the people (*laos, populus*); though not a priest he had a special sacral role. To us it is remarkable but the Fathers were able to see in the saying 'here are two swords' (Luke 22.38) a prefiguring of the twin powers of Church and state. Lastly, it is most important to note that the Christians (as well as everyone else) totally accepted the view that finally Church and State was a place where God (gods) and Devil (demons) met and contended.

Jesus suffered under Pontius Pilate in the reign of Tiberius 14–37. Under the next emperor, Claudius, it is reported that at Rome in 49 the Jews, stirred up by one Chrestus (Christus?), were rioting and were expelled for a while.[5] The Jews still had their special position under the agreements of the previous century and the authorities (along with many others) tended to confuse the Christians with them. The genocides of 66–70, 115, and 132–135 differentiated the two, and modified the position of the Jews. So far as we can tell there was no definition of the position of the Christians.

Under Nero (54–68), according to a number of reliable church traditions, Peter died by crucifixion and Paul by the sword.[6] Tacitus (died *c.* 116), an experienced Roman public servant, writing in the latter part of his life, records that a great number of Christians were put to death with particular cruelty by Nero as a means of diverting responsibility for the Great Fire of Rome in 64.[7] Again there seems to be no full-scale follow-up, but a precedent had been set. Some think a general law was passed, but most of the specialist scholars doubt its existence.

Coming in about 112 from the side of the Roman state, Pliny's *Letter to Trajan* (98–117) in its robust rhetorical Latin brings us to some firmer ground.[8] Pliny had investigated the Christians as part of his task as a special commissioner in Bithynia-Pontus on one of the lines of communication for action against Persia. He reports his findings, reviews his methods, and asks for further instructions. For him the basic problem seemed to be whether Christianity in itself was a crime or just a 'depraved and immoderate superstition'. The emperor in reply said Pliny had done well. He cites no definite rule beyond saying that if people were accused and convicted they had to be dealt with. From the legal point of view this is a somewhat slippery reply. Other such material and gleanings concerning the legal position are available, and have given rise to a lively and complicated modern critical debate which should be followed up as opportunity permits.[9]

On the Christian side, the martyrdom literature begins to flow in from the mid second century onwards. It is rich in phenomena reflecting Church-state relations at every level. It includes *Acta*, that is reports of trials, as well as 'Martyrdoms' proper, write-ups, usually by a contemporary, with comment. It has to be remembered that the purpose of the latter is hagiographic, seeking to establish a saint-hood, rather than to narrate history, though they may do that too. As a whole they form one of the best examples of a subaltern literature, that is, material coming from an under-class which is normally voiceless. The accounts we get of martyrdoms in connection with military service which trickle and then flow in from the late second century onwards are of particular value to anyone studying the relationship of Christianity and the use of force and violence.

The Apology literature also begins to become available. As early as Melito of Sardis (extracts from whose *Apology*, written in the 170s, are extant in Eusebius) we can discern the theory that Christianity and the Roman Empire are partners, that good emperors could not harm Christians unless they were deceived, and that both Church and Empire began under Augustus and the presence of the Christians has prospered the Romans. Justin (martyred in 165) shows in his *Apology* how compatible Christianity is with Greek philosophy and much of Graeco-Roman life and culture. In the East this literature is continued in part in the work of Origen (died as a result of torture in persecution, *c.* 253/4) and Eusebius. It owes much to Philo and Platonic thought as well as to Luke/Acts. The Latin Apologists such as Tertullian are not as friendly to the Roman state but insist Christians are not a menace to it.

A HALF-CENTURY OF CONFRONTATION AND PEACE (235–85)

Our notes on the legal situation and the martyrdom and apology literatures have carried us to the reign of Marcus Aurelius (161–80). The time of his successor, Commodus (180–92), was in the main peaceful for the Church. From these times forward the writings of major figures like Irenaeus of Asia Minor and Gaul (*c.* 130–*c.* 200), Origen of Egypt and Palestine (*c.* 185–253/4) and Tertullian of Roman Africa (*c.* 160 until after 220) and many great successors in the tradition become available, providing a great deal of between-the-lines information about the Church's attitude to the state as well as general background.

Commodus was followed by Septimus Severus (193–211), a soldier from Africa. He seems to have determined to inhibit conversion, for most of the martyrs of whom we hear are either in training or newly baptized. The rest of his dynasty which lasted to 235, were friendly to Christianity. Up till this third decade of the third century the Empire had enjoyed a period of relative prosperity. The government had felt strong and secure enough to be tolerant of a good measure of non-conformity; then disastrous internal and external threats arose. In 260 the Persians captured the Roman emperor

247

himself and displayed him in a cage till executed. A Gothic break-through led on to an attack on Rome in 248 and the invasion of Cappadocia in 254. In 252 there was a frightening outbreak of the plague. This was the very time when the Church was suddenly increasing in numbers, resources and confidence, especially in Africa, Egypt, Syria, Palestine and Asia Minor.

Between 235 and 260 a succession of very powerful assault on the Church was launched by the state. Here there is only room to mention that in 247 the Thousand Year Celebrations of Rome were held. Soon after that Decius (249–51), a conscious reviver of the old Roman virtues, demanded that everyone sacrifice to the Roman gods and obtain a *libellus* (certificate) to that effect. (Some of them in their original papyrus form have come down to us.) The onus for the task was placed on the local authorities, who responded with energy and enthusiasm. In 251 Decius was killed in the noble Roman occupation of fighting barbarians. Although his immediate successors did not continue persecution, in 257 Valerian in his turn rounded on Christians and in the next years took sterner and more systematic measures, but in 260 he was captured by the Persians. His son Gallienus (260–8) gave the Christians peace. He restored their property, and they now clearly had the right to exist as a corporate property-owning body.

That peace lasted to the end of the century. It is worthy of note that Aurelian (270–5), who seems to have led Roman religion towards a vague sun-god monotheism, was petitioned by the Greek-speaking bishops of the area to decide whether Paul of Samosata, whom they had deposed, was to be allowed to go on living at Bishop's House at Antioch. Paul as a bishop of Antioch had been friendly towards Zenobia, Queen of the Arabs whom Aurelian had defeated and led captive. The emperor ruled that whoever the bishops of Rome and Italy approved of should take possession. Beneath Constantine's basilica on the Vatican a mosaic of about this time can be seen which depicts Christ with the rays and the chariot of the sun-god. There seemed to be some alternative ways of symbiosis between Church and state opening up; but then at the end of the century the Empire again turned on the Church with the fiercest and most sustained effort to obliterate it that had been tried so far.

FROM THE DIOCLETIANIC RECONSTRUCTION TO THE PROSCRIPTION OF PAGANISM (285–392)[10]

On coming to the purple in 285 Diocletian was determined to save the Empire. He set out to reorganize everything from top to bottom, including the supreme rulership itself. Inevitably state policy towards Christianity would have to come on the agenda. One answer would have been to impose what William Frend had well termed the *millet* system. By this, religious groups which did not follow the official religion were placed under their own head who had power over them but was responsible for their good behaviour. It is the kind of policy which could be behind the one, of toleration and freedom for all pursued by Galerius, which the Church Fathers Athanasius and Hilary of Arles advocated in the 340s, or that pursued by Valentinian I (364–75).[11] Whatever may have been the case, Diocletian let himself be sucked into a long drawn-out attack on the Christians. Terrible as it was to the Christians of the day, a latter-day wisdom can point out that it was never enforced Empire-wide, nor kept up consistently in any one place for a sufficient period of time, nor did it make effective use of the local and popular support which would have been easily available. The era of persecution was ended by Galerius' Edict of 311 and the Edict of Milan of Licinius and Constantine of 313.

The discussion as to why the Roman government did not wipe out Christianity will never be settled. Constantine, who since 306 had first in the west and then on a wider scale shown friendliness and favour to Christianity, felt his way to a means by which he as Roman emperor could gain the enthusiastic support of the Church. This is not to question his sincerity nor his megalomania for Rome as well as for Constantine. In 324 he defeated his last military opponent and became sole ruler of the Roman world. He called a council, which met at Nicaea in 325 and gave the Church decisions which are to this day definitive for the majority of Christians. His patronage of Christian charitable and welfare institutions and scholarship had indelible effects on the religion. In Eusebius of Caesarea he found a Christian thinker, writer and organizer who could help him lay out ideas.

While remaining first and foremost a Roman emperor he began the Christianization of the imperial system. He made Constantinople, a city with few visible traces of its non-Christian past, the new

Rome, which retained the old traditions and yet could last till 1453. There he set up a cultus of emperor veneration which was a transposition of the Diocletianic system and which apparently most Christians could accept. The Christians were comparatively few in number, the old gods still had vast riches and power and could mount a powerful army as late as 394, but even so the energy and new life for Rome that the Christians brought was immense. Yet from his nephew Julian to many in our own day who love Christianity or admire Rome, he was an unutterable villain. As for what happened to the Church thanks to Constantine, one may cite the venerable chestnut of the Oxford Examination Schools: '"Constantine's career was the erratic boulder that diverted the stream of Christian History." Discuss.' From the beginning some Christian voices were raised against the Constantinian take-over, not all with the robust ring of the African Donatist question: 'What has the Emperor to do with the church?'[12] But the same commands to obedience and submission to worldly authority, so long as it does not cut across God's requirements, which could so easily fetter Christians under non-Christian authorities, could as easily shackle them under rulers and powers that called themselves Christian.

At about the time of Constantine important additional sources which greatly enrich our understanding become available in a sufficient quantity for us to make easy use of them. Non-literary remains become more plentiful. It is one of William Frend's most eminent contributions to our subject that for over forty years he has consistently used them and pointed out their importance. In his case also it is based on field-work which few can match. Archaeological remains tell us of the strength, vigour and growing prosperity of the Church. Sarcophagi, ivory carvings, gold and silver objects, and mosaics tell of a vast inflow of finance and artistic talent. Coins are highly interesting though it is sometimes hard to interpret their significance. Another valuable source which becomes available from Constantine onward to Theodosius II is the *Theodosian Code*. This collects the laws passed by the emperors giving date and place of issue. Book XVI is devoted to church affairs. It is indeed an eerie sensation to find Christian tenets being promulgated in this way and the methods of the Roman police state being applied.[13]

FROM THE THEODOSIAN SETTLEMENT AND THE BARBARIAN INVASIONS ONWARDS TOWARDS ISLAM

Bearing in mind the metaphor of the Church's stream being diverted by an erratic boulder (Constantine) we may glance over what happened in the rest of the fourth century as the Roman Empire went on its way as Christian Roman Empire, and the Church which took its rise in Galilee and Judaea received the full effluence of the Graeco-Roman world. Constantine's son, Constantius II, continued his father's policies in his own way.[14] It is alleged that he exclaimed, 'Let my will be the canon.'[15] It is certain he gave a great deal of informed thought to theology, and indeed, there is reason to believe that he represented the views of many Christians as faithfully as Athanasius, Hilary and their friends represented others. Julian (360/361–3) succeeded Constantius, apostatized from Christianity and set out to resuscitate the old religion, but he was soon killed in battle against Persia. Even so he showed how much life 'paganism' still had.[16] His successor, Jovian, reigned but a short time. Valentinian (364–75), as mentioned above, chose freedom of religion for all. His brother and colleague Valens (364–78) moved in a more Arian direction. The empress Justina, Valentinian's second wife and widow, guardian of the young Valentinian II, was also of Arian tendency. She met the implacable opposition of Ambrose, bishop of Milan (373–97). The empress had to back down.

When in 378 Valens was struck down by the Goths in the greatest defeat the Roman arms had suffered since Hannibal, Valens' son Gratian called Theodosius (379–95) to the purple. He had grown up in a Christian family and was under strong non-Arian, Nicene, influence. Early in his reign, being in fear of death by illness, he received baptism. At the Council of Constantinople in 381 he re-expressed through the bishops the decisions of Constantine's Council of Nicaea of 325. Through the law and the use of *coercitio* (coercion) strenuous efforts were made to follow up the decisions, so that the officially recognized party would possess the property, collect the largesse and have the opportunity of teaching the hordes who flocked in.

Theodosius came twice from Constantinople, his definitive capital, to the West. A study of the encounters between Ambrose of Milan and Theodosius tells us a great deal about the thinking which lies behind the Church and State relationship at this time. At one side

251

there is Theodosius as a Roman ruler who is a Christian. In 390 in a fit of rage he had ordered a massacre at Thessalonica. Ambrose forced him to do penance and ask forgiveness. Ambrose's honour-giving and diffidence is evident throughout. But he clearly indicates that officials (*comites*) and bishops have separate spheres. Where they break in on one another, the churchman is superior, just as God is superior to Caesar. It is also enlightening to carry out a comparison of the views and fate of Ambrose with those of John Chrysostom, bishop of Constantinople from 398 to 404. He was force-marched to death in the snow for having dared to denounce the empress Eudoxia as a Jezebel and Herodias.

Towards the end of his reign (391–2) Theodosius issued laws against paganism.[17] Christian mobs had already been allowed in parts of the Empire to demolish temples. In 391 the great Serapeum at Alexandria was sacked. On their side the pagans at last came out in battle array against Theodosius and the battle of the Frigidus in 394 was seen by both sides as a life and death struggle between Jupiter and Hercules against Christ. The Roman Empire and the Roman religion had in-theory once more been made one thing; whether religion or politics had triumphed no one can say. Nor indeed was the writ of the Empire valid everywhere. Rome fell before the Germanic tribes in 410. The western Empire weltered down to centuries of barbarian chaos where often the local church had to take on government functions. The Goths, thanks to Constantius II and Justina, were Arians, and so the elision of Catholic sacral monarch and Germanic sacred kingship had to wait for the conversion of pagan tribes like the Anglo-Saxons and Franks. In the meantime together with the use of purple, the title Pontifex Maximus, the tendency to bureaucratic centralization and the buildings and pre-stige of old Rome, the papacy, while remaining basically grounded in the spiritual, could take over a great deal of Roman emperorship. Now in the West the doctrine of the two swords could be taken up, with the pope sometimes carrying both. The stage was set for the great medieval drama of pope and Holy Roman emperor. However, we must never suppose that there was no separation of Church and state in the East and no 'Byzantine caesaro-papism' (or papal-caesarism) in the West.

In the East at Constantinople the Christian Roman Empire settled down to a way of life which went on till 1453, and in some ways in Russia till 1917. Church and state were very closely involved with one another. Questions of doctrine were reflected in politics and in the faction struggles in the hippodrome. Equally, politics were reflected in the inmost life of the Church. Amongst other things, suddenly for a while the veil is lifted from at least a fraction of women's power, majesty and sacrality in Church affairs.[18] Perhaps a greater than Constantine is to be discerned in the Augusta Pulcheria (399–451) who was vastly influential in two ecumenical councils, Ephesus 431 and Chalcedon 451. As the emperorship was demilitarized, she was able to use virginity and charity as mighty political weapons.

This has been a survey of Church and state in the Roman Empire in the first four centuries. It is valuable to remind ourselves that Armenia was a Christian state from the time of King Tiridates (274–316). We may compare Christianity in Ethiopia. We may contrast the position of Christians in Persia as they poised themselves for their outreach across Asia to China. We have barely mentioned the position of the Christians in the East (one could add Egypt and North Africa) when the Muslims came. In India we may speculate that the Christians of St Thomas found a way of survival and service.[19]

As the stream of the Church enters a new century when most of its volume will flow in from Africa and Latin America (may we hold Constantine and his ilk responsible for the omission of China and India?), Christianity as well as her opponents look back to the first centuries. On her part this is not to learn to imitate or to find precedents but to discover the mind which guided her spiritual ancestors in their situation. It is possible that Christians have not changed much between on the one side the *ministrae* (women clergy, slave girls?) who stood up so well to Pliny's tortures and Janani Luwum, archbishop of Uganda, who, calling on Christ, at Amin's order was shot in the groin by a henchman with trembling hands, and had to be despatched by the master himself. On the other are the *libellatici* with their little certificates obtained by betrayal or bribery or some televangelists with their 'checks'.

NOTES

1   '*Mothers and* Fathers': a wonderful band of younger Church historians are continuing the work of indicating that the 'Mapatristic' Age was no male preserve nor indeed a bedroom whence females manipulated

husbands and sons. However for brevity the older expression will be used as a collective term. Again it is not used in the 'Dads and Bads', sense of 'orthodox' versus 'heretic' or 'schismatic'.

2 The reader should fill out this brief and summary survey with a standard early Church history such as W H C Frend's *The Rise of Christianity* (London, Darton, Longman & Todd, 1984), supplemented for the period before Constantine by his *Martyrdom and Persecution in the Early Church* (Oxford 1965). It is also most valuable to read the related documents in the editions and translations now available or at least in collections such as those of Stevenson.

3 Eusebius of Caesarea in Palestine *c.* 269–*c.* 339. On most of the names mentioned, see F L Cross and E A Livingstone, eds, *Oxford Dictionary of the Christian Church* (Oxford University Press 1974).

4 For a summary of the Church's inheritance on the subject see T M Parker, *Christianity and the State in the Light of History* (London, A & C Black, 1955). Considerations of space have forced us to omit a long section on the history of exegesis (*Auslegungsgeschichte*). The *Centre national de la recherche scientifique* is publishing a kind of concordance of the patristic use of the Bible. *Biblia Patristica* (vol. 1, Paris, appeared in 1975 and others have followed). Much more computer-based wizardry is expected. For an expert's use of this art or science see Aland in the article cited in the Bibliography.

5 Suetonius, who died in 140, and served as a high official under Hadrian, writing in his *Life of Claudius*, 25.4.

6 Clement of Rome, *First Letter to the Corinthians*, 5–6; Tertullian, *On the Prescription of Heretics*, 36; Eusebius, *Ecclesiastical History*, 2.25.5–8; and apparently continuous local tradition.

7 Tacitus, *Annals*, 15.44.2–8. Compare Suetonius, *Life of Nero*, 16.2.

8 Pliny, *Letters*, X 96. Trajan's reply is No. 97.

9 For full details of the many encounters and documents not mentioned by us (including possible events under Domitian especially in the year 96) and the *Letters* of Ignatius of Antioch, the rescripts of Antoninus Pius and Marcus Aurelius as well as a *senatusconsultum* ('*decree*') relevant to persecution in *c.* 177, see P Keresztes in 'The Imperial Roman Government and the Christian Church', in the volume of *Aufstieg und Niedergang* mentioned below.

10 W H C Frend in *The Rise of Christianity* gives this period detailed description and analysis; for he considers that the fundamental victory of the Christians came during these events.

11 Ammianus Marcellinus, XXX.9.5: '*inter religionum diversitates medius stetit*', 'He stood in the middle between the diversities of the religions.'

12 *Quid est imperatori cum ecclesia?*, quoted in Optatus of Milevis, *On the Donatist Schism*, 3.3., PL 11.999.

13 The best text remains T Mommsen, and P M Meyer (3 vols in 2, Berlin, 1905); for a translation see C Pharr, *The Theodosian Code* (Princeton 1952).

14 See especially S L Greenslade, *Church and State from Constantine to Theodosius*, London, Greenwood Press, 1981.

15 Anthanasius, *History of the Arians*, 33, PG 25.732.

16 The word 'pagan' is not used pejoratively; it is a useful short label to indicate the followers of the old gods.

17 *Theodosian Code*, 16.10.10 and 11 of 391 stopped sacrifices in Rome and Alexandria. 16.10.12 from late in 392 was more of an all-out attack and proscription.

18 K G Holum, *Theodosian Empresses, Women and Imperial Dominion in Late Antiquity* (Berkeley, University of California Press, 1982), gives an excellent lead in to the study of some of these women.

19 W H C Frend's *Rise of the Monophysite Movement* (Cambridge University Press 1972) brilliantly covers the ground to Justinian's age (527 –65), goes forward to Pope Gregory (d. 604) and comes to the emperor Heraclius' 'long farewell' to the lands south of the Mediterranean as Islam takes over.

BIBLIOGRAPHY

Aland K, 'Das Verhältnis von Kirche und Staat in der Frühzeit', in *Aufsteig und Niedergang der Römischen Welt* 2, 23, 1, eds. W. Haase and H Temporini (Berlin and New York, Walter de Gruyter, 1979), pp. 60–246.

Frend, W H C, *Martyrdom and Persecution in the Early Church*. Oxford, Basil Blackwell: New York, New York University Press, 1965 and 1967.

——, 'Church and State, Perspectives and Problems in the Patristic Era', in E A Livingstone, ed., *Studia Patristica*, vol. XVIII (Oxford and New York, Pergamon Press, 1982), pp. 38–54.

——, *The Rise of Christianity*. London, Darton, Longman & Todd, 1984.

Stevenson, J, new edn rev. Frend, W H C, *A New Eusebius: Documents Illustrating the History of the Church to AD 337*, London, SPCK, 1987.

——, ed., new edn rev. Frend W H C, *Creeds, Councils and Controversies: Documents Illustrating the History of the Church, AD 337–461*. London, SPCK, 1989.

22

Christian Attitudes to Poverty and Wealth

BONIFACE RAMSEY OP

The reader of the New Testament will discover there five data that are pertinent to any discussion of poverty and wealth in the early Church. They are, first, scattered allusions to the existence of both rich and poor among the first generations of believers, such as can be seen in Jas. 2.1–7; second, a concern for alleviating the plight of the poor, which is evident, for example, in Paul's discussion of an 'offering for the saints' in 2 Cor. 9; third, an occasional but marked predisposition in favour of the poor (and against the rich), which is perhaps clearest in Luke 1.46–55, Mary's 'Magnificat'; fourth, the proposing of an ideal of voluntary poverty for the sake of Christ, as appears in Matt. 19.16–30; and fifth, two descriptions of the early Christian community, in Acts 2.44–7 and 4.32–6, which indicate that the Christians of apostolic times in Jerusalem possessed all things in common and that none of them were in need. These data, found already in the scriptural writings of the first century, were of importance throughout the history of the early Church, and how they were viewed and treated by that Church's leaders and thinkers constitutes a theme of profound and enduring significance.

It is quite understandable that, despite a sprinkling of fairly well-off persons, the Church of the first and second centuries would have been composed predominantly of the poor and the simple. Some pagan writers found fault with Christianity precisely because of its attractiveness to slaves and others without influence in the world. To Celsus, for example, in his book against Christianity in the second half of the second century, it was an indication of the new religion's fundamental lack of credibility that it did not succeed in drawing to itself a larger number of more sophisticated persons.[1] Most Christians, however, saw the matter differently. It was all the more remarkable, they asserted, that a religion claiming a crucified criminal as its founder and propagated by poor and ignorant men should have spread as quickly as it did.

Moreover, consonant with and enlarging upon the New Testament notion that the poor enjoyed God's favour in a way that the rich did not, Christian thinkers attributed great intercessory power to the prayers of the poor and declared that the rich who were generous to the poor would be saved by their beneficiaries' appeals to God on their behalf. In this regard the second-century visionary Hermas developed a famous image that may serve as representative of much of early Christianity's attitude toward the respective positions of rich and poor. Hermas said that the poor were like a vine and that the rich were like an elm tree. The vine, in order to produce healthy fruit, needs to climb up the elm tree; it is thus, vicariously, that the elm tree bears fruit, for by itself it is barren. So the rich, who are themselves spiritually lacking but who support the poor, make it possible for the poor to produce enough spiritual fruits for both of them. It is clear from this, as from numerous other early Christian writings, that a sort of mystique enveloped the persons of the poor. So true was this, indeed, that some writers and preachers felt obliged to point out that mere poverty was of itself not equivalent to holiness and that the poor could be as capable of wrongdoing and of avarice as the rich.

In this kind of atmosphere the rich found it necessary to justify their possession of wealth. The urgency to do so was all the greater in view of Christ's words in Matt. 19.24 to the effect that a rich person could no more be saved than could a camel go through the eye of a needle. It fell to Clement of Alexandria, in a sermon delivered at the end of the second century and known to posterity as *The Rich Man's Salvation* (*Quis dives salvetur?*), to relieve the unease of the rich and to offer the first extended argument in favour of the Christian possession of wealth. Commenting on the gospel story of the rich young man in Mark 10.17–30, Clement confidently asserted that Christ's words there about the dangers of wealth were to be taken in a spiritual and not a literal way. Christ was concerned not lest Christians own wealth but lest they be preoccupied with it. He could not possibly have intended that the rich give up all their possessions, for, if they did, they would no longer be able to accomplish the good that can only be accomplished by those who have many resources at their disposal. This reasonable interpretation of the gospel message, which however removed all of its passion, became in one form or other the classic justification for the ownership of wealth by Christians. Not everyone accepted it, however, and Clement's exegesis existed in a sometimes very uneasy tension with the more literal interpretation of Christ's words.

Clement's argument on behalf of wealth, which was embraced by the vast majority of the Church's members, turned on the understanding that wealth was legitimate if it was used for the achievement of good. This good use of wealth was known as almsgiving, but often it was referred to in more theological fashion as 'mercy' or 'charity'. Several treatises, beginning with Cyprian of Carthage's mid-third-century *On Good Works and Almsgiving*, and hundreds of sermons devoted to this practice have survived from Christian antiquity. Besides telling us that wealth has its raison d'être in helping the poor, they also inform us that the poor themselves were obliged to give alms to those who needed them, if not in the shape of money then in some other way. Augustine provides perhaps the most extensive list of possible almsdeeds in his *Enchiridion*, including not only feeding the hungry and clothing the naked but also carrying the crippled and comforting the sorrowful, which were things that those without monetary resources could do.[2] Almsgiving, it may be said, was the ordinary way of evening out at least some of the inequities caused not only by social status but by nature and the human condition as well. Its practice was recommended throughout the year; indeed, the earliest detailed description of the eucharistic liturgy, given by Justin Martyr in the middle of the second century, tells us that a collection for the poor was taken up every Sunday on a voluntary basis. In Lent, though, almsgiving was urged on Christian congregations with particular insistence. The sermons preached at that season rarely fail to mention it, and they frequently link it with two other practices – namely, prayer and fasting – to form a kind of canonized triad of good works. Yet, of the three, almsgiving was by far the most important. 'Almsgiving is to fasting what the sun is to the day', declares the fifth-century preacher Peter Chrysologus.[3] And the late fourth-century Chromatius of Aquileia tells his listeners that 'if we wish our prayers to be heard by the Lord we ought to commend them with good works and alms'.[4]

It is in the context of appeals to give alms that we read the most vivid descriptions in early Christianity of the condition of rich and poor. 'As I was crossing the squares and streets of the city in order to come to your gathering', John Chrysostom relates to his congregation at Antioch in a late fourth-century sermon, 'I caught sight of the wretches lying in the cross-roads, some of them missing their hands and others their eyes, still others covered with ulcers and incurable sores, displaying parts of their body that they ought to have covered because of the matter running from them, and I thought that it would be utterly inhuman not to mention this to your charity.'[5] Ambrose's depictions of poverty in his treatise *On Naboth* (which seems originally to have been homiletic material) are striking. In one passage he contrasts vividly the dire need of the poor and the heartless indifference of the rich: 'A naked man cries out before your house and you ignore him. A naked man cries out and you worry about what kind of marble to clothe your floor with. A poor man asks for money and you have none. Someone is looking for bread and your horse champs on a golden bit. Your precious ornaments delight you, while others want for grain.'[6] And if the condition of the poor was tragic, that of slaves was even worse, since they had very little recourse from cruel masters. The early fifth-century bishop Maximus of Turin complains in a sermon:

> These days a Christian master does not spare his Christian slave ... There are many who, on returning from the hunt, pay more attention to their hounds than to their slaves. Not caring if their slaves die of hunger, they have their hounds recline or sleep next to them while they themselves feed them a daily portion. And, what is worse, if the food has not been well prepared for them, a slave is slain for the sake of a dog. In some homes you may see sleek and fat dogs running around, but human beings going about wan and faltering. Will such persons even take pity on the poor when they are without mercy for their own households?[7]

Allowing for some rhetorical exaggeration, we have every reason to believe that such descriptions were basically true to the facts.

In the face of the injustices that the leaders of the Church of the fourth and fifth centuries in particular speak and write eloquently about, few offered solutions more radical than almsgiving. Some of them, most notably Ambrose and John Chrysostom, suggested that wealth was wicked at its very source because it represented the usurpation by a very few people of goods that God had originally intended to be at the disposition of everyone. Such leaders might occasionally preach a sermon espousing a return to the condition of perfect commonalty that they felt sure had primordially existed, but this was just as often offset by other words elsewhere, from the very same preachers, to the effect that private wealth was legitimate so long as it was properly used.

It is important to observe here, by way of explanation, that early Christian social thought was by and large conservative. It would be a mistake to attribute this conservatism exclusively or even principally to the fact that from the beginning some Christians were rich and owned slaves and that certainly by the middle of the fourth century, if not before, the Church itself could boast of possessing extensive and valuable property, and its priests and bishops had in many places become persons of the highest social status, thanks to the pro-Christian policies of Constantine and most of his successors. We know that the pursuit of wealth and status contributed to the Church's decadence. Cyprian complained that their frantic acqui-sition of property was the reason why so many Christians, including bishops, renounced their faith in the Decian persecution of the early 250s; they were more willing to give up their faith than to part with their wealth. More than a century later the pagan historian Ammianus Marcellinus wrote critically of Roman clergy who 'are enriched with gifts from matrons, go about seated in carriages, are clothed in style and serve banquets so rich that their suppers outdo the tables of kings'.[8] It is true that the existence of such wealth within the Church, or at least the access to such wealth, must have helped make the Church socially conservative. But it is also true that this conservatism was part and parcel of the ancient mentality – Chris-tian, pagan and Jewish – and that it was highly uncommon for the basic structure of the social order to be questioned even by those who suffered the most from the consequences of that order. Christians and others were more likely to accept social inequalities simply as belonging to the divine arrangement of things, which was an attitude that could have a fatalistic tinge to it. Christians in particular would have believed, in any event, no matter how they behaved to the contrary, that everything which pertained to this earth was only transitory and that one's status in eternity was far more important than one's status in time. This belief served, at least to some degree, to relativize the sufferings of life and to make attempts to eliminate them seem gratuitous. Added to this conservatism was an occasional tendency, inherited from Stoic thought, to romanticize the lot of the poor and to compare it favourably with the worries and preoccupations of the rich. Finally, as has already been mentioned, many held that the poor were indeed spiritually better off as they were.

In contrast to this widespread view of poverty and wealth, which tolerated the existence of poverty and was not adverse to that of wealth, there stood – leaving aside a few inconsistent statements by men like Ambrose and Chrysostom – two important movements, both ascetical, but one unorthodox and the other orthodox. For neither of them was mere almsgiving an adequate response to the reality of things.

The unorthodox movement, to call it such, was in fact represented by several different groups which insisted that the possession of wealth was incompatible with the pursuit of a Christian life. In the middle of the fourth century Cyril of Jerusalem alludes to heretics, otherwise unnamed, who considered riches accursed. At about the same time a synod held in Gangra in Paphlagonia (in present-day north-central Turkey) condemned a group of ascetics known as Eustathians, who held more or less the same opinion. At the beginning of the fifth century the Pelagians, or at least some of them, taught that Christ's words in Matt. 19.21 ('If you would be perfect, go, sell what you possess . . .') had to be observed literally by those who wished to be saved. Yet even the Eustathians, the Pelagians and others were ultimately more concerned with saving the rich than with helping the poor; theirs was a call not for the radical restructuring of society but rather for the re-establishment of an inner moral order that happened to have outer ramifications. In other words, according to them, the wealthy would have had to divest themselves of their riches even if the poor did not exist. In any event, this radical rejection and condemnation of wealth never succeeded except at the fringes of Christian society; mainstream Christianity could in principle accept the rejection of wealth, but it could never agree to its condemnation.

The second, orthodox, movement, on the other hand, penetrated, into the very fibre of Christianity. Although it too was concerned more with eternal salvation than with temporal society, it in fact made an enduring impression upon the latter. This movement was monasticism.

According to one of the key documents of primitive monasticism, *The Life of Saint Antony*, written by Athanasius of Alexandria in the 350s,[9] the movement effectively began when Antony, then a middle-class adolescent in rural Egypt, was musing one day on his way to church over the description in the Acts of the Apostles of the earliest Christians' communal life. When he finally arrived in church he heard Matt. 19.21 being read and, feeling that the passage was being addressed directly to him, forthwith determined to take it seriously, and so sold his property and went off into the desert. The model of the early Christian community and Christ's own words about voluntary poverty are thus crucial elements in the formation of monasticism; and with these two elements, among others, the monastic founders built a system that perhaps came closer than any other to being the ideal Christian society.

Antony and the disciples that he eventually gathered around himself were solitaries, but other founders, notably Pachomius and Basil the Great, established coenobitic (or communal) monasteries. Pachomius' foundation in Egypt was marked by a rigid organization and by a striving for an austere material self-sufficiency. Basil's, outside Caesarea in Cappadocia, had a social thrust and included the operation of facilities for the sick and for travellers. Both involved hundreds and even thousands of monks, all living in accordance with what they perceived to be the apostolic ideal, none of them possessing anything much more valuable than a few books. In these communities, as well as among the solitaries, the breaking of one's commitment to voluntary poverty was looked upon with severity, and a dead monk in whose cell some gold coins had been found might be denied Christian burial and considered as good as damned. With time, however, even the strictest monasteries, like the Church at large, came to possess extensive property and to enjoy a corresponding prestige. This seemed to be an inevitable development.

It has been remarked by several scholars that the beginning of the monastic movement coincided with a period of terrible financial decline in the Roman Empire, and that many of the earliest monks were men whose primary preoccupation was to escape the burdens of taxation and of a static society that offered little or no opportunity for advancement. Some of the surviving texts in fact suggest this, but we must also give credit for idealism to these early monks, for among them there were persons who had formerly held high positions in the Empire or who had been very rich and who had no reason to flee from economic turmoil.

Concomitantly with the rise of monasticism, in the second half of the fourth century, there occurred a series of remarkable conversions that had as their most stunning aspect an option for poverty that often appeared extravagant to contemporary society. In this connection one must mention in particular Melania the Elder, Melania the Younger and her husband Pinian, the Roman senator Pammachius, and Paulinus of Nola and his wife Therasía. All of these came from noble families from Rome or elsewhere, but they rejected their pedigrees in favour of an ascetic if not precisely monastic life. Some, like Melania the Younger and Pinian, disposed of their vast wealth prodigally; others, like Paulinus and Therasía, seem to have abandoned most of theirs but still lived rather comfortably. Thanks to the monks and to persons such as these, voluntary poverty as an ascetic practice acquired a permanent place in Christian spirituality.

At about this time and in this atmosphere there began to develop, especially in the West, the notion of the poor Christ. In a famous expression that would be repeated into the Middle Ages, Jerome described the monk as one who, naked, followed the naked Christ.[10] A text from Augustine best elaborates the image. Christ, Augustine declares, is

the true poor man . . . the devout humble man who does not rely on himself, the true poor man, the member of the poor who became poor for our sake, although he was rich . . . Let us consider his poverty, lest we who are poor fail to grasp it. He is conceived in the virginal womb of a woman, enclosed in his mother's body. O poverty! He is born in a narrow shelter, placed in swaddling clothes in a manger, becoming fodder for the poor beasts. Then the Lord of heaven and earth, the creator of the angels, the one who established all things visible and invisible, takes suck, cries, is nursed, grows up, gets older, hiding his majesty all the while. After that he is seized, condemned, beaten, mocked, spat upon, struck, crowned with thorns, hung on a tree, pierced with a lance. O poverty![11]

The Sunday collection for the poor, which existed in the second century and which has already been mentioned, continued to be taken up in succeeding centuries. Tertullian writes at the end of the second century in a famous passage that it was used for the burial of paupers, the support of orphans and of old people, and the relief of those imprisoned for the faith. By the fourth century larger donations from many sources were building hospital and hostelries, known as *xenodocheia*. From the very beginning the Church also took care of widows and provided meals for the needy. Sometimes money was raised for such activities as the ransoming of hostages by selling gold and silver chalices and other altar vessels; indeed, numerous bishops recommended this. Although bishops were chiefly responsible for the poor of their dioceses, it was usually deacons who bore the brunt of the responsibility. The best known of these was Laurence, who was martyred along with Pope Sixtus II at Rome in 258 and who, according to writers a century later, had a particular love for the poor.

It may be said, in a word, that the Church did virtually everything that a large organization with charitable interests would be expected to do in the face of poverty. So formidable was its reputation in this regard that by the early 360s the pagan emperor Julian asserted that concern for the poor was a decisive element in Christianity's success in gaining converts, and he urged pagan priests to imitate their Christian counterparts in providing for the needy. But, for all its charitable work, the Church at large was never able to recapture completely the spirit of the first Christian community in Jerusalem, as described so memorably in the Acts of the Apostles. At best only restricted groups within the Church, like the monastic communities, succeeded in doing so, and even they often eventually succumbed to the temptations of property, sometimes with the best intentions and sometimes because there seemed to be no alternative. Could anything more have been realistically expected? Yet, while early Christianity may not have eliminated poverty or established a universal community of property among its adherents, it at least made a permanent contribution to eliminating the opprobrium of poverty, both material and spiritual, and to fostering the ideal of a true sharing of resources.

NOTES

1 ap. Origen, *Against Celsus*, 3.44, 55, PG 11.976–977, 993.
2 cf. *Enchiridion*, 19.72, PL 40.266.
3 *Sermon*, 8, PL 52.209.
4 *Sermon* 3.2, Corpus Christianorum: series Latina = CCSL 9A.13.
5 *Sermon on almsgiving*, 1 PG 51.261.
6 *On Naboth*, 13.56, PL 14.784.
7 *Sermon* 36.3, CCSL 23.142–3.
8 *Res gestae*, 23.3.14, Loeb Classical Library (1940), vol. 316.
9 *Life of St Antony*, 2–3, PG 26.841–5.

10   cf. *Letter*. 125/20, PL 22.1085.
11   *Sermon* 14.9, PL 38.115–16.

BIBLIOGRAPHY

Avila, C, *Ownership: Early Christian Teaching*. London, Sheed & Ward; Maryknoll, NY, Orbis, 1983.

Hengel, M, *Property and Riches in the Early Church*, tr. J. Bowden. London, SCM, 1973; Philadelphia, Fortress, 1974.

Phan, P C, *Social Thought*, Message of the Fathers of the Church 20. Wilmington, Del., Michael Glazier, 1984.

Ramsey, B, 'Almsgiving in the Latin Church: The Late Fourth and Early Fifth Centuries', *Theological Studies* 43 (1982), 226–59.

Walsh, W J, and Langan, J P, 'Patristic Social Consciousness – The Church and the Poor', in J. Haughey, ed., *The Faith that Does Justice* (New York, Paulist, 1977), pp. 113–51.

PART SEVEN

Finding the Early Church

23

Patristic Historiography

JILL HARRIES

Ecclesiastical history was a new way of looking at the past which sprang, fully-formed, from the head of Eusebius of Caesarea early in the fourth century AD. That great figure stands in isolation at the start of the evolution of various forms of Christian history but it was the history of the Church that he made his own and the rules he laid down remained virtually unchanged for a century after his death. But during that century the relationship of the Church and the world was radically transformed and in the Constantinople of Theodosius II in the 430s new ideas on the purpose and identity of church history became the subject of vigorous debate. This chapter examines the historiographical achievement of Eusebius and its fate in the hands of his successors.

The reign of the pious Theodosius II from AD 408 to 450 was the longest in Roman imperial history and till recently it was regarded as one of the least distinguished. Bullied by Attila the Hun, manipulated by his wife and sisters, dominated by eunuchs and dogged by ecclesiastical controversy, Theodosius was personally uninspiring. But his reign was also a cultural watershed. In his time and partly thanks to his patronage, the Roman Empire in the Greek East witnessed an explosion of literary talent, which was particularly apparent in the field of historiography. Theodosius was the dedicatee of the pagan historian Olympiodorus of Thebes, whose account of affairs in the eastern and western Roman Empires closed with Theodosius' triumph over western usurpation in 425; and the Christian historian Sozomen, writing in or just after 443, devoted a laudatory preface to the emperor's piety, in which he showed his respect for the classical Hellenic tradition by a comparison of Theodosius with Alexander the Great, and for imperial encouragement by pointed mention of previous rewards granted to the eloquent.

It was in this complex context of the Theodosian renaissance that a major re-evaluation took place of the rules of ecclesiastical historiography laid down by Eusebius in the reigns of Diocletian and Constantine over a century before. This genre was recognized at the time as being distinct from, and narrower than, other forms of Christian history, a term which could apply to any version of past events concocted for Christian purposes. Christian histories could have a polemic purpose: soon after Augustine's attack on pagan views of the past in the *City of God* the Spanish priest Orosius wrote in 417 at the request of Augustine a seven-book history *Against the Pagans* in Latin, which used sources such as Livy, much revered by the pagans themselves, to prove that the Roman Empire had been far more subject to catastrophes under the pagans' gods than in the centuries since the birth of Christ. The object of other Christian histories is less clear. Philip of Side's Greek *Christian History* of the period from the creation to AD 430, now lost, was an encyclopaedic account in nearly a thousand volumes of everything that interested him in the world, complete with geographical and scientific excurses. The church historian Socrates, writing in Constantinople *c.* 440, emphasized that Philip's work was a Christian, not an ecclesiastical, history, and was scathing on the irrelevance of much of its contents, 'for it contains a medley of geometrical theorems, astronomical speculations, arithmetical calculations and musical principles, with geographical delineations of islands, mountains, forests and various other matters of little moment.'[1] The loss to posterity of what R A Markus described as this 'loose baggy monster' may be accepted with equanimity.

One especially important form of Christian historical writing was the *Chronicle*, which took the form of the listing of significant events, year by year. Eusebius' preoccupation with problems of chronology, a necessary preparation for the composition of his *Ecclesiastical History*, led him to become also the father of Christian chronography. Eusebius' *Chronicle* (which survives only in an Armenian version and through Jerome's translation of it into Latin) consisted of a collection of raw source material, the *Chronography*, and the *Canons*, a series of parallel chronological lists bringing Jewish/Christian history into line with the events of classical history familiar to the educated élites of the Roman world. In terms of its own time, the late third century, this assertion of an 'alternative history' was a revolutionary undertaking. The Jews, although scattered over much of the empire, had kept their history to themselves; Christians numbered perhaps one tenth of the total population of the Empire; and Jerusalem itself, renamed Aelia Capitolina in the second century, was an obscure outpost on a remote and troublesome frontier. It was a symptom, as well as in part a cause, of the cultural transformation effected by Constantine and his successors in the fourth century that continuations of Eusebius' *Chronicle*, which began with that of Jerome down to 379, were so often compiled. These continuations of Jerome and Eusebius were not mechanical records of events but reflected the interests of their authors and their personal, sometimes idiosyncratic interpretations of contemporary events. The fifth-century chronicler Hydatius, for example, relatively isolated in his Spanish bishopric, compiled a Latin continuation of Jerome down to 468, which reflected the bishop's own views of barbarian invaders and Romans and closes with a foreshadowing of the apocalypse. Another chronicler with Pelagian sympathies, writing at Marseilles after 452, complained about Augustine's 'heresy' on predestination. All such interpretations, whatever their stance on specific questions, were concerned with the underlying *providentia* of God and were an attempt at explaining his ways to men.

Although distinct in genre, Christian historiographical writings had an important bearing on church historians. They voiced the interpretations of the (often recent) past, which were current at the time of writing and which readers of, or listeners to, new works would want to hear discussed. For writers of church history in the intellectual hot-house that was fifth-century Constantinople, it would not be enough to regurgitate an updated Eusebius. Since the time of the bishop of Caesarea, the relationship between *ecclesia* (Church) and *basileia* (imperial state) had undergone a fundamental transformation. Due to the process begun by Constantine, the separation between the two was no more, and increasingly the life of the Church, which Eusebius had had no difficulty in treating as a separate entity, had permeated the life of the world. And the process had been two-way: the life and culture of the world had entered that of the Church and the great divide between Christ and Cicero, which had so tormented Jerome in the late fourth century, was now of little real importance. Eusebius himself was beyond challenge: the nearest approach to a rework of the *Ecclesiastical History* itself was a

271

two-book summary by Sozomen. But how far could the rules for the genre, laid down by the founding father of church history, survive the pressures of a changing secular and religious environment? If they were left untouched, due to characteristic Roman (and Christian) reverence for tradition, the genre might become narrow to the point of irrelevance; but, if diluted, church history might disappear altogether.

Eusebius set the pattern for subsequent church historians in two spheres, literary form and subject-matter. Following the practice of the Jewish historian Josephus, he departed from the conventions of classical historiography in his extensive citations of the texts of documents, the purpose of which was to establish the authority of his account. For the same reason he excluded the invented speech, much indulged in by classical historians, and the entertaining anecdote. As an educated man, he of course knew what classical history writing was supposed to be like, and his rejection of it was deliberate. Just as the Christian Church was an unprecedented subject for an historical account, so the style and methods of the historian had to mirror his innovatory approach. Among Christian writers, too, he had no real predecessors, although he pays tribute to the work done by, among others, the chronographer Julius Africanus (AD 221) and the apologist Hegesippus (*c.* 150).

The church historians who came after Eusebius followed his practice in the citation of documents, but to different degrees. Sozomen, the jurist from Gaza (published *c.* 443), perhaps the most readable of fifth-century church historians and one much influenced by classicizing stylistic considerations, avoided extended quotation of documents already cited by his coeval Socrates, both out of courtesy and for literary effect, and employed paraphrase rather than direct citation on other occasions as well. Sozomen was also more adventurous in other respects. Where Eusebius, his Latin continuator Rufinus of Aquileia, and Socrates all showed scrupulous regard for chronology, Sozomen allowed himself thematic excursuses which took him beyond the chronological bounds of his subject; thus a description included under the reign of Constantine of the persecution of Christians in Persia deals with the whole subject down to the late 370s.[2] Nevertheless, Sozomen was scrupulous in adhering to the two basic literary practices of Eusebius, the use of documentation to support authenticity (many texts quoted verbatim in Sozomen survive in no other source) and the avoidance of invented speeches. And documents remained essential supports to church history down to the time of the late sixth century historian Evagrius Scholasticus, although Evagrius, like Sozomen, was open to the stylistic influence of the classicizing historians – in his case, Procopius and Agathias – and relegated the documentation of his *Ecclesiastical History* to a separate book.

In terms of literary form, then, the heritage of Eusebius, although modified by his successors, remained recognizable. More serious were the problems that arose with the need to adapt the subject-matter of church history as defined by Eusebius to the changed situation of the church itself. Although Eusebius completed and produced a second edition of his *Ecclesiastical History* under Constantine and was fully aware of the momentous change effected by that emperor, the first seven books of his work was generated by the situation of the late third century: this was to culminate in persecutions under Diocletian and Galerius between 303 and 311, which were covered in Books VIII and IX. For readers of Eusebius' final version the identity of the Church was defined by her succession of orthodox bishops and the steadfastness of martyrs under persecution and torture at the hands of a hostile and alien state.

He was obliged to define his topic because his work was new: 'We are the first to enter on this subject, starting out as on some trackless desert way', with only a few 'raising their voices from far off like beacons and calling ... as from a distant watch-tower.'[3] In his prefatory chapter, Eusebius summarized his subject: a first group of topics related to the internal history of the Church, that is the succession from the apostles to Eusebius' own day, the events of church history, the most notable bishops in the most distinguished sees, and oral and written witnesses to the divine Word; secondly he would discuss heretics who 'because of yearning for innovation, proclaimed themselves authors of knowledge, falsely so-called', and who represented discontinuity with the orthodox tradition of the true apostolic Church, coming from the outside and 'ravaging the flock of Christ like fierce wolves'; and thirdly he would describe the Church's relationship with the outside world through the history of the Jews after the crucifixion, attacks made by the pagans, and the sufferings of the martyrs. Much of this could be adapted to a fourth- and fifth-century word, even though there were no longer martyrs (except under Julian's short-lived persecution). As Sozomen's

273

introductory chapters show, the Jews were still objects of Christian attack; pagan mobs and writers were still, nominally, a threat; and famous bishops, heretics and controversies were as present in the history of the Church under the Christian Empire as they had been earlier. In all these fields, continuity of subject (although not always of treatment) could be maintained without difficulty.

Eusebius was also to influence his successors in one further field, in addition to those of chronography and church history. Soon after the death of Constantine in 337, Eusebius produced his *Life of Constantine*, which was not so much a biography as a hagiography of the first Christian emperor. In this turgid exercise, Constantine, that most ruthless of emperors, was praised as the model of Christian piety, his successes were ascribed to the favour of God, and many of his laws and public letters sent to officials promoting Christianity were quoted *in extenso*. Its reception by later writers was mixed. On the one hand, it provided the model for praises of the '*pius princeps*' (godly prince) which could be reused, for example by Sozomen in his laudatory preface addressed to Theodosius II (whose piety was certainly more in evidence throughout his life than was that of Constantine). Eusebius' *Life* also provided much of the raw material that was to be transposed by his successors from the genre of biography to that of church history. On the debit side, however, Eusebius' *Life of Constantine* did not inspire other *Lives* of Christian emperors. Creators of Christian role-models turned instead to saints from the desert. Athanasius' *Life of St Antony*, published in *c.* 360, quickly won a wide readership in both East and West, including members of the imperial court, and set the tone for a new kind of literature celebrating the lives, sayings, and miracles of holy monks. Monasticism became a proper subject for such histories as that of Palladius, dedicated to Theodosius II's chamberlain Lausus in 420, and was accepted by the Christian writers of the 430s and 440s as a proper topic for church history.

Moreover even as history some found Eusebius' *Life* unsatisfactory: Socrates justified his decision to continue Eusebius from Constantine's accession on the grounds that Eusebius had said little about the Arian controversy in his account of the emperor, 'being more intent on the rhetorical finish of his composition and the praises of the emperor than on an accurate statement of the facts.'[4] Socrates was perhaps unfair, in that biography (or hagiography) was a distinct genre in classical literature and its conventions differed from those of history. But genres, particularly experimental ones, were not watertight in all respects. Eusebius used the citation of documents in his *Life of Constantine* on the same principles as he had employed them in his *Ecclesiastical History*; and his successors plundered the *Life* for the source materials on which the opening books of their own histories of the Church were based. Eusebius, then, was not infallible. How far were subsequent writers free to modify the genre of church history of which he was the father without destroying it altogether?

As late as the early sixth century, writers of ecclesiastical history were still perceived as a distinct group. Theodore *lector*, in the East, produced a synthesis of earlier ecclesiastical historians as, in the West, did Cassiodorus' monk, Epiphanius, with his *Historia Tripertita*, a collation of Socrates, Sozomen and Theodoret. A little earlier, one Gelasius of Cyzicus compiled a *Syntagma*, synthesis, of Eusebius, Socrates, Sozomen, Theodoret, Rufinus of Aquileia and Rufinus' probable source for the fourth century, Gelasius of Caesarea. One church historian was excluded from the canon: Philostorgius, whose *Ecclesiastical History* survives in the fragments preserved by the Byzantine patriarch Photius, was a follower of the heresiarch Eunomius and his history was designed to glorify his hero and thus was unsuitable for incorporation into the works of the orthodox.

What this uniformity imposed by later compilers tends to conceal is, firstly, the elements of discontinuity in the church historiographical tradition and, secondly, the experiments that took place within it. The discontinuity resulted partly from the disruption caused by the barbarian invasions of the West in the early fifth century and the subsequent slow drifting apart of the imperial administrations of East and West. In the West, Eusebius was translated into Latin and continued by Rufinus of Aquileia down to Theodosius I's triumph over paganism at the battle of the Frigidus in September 394, a victory that was naturally ascribed more to the emperor's prayers than to military might. But Rufinus had no direct successors in the Latin West and no continuators in the Greek East, where Socrates and the other historians sometimes used him but all began from where (in their view) Eusebius left off. Rufinus was also ignored by Cassiodorus, who turned to the Byzantine trio, Socrates,

Sozomen and Theodoret, for his *Historia Tripertita*, thus giving their work a limited circulation in the West.

The activities of the later epitomators also obscured the extent of experimentation in the fifth-century church historians, in particular Socrates and Sozomen. The third of the trio, Theodoret, bishop of Cyrrhus, although learned in style with references to the Greek tragedians of the fifth century BC, confined himself rigorously to the subjects of church history in its narrowest sense, as defined by Eusebius; as he was writing probably after the other two, in the late 440s, his work may have been a reaction against theirs. Socrates and Sozomen, however, were not only bolder in tampering with the genre; they were also a different breed of church historian. Unlike the bishop Eusebius, the priest Rufinus or the deacon Philip of Side, Socrates and Sozomen were laymen and, although in theory much opposed to heresy, were comparatively tolerant of diversity; Socrates had a weakness for the Novatians, which he did not scruple to acknowledge. Moreover, Socrates probably and Sozomen certainly were jurists and Sozomen had at least one friend at court. Both were writing in Theodosian Constantinople, where the vibrant intellectual atmosphere of the eastern capital may have encouraged them to take the risks that would be consciously avoided by the cautious provincial, Theodoret. Their world was that of men educated in the classical tradition, both Christians and pagans, like the swashbuckling classicizing historian Olympiodorus of Thebes, whose paganism had not debarred him from serving on imperial embassies to the Huns in 412 and to Rome in 425. Constantinople in the 420s was the city of culture and of law: its university was reorganized in 425. In 429 and 435, Theodosius organized the two stages of a great project to collect and publish imperial constitutions from the time of Constantine, and the result was the great *Theodosian Code* of 438. It is probable that Sozomen at least was directly inspired and influenced by the appearance of the *Code* in the writing of his history, of which, as he made a point of stating, law was a part.

The *Ecclesiastical History* of Socrates emerged in instalments in the late 430s and his inclusion of matters such as wars alien to the genre seems to have caused controversy. To answer his critics, he prefaced Book V with an explanation stating that his aim was to give readers the facts, that constant repetition of the disputes of bishops with each other could become tedious, and that 'whenever the affairs of the state were disturbed, those of the Church, as if by some vital sympathy, became disturbed also'. Examples of this in earlier books were his linking of Constantius II's Persian wars, and the usurpation of Magnentius in 350 with the troubles over Athanasius,[5] and his association of Valens' problems over the usurpation of Procopius in 365 with earthquakes and floods, and disturbances caused by the Macedonian heretics.[6] The 'vital sympathy' idea was closely linked to the traditional Eusebian view (which was shared by Constantine himself in his public pronouncements) that the character and actions of the emperor determined the fate of the state. That view Socrates also held, believing that an emperor who governed the Church well would also succeed in his secular undertakings, whether they were subjugation of barbarians or the averting by prayer of a violent snowstorm.[7] Such portraits of pious rulers were also a response to pagan lists of 'good emperors'. Indeed Socrates may deliberately have juxtaposed a reference to the pagan Themistius' consular oration in praise of the emperor Jovian in 364 with the observation that, if Jovian had lived, the state would have prospered as 'both civil and ecclesiastical affairs would have been happily administered'.[8]

Writing a few years later, Sozomen was more aggressively experimental than all his predecessors in his approach to classical norms of style and subject. He had the casual layman's attitude to dogma, which was to be excluded: the function of history 'is to treat of what is, without introducing personal opinions'.[9] As a lawyer he was self-conscious in continuing the Eusebian practice of citing laws 'passed in aid of the honour and establishment of worship',[10] and took the opportunity to correct and amplify the version of his predecessor in this area. In his adherence to classical literary conventions, his casual attitude to chronology and, perhaps most striking of all, his hijacking in Book IX of lengthy extracts from Olympiodorus' history on secular events in the West in the early fifth century, Sozomen showed himself the most secular of church historians. But his broadening of the scope of church history had its justification. Like Socrates, he sought to highlight the connections between dissensions in the Church and disturbances in the state,[11] and emphasized that the piety of emperors brought peace, prosperity, and the discovery of holy relics.[12] In effect, Sozomen was seeking to mount a takeover of secular history, with the implied claim that Olympiodorus' material could all be absorbed by the church historian – provided the right interpretative notes were attached.

If his onslaught on Olympiodorus was by implication, his attack on the polemical pagan historian, Eunapius of Sardis was more explicit. Here again, Sozomen took on the pagan writers on their own ground. The Eunapian versions of the conversion of Constantine (ascribed to guilt over the murder of his son Crispus in 326), and the 'philosophers' conspiracy' against Valens in the early 370s were shown to be wrong by reference to the pagans' own heroes, to Heracles, the philosopher Sopater under Constantine and, by contrast with Valens' philosophers, Socrates the Athenian.[13] All this no doubt appealed to the Hellenic literati of Constantinople. Yet, as the conservatively minded Theodoret of Cyrrhus implied by his return in the late 440s to the strict Eusebian criteria, the integrity of the genre itself was in danger of being undermined.

Never again after the reign of Theodosius II was there to be so vigorous a debate on the nature of church history. But there was a sequel. Late in the sixth century another layman and lawyer, Evagrius Scholasticus, picked up the story where the Theodosian historians had left off with an *Ecclesiastical History* spanning the period from the outbreak of the Nestorian controversy in the 420s down to 594. By then it was virtually impossible to observe the dichotomy between church and secular histories. Evagrius' language was that of the classicizing historians; he included secular material taken from Procopius and Agathias, whom he perceived as being as much his predecessors as were the ecclesiastical writers; and he even flouted Eusebian convention by including an invented speech. His half-hearted inclusion of anti-pagan polemic and praise of the martyrs at a time when neither any longer existed illustrates how the conventions of the genre had been overtaken by social change. Not surprisingly, Evagrius was the last of his line.

Eusebius was indisputably one of the most revolutionary writers of antiquity. He recast the science of Christian chronography, established the criteria for the ideal Christian ruler and defined for future generations the genre of church historiography. His rigorous use of documentation as part of his historical method was an innovation with long-term consequences: as Momigliano observed, we may owe to him our use of footnotes and appendices. The church historians as a group were preoccupied with one central issue, the place of the Church in the world. Increasingly after Constantine it became clear that the history of the Church – and of Christianity – is bound up with its secular context. As William Frend's work has shown over the years, that part of Eusebius' heritage is also with us still.

NOTES

1 Socrates, *Ecclesiastical History*, VII.27, in Migne PG 67. 800–801. This vol. also contains Sozomen. Theodoret's *Ecclesiastical History* is in PG 82. 881–1280. The *Histories* of Socrates and Sozomen are translated in the Library of Nicene and Post-Nicene Fathers 2nd series vol. II (1892).

2 Sozomen, *Eccl. Hist.*, II.9–14, PG 67, 956–969.

3 Eusebius, *Eccl. Hist.*, I.1.3, PG 20.48; t. in Library of Nicene and Post-Nicene Fathers 2nd series vol. I, (1890); now readily accessible in Penguin Classics.

4 Socrates, *Eccl. Hist.*, I.1, PG 67.33.

5 id., *Eccl. Hist.*, II.25, PG 67.264–5.

6 id., *Eccl. Hist.*, IV.4, PG 67.468–9.

7 id., *Eccl. Hist.*, V.10 and VII.22, PG 67.584 and 784–8.

8 id., *Eccl. Hist.*, III.26, PG 67.457.

9 Sozomen, *Eccl. Hist.*, III.15, PG 67.1086.

10 id., *Eccl. Hist.*, I.8, PG 67.875.

11 e.g. Sozomen, *Eccl. Hist.*, VIII.25, PG 67.1580–4.

12 id., *Eccl. Hist.*, IX.1 and 16, PG 67.1598 and 1628.

13 On Constantine, see Zosimus, *Historia Nova: The Decline of Rome*, tr. J B James (San Antonio, Trinity University Press, 1967) II.29, and Sozomen, *Eccl. Hist.*, I.5, PG 868–72; on Valens and the philosophers, see Eunapius, frag. 38 (in K Müller, *Fragmenta Historicorum Graecorum* IC, (Paris, Firmin Didot, 1851) p. 28) and Sozomen, *Eccl. Hist.*, VI.35, PG 67.1397–1400.

BIBLIOGRAPHY

Allen, P, *Evagrius Scholasticus: The Church Historian*. Louvain, Spicilegium Sacrum Lovaniense, fasc. 41, 1981.

Barnes, T D, *Constantine and Eusebius*. Cambridge, Mass., Harvard University Press 1981.

Chesnut, G F, *The first Christian Histories: Eusebius, Socrates, Sozomen, Theodoret and Evagrius*. Macon, G A, Mercer University Press, 1986[2].

Grant, R M, *Eusebius as Church Historian*. Oxford University Press, 1980.

Markus, R, 'Church History and Early Church Historians', in D Baker, ed., *The Materials, Sources and Methods of Ecclesiastical History: Studies in Church History*, vol. 11 (Oxford, Blackwell, 1975), pp. 1–17.

Momigliano, A D, *The Conflict between Paganism and Christianity in the Fourth Century*. Oxford University Press, 1963.

24

Archaeology

KENNETH PAINTER

Archaeology is concerned with material culture. It can interpret only factual evidence preserved in the ground or in buildings or in objects; but this of course provides a vast quantity of evidence to be incorporated into the historical record, and indeed the archaeological evidence can supplement and even alter the record derived from the written sources. The archaeology of the early Church is a vast subject, as large as the activities of its members, and so the examples of the following pages will try to give some idea of its variety and breadth.

Very little evidence of the holy places mentioned in the Gospels or of the events of the first century AD recorded in the New Testament can be expected to survive, particularly in view of the Roman destruction of Jerusalem, including its public buildings, by Titus in AD 70. As the following selected examples show, the main contribution of archaeology for this early period is to demonstrate both Herod the Great's Romanization of the province, which had become part of the Empire in 63 BC, and also the underlying Jewish culture, attested by such remarkable evidence as the Dead Sea Scrolls and the monastery of Qumran.

The long-standing differences between north and south at every stage in the history of Palestine are reflected in the different reactions of the two areas to the spread of Hellenization. In the north it was accepted readily, and towns of Hellenistic type appear. Samaria had Hellenistic buildings as early as about 300 BC, and most of the domestic pottery used during the last centuries BC was Greek or local copies of such imports. The Maccabees destroyed the city in 107 BC; but it was rebuilt about 60 BC and remained a Hellenistic town. The inhabitants of Samaria, therefore, found nothing alien in the Roman-style public buildings with which Herod sought to enhance the town's status. Two were of special importance. One was the temple of Augustus, founded on the platform which had been created for the palace and royal quarter of the Israelite kings. A considerable part of a large stone statue of Augustus was found in the excavations of 1908–10. The other was the typical Roman civic centre, the Forum and Basilica, constructed to the east of the royal quarter. To this building an aqueduct 4400 metres long brought water from a spring on the adjacent hill, which crossed the valley on a bridge 50 metres high. A Herodian stadium for athletic sports was built on the lower slopes of the hill, and a later theatre, of classical form, just below the summit of the hill, probably lies over a Herodian theatre. Herod was therefore able to build at Samaria a town which would have met with the approval of his Roman friends. He changed its name to Sebastie, the Greek equivalent of Augusta, in honour of his patron.

In the xenophobic south, and especially in Jerusalem, Herod had to modernize very cautiously. His major undertaking was the rebuilding of the Temple in the north-east of the Maccabaean city. Of the building itself nothing survives, for the platform on which it stood is now occupied by the Moslem sanctuary of the Dome of the Rock; but the platform is Herodian work, and so something of the appearance from the south of the enclosing colonnades, gates, ramps and roads of the Temple can be recreated archaeologically.

On the western ridge within the city a second major Herodian building, his palace, can be identified. The lower courses of the so-called Tower of David are of Herodian masonry, and can be recognized as the tower in the palace called Phasael, one of the three described by Josephus. The rest of the palace lay to the south, and may have covered much of the south-western sector of the present Old City, but little more has survived than fragments or walls supporting the terrace upon which stood the buildings, gardens, pavilions and canals described by Josephus. Between the Temple and the palace the city may have differed from today's view only in that, in the early first century AD, the dip towards the central valley was much greater. The main levelling-up of this area came with the lay-out of Aelia Capitolina in the second century AD.

Herod's Romanization was little more than a veneer over the Jewish culture of much of Palestine of the first century AD. Only rarely, however, is evidence found of the Jewish religious background of New Testament times. The outstanding exception has been the discovery of the Dead Sea Scrolls and of the abode of the community to which they had belonged.

In 1947 seven old rolls of inscribed sheepskin were found by shepherds in a cave of the Judaean Wilderness, in the vicinity of Khirbet Qumran. The cave is one of many in the cliffs at the base of the mountains fringing the north-west end of the Dead Sea. Fragments of manuscripts were found in eleven of them in locations radiating out from Khirbet Qumran. On a plateau at the base of the cliffs, slightly above the narrow plain along the shore, are the ruins of a monastery, and their excavation between 1951 and 1956 by Roland de Vaux OP proved them to be the home of the community to the library of which the scrolls had belonged.

The monastery and its library belonged to one of the ascetic sects of the Jews at this period, generally accepted to be that of the Essenes, of which John the Baptist might at one stage have been a member. The sect probably protested against the perpetuation of the high priesthood in the family of the Maccabees, and also against the Maccabees' policy of seeking closer ties with Rome. The Maccabees persecuted the Essenes and their leader, 'the Righteous Teacher', and so the sect fled to the wilderness and turned to apocalyptic visions of the overthrow of the wicked priests of Jerusalem as well as the evil nations of the world, and to the establishment of their community as the true Israel, the Elect of God, in the dawning Messianic Age. The final stage of the Qumran community coincides exactly with Jesus' ministry and the establishment of the first Christian communities. The importance of the finds at Qumran is that they illuminated by their differences the distinct nature of the Christians, who must at first have appeared as only one more sect within a very diverse Judaism. Christians and Essenes together, however, provide evidence of the Jewish religion and culture to set against the veneer of Roman civilization of the Herodian period.

The apostolic period, like that of the Gospels, is unlikely to have any direct archaeological evidence. The great nineteenth-century advances in the study of epigraphy, however, led to progress in the scientific establishment of the accuracy of Luke–Acts long before the most significant archaeological discoveries in Palestine itself. In the 1880s W M Ramsay and C S Sterrett began their travels in Anatolia. Their original idea was to demonstrate the historical truth of Acts, and in particular the 'south Galatian' theory of the Pauline missionary route, by close observation of sites on the ground. In this they succeeded. The inscriptional material showed that the Pauline cities were there to be explored in the Roman province of Galatia, solving apparent contradictions between Acts and the Pauline Epistles. Similarly, Luke was clearly well informed about the provincial administration in the time of Claudius and Nero. In the words of Ramsay: 'The officials with whom Paul and his companions were brought into contact are those who would be there. Every person is found just where he ought to be: proconsuls in senatorial provinces, asiarchs in Ephesus, strategoi in Philippi, politarchs in Thessalonica, magicians and soothsayers everywhere.'

In the second and third centuries AD, Christianity developed from being a branch of Judaism into an independent religion spread throughout the Roman world. Archaeological evidence for the sect is rare, as might be expected for a sect which had relatively small numbers and which from time to time found itself in conflict with the authorities. Nevertheless, for the first time, archaeological evidence does begin to be available, in inscriptions, papyri, cemeteries, buildings and even the beginnings of a distinctive Christian art.

Overtly Christian inscriptions of the second and third centuries AD are rarely found outside such places as the catacombs of Rome. Down to the moment of Constantine's victory most Christians were discreet about their beliefs. Occasionally, however, illuminating evidence occurs. The epigraphical explorations of Ramsay and his colleagues in Asia Minor, for example, did not only produce evidence for the sub-apostolic periods of the late first and early second centuries. At Ishekli, the site of the town of Eumeneia in Phrygia, he and Calder discovered a series of third-century epitaphs, whose dedicators threatened that anyone who sought to insert an unauthorized body into their tomb made himself liable to the judgement of 'the living God'. The imprecation is more likely in its context to be Christian than Jewish: but its very discreetness shows how the well-established communities in the towns, attested by the church councils, did not draw attention to themselves. Less discreet were the Phrygian countryside inhabitants of the imperial estate in the Tembris Valley. Ramsay and his pupil, J G C Anderson, found there the remarkable series of 'Christians for Christians' funerary inscriptions, dating from AD 249–304. They identified them as belonging to the militant Montanist movement, which came into being in the last third of the second century, and the conclusion was reinforced by another of Ramsay's discoveries, the epitaph of Abercius Marcellus, the anti-Montanist Bishop of Hieropolis. The difference in attitude, however, between the town congregations and the rural Montanists is perhaps explained by the fact that these 'soldiers' retained an apocalyptic and prophetic outlook long after the town communities had begun to come to terms with their environment.

In the 1890s, while Ramsay was exploring Asia Minor, another group of scholars had realized the wealth and importance of the fragments of papyri preserved in the dry sands of Egypt. The Egypt Exploration Fund decided to organize systematic expeditions to search for papyri, and in 1896 Grenfell and Hunt began work at Bahnasa, Oxyrhynchus. One of the earliest finds was a leaf of a papyrus book containing hitherto unknown Sayings of Jesus. Other fragments of the Sayings were found; but it was not until the 1950s that they were identified as part of the apocryphal Gospel of Thomas. This was the result not of a planned expedition but of the chance discovery in 1945 or 1946 at Nag Hammadi in Upper Egypt of a mass of writings in Coptic, which provided a wealth of new material for the reconstruction of the Gnostic system as it had developed by the middle of the second century.

Since 1914 the Egypt Exploration Society has sponsored no excavation specifically to search for papyri; but remarkable texts have continued to be found, either by chance, as at Nag Hammadi, or as a result of broader expeditions. The biblical papyri in the Chester-Beatty group, for example, written about AD 200, included large sections of the New Testament and carried evidence for the text of the New Testament a hundred years earlier than any manuscript previously in our possession. In 1934 the chance offer of a collection of papyri to the British Museum revealed a fragment of an unknown Gospel, dated about AD 100–50, which rewrites the gospel story, embodying fragments of the canonical Gospels and making legendary additions. About the same time was published a tiny fragment of St John's Gospel, which can be dated to not later than AD 130, a date within a very few years of the actual writing of the Gospel. These fragments are virtually the only archaeological record we have of the spread of Christianity in Egypt during the second and early third centuries. The middle of the third century, however, produced the first reliably documented official persecutions of Christians in Egypt. Under the emperor Decius, people were required to produce documentary proof of the fact that they were not practising Christians, and several of these declarations have survived. Papyrus 2457 at the British Library, for example, is a declaration to the commissioners of sacrifices at Oxyrhynchus by Aurelius Gaion, on 27th June, AD 250, that he and his family had made the customary sacrifices to the gods. Chance finds like these, or the important discovery of 1940 made in the Tura quarries near Cairo, continue to be made. They are, however, a rare and heady element in archaeological research.

The persecutions of the third century help us to understand why Christians would not be inclined to advertise their affiliation, and for the same reason it has proved difficult in modern times for archaeologists to identify the buildings where Christians met. The only certain house-church is that excavated by M I Rostovtzeff between 1931 and 1932 at Dura Europos, situated in the Syrian desert on the Euphrates frontier. The town was occupied by the Romans in AD 165, but fell after a siege by the Persians in AD 257. The Christian church was located in the same street as a temple of Mithras and a synagogue, from which it does not differ greatly in form. The building began as a middle-class home. It is arranged around a paved court, and two rooms on the south side, discreetly invisible from the street, were combined to form an assembly-room and to change the building from house to church. At right angles to the assembly-room is a smaller, plain room, which might have been for the catechumens, and from this room a doorway led into the baptistery chapel. The paintings on the walls are of biblical episodes which illustrate the fact that baptism itself is the guarantee of a new life: the healing of the paralytic, St Peter's rescue from sinking into the Sea of Galilee, Christ's conversation with the woman of Samaria, David and Goliath, and, possibly, the visit of the three Marys to the Holy Sepulchre on the first Easter morning. In the West, by contrast, third-century Christian art is preserved only as funerary art. Based most probably on prayers for salvation, a repertory of salvation scenes on wall and ceiling paintings in the Roman catacombs, was abbreviated about AD 220–30 to the essential details. It was transferred to sarcophagi from AD 250 onward.

The second and third centuries AD are thus a period of enormous advance for the Church. It began to separate itself from the world of Judaism; but visible links remain, whether in the apocalyptic nature of Montanism or in the artistic links between the paintings of Dura Europos and the synagogue. Direct archaeological evidence for

Christianity begins to appear; but it is very sparse, and it thus reflects both the relatively small numbers of the sect and the discreet way in which they practised their beliefs.

With the Edict of Milan in AD 313 the emperor Constantine recognized Christianity and made the Church the dominant religious power within the Roman Empire. Now every village and parish had its own clergy, and every town its own bishop, while above them rose the major sees of Carthage, Trier, Aquileia, Antioch, Caesarea in Cappadocia, Milan, Alexandria, Rome and Constantinople. Material evidence for Christianity now appears in gradually increasing quantity in the archaeological record. Manuscripts, for example, have survived, either above ground in monasteries and libraries, or in the dry ground of Egypt as fragments. The most spectacular range from the fourth-century Codex Sinaiticus (from the monastery of St Catherine in Sinai), written in Caesarea or Alexandria, to the Codex Amiatinus (Laurentian Library, Florence), written at the end of the seventh century in Monkwearmouth or Jarrow when Bede was a young man there. A comprehensive Christian art also comes into being, in painting, metal, stone and textile, from Syria in the east to Britain and Ireland in the west. Even in the surviving remains, however, the most visible change which resulted from this development was the creation, within the existing cities, towns and villages of the Empire, of a distinctive parish and monumental architecture, including cathedrals, palatine and parish churches, or of spaces for the dead, whether funeral buildings or martyria or cemeteries and catacombs.

The emperor Constantine and his family led the way, building huge churches which acknowledged the ever-growing cult of martyrs and holy sites. About AD 320 outside Rome on the Vatican Hill he housed the shrine of St Peter in a huge basilica which would hold thousands of pilgrims. In AD 325–6 the dowager empress Helena visited the sites in the Holy Land where the Godhead had revealed itself, and during the last twelve years of his reign Constantine donated church buildings on these sites, at the grotto of the nativity at Bethlehem, on the site of the resurrection and crucifixion, at the place on the Mount of Olives and at Mambre where Christ had taught the disciples, and near the terebinths at Mambre where the Lord had spoken to Abraham. In the martyria of the Holy Land, the object of veneration remained outside the main hall where the faithful had gathered. At St Peter's, however, excavations begun in

1939 to prepare a tomb for Pius XI have shown that the second-century memorial of St Peter, which stood in a large cemetery, was incorporated within the church, which was both a martyrium shrine for the visiting pilgrims and also a funeral banqueting hall for the relatives of those who had been buried near the saint.

St Peter's was not the first major church built by Constantine at Rome. The Lateran church, now S. Giovanni in Laterano, had been begun for the bishop of Rome in AD 313 on a site in the south-east corner of the city. As later at Constantinople Constantine did not attempt to create a Christianized city. In Rome's pagan heart he erected public buildings like those of any other emperor. The Lateran cathedral was erected within the walls, but discreetly in the green belt on the city's edge. As a counter to the vigorous paganism of late fourth- and fifth-century Rome the popes beautified the Lateran church and embarked on a church-building programme, perhaps even marking out a papal enclave in that part of the city, bounded by the subsidiary cathedrals of S. Maria Maggiore, S. Croce in Gerusalemme and S. Stefano Rotondo. The real threat to this plan, however, came not from paganism but from the rival popularity of St Peter's, situated in the thriving north-west corner of the city and always most popular with pilgrims. Not until the Renaissance did the popes give up the struggle and move their headquarters to St Peter's and the Vatican.

Forty years of excavation and survey in Milan have revealed the next major development in the history of the Church. After the death of Constantine the senior rulers of the Western Roman Empire for strategic reasons made Milan rather than Rome their base in Italy. Their almost continuous presence there from AD 340 to 402 coincided with the bitter politico-theological wars between orthodox and Arians, and the historical record is mirrored in the story of fourth-century church building in the city. Imperial favour towards the Church is shown first in the choice of site for the cathedral, S. Tecla, which about AD 350 was placed not on the edge of the city, like the Lateran cathedral in Rome, but in its heart, demanding the sacrifice of a considerable amount of property. In AD 355 the emperor Constantius, at a synod in Milan, forced through an Arianizing, anti-Nicene, creed, and for the next twenty years Milan was an Arian island in an otherwise anti-Nicene West. In AD 374, however, bishop Auxentius, a Cappadocian anti-Nicene, died. His successor, Ambrose, fought against Arianism, in spite of its continued popularity at the near-by court, and sought to free the Church from temporal power, rejecting the emperor's implied claim to stand at the head of the church. This is reflected in his building programme. Ambrose built round the city a ring of sanctuaries of martyrs (S. Ambrogio, S. Nazaro, and S. Simpliciano) which match those built by Constantine and his successors round Rome. Moreover, the Basilica Apostolorum (S. Nazaro) seems to be a deliberate echo of Constantine's Apostoleion in Constantinople, and even the relics, of Andrew, Thomas and John the Evangelist, are likely to have been brought to Milan from the same church. For Ambrose, stressing the bonds to Constantinople and to Rome was essential in his fight during the 380s against the anti-Nicenes of the court.

Just like the greatest cities, the Christian development of the ordinary, smaller towns was a matter of slow evolution. Gerasa (Jerash) in Jordan, for example, is known from the investigations of the 1930s to have been a Hellenistic foundation, to have developed during the Roman period, even gaining a hippodrome for 15,000 spectators, and to have become a bishopric in the fourth century. Not until the middle of the fifth century, however, do the temples seem to have gone out of use, their functions being replaced by a vast ecclesiastical complex which was built directly to the south of the temple of Artemis and grew over two centuries. Churches and martyria were built elsewhere in the town, and inscriptions show that the bishop became the leader of religious and non-religious life.

The same kind of development took place throughout the Empire. In Africa, for example, excavations have revealed the history of the basilicas at Ammaedara (Haïdra), which range in date from the fourth to the seventh centuries. Basilica II is a martyrium, begun in the fourth century; but basilicas I, III and IV were built in the sixth century, at a time when the territory was controlled by the Arian Vandals, who did not give the orthodox Catholics an easy time. The Catholics themselves, however, had in their turn made life difficult in the fourth century for the Donatists. The conflict was resolved by the Catholic Augustine of Hippo's victory over them at the Council of Carthage in AD 411, though the schism survived until the seventh century. The archaeological evidence for Donatism is slim; but at Timgad (Numidia) the south-western suburbs include the unique complex of the Donatist quarter, the seat in the late fourth century of the 'mitred bandit', bishop Optatus, the bête noire of Saint Augustine. His headquarters was like a great monastery, containing his cathedral, a chapel, apsidal rooms, the bishop's own house and a baptistery. At the same time the north-west corner of the town contains an elaborate orthodox Christian complex, with its own church, baptistery and courtyard.

Some Christian communities did not develop on ancient sites but moved to new ones. These include not only monasteries in places like Egypt and Syria, but settlements which shifted to cluster near a saint's remains. At Ephesus it is Ayasaluk at the tomb of St John which has survived, leaving the ancient city deserted. Medieval Augsburg grew up around the cemetery church of Saint Ulrich and Saint Afra. At Tours, St Martin drew around himself a separate and eventually fortified settlement, the Bourg St Martin. Xanten (*ad sanctos*) stands at the double grave of two executed men outside the now deserted site of Colonia Ulpia Traiana. Bonn clusters round the grave of another martyr well to the south of Castrum Bonna, and in Britain St Alban has attracted the living to his hilltop city, leaving Verulamium deserted in the valley beneath.

So short a survey can do little justice to a subject as vast as the archaeology of the early Church. No mention has been made of a multitude of topics, of which the catacombs of Rome and Justinian's churches in Turkey, Italy and Africa are but two. Britain could have supplied a chapter in itself, with house-chapel wall paintings in the villa at Lullingstone, floor-mosaics in the villas of Dorset, the cemetery of Dorchester revealing about a quarter of the fourth-century population to be Christian, the earliest liturgical silver at Water Newton, martyr-churches at St Albans, Exeter and Wells. This takes no account of the early Celtic church in Ireland, Wales, Scotland and the north of England, let alone the Anglo-Saxon developments from the seventh century. The same catalogue could be drawn up for any part of the late Roman or early medieval world. In Asia Minor, Nubia, Africa, Britain and all his published works William Frend has been a pioneer in combining the disciplines of archaeology and examination of the written sources. They are now equal partners in the recreation of the history of the early Church.

BIBLIOGRAPHY

Frend, W H C, *Archaeology and History in the Study of Early Christianity*. London, Variorum Reprints, 1988.

Kenyon, K M, *The Bible and Recent Archaeology*. London, British Museum Publications, 1986.

Krautheimer, R, *Early Christian and Byzantine Architecture*. Harmondsworth, Penguin, 1979.

Milburn, R, *Early Christian Art and Architecture*. Aldershot, Scolar Press,
1988.

Thomas, A C, *Christianity in Roman Britain*. London, B T Batsford, 1985.

Weitzmann, K, *Age of Spirituality. Late Antique and Early Christian Art, Third
to Seventh Century*. New York, Metropolitan Museum of Art and Princeton University Press, 1979.

25

The Early Church in the Renaissance and Reformation

IRENA BACKUS

It will be many years before the reception of the early Church by the fifteenth and sixteenth centuries can be assessed fully. The present study will cover three aspects of the question: (1) use of the church Fathers by theologians of the Reformation period: (2) editions of the Fathers available from the fifteenth century onwards, with Origen (*c.* 185–*c.* 254), Basil of Caesarea (329–79) and Jerome (*c.* 342–420) serving as examples; (3) wider availability of the patristic writings in Protestant territories, and recourse to the early Church as model for practical reform.

THE 'RENAISSANCE' AND THE 'REFORMATION'

We normally mean by the 'Renaissance' cultural events which took place between *c.* 1300 and the end of the sixteenth century. One of their most interesting features was an increase of interest in classical, including early Christian, literature. As will be seen, many of the fifteenth- and sixteenth-century translations and editions of the Fathers were the work of classical scholars and not of 'trained' theologians.

The 'Reformation' can be defined as a series of religious reforms, starting with Martin Luther's publication, in 1517, of his ninety-five theses criticizing the indulgences of the Church of Rome, and carrying on into the second half of the sixteenth century. Luther's criticisms resulted in the split between the Roman and the various Protestant Churches. Moreover, some fairly far-reaching changes took place within the Church of Rome itself, culminating in the Council of Trent (1545–65).

Close attention will be paid to the effect that these confessional divisions may or may not have had on the reception of the writings of the Fathers.

USE OF THE CHURCH FATHERS BY THEOLOGIANS OF THE REFORMATION PERIOD

The crucial issues which divided the Roman Catholics and the Protestants were the papacy, the role of tradition, the sacraments, the real presence, the relative importance of faith and good works, free-will, predestination, monastic vows and the cult of the saints.

Since one of Luther's complaints was that the Roman Church relied too much on human institutions and not sufficiently on the Scripture, one would expect the Reformers to discount patristic writings as a 'human superstition'. However, this was very far from being the case.

MARTIN LUTHER (1483–1546)

Luther himself, whose education had not been strongly influenced by the Renaissance, came out in favour of patristic tradition in his 1523 Order of Service entitled *Formula missae et communionis pro ecclesia wittenbergensi* (The Form for the Mass and Communion to be adopted by the Wittenberg Church). There he states that the object of the Reformation is not to abolish church services but to free them from unnecessary, human additions. The Eucharist was instituted by Christ and observed in all simplicity by the apostles, before being corrupted. However, Luther expresses strong approval of additions to the service made by what he calls 'the first Fathers'. He claims that it was Athanasius (*c.* 296–373) and Cyprian (d. 258) who added the psalms to be sung before the benediction. The addition of the *Kyrie Eleison* (lit. 'Lord have mercy', a brief prayer for divine mercy) is also approved of; according to the Reformer it was part of the service during the time of Basil of Caesarea. (Luther's sources for this pronouncement are dubious: Athanasius is mentioned by Augustine in the *Confessions* (10, 33) as singing during the Eucharist service; the mention of Cyprian cannot be explained and the reference to Basil can be traced back to a medieval source.)

ULRICH ZWINGLI (1484–1531)

Ulrich Zwingli, the Reformer of Zurich, had, unlike Luther, undergone a humanist education and his personal library, still extant, contains a large number of editions of the Fathers (notably Origen, Jerome and Augustine) with Zwingli's own annotations. Moreover, the Fathers are frequently cited by him. Naturally Zwingli does not use patristic material in a way that a modern scholar would. He is interested neither in the best (most accurate) text, nor particularly in the question of correctly identifying its author, the writings of the Fathers being sometimes wrongly attributed in the course of their transmission. What is of primary importance to Zwingli is to find arguments in the writings of the early Church which bear out the doctrines of the Reformation.

JOHN CALVIN (1509–64)

John Calvin puts up a vigorous defence of patristic testimony in the introduction (entitled 'Epistle to the King') to the first edition of his *Institutes of the Christian Religion* (1536). Calvin's main argument is that the doctrines of the Fathers are also those of the Reformers. He claims that all the Fathers 'held in abomination the contamination of the Holy Scripture by sophistical subtleties and philosophical wranglings'. A little further on he cites Hilary of Poitiers (*c.* 315–67) whose example should be followed in condemning excessive reverence accorded to ecclesiastical officials with no attention paid to their moral virtues.

THEODORE BEZA (1519–1605) AND THE ANTI-TRINITARIANS

It was in a very similar spirit that Calvin's successor in Geneva, Theodore Beza, published in 1570 the Greek text of *Dialogues on the Trinity*, which he attributed to Athanasius, together with a Latin translation and other patristic pieces.

Beza's aim was twofold. Firstly, he was using the Fathers to show the sixteenth-century antitrinitarians that their teachings were contrary to those of the Fathers and therefore heretical. Secondly, he was demonstrating to the Polish Roman Catholic Church that the trinitarian doctrine of the Reformers was that of the Fathers and therefore, accusations of the Polish prelates to the contrary, could not have given rise to antitrinitarianism. Questions of attribution were of little interest to Beza.

It is interesting to see that the Transylvanian antitrinitarians in their manifesto entitled *The true and false knowledge of God the Father, the Son and the Holy Spirit*, which came out in 1568, also used patristic models to show that their doctrine of the Trinity was the correct one. Far from identifying themselves with the heretic Arius (*c.* 250– *c.* 336) they cite as primary authority Augustine's *On the Trinity* or, more exactly, a digest of it compiled by one of their number.

PATRISTIC TESTIMONY IN RELIGIOUS CONTROVERSIES OF THE REFORMATION

The same principle, which can be summarized as 'my doctrine is the patristic doctrine and therefore orthodox', applied to the attacks of the Roman Church against the Protestants and to disputes among Protestants themselves. Two examples will suffice. John Eck (1486–1543), one of the most prominent Roman Catholic adversaries of Protestantism has consistent recourse to the Fathers to show that Lutheran and Zwinglian teachings enter into direct conflict with any and all patristic doctrines.

Even more interesting is the use of the Fathers in the eucharistic controversy between Zwinglians and Lutherans in the years 1526– 36. The Zwinglians affirmed that Christ's presence in the Eucharist was purely symbolic as, after the ascension, his human body was to be found in heaven on God's right hand and nowhere else. Luther and his followers claimed that Christ in his human nature was present everywhere after the ascension. He can thus be found both on God's right hand and in the Eucharist.

One of the biblical passages which served as point of reference for the controversy was John 6.63 'the flesh is of no avail'. Luther claimed to follow Chrysostom (*c.* 347–407) on this point referring 'the flesh' to human understanding. The Greek Father in his *Commentary on the Fourth Gospel* does indeed refer 'the flesh' to the weakness of human understanding; he urges a spiritual understanding which would enable us to perceive the divine nature of Christ in spite of his human form. Luther, however, asserts that Chrysostom is saying: 'Just because humans cannot understand the concept of spiritual eating, it does not follow that Christ's flesh, being spiritual, cannot be present in the Eucharist.' He thus imposes his own exegesis upon that of Chrysostom.

However, it would be quite inappropriate to accuse Luther of 'cheating' or of deliberately perverting patristic sources. His attitude is an excellent example of the epoch's unhistorical approach to the early Church. Having found in Chrysostom's exegesis an isolated element that can be used to support his own teaching, Luther automatically takes the teaching to be 'patristic' and therefore orthodox.

THE ABSENCE OF CRITICAL APPROACH

This tendency to select from the Fathers without looking to the context could well be a hang-over from the Middle Ages, when relatively few complete patristic writings were available and knowledge of the Fathers often amounted to knowing excerpts from their works. Those were available in *florilegia* (collections) such as the *Decree of Gratian* (a collection of nearly 4000 patristic texts, conciliar decrees and papal pronouncements touching on all fields of church discipline), the glossed (or annotated) Bible, the *Sentences* of Peter Lombard (standard theological text book), and the *Catena aurea in quattuor Evangelia* (The Golden Chain on the four Gospels) by St Thomas Aquinas. Those collections continued to be used throughout the fifteenth and the sixteenth centuries. There was no substantial difference between the Reformers' attitude to the Fathers and that of their opponents. All theologians attempted to show that their own doctrine, as opposed to any other, represented the true and therefore the patristic teaching. This meant that although different Fathers, or different extracts from the same Father, were used in debates, there was no question of holding a theological debate without having recourse to the writings of the early Church as well as to the Bible. The currently received view on the primacy of Scripture for the Reformers cannot be accepted without this qualification.

Questions of attribution and textual criticism were by and large of secondary importance. The researches of Erasmus of Rotterdam (*c.* 1469–1536), although not an isolated phenomenon, were nonetheless very far ahead of their time. Much more typical of the 'spirit of the age' is the Strasbourg Reformer's, Martin Bucer's (1491–1551) remark apropos the incident of the woman taken in adultery recounted in the Gospel of John. The passage, remark the editors of the *New English Bible*, has no fixed place in the best witnesses and some do not print it at all. Bucer was aware of this problem (from his reading of patristic commentaries) already in 1528. However, in his own *Commentary on the Gospel of John* he inserts the incident arbitrarily at the beginning of chapter eight and comments that 'as the story contains nothing unworthy of Christ, it can certainly be read with profit'.

EDITIONS OF THE FATHERS AVAILABLE IN THE FIFTEENTH AND SIXTEENTH CENTURIES. SOME EXAMPLES.

The amount of patristic material available to theologians increased even before the invention of printing (*c.* 1450) and the Fall of Constantinople (1453) (the latter did mean, however, that a large number of Greek, including patristic, manuscripts was brought into Western Europe, particularly Venice, by Greek refugees) due to continued cultural exchange between Italy and the East. This meant that Italian scholars such as Guarino of Verona (1374–1460) and Leonardo Bruni (1369–1444) could learn Greek and put it to good use by translating not only pagan authors but also some Fathers into Latin. In spite of their poor quality, translations made by the Greek, George of Trebizond (1395–1472/3) enjoyed great popularity.

The general revival of antique literature also brought about an interest in the Latin Fathers, and the invention of printing made their writings more widely available. As the listing of all the patristic editions of the period would require several volumes, I have chosen Origen and Basil of Caesarea as a representative sample of the Greek Fathers and Jerome as an example of the Latin. Before embarking on this brief survey, it is worth noting that most writings of the Greek Fathers, at least in the first half of the sixteenth century, were first published in a Latin translation. New (often mediocre) Latin translations continued to be produced even after the publication of the Greek text. Translations into the vernacular, on the other hand, tended to be late and rare. Moreover, they were frequently translations of extracts from a work and were done for a particular occasion.

ORIGEN

The question of Latin translations is less important when we come to consider the Alexandrian biblical scholar as many of his works survived only in Latin translations made in the two centuries immediately after his death. The history of the survival and reception of his works is closely linked with the Italian Renaissance. It is particularly interesting because of the Alexandrian's dubious reputation in antiquity.

Certain works of Origen, notably excerpts from his New Testament *Commentaries* were known already in the Middle Ages thanks to compilations such as Aquinas' *Catena aurea*. However, the Alexandrian's doctrines aroused no particular interest. It was the late fifteenth century that marked the Origen revival and the controversies that went with it.

In 1481 the Vatican librarian, Cristoforo Persona (*c.* 1416–85) published in Rome his own Latin translation of Origen's famous defence of Christianity, *Against Celsus*. Persona's prefaces suggest no deep knowledge of Origen's theology. The preface addressed to Pope Sixtus IV, which survives in some of the extant copies, is a simple request for money. The preface in the other extant copies, addressed to the Doge of Venice, is no more than a call for a crusade against the Turks.

The high spot of the Origen revival is reached in the years of what is commonly known as Florentine Platonism or Neoplatonism. As Origen's theology bore the stamp of both Plato and of Neoplatonist philosophy, it is not surprising that he was viewed favourably by thinkers such as Marsilio Ficino (1433–99) or Giovanni Pico della Mirandola (1463–94). The latter put forward a defence of Origen in 1486 and 1487 and was condemned for it by a papal commission.

This incident put a stop to Italian publications of Origen's writings until 1503 when the Venetian printer, Aldus Manutius, printed his *Homilies* on the five books of Moses and on the books of Joshua and Judges. In 1506 Origen's *Commentary on Romans* appeared, also in Venice. Its editor, Theophilus Salodian, praises the Alexandrian for his learning and for his moral qualities without referring to any scandals surrounding his doctrine. In 1514 Origen's most important theological work *De principiis* (*On First Principles*) also became available. Whereas Italian Renaissance scholars were interested in Origen because of his Platonism and because of his moral qualities, their French counterparts took an interest in him because of his mastery of allegorical exegesis of the Bible. Thanks to the efforts of the Italians and to those of the Parisian doctor of theology, Jacques Merlin (d. 1541 ?), most of Origen's authentic works together with a large number of inauthentic ones were available already before the Reformation.

The most authoritative Latin edition was, however, that of Erasmus which appeared in 1536. In his notes Erasmus drew the reader's attention to several incorrectly attributed works and praised Origen highly for his exegetical method. The Reformers' attitude to Origen tended to be ambivalent. Certain aspects of his theology (e.g. his defence of infant baptism) were much admired, others (e.g. his liking for interpreting the Bible allegorically) were overtly condemned. The Roman Catholics did not adopt him whole-heartedly either. There was no reliable edition of Origen's Greek works until 1668.

BASIL OF CAESAREA

It was primarily the Reformation that brought about a revival of interest in his works. One of the three Cappadocian Fathers, defender of the orthodox doctrine of the Trinity and reorganizer of the Caesarean Church, Basil, although a remarkable stylist, did not attract the attention of the Italian humanists. The only exception was his short treatise on the usefulness of pagan authors in Christian education, *Ad iuvenes* (To young people). This was translated in the fifteenth century by the Florentine, Leonardo Bruni, and came to be considered as a standard work on education. It underwent innumerable editions in the fifteenth and in the sixteenth centuries, independently of any confessional prejudices.

Confessionally-oriented interest in Basil dates from the Council of Florence (1439) when excerpts from his treatise *Against Eunomius* were used by the eastern and by the western Church delegates to show respectively that the Holy Spirit proceeds from the Father only or from both the Father and the Son.

In the sixteenth century Basil's (liberal) *Monastic Rule* appeared in Greek as early as 1535. The Roman Catholic editors of the volume, judging by their preface, considered Basil as a precursor of the pre-Tridentine party within the Roman Catholic Church that wanted certain reforms while considering that Luther had gone too far. They claim that the publication of Basil's *Rule* will help bring about the necessary reforms and stop the faithful from defecting to the Lutheran side.

In 1540 the reformer of Augsburg, Wolfgang Musculus (1497–1563) published his own Latin translation of Basil's *Rule* as part of his edition of the Cappadocian's *Complete Works*. Musculus sees in Basil a direct precursor to the Reformation. His Rule is in no sense intended for monks or nuns; it provides ethical norms for all non-monastic Christian communities. While Musculus' interpretation of the *Rule* cannot be called totally mistaken, it is certainly not correct. It is true that Basil sets out to address all Christian communities. His aim, however, is not to ask them to remain secular but to impose a monastic life-style upon them. The perfect Christian is to Basil a monk or a nun! It is no wonder that John Cochlaeus (1479–1552), Musculus' Roman Catholic adversary, accused the Augsburg Reformer of bad faith!

The spirit of religious controversy continued to surround the Latin works of Basil until 1565, although some of his homilies did appear separately in pocket-sized editions intended to edify their readers, regardless of creed.

JEROME

Although Jerome, author of the Latin Vulgate Bible, had always enjoyed a certain cult, appreciation of him as biblical scholar and man of letters underwent a revival from about the middle of the fourteenth century. It was around that time that the canonist Giovanni d'Andrea drew up a list of Jerome's writings in the fourth volume of his manuscript work *Hieronymianus* also known as *De laudibus sancti Hieronymi* (On the praises of St Jerome). The list naturally contained much spurious material.

Teodoro de' Lelli, bishop of Feltre and Treviso, prepared a two-volume collection of Jerome's letters and treatises before his death in 1466. He was very concerned to order the material systematically but was not at all interested in questions of attribution. The manuscript was the chief source of the most influential early printed edition of Jerome's works (Rome 1468) which became the received text. Although it was emended by later editors, its general outline is recognizable in the successive landmark editions, from Erasmus (Basel 1516) to Domenico Vallarsi (Venice 1766–72) whose text is reproduced in Migne's Patrology. Only in the nineteenth century did textual studies of Jerome advance sufficiently for a definitive text to be established.

In the early part of the fifteenth century, Ambrogio Traversari (1386–1439), a Camaldulensian monk interested in patristic sources, was instrumental in discovering Jerome's translation of Origen's *Homilies on Luke.*

To the Roman Catholics Jerome was a touchstone of orthodox i.e. anti-protestant belief. Various treaties of his were published regularly to defend the cult of the Blessed Virgin or of the veneration of saints. *Lives* of Jerome frequently had an apologetic purpose: he was to be imitated as the monk, the celibate, the ascetic, in short the perfect Christian.

His Latin translation of the Bible, however, which became known as the Vulgate in the 1530s, caused some controversy among Roman Catholic theologians. As knowledge of Greek and Hebrew became more widespread (at least among scholars) the imperfections of the translation were noticed, first by the famous Italian humanist Lorenzo Valla (*c.* 1406–57) then by the French biblical critic Jacques Lefèvre d'Etaples (*c.* 1455–1536). The latter in fact, argued, as did Erasmus and others after him, that the Vulgate translation was too poor to be considered the work of Jerome. Defenders of the traditional attribution, however, were not wanting. They argued that a bible translation could not be judged by the standards of secular rhetoric, and that, although the translation contained straightforward errors, it accurately reproduced the Greek and Hebrew originals in everything touching faith and morals. The Council of Trent reaffirmed the authority of the Vulgate in April 1546. (Modern scholarship considers that Jerome translated most of it himself.)

The Protestants naturally preferred the Bible either in the original Greek and Hebrew or in their own vernacular translations. However, their attitude to Jerome as theologian and biblical commentator was far from being entirely negative. Few Reformers echoed Luther's open dislike of him; men like Philip Melanchthon (1497–1560) or John Calvin tended to believe that Jerome should be used with discrimination but not ignored. Calvin particularly praised Jerome's doctrine of the Eucharist as it did not advocate transubstantiation.

PATRISTIC FLORILEGIA AND VERNACULAR TRANSLATIONS

Collections of excerpts from the Fathers on one or several points of doctrine were also popular during the Reformation period and circulated in manuscript or printed form among Protestant and

Roman Catholic theologians alike. Some, such as *Unio dissidentium* (reconciliation of theological controversies through relevant extracts from the Fathers) published in 1531 by the mysterious 'Hermannus Bodius', were intended for publication. Others remained in manuscript for the private use of particular theologians. Martin Bucer possessed at least two such *florilegia* of which one is still extant.

Vernacular translations of the Fathers were rarely available until the seventeenth century. When available they were printed in the form of extracts. A good example of this is excerpts from Cyprian's treatise on female clothing, printed with Calvin's sermons on the same subject in 1561.

DIFFUSION OF PATRISTIC WRITINGS IN PROTESTANT TERRITORIES DURING THE REFORMATION AND USE OF THE EARLY CHURCH AS MODEL FOR PRACTICAL REFORMS

Did the writings of the Fathers reach the wider mass of the Protestant clergy and such faithful as could read Latin? Church ordinances from the 1520s and the 1530s would suggest that an effort was being made, especially in some parts of Germany. In his plea of 1527 for Reformation in Silesia, Duke Frederick II of Liegnitz asserts that patristic writings should be studied regularly although they will always remain subordinate to Scripture. In the 1528 Visitation articles of Saxony, it is stated that the Saxon duke, Johann, should watch over the orthodoxy of the reforms being carried out, just as emperor Constantine the Great (d. 337) imposed the orthodox (trinitarian) doctrine upon the bishops assembled at the Council of Nicaea in 325.

The Brunswick Church Ordinance, drawn up by Luther's confessor, Johann Bugenhagen (1485–1558) contains a section on parish libraries which should contain the works of Augustine, Ambrose of Milan (*c.* 339–97) and Jerome. The Church Ordinances of Soest (1532) and Bremen (1534) contain a similar injunction without explicitly naming the Fathers who are to be read.

THE EARLY CHURCH AS MODEL FOR PRACTICAL REFORMS

The practices of the early Church were considered by Luther and his followers as a direct model for the Reformation of church government, discipline and liturgy. For example, John Calvin in his *Institutes of Christian Religion* invokes various patristic sources in support of his doctrine of the ministry. The fourth-century *Apostolic Canons* are used by him as a textbook of morals of the clergy. The Genevan reformer further cites the example of the emperor Theodosius' submission to Ambrose (390) to show that not even princes are to be exempted from church discipline.

In stressing preaching and making it part of the liturgy all the Reformers believed themselves not only to be obedient to Scripture but also to be following the practice of the ancient Church. Preaching on a book of the Bible, chapter by chapter or even verse by verse as done by Zwingli in Zurich became standard reformed practice, and derived from the practice of Chrysostom and Augustine.

Pliny's letter on the Christians to Trajan (*c.* 112) was frequently cited to show that the earliest Christians sang hymns in their worship, and Tertullian's (*c.* 160–*c.* 225) *Apology* was one of the important sources of the Reformers' knowledge of the Prayer of Intercession especially for civil authorities.

CONCLUSION

The revival of patristic studies in the fifteenth century can be considered a by-product of the general interest in the writings of antiquity, itself a hallmark of the Renaissance. Patristic editions were frequently the work of Roman Catholic scholars even during the Reformation period when attempts to reform the Roman Church from 'within' (notably through the Council of Trent) led to an increased interest in the Fathers. However, some works of some Fathers, notably those of Basil of Caesarea, were *also* edited and published by Protestants. There is extensive evidence to show that the Reformers themselves considered patristic tradition as second only to biblical authority and used it, more or less selectively, to vindicate their own doctrines. Moreover, provision was made in some Protestant church ordinances for patristic literature to be made available in parishes. In short, the Protestant attitude to the early Church could not be considered as substantially different from the Roman Catholic attitude although the two sides tended to cite different Fathers or different excerpts from the same Father in defending their own doctrine, and the Protestants did officially reject the Vulgate. Questions of authenticity and textual criticism played a very subordinate role in these controversies and it must be said that the Fathers were cited as often from medieval collections (*Decrees of Gratian*, etc.) as from more recent editions. The practices of the early Church, in so far as they were known, were considered by the Protestants as a direct model for the Reformation of church government, discipline and liturgy.

BIBLIOGRAPHY

Backus, I, *Les traductions latines de Basile de Césarée publiées entre 1439 et 1618.* Paris, Etudes Augustiniennes, 1990.

Fraenkel, P, *Testimonia Patrum: The Function of the Patristic Argument in the Theology of Philip Melanchthon*, Travaux d'Humanisme et Renaissance, vol. 46. Geneva, Librairie Droz, 1961.

Kristeller, P O, and Cranz, F E, eds.-in-chief, *Catalogus translationum et commentariorum: Mediaeval and Renaissance Latin Translations and Commentaries. Annotated Lists and Guides.* Washington, Catholic University of America Press, 1960.

Old, H O, *The Patristic Roots of Reformed Worship*, Zürcher Beiträge zur Reformationsgeschichte, 5. Zürich, Theologischer Verlag, 1975.

Rice, E F, *Saint Jerome in the Renaissance.* Baltimore and London, Johns Hopkins University Press, 1985.

Stinger, C L, *Humanism and the Church Fathers: Ambrogio Traversari (1386–1439) and Christian Antiquity in the Italian Renaissance.* Albany, State of New York Press, 1977.

PART EIGHT

Aids for Further Study

Select Bibliography

MAIN SOURCE COLLECTIONS IN ENGLISH

Ancient Christian Writers, eds J Quasten and J C Plumpe. Westminster, Maryland, and New York, Newman Press; London, Longmans Green, 1946–75.

Ante-Nicene Christian Library, ed. A Roberts and J Donaldson. Edinburgh, T & T Clark, 1867–72. Additional vol., New York, Christian Literature Co., 1897. American edn: *Ante-Nicene Fathers*. New York, 1926.

The Fathers of the Church. Washington, Catholic University of America Press, 1947– .

Library of Christian Classics, eds J Baillie, J T McNeill and H P van Dusen (Philadelphia, Westminster; London, SCM, 1953–69), certain vols. only.

Loeb Classical Library (Cambridge, Mass., Harvard University Press; London, Heinemann, 1912–), certain vols. only.

The Oxford Library of the Fathers, ed. M Dods. Edinburgh and New York, T & T Clark and Eerdmans, 1838–81.

A Select Library of Nicene and Post-Nicene Fathers of the Christian Church, eds P Schaff and H Wace. Oxford, Buffalo and New York, 1887–92 (first series); Oxford, J H Parker, 1890–1900 (second series); repr. Grand Rapids, MI, Eerdmans, 1975ff.

Translations of Christian Literature, eds S Simpson and L Clarke, London and New York, SPCK, 1919ff.

OTHER SOURCES (selection)

Abramowski, L and Goodman, A E, eds, *A Nestorian Collection of Christological Texts*. Vol. 2, Cambridge, Cambridge University Press, 1972.

Augustine, *Confessions*, ed. R Pine-Coffin. London, Penguin Classics, 1961.

——, *The City of God*, new edn by H Bettenson, London, Penguin Classics, 1984.

——, *On Free Choice of the Will. On Christian Doctrine*. The Library of Liberal Arts. Indianapolis etc., Bobbs-Merrill, 1971.

Ayerst, D and Fisher, A S T, eds, *Records of Christianity*. 2 vols., Oxford, Blackwell & Mott, 1971.

Bettenson, H, ed., *The Early Christian Fathers*. Oxford, London and New York, Oxford University Press, 1969.

——, ed., *The Later Christian Fathers*. London, New York and Toronto, Oxford University Press, 1970.

Bindley, T H and Green, F W, eds, *The Oecumenical Documents of the Faith*. London, Methuen, 1950.

Celsus, *On the True Doctrine: a discourse against the Christians*, ed. R J Hoffmann, New York and Oxford, Oxford University Press, 1987.

Chrysostom, John, *Chrysostom and His Message. Selections from his Sermons*, tr. S Neill. London and New York, London Society for Christian Literature, 1962.

Clarkson, J F et al., eds, *The Church Teaches. Documents of the Church in English Translation*. Rockford, Ill., Tan Books, 1973.

Classics of Western Spirituality (series), ed.-in-chief R J Payne. Ramsey, N J, Paulist Press; London, SPCK, 1978– .

Early Christian Writings (Apostolic Fathers), rev. edn by M Staniforth and A. Louth. Penguin Classics, 1987.

Eusebius of Caesarea, *The History of the Church from Christ to Constantine* (= *The Ecclesiastical History*), tr. G Williamson. Harmondsworth, Penguin, 1965; New York, 1966.

——, *In Praise of Constantine: A Historical Study and New Translation of Eusebius' Tricennial Orations*, by H A Drake. London and Berkeley, University of California Press, 1976.

Grant, R M, *Gnosticism: A Sourcebook of Heretical Writings from the Early Christian Period*. London and New York, Harper & Row, 1961.

Gregory of Nyssa, *From Glory to Glory. Selection of Mystical Writings*, tr. H Musurillo. New York, Scribner, 1961; London, J Murray, 1962.

Gwatkin, H M, ed., *Selections from Early Writers Illustrative of Church History to the Time of Constantine*. London and New York, Macmillan, 1905.

Haines, C R, *Heathen Contact with Christianity during its First Century and a Half*. Cambridge, Deighton, Bell, 1923.

Hillgarth, J N, ed., *Christianity and Paganism* AD *350–750: The Conversion of Western Europe*. rev. edn, Philadelphia, University of Pennsylvania Press, 1986.

Hoare, F R, ed. and tr., *The Western Fathers* (Lives of SS. Martin of Tours, Ambrose, Augustine of Hippo, Honoratus of Arles and Germanus of Auxerre). London and New York, Sheed & Ward, 1954.

Kidd, B J, ed., *Documents Illustrative of the History of the Church*. 2 vols., London, SPCK, 1920, 1923.

Lightfoot, J B, ed., *The Apostolic Fathers*. London, Macmillan, 1926.

Merton, T, ed., *The Wisdom of the Desert: Sayings from the Desert Fathers of the Fourth Century*. Norfolk, Conn., James Laughlin, 1960; London, Hollis & Carter, 1961.

Musurillo, H A, ed., *The Fathers of the Primitive Church*. New York, New American Library, 1966.

Neuner J and Dupuis, J, eds, *The Christian Faith in the Doctrinal Documents of the Catholic Church*. Rev. edn, London, Collins, 1983.

Origen, *Contra Celsum*, ed. H Chadwick, Cambridge, Cambridge University Press, 1953.

Oxford Early Christian Texts (series), ed. H Chadwick, Oxford, Clarendon Press, 1970– .

Pharr, C, ed., *The Theodosian Code*. Princeton, Princeton University Press, 1952.

Rusch, W G, ed., *Sources of Early Christian Thought*. 5 vols., Philadelphia, Fortress, 1980ff.

Stevenson, J, ed., *A New Eusebius: Documents Illustrating the History of the Church to* AD *337*, rev. with additional documents by W H C Frend. London, SPCK, 1987.

——, ed., *Creeds, Councils and Controversies: Documents Illustrative of the History of the Church* AD *337–461*, rev. with additional documents by W H C Frend. London, SPCK, 1989.

Toal, M F, tr. and ed., *Patristic Homilies*. Cork, Mercer, 1955.

——, tr. and ed., *Sunday Sermons of the Great Fathers*. 3 vols., London and New York, Longmans; Chicago, Henry Regnery, 1958–63.

Tugwell, S, *The Apostolic Fathers*. Outstanding Christian Thinkers series. London, Geoffrey Chapman, 1989.

Waddell, H, ed., *The Desert Fathers*. London and New York, Constable, 1936; Ann Arbor, University of Michigan Press, 1957.

Ward, B, *Lives of the Desert Fathers*. Oxford, Mowbray, 1981.

Wiles, M F and Santer, M, eds, *Documents in Early Christian Thought*. Cambridge and New York, Cambridge University Press, 1975.

Wright, F A, ed., *Fathers of the Church: Selected Writings of the Latin Fathers*. London, Routledge, 1928.

REFERENCE BOOKS

Altaner, B., *Patrology*, tr. H C Graef from the 5th German edn. Freiburg, Herder; Edinburgh and London, Nelson, 1960.

Bishop, P and Darton, M, eds, *The Encyclopaedia of World Faiths*. London and Sydney, Macdonald Orbis, 1987.

Cross, F L, *Early Christian Fathers*, Studies in Theology No. 57. London, Duckworth, 1960.

——, and Livingstone, E A, eds, *The Oxford Dictionary of the Christian Church*, London, New York & Toronto, Oxford University Press, 1974[2].

Ferguson, E, ed., *Encyclopaedia of Early Christianity*. New York, Garland, 1989.

Jedin, H, Latourette, K S and Martin, J, eds, *Atlas zur Kirchengeschichte*. Freiburg etc., Herder, 1987[2].

Labriolle, P de, *The History and Literature of Christianity from Tertullian to Boethius*. London, Kegan Paul; Trench, Trübner, 1924.

Meer, F van der and Mohrmann, C, eds, *Atlas of the Early Christian World*. London, Edinburgh etc, Nelson, 1958.
Milburn, R L P, *Early Christian Art and Architecture*. Aldershot, Scolar, 1988.
Quasten, J, *Patrology*. 3 vols., Utrecht and Antwerp, Spectrum; Westminster, Maryland, Newman Press, 1962–4.
Rusch, W G, *The Later Latin Fathers*. Studies in Theology. London, Duckworth, 1979.
Warrington, J, *Everyman's Classical Dictionary 800 B.C.–A.D. 337*. London and Melbourne, J M Dent, 1961.
Young F, *From Nicaea to Chalcedon: A Guide to the Literature and its Development*. London, SCM; Philadelphia, Fortress, 1983.

GENERAL SURVEYS

BRIEF AND INTRODUCTORY

Chadwick, H, *The Early Church*. Harmondsworth, Penguin, 1967; Grand Rapids, MI, Eerdmans, 1969.
Comby, J, *How to Read Church History*, vol. 1. London, SCM, 1985; New York, Crossroad, 1989.
Frend, W H C, *The Early Church*, Philadelphia, Fortress; London, SCM, 1982[2].
Lohse, B, *A Short History of Christian Doctrine: from the First Century to the Present*. Philadelphia, Fortress, 1966, c. 1985.
MacCulloch, D, *Groundwork of Christian History*. London, Epworth, 1987.
Ramsey, B, *Beginning to Read the Fathers*. Mahwah, NJ, Paulist Press, 1985; London, Darton, Longman & Todd, 1986.
Urban, L, *A Short History of Christian Thought*. Oxford and New York, Oxford University Press, 1986.

COMPREHENSIVE

Aland, K, *A History of Christianity*, vol. 1, Philadelphia, Fortress, 1985.
Brown, P, *The World of Late Antiquity*. London, Thames & Hudson, 1971; New York, Harcourt Brace Jovanovich, 1971.
Caird, G B, *The Apostolic Age*. London, Duckworth, 1955; New Haven, Longwood, 1982.
Campenhausen, H von, *The Fathers of the Greek Church*, London, A & C Black, 1963; New York, Pantheon, 1959.
——, *The Fathers of the Latin Church*. London, A & C Black, 1964; Stanford University Press, 1964.
Carrington, P, *The Early Christian Church*. 2 vols., New York and Cambridge, Cambridge University Press, 1957.

Cave, S, *The Doctrine of the Person of Christ*. London, Duckworth, 1925.

Daniélou, J, and Marrou, H I, *The Christian Centuries. 1: The First Six Hundred Years*. London, Darton, Longman & Todd, 1964; New York, McGraw-Hill, 1964.

Frend, W H C, *The Rise of Christianity*. Philadelphia, Fortress; London, Darton, Longman & Todd, 1984.

McGiffert, A C, *A History of Christian Thought*. 2 vols., New York and London, C Scribner, 1932–3.

Harnack, A von, *The Mission and Expansion of Christianity in the First Three Centuries*, tr. J Moffatt. London, Williams & Norgate, 1908; repr. Gloucester, Mass., Peter Smith, 1963.

Jedin, H, and Dolan J P, eds, *History of the Church*. vol. 1–2. New York, Crossroad, 1980; London, Burns & Oates, 1980–1

Kelly, J N D, *Early Christian Doctrines*. 5th rev. edn, London, A & C Black, 1977; New York, Harper & Row, 1978.

Latourette, K S, *History of the Expansion of Christianity. 1: The First Five Centuries*, London, Eyre & Spottiswode, 1938; rev. edn, New York, Harper & Row, 1975.

Lietzmann, H, *A History of the Early Church*, 4 vols., tr. B L Woolf, London, Lutterworth, 1953^3; New York, Schribner, 1952^3.

Lindsay, T M, *The Church and the Ministry in the Early Centuries*, Cunningham Lectures, Edinburgh. New York, G H Doran, *c.* 1900.

MacMullen, R, *Christianizing the Roman Empire A.D. 100–400*. London and Haven, Yale University Press, 1984.

Pelikan, J, *The Christian Tradition: A History of the Development of Doctrine. Volume 1: The Emergence of the Catholic Tradition (100–600)*. Chicago and London, University of Chicago Press, 1971.

Troeltsch, E, *The Social Teaching of the Christian Churches*, 2 vols., London, Allen and Unwin; New York. Macmillan, 1931.

311

Glossary

Adoptionism A christological heresy seeing Christ as a normal human being, gifted at his baptism with divine powers and adopted into the Godhead after his resurrection.

Apocalyptic From the Greek word *apokalypsis* ('revelation' or 'unveiling'). Usually used of literature containing revelations concerning the events associated with the end of time, e.g. the Book of the Revelation of John the Divine. Also used of certain religious tempers and movements.

Apocryphal Writings Used to refer to writings similar in style to biblical texts but excluded from the canon of the Old or New Testaments as not being authentic.

Apollinarianism A christological heresy named after Apollinaris, bishop of Laodicea, who maintained that Christ possessed a human body but not a human spirit, the latter being replaced by the divine Logos.

Apologists The name given to the group of second-century Christian writers who first attempted to present a reasoned exposition of Christianity for the benefit of non-Christians. To this end, categories and concepts of current philosophy were often employed (see *Platonism*).

Apostasy Abandonment of the faith, lapsing.

Apostolic Age Name given to the first period in Church history, loosely corresponding to the lifetime of the apostles.

Apostolic Fathers Name given to leading church figures of the generation immediately succeeding the apostles and whose writings are extant.

Arianism A heresy named after Arius, an Alexandrian presbyter, who maintained that the Son of God had been created by God and was therefore neither eternal nor fully divine. While Arius' Christ was less than God, he was more than human, being as Logos pre-existent.

Aristotelianism Derived from the Greek philosopher, Aristotle, this way of thought stressed attention to the external world of nature and historical experience. At the same time it cultivated a natural or philosophical theology directed to the supreme or divine being. It stressed the unity of spirit and matter and so rejected the traditional dichotomy between body and soul. Except in the area of logic and dialectics, Aristotelianism had little influence on early Christian theology, though it helped to determine the anti-allegorical method of biblical interpretation identified with Antioch.

312

Glossary

Asceticism From the Greek word *askēsis* ('exercise' or 'training'). Used to describe a way of life based on rigorous self-denial to achieve holiness, as in monasticism.

Baptism Christian rite or sacrament of initiation. Until about AD 330, baptism was usually for instructed adults and by total immersion.

Barbarian Originally used of someone who did not speak Greek but later used to refer to peoples living outside the boundaries of the Roman Empire and therefore allegedly ignorant of Graeco-Roman culture.

Canon Name given to the list of biblical books regarded by the early Church as the authoritative Scriptures. Also used to refer to liturgical rules and laws governing the life and discipline of the Church.

Cappadocian Fathers Collective name given to Basil of Caesarea, his brother Gregory of Nyssa and their friend Gregory of Nazianzus, who came from the province of Cappadocia and became leading figures in the Church of the fourth century AD.

Catechetics Instructions given to those preparing for baptism (cathechumens).

Chalcedonian Pertaining to the Council of Chalcedon, AD 451, which rejected the christological views of Nestorius and Eutyches as heretical. It is famous for formulating the orthodox view of Christ as perfect man and perfect God, distinct natures united in one person.

Christology The study of the person and status of Christ with particular reference to the relationship between Christ and God on the one hand, and Christ and humanity on the other.

Constantinian After the emperor Constantine, usually with reference to the state or imperial Church instituted by him and maintained by his successors.

Creed Concise, formal statement of faith. Alternatively called 'confession' or 'symbol'.

Diophysitism The orthodox doctrine that the incarnate Christ was both fully human and fully divine.

Donatism North African schism named after one of its early leaders, Donatus. Originally split from the Catholic Church over the recognition of the consecration of Caecilian, bishop of Carthage. The Donatists considered this consecration was rendered invalid by the participation of a bishop who was alleged to have lapsed during Diocletian's persecution.

Docetism Notion that Jesus Christ's human body was only apparent and not real, from the Greek *dokēsis* ('phantom', 'semblance').

Dualism Belief that the mind and body are distinct entities and that the material world is inferior to the spiritual, and even evil.

Ecumenical (or 'Oecumenical'), from the Greek *oikoumenē*, 'the whole inhabited world': general, universal, catholic, belonging to or involving the entire Christian Church.

Eschatology From the Greek *eschatos* ('last'). Doctrine of the last things.

Eucharist or Lord's Supper, or Mass. Ritual sacramental participation in the body and blood of Christ by means of eating and drinking the consecrated symbols of bread and wine. It is the climax of Christian worship.

Eutychianism   A christological heresy named after its originator, Eutyches. He maintained that Christ had only one nature which was divine.

Exegesis   The exposition of biblical (or other) texts.

Gnosticism   From the Greek *gnōsis* ('knowledge'). Complex esoteric movement within the second-century Church, originating in pagan religious thought and which placed particular emphasis on revealed but cryptic knowledge of God. Opposed by Christian writers.

Godhead   Deity.

Hellenistic   Pertaining to the period after the conquests of Alexander the Great (died 323 BC) when the Greek language and culture were spread throughout the Mediterranean world and were modified by contact with other cultures.

Heresiologist   Orthodox writer who devotes polemical works to the identification, classification, and refutation of heresy.

Heresy   Deviation from any defined doctrine of the Catholic or orthodox faith.

Homoousian   from the Greek *homoousios* ('of the same essence' or 'being'), adherent of formula adopted at the Council of Nicaea devised to affirm that the Father and the Son were of the same essence or being. Usually translated into Latin as *substantia*.

Islam   Religion founded by Muhammad (AD *c.* 570–629).

Logos   A Greek word meaning 'word' or 'reason'. In Stoic philosophy it was seen as the active principle permeating and determining the world. Used in Christian theology to refer to the second person of the Trinity, the Son of God being God's Logos or Word.

Manichaeism   Dualist religion of Persian origin named after its founder Manes (AD *c.* 215–75). It attributed the existence of evil to an evil power which controlled the material world. Gnostic related, it became the first post-Christian world religion.

Marcionism   A second-century heresy named after its founder Marcion. He claimed that the God of the Jews was other than the superior God of love revealed by Jesus. He therefore rejected the whole Old Testament as well as much of the early Christian literature later included in the New Testament as being alien to the gospel.

Martyrdom   Suffering, and supremely death, in witnessing to the faith. The bodies of martyrs, living or dead, were considered to have been vessels of the Holy Spirit, and so venerated.

Melitianism   A fourth-century schism named after Melitius, bishop of Lycopolis in Egypt. He split from the Catholic Church because he regarded their attitude to those who had lapsed from the faith during the Diocletian persecution as too lax.

Mithraism   Worship of the Persian sun-god, Mithras. A mystery religion with some elements in common with Christianity, e.g. baptism and ritual meals.

Monarchianism   Second- and third-century concept which, in attempting to preserve the unity or oneness of the Godhead saw the Father as pre-eminent and sole seat of authority and power within the divine Triad or Trinity. It was judged as failing to do justice to the eternity and co-equality of the other persons of the Trinity. (See also *Adoptionism* and *Sabellianism*.)

Monarchical episcopacy   Hierarchical system of church order or government whereby extraordinary apostolic and supervisory authority is bestowed upon one church leader in a region, traditionally called a 'bishop' (Greek *episkopos*, 'overseer').

Monasticism   A way of life involving separation from the world in order to attain personal sanctification, usually in a community with others.

Monophysitism   From Greek *monos* ('single', 'one') and *physis* ('nature'). The doctrine that in the person of the incarnate Christ there was only one (divine) nature. (See also *Apollinarianism* and *Eutychianism*.)

Montanism   An apocalyptic movement originating in Phrygia in the latter half of the second century and named after its leader Montanus. It laid particular emphasis on prophecy, based on direct communication with the Holy Spirit, and adherence to a strict moral code. Revelation was seen as not confined to Scripture.

Mystery Religions   Religions or cults with secret initiation ceremonies. There was a proliferation of mystery religions during the Hellenistic period, many originating from the Orient. Common features included sacred rites and symbols, asceticism and belief in an after-life.

Nestorianism   The doctrine that in the incarnate Christ there were two separate natures, one human and one divine. In stressing this separateness, the unity of Christ's person was jeopardized. Named after its chief proponent Nestorius, bishop of Constantinople AD 428–31.

Nicene   Pertaining to the Council of Nicaea, AD 325. Usually used to refer to the creed formulated at this Council.

Novatianist   After the schismatic bishop of Rome, Novatian (AD 251), who favoured a hard line against those who had lapsed in the face of persecution.

Origenism   Name given to the theology of Origen of Alexandria (AD *c*. 185–253/4) during the fourth-century debate over the orthodoxy of some of his teachings.

Orthodoxy   From the Greek *orthos* ('right', 'straight') and *doxa* ('opinion'). Right belief as defined by the Catholic Church at an ecumenical council.

Paganism   From the Latin *paganus* ('rustic' or 'country-dweller') as used by early Christians to refer to non-Christians, either because as 'civilians' they were not 'soldiers of Christ' or because the countryside was predominantly non-Christian.

Patristic   Pertaining to the age and writings of the Fathers (Latin, *patres*) of the Church, i.e. the leading Christian teachers of the first eight centuries. A distinction is usually made between the Latin, Greek and Oriental (Syriac) Fathers.

315

Pelagianism   A fifth-century heresy named after the British monk, Pelagius, who was opposed by Augustine of Hippo. The main tenets of his belief were that the radical demands of Jesus should be obeyed literally; that each man was responsible for his own sin and for working out his own salvation; that Adam's sin affected him alone and not the entire human race.

Pentateuch   Collective named given to the five 'Books of Moses', Genesis, Exodus, Leviticus, Numbers and Deuteronomy in the Old Testament.

Petrine Claim   Claim made by the bishops of Rome to be the living embodiment of the apostle Peter through the apostolic succession and therefore to have authority over other metropolitan bishops.

Platonism   Derived from the Greek philosopher, Plato (427–347 BC), this way of thought understands true reality in terms of metaphysical 'Forms' or 'Ideas'. From the ultimate 'Form' of the Supreme Good everything emanates. Associated are the notions that the human soul is immortal and incorporeal, that it recollects and strives for ultimate reality or truth by contemplating the Forms or Ideas, stimulated by the external world. This way of thinking had a potent influence on Christian theology and piety, seen by some as compromising, due to the adoption of non-biblical dualism and to its devaluation of created matter and this world.

Presbyter   From the Greek *presbyteros* ('senior'), meaning either elders or priests.

Proselytising   From the Greek *prosēlytos* (convert): the act of converting someone to a faith or cult.

Sabellianism   A Monarchian heresy named after one of its chief proponents, Sabellius, holding that the only differentiation within the Godhead was a succession of modes or operations whereby the Father appeared in disguise as the Son and then as the Holy Spirit. (See also *Monarchianism*.)

Schism   A division within the Church based not so much on doctrinal issues as on issues of practice. But doctrinal schisms also occurred.

Septuagint   The most important Greek version of the Old Testament, allegedly translated by seventy-two scholars for Ptolemy Philadelphus (285–246 BC) in Alexandria. It was the version of the Old Testament most widely used by the early Church Fathers.

Stoicism   A Graeco-Roman school of philosophy founded at Athens by Zeno (335–263 BC). It emphasized the benevolent divine rule of the world and described God as an immanent force of reason within the world and the human soul. The emphasis of Stoic ethics was the concern to live according to nature and reason and to avoid being troubled by emotions or experiences.

Trinity   Orthodox normative Christian doctrine, which understands God and his relationship to the world in terms of three co-equal persons, the Father (Creator), the Son (Redeemer) and the Holy Spirit (Comforter), all fully sharing in the one and the same deity or divine substance.

Conspectus of Early Church History to AD 600

DATE	GENERAL HISTORY – EMPERORS	RELIGIOUS EVENTS – PERSONALITIES	THEOLOGICAL LITERATURE
c. 30	Execution of **Jesus**.	**Peter** and **James** leaders of Christian community in Jerusalem.	
c. 38		Conversion of **Paul**.	
c. 45–64		Paul's mission among Gentiles. Controversy over Jewish legal requirement for Gentile Christians.	Pauline *letters*.
64	**Nero.** Great fire of Rome.	Persecution of Christians in Rome. Possible martyrdom of Peter and Paul.	
70	Fall of Jerusalem. Destruction of Temple.		**Mark's** *Gospel.*
79	Destruction of Pompeii.		
c. 85			*Gospels* of **Matthew** and **Luke**. *Eighteen Benedictions* – Jewish document expelling Christians from Synagogue. Jewish Old Testament Canon.
c. 90			**John's** *Gospel.*
90–95	**Domitian** demanded worship as a god.	Persecution of Christians.	*Revelation* of **John**.
97–117	**Trajan.**	Growth of **Gnosticism**.	*Letters* of **Clement of Rome**.

317

DATE	GENERAL HISTORY – EMPERORS	RELIGIOUS EVENTS – PERSONALITIES	THEOLOGICAL LITERATURE
			Letters of Ignatius of Antioch.
110		Martyrdom of **Ignatius of Antioch**.	
112			**Pliny's** *letter* to Trajan.
117–138	**Hadrian.**		**Aristides'** *Apology* (no longer extant) addressed to Hadrian.
144+		**Marcion** active in Rome.	Marcion's expurgated *New Testament.*
c. 160		Martyrdom of **Polycarp**.	
161–180	**Marcus Aurelius**, emperor and Stoic philosopher.	Widespread persecution of Christians.	
		Growth of **Montanism**.	**Tatian's** *Diatessaron.*
168		Death of **Justin Martyr**.	Justin's works include
177		Massacre of Christians at Lyon.	*Against Heresies, Against Marcion, Apology.*
c. 178			**Celsus'** *True Word* against
		Growth of **Sabellianism**.	Christians.
c. 197			**Irenaeus'** *Against Heresies.*
		Quartodeciman Easter controversy.	Tertullian's *Apology* .
c. 215		**Tertullian** becomes Montanist.	**Clement of Alexandria**, *Exhortation*
c. 216		**Mani**, founder of Manichaeism	*to Greeks, The Pedagogue,* etc.
			Hippolytus' *Apostolic Tradition.*
218		**Origen**, teacher in catechetical school of Alexandria.	Origen's works include *Against Celsus, On First Principles* and many biblical commentaries.
249–251	**Decius**.	Decian persecution. Growing controversy between Carthage and Rome over the treatment of returning lapsed Christians.	
253–260	**Valerius** and **Gallienus** emperors.	Valerian persecution.	

DATE	GENERAL HISTORY – EMPERORS	RELIGIOUS EVENTS – PERSONALITIES	THEOLOGICAL LITERATURE
c. 254		Death of Origen.	
258		**Cyprian of Carthage** martyred.	Cyprian's *On the Unity of the Church.*
260	**Gallienus** sole emperor.		
293	Tetrachy: **Diocletian, Maximian, Constantius** and **Galerius.**	Diocletian persecution. Emergence of monasticism, **Antony, Pachomius.**	
310		**Armenia** becomes first officially Christian state.	
311		Galerius' edict of toleration.	
312	**Constantine** wins *Battle of Milvian Bridge.*	New relationship between emperor and Christianity. Beginning of **Donatist schism** in Carthage.	
313		**Edict of Milan** – universal toleration.	
314		Council of Arles deals with Donatist schism, though not conclusively. **Arian controversy** breaks out.	
319		Toleration for Donatists.	
324	Constantine defeats **Licinius.**	Religious toleration extends to the East.	
325		Universal Church **Council of Nicaea,** summoned by emperor.	**Eusebius'** *Ecclesiastical History.*
328		**Athanasius,** bishop of Alexandria, chief defender of Nicene orthodoxy.	Athanasius' works include *On the Incarnation of the Divine Word, Orations against the Arians, Against Apollinarius.*
337	Constantine baptized on his death bed.		
337	**Constantine** II, **Constantius** II and **Constans** emperors.		
c. 340		First conversion of Goths by Pro-Arian **Ulfilas.**	Ulfilas' *Gospels* in Gothic.

DATE	GENERAL HISTORY – EMPERORS	RELIGIOUS EVENTS – PERSONALITIES	THEOLOGICAL LITERATURE
		Proliferation of councils and creeds in continuing Arian controversy.	
356–360		Arian supremacy.	
361–363	**Julian the Apostate**. End of Constantinian dynasty.	Paganism restored.	
370–379		**Cappadocian Fathers** Basil of Caesarea.	Writings defending
374–384		Gregory of Nyssa.	trinitarian doctrine.
379–381		Gregory of Nazianzus.	
c. 374–397		**Ambrose**, Bishop of Milan.	
381		**Council of Constantinople** curtails Arianism. Patriarch of Constantinople given primacy alongside bishop of Rome.	
385		**Priscillian** and others executed for heresy at Trier.	
386		Conversion of **Augustine** at Milan.	
395	Death of **Theodosius**. Split of Empire into East and West.	Earliest testimony to present New Testament Canon.	
395–430		**Augustine**, bishop of Hippo.	Augustine's works include *Confessions, City of God, On the Trinity.*
c. 400		**Ninian's** mission to Picts.	
410	**Alaric's** invasion of Rome.		
411		Successful condemnation of Donatism by **Council of Carthage**.	
	Increasing discrimination against pagans.	Rise of **Pelagianism**.	**Pelagius'** *In Favour of Free Will.* Augustine's *On Nature and Grace, On Heresies, On Original Sin.*

DATE	GENERAL HISTORY – EMPERORS	RELIGIOUS EVENTS – PERSONALITIES	THEOLOGICAL LITERATURE
412–444		**Cyril**, bishop of Alexandria.	
428–431		**Nestorian controversy**.	
429	Vandal invasion of Africa.		
431		**Council of Ephesus** condemns Nestorius and Pelagius.	
c. 435		**Patrick's** mission to Irish.	
440–461		**Leo**, bishop of Rome. Rise of **Monophysitism**.	
451	Temples to remain closed. Pagan rites forbidden.	**Council of Chalcedon** condemns Monophysitism.	**Chalcedonian Definition**. **The Tome of Leo** concludes the christological controversy.
		Monophysite schism.	
476	**Odoacer** deposes **Romulus**, last emperor in the West.		
		Increasing tension in theology and Church polity between East and West.	
484–519		**Acacian schism** between Constantinople and Rome.	
499		Conversion of **Clovis** and Franks.	
524		Execution of **Boethius** for treason.	Boethius' writings include *The Consolation of Philosophy*.
527	**Justinian** made emperor.	**Council of Orange** condemns Pelagianism.	
534	Publication of Justinian's *Institutes*.		
553		**Council of Constantinople** discusses interpretation of Chalcedonian definition.	
c. 563		**Columba's** mission to the Scots.	

DATE	GENERAL HISTORY – EMPERORS	RELIGIOUS EVENTS – PERSONALITIES	THEOLOGICAL LITERATURE
565	Death of Justinian.		
c. 570		Birth of **Muhammad**.	
590–604		**Gregory the Great**, bishop of Rome.	Gregory's writings include *Magna Moralia, Dialogues*.
c. 600		**Augustine of Canterbury's** mission to the Angles and Saxons.	

WHC Frend: Select Bibliography

The Donatist Church: A movement of protest in Roman North Africa. Oxford, Clarendon Press 1952.

ibid., 2nd ed., reprint with corrections and additions to the bibliography. Oxford, Clarendon Press 1971.

ibid., reprint of 2nd ed. Oxford, Oxford University Press; New York, AMS Press, 'Orthodoxies and Heresies in the Early Church' series 1985.

The Early Church. London, Hodder & Stoughton, 'Knowing Christianity' series 1965.

The Early Church from the Beginnings to 461 A.D., reprint with new preface. London, SCM Press; Philadelphia, Augsburg Fortress 1982.

Martyrdom and Presecution in the Early Church: A study of conflict from the Maccabees to Donatus. Oxford, Blackwell 1965.

The Rise of the Monophysite Movement: Chapters in the history of the Church in the fifth and sixth centuries. Cambridge University Press 1972.

The Rise of Christianity. London, Darton, Longman & Todd; Philadelphia, Augsburg Fortress 1984.

Saints and Sinners in the Early Church: Differing and conflicting traditions in the first six centuries. London, Darton, Longman & Todd; Wilmington, Delaware, Michael Glazier, 'Theology and Life' series 11, 1985.

A New Eusebius: Documents illustrating the history of the Church to AD 337. Ed. by J Stevenson. Revised with additional documents by W H C Frend. London, SPCK 1987.

Creeds, Councils and Controversies: Documents illustrating the history of the Church AD 337–461. Ed. by J Stevenson. Revised with additional documents by W H C Frend. London, SPCK 1989.

Seventy-one articles are collected and republished in the following volumes:

Religion Popular and Unpopular in the Early Christian Centuries. London, Variorum Reprints, 'Collected Studies' series 45, 1976.

Town and Country in the Early Christian Centuries. London, Variorum Reprints, 'Collected Studies' series 110, 1980.

Archaeology and History in the Study of Early Christianity. London, Variorum Reprints, 'Collected Studies' series 282, 1988.

Below is a selection of notable individual articles and contributions by William Frend falling outside the scope of the Variorum collections:

'A third-century inscription relating to the Angariae in Phrygia'. *Journal of Roman Studies* 46 (1956), pp. 46–56.

'Hitler and his Foreign Ministry'. *History* 42 (1956), pp. 118–29.

'Some aspects of the Christian view of immortality'. *The Modern Churchman*, n.s. 3 (1959), pp. 47–59.

'A Byzantine church at Knossos'. *Papers of the British School at Athens* 61 (1962), pp. 186–238.

'The Christianization of Roman Britain'. In: *Acts of the Congress of Archaeologists at Nottingham* (1967), Leicester University Press (1968), pp. 37–49.

'Christianity in the Middle East: Survey down to 1800'. In: *Religion in the Middle East*, ed. A J Arberry, Cambridge 1969, pp. 239–96.

'The Christian Period in Mediterranean Africa'. In: *The Cambridge History of Africa* 2, ed. J D Fage, Cambridge 1979, chap. 2.

'The Fall of Macedonius in 511, a suggestion'. In: *Kerygma und Logos*, Festschrift für Carl Andresen, Göttingen 1979, pp. 183–96.

'Augustine and State Authority; the example of the Donatists'. In: *Agostino d'Ippona. Quaestiones Disputatae*. Augustiniana – Testi e Studi IV, Palermo 1989, pp. 49–73.

'The Church in the reign of Constantius II (337–361): Mission – Monasticism – Worship'. In: *L'Eglise et l'Empire au IVe Siècle*, ed. A Dihle, Geneva 1989, pp. 73–112.

' "And I have other sheep". John 10, 16'. In: *The Making of Orthodoxy*. Essays in Honour of Henry Chadwick. Cambridge 1989, pp. 24–39.

'Fragment of a version of the *Acts S. Georgii* from Q'asr Ibrim'. *Jahrbuch für Antike und Christentum* 32, Münster 1989 (1990).

INDEX OF BIBLICAL REFERENCES

INDEX OF REFERENCES TO ANCIENT WRITINGS

INDEX OF PERSONAL NAMES AND PLACES

Index of Personal Names and Places

SUBJECT INDEX